Emerging Themes in Information Systems and Organization Studies

A Tribute to Marco De Marco

Andrea Carugati • Cecilia Rossignoli
Editors

Emerging Themes in Information Systems and Organization Studies

Physica-Verlag

Editors
Andrea Carugati
Department of Business Administration
Aarhus University, Business and Social Sciences
Haslegaardsvej 10
8210 Aarhus V
Denmark
andreac@asb.dk

Cecilia Rossignoli
Department of Business Administration
University of Verona
Via dell'Artigliere 19
37129 Verona
Italy
cecilia.rossignoli@univr.it

ISBN 978-3-7908-2738-5 e-ISBN 978-3-7908-2739-2
DOI 10.1007/978-3-7908-2739-2
Springer Heidelberg Dordrecht London New York

Library of Congress Control Number: 2011930135

Cover design: SPi Publisher Services

Printed on acid-free paper

Physica-Verlag is a brand of Springer-Verlag Berlin Heidelberg
Springer-Verlag is part of Springer Science+Business Media (www.springer.com)

Table of Contents

Part III
ICT in Organizational Design and Change

Part IV
ICT and Social Impact

Part V
ICT and Productivity

Part VI
E-government

Biography of the Editors

Andrea Carugati is an Associate Professor and Director for the Information Systems Research Group at Århus School of Business and Social Sciences, in Århus, Denmark. Andrea received a Ph.D. from the Technical University of Denmark in 2004. In his career he has held permanent positions in IESEG School of Management and visiting positions in various universities including MIT, Grenoble School of Management, LUISS University, LIUC University. Andrea's research focuses on the use of information technology in organizations and on IT driven organizational change. Andrea Carugati has published, among others, on the European Journal of Information Systems, Database for Advances in Information Systems, Electronic Markets, at the International Conference on Information Systems, EGOS, and at the European Conference on Information Systems.

Cecilia Rossignoli is an Associate Professor of Organization Science at the University of Verona (Italy). Previously she taught and researched Information Systems at the Catholic University of Milan, where she began as a researcher in 1995. She has been the Director of the Masters Program in Business Intelligence and Knowledge Management at the University of Verona since 2003. She is a member of AIS and also a member and cofounder of ItAIS (Italian Chapter of Association for Information Systems). She served in the Organizing Committee of the 17th ECIS 2009, "Information Systems in a Globalizing World: Challenges, Ethics and Practices", held in Verona in June, 2009. Her research interests cover the areas of IS and organizational change, the role of IS in inter-organizational information systems, electronic markets and the impact of Business Intelligence Systems in organizations. On this subject she has published more than 50 papers and books. Her latest works were published in the Journal of Electronic Commerce Research, the Journal of Information Systems and e-business Management and Electronic Markets.

Biography of Marco De Marco

Marco De Marco is a Full Professor of Organization and Information Systems at the Università Cattolica in Milan. He also teaches the Business Organization course at the LUISS Guido Carli University in Rome. Before embarking upon his academic career he worked as a research engineer and product planning manager in the aerospace (Boeing) and computer (IBM, GE, and Honeywell) industries. He is the author of four books and numerous essays and articles; mainly on the development of information systems and the impacts of technology on organizations. Marco De Marco has worked as a consultant for a wide range of important public institutions, such as the Venice City Council, the Rome City Council, the Lombardy Regional Government, the Hospital Administration Authority, and the Ministry of Justice as well as the Italian parliament. He has also been a consultant to the major trades unions of Italian bank employees. He is a member of the editorial board of several academic journals, including the Journal of Information Systems, the Journal of Digital Accounting Research, Banking and Information Technology, Information Systems and e-Business Management. Marco De Marco was a founder in 2003 and former President of the Italian Association for Information Systems (ITAIS), the Italian Chapter of the Association for Information Systems. In 2008 and 2009, he was a Board committee member of the Association for Information Systems, representing Europe, Africa, and the Middle East. He is the editor-in-chief of the Informatica e Organizzazioni book series published by Franco Angeli. He has worked on several projects of European breadth and has served as ECIS conference officer, acting as conference chair at ECIS2009 in Verona. In the past, his main research interests have included information system development and performance measurement methodologies, while bank information systems and their specificities were a particular study and focus. More recently, he has investigated the impact on organizations of information systems and Information Technology generally, leading him to focus on the themes of ERP systems due to their strong influence on the organization of companies and Business Process Management, perceived as a fundamental aspect in optimizing the delivery of services. Marco has been a driving force in getting the Italian scientific community to integrate with the international community, a success attested to by the fact that both ECIS 2003 and ECIS 2009 were staged in Italy, where also ICIS 2013 will be held.

Biography of the Contributors

David Avison is Distinguished Professor of Information Systems at ESSEC Business School, near Paris, France. In 2008-2009 he was President of the *Association of Information Systems (AIS)*. He is joint editor (with Guy Fitzgerald) of the *Information Systems Journal*, one of the AIS basket of six top IS research journals. So far, twenty-five books are to his credit along with many research papers. He researches in the area of information systems development and more generally on information systems in their natural organizational setting, in particular using action research, though he has also used a number of other qualitative research approaches.

Barbro Back is Professor in Accounting Information Systems at Åbo Akademi University in Turku, Finland. Her research interests include business intelligence, neural networks, data mining and text mining. She has presented her research amongst others in Journal of Management Information Systems, Accounting Management and Information Technology, European Journal of Operations Research. She currently serves on the editorial boards of various international journals including the International Journal of Business Information Systems.

Joerg Becker is Professor of Information Systems and Information Management, head of the Department of Information Systems at the University of Muenster, managing director of the European Research Center for Information Systems (ERCIS) and principal shareholder of the Prof. Becker GmbH. His research focuses on information management, management information systems, information modeling, e-business management, e-government, data management, logistics and industry information systems, workflow management and retail information systems.

Alinaghi Ziaee Bigdeli is a PhD researcher in the Department of Information Systems and Computing at Brunel University (UK). His current research focuses on the area of inter-organisational information integration and sharing in e-Government. Alinaghi is involved in teaching undergraduate and postgraduate courses within the Department of Information Systems and Computing.

Alessio Maria Braccini holds a PhD in Information Systems for the LUISS Guido Carli University (Rome, Italy) where he is currently working as a research fellow at the Research Centre on Information Systems (CeRSI). He is actively involved in national and international research projects and he contributes as an author and as a reviewer to several national and international conferences and journals. His research interests include: IT business value, open source software, organizational aspects of information systems.

Leonardo Caporarello holds a Ph.D. in Management Information Systems, LUISS University (Rome). He is Research Fellow of the Department of Management and Technology at the Bocconi University, and Professor of Leadership and Organization at SDA Bocconi School of Management, where he is also the Director of the Learning Lab. Leonardo is Faculty member of the MBA full-time and Executive MBA Programs. His research interests include: managing complex IT projects; project and change management; organizational governance.

Maurizio Cavallari graduated at Università Cattolica, Milan, where he has been serving as Adjunct Professor on Information Systems since 1992. He has been a visiting lecturer at University of Vaxjo (Sweden) and a visiting scholar at Templeton College – Oxford University (UK); He is appointed at several board of directors in banks and industry in Italy and had been working since 1989 as a consultant for private and public organizations on information systems security and organizational matters.

Yu Chen is Professor at Information School of Renmin University of China since 1990. He got his master degree on Computer Science and Application at 1981. His main work is on Management Information System, both in teaching and research. He has published more than 10 textbooks and about 70 papers. He has worked as consultants for many important projects in China, and has been at several leading position in organizations like the Chinese National Representative in IFIP TC8, the Chinese Information Economics Society, and CNAIS.

Alessandro D'Atri is a Full Professor of Information Systems and Director of the IS Research Centre at LUISS Guido Carli University of Rome. He is the Vice-President of ItAIS, the Italian Chapter of the International Association for IS. He is a member of the Editorial Board of the *Journal on IS and e-Business Management* and of the *Journal on Information, Communication and Ethics in Society.* His main research interests include: IS, virtual enterprises, e-commerce, telemedicine, databases, computational complexity, and graph theory. In these fields, he has more than 100 articles published in journals and books.

Sergio de Cesare is Lecturer and Director of Postgraduate Studies in the Department of Information Systems and Computing at Brunel University. Sergio's work focuses on the adoption of ontologies in IS development. Sergio has over 50 peer-reviewed publications in leading journals and conferences and has organized several international events related to modeling in IS development. Sergio is also currently the Managing Editor of the European Journal of Information Systems.

Meiqi Fang is Professor at Information School of Renmin University of China since 1993. She got her M.D. on Computer Science and Application at 1981 on RUC.. Her B.D. on mathematics has been received at 1967 at Tsinghua University. Her main work is on MIS in teaching and research. She has published more than 15 textbooks and about 80 papers in MIS, EC and computer simulation Her "Introduction of Electronic commerce" is main text book on EC in China. She has been Vice Chairman of Chinese Information Economics Society, Vice Chairman of MIS group in Chinese System Engineering.

Antonella Ferrari has a Business Administration degree from the Catholic University and a Phd in Information Systems at Guido Carli – Luiss University, Italy. She's been teaching since 1992, first at Catholic University of Milan and University of Trento and now at Politecnico of Milan. She researches in the area of information systems organizational impacts and more specifically on Business Intelligence organizational implications.

Guy Fitzgerald is Professor of Information Systems in the Department of Information Systems and Computing (DISC) at Brunel University, UK. His research interests are concerned with the effective management and development of information systems and he has published widely in these areas. He is founder and co-editor, with David Avison, of the *Information Systems Journal (ISJ)*, he is the author (also with David Avison) of *Information Systems Development: Methodologies, Techniques and Tools*, and is Vice-President of Publications of the Association for Information Systems (AIS).

Cyrus (Chuck) Gibson is a Senior Lecturer at the MIT Sloan School of Management where he teaches primarily in executive education programs. He is associated with the Center for Information Systems Research. His teaching, research, and consulting focus on IT-enabled business change. He is author or co-author of three books and more than forty case studies and articles. Prior to coming to MIT in 1996, he was a senior vice president at CSC Index. He worked as an associate professor at the Harvard Business School where he conducted research on the impact of new IT systems on work behavior.

Nobuyuki Ichikawa graduated from Department of Civil Engineering, Tokyo University of Science in 1995 and worked in Japan Highway Public Corporation. He is currently a project Lecturer in Graduate School of Interdisciplinary Information Studies, the University of Tokyo, Japan. His research interests are in "Advanced Infrastructure with ICT" to achieved the efficiency improvement of infrastructure maintenance that takes care about the flow of information.

Yusho Ishikawa holds a doctorate in Engineering from the University of Tokyo in 2005. He was a manager of Tokyo highway office in Ministry of Land, Infrastructure and Transport and a chief information officer of Kochi Prefecture. He is currently a project professor in Graduate School of Interdisciplinary Information Studies, the University of Tokyo. His interests are in "Advanced Infrastructure with ICT" in the future, and "Public Involvement" for policy making.

Pertti Järvinen is a former IT mathematician in OVAKO steel factory 1963-67, chief in the Computing Centre of University of Tampere 1967-1970. He is a Permanent Professor at the University of Tampere 1970-1974, at the University of Jyväskylä 1974-75 and at the University of Tampere 1976-2003. He served as Secretary 1990-95) and Chairman (1996-98) of International Federation of Information Processing Technical Committee 9 (Computers & Society); he is one of the founders of IRIS.

Eirini Kalliamvakou is a research officer and a PhD candidate in the Department of Management Science and Technology at the Athens University of Economics and Business (AUEB). Her research interests concern the communication and coordination processes in global software development projects active in Open Source Software development. She has been involved with digital identity in the eGovernment environment.

Minna Kallio is a Ph.D. student at the Department of Information Technologies at Åbo Akademi University. She has received her master degree from Turku School of Economics. The topic of her doctoral thesis will be the use of self-organizing neural networks in selecting companies for tax auditing.

Kalinka Kaloyanova is Associate Professor, Faculty of Mathematics and Informatics, at University of Sofia. Her research interests are Database Systems, Data Mining, Software Engineering, Project Management. She has more than 40 publications on these topics. Dr. Kaloyanova participated in industrial and research projects and is member of Association of Information System and the President of Bulgarian Chapter of AIS.

Claudia Loebbecke is Director of the Department of Media and Technology Management at the University of Cologne. In 2005-2006 she served as President of the Association for Information Systems (AIS). Her research focuses on business models and management aspects of digital and creative goods and on the innovative use of new media covering aspects such as electronic business, knowledge management, and new organizational forms.

Piercarlo Maggiolini is Associate Professor at the Politecnico di Milano. He carried out research activity in the field of the management and economic and socio-organizational assessment of information systems in business organizations and Public Administrations. At present his mainly research activity is concerning Computer Ethics, Business Ethics and Corporate Social Responsibility, e-Government.

Marcello Martinez is a Professor of Organization Studies at the University of Naples, Italy, Economics Faculty. He obtained his PhD in Business Administration and Management at the University of Catania. He specialized in Public Transportation Service at the Massachusetts Institute of Technology. In his academic research, he has explored the governance and organization of public utilities, the organizational change processes within the railway industry, and the impact of information systems on organizational dynamics and structures.

Antonio Marturano is an Adjunct Professor of Business Ethics at the Sacred Heart Catholic University of Rome and Visiting Lecturer in Leadership and Communication at the LUISS University of Rome. Previously Dr. Marturano has worked at the Jepson School of Leadership, University of Richmond, at the Centre for Leadership Studies, University of Exeter (2003-2007) and Lancaster University (2000-2002). He has published extensively on leadership and computer ethics.

Lapo Mola is Assistant Professor in Organization Science at the University of Verona where he undergraduate and graduate courses. He is member of the scientific committee of the master program of Business Intelligence and Knowledge Management. He is coauthor of several papers presented in international conferences (ECIS, ICIS, itAIS, Academy of Management) and journals (Sinergie, Electronic Commerce). His research focuses on the organizational impact of ICT and organizational design

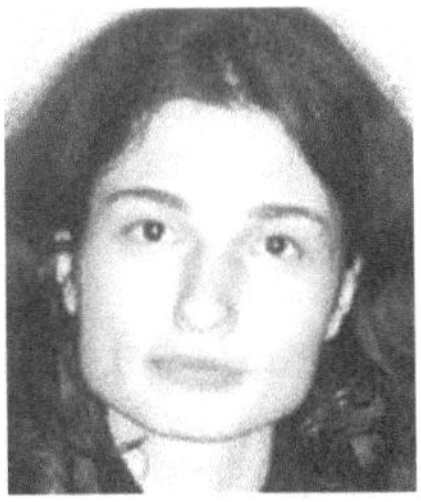

Ina Naydenova is a Ph.D. student at the Sofia University. Her teaching and research interests are in the fields of relational databases, data-warehousing and OLAP technologies.

Hanne Westh Nicolajsen is an Associate Professor at the Department for Communication and Psychology, Aalborg University. Hanne Westh Nicolajsen teaches within the fields of organizational learning and organizational implementation and use of new communication technologies. In the later years her research focused on service innovation and user involvement in service innovation.

Toshie Ninomiya worked in Toyota Motor Corporation, Keio University, Ibaraki University and University of Electro-Communications. She is currently a project researcher in Graduate School of Interdisciplinary Information Studies, the University of Tokyo, Japan. Her research interests are in "environment and governance" to increase social capital of human network, and "architecture" of expert support system in social infrastructure maintenance.

Fernando Pennarola is an Associate Professor of Organization and Management Information Systems at Bocconi University, Milan. Delegate Rector for E-Learning at Bocconi University. Chairman of the Board of Directors of ISBM (International Schools of Business Management). His research focus on MIS productivity and change initiatives initiated by IS.

Angela Perego is lecturer at SDA Bocconi School of Management. She received her Ph.D from Luiss University of Rome and the Paris-Dauphine University. She is member of the faculty of Masters in Information Systems Management and in Energy and Management of Transport, Logistics and Infrastructure at Bocconi University. Main research interests include: IS performance measurement and management, decision making process and IT, data warehouse and business intelligence systems and customer relationship management.

Athanasia (Nancy) Pouloudi is an Associate Professor in Information Systems Management at the Athens University of Economics and Business. Her research focuses on organizational and social aspects in information systems adoption. She serves on the editorial boards of the European Journal of Information Systems, IT & People and Information & Management. She is currently Representative of Region 2 (Europe-Middle East-Africa) in the Association for Information Systems (AIS).

Soley Rasmussen is a researcher at the Center for Applied ICT at Copenhagen Business School and at the Danish media company JP-Politikens Hus A/S. She holds an MA in Philosophy of Education. Since 2004 her professional focus has been on innovation, media and ICT. Her primary research interests are Web evolution, social media, media-asaservice and the innovation methods and business models of the networked economy.

Tapio Reponen is Professor of Information Systems at the Turku School of Economics, University of Turku, Finland. Currently he is the Vice-Rector of the university. His research interests are: information management, strategic information systems, organizing the IS function and knowledge management. He has published, reviewed and edited articles and books linked to these themes.

Francesca Ricciardi is a lecturer in ICTs and Information Society at the Catholic University in Milan and Brescia, Italy. Her main research interests span epistemological problems in IS and organizational studies, network theories and territorial networks, e-government, e-tourism, organizational and technological innovation for the ageing society.

Frantz Rowe is the co-Editor of the European Journal of Information System. He is the founding Director of the graduate program in IS at the University of Nantes. He is the President of the French-speaking IS Association. Professor Rowe's principal research interests pertain to organizational transformations and performance especially as related to information systems projects and use.

Ada Scupola is an Associate Professor at Roskilde University, Denmark. She holds a Ph.D in social sciences from Roskilde University, an MBA from the University of Maryland at College Park, USA. She is the editor-in-chief of The International Journal of E-Services and Mobile Applications.

Maddalena Sorrentino researches in organisational change, particularly in the public sector, at the University of Milan, Italy. She is professor of e-Government. Maddalena has been published in academic proceedings, such as EGOS, ECIS, EURAM, DEXA-eGOV, Bled eConference, journal articles and books. She is a member of the editorial boards of the "Government Information Quarterly" and the "Information Systems and e-Business Management".

Dov Te'eni is the Mexico Chair for Information Systems at Tel Aviv University. Dov studies how computers support people deciding, communicating, sharing knowledge and interacting. He was elected President of *AIS*, has served Senior Editor for *MIS Quarterly, AIS Transactions of HCI,* and associate editor for *Journal of AIS*, *Information and Organizations*, *European Journal of IS*, and *Internet Research*. Dov was awarded *AIS Fellowship* in 2008.

Manfred Thaller is Professor of Humanities Computer Science at the University of Cologne, Germany. He is in the Library Committee of the German National Research Council and participated in more than 20 projects in the digitization of the Cultural heritage including 3 in digital long term preservation.

Duane Truex is an Associate Professor at Robinson College of Business, Georgia State University and Professor and Chair of Industrial Economics, Mittuniversitetet (MidSweden University). Duane researches the social impacts of IS and how emergent properties of organizations are reflected in emergent ISD, and enterprise architectures. He is currently examining the construct called 'scholarly influence' and the nature knowledge dissemination and uptake in academic communities.

Francesco Virili, is tenured Assistant Professor a the University of Cassino, Italy. He published in peer reviewed international journals including the *International Journal of Information Management,* the *Journal of Information Systems and e-Business Management*, and *Computational Statistics*. He had five accepted papers at the *European Conference on Information Systems* and one accepted paper at the *International Conference on Information Systems*.

Jan vom Brocke holds the Martin Hilti Chair in Business Process Management (BPM) at the University of Liechtenstein. He is Director of the Institute of Information Systems and President of the Liechtenstein Chapter of the Association for Information Systems (AIS). He is a standing member in the EU Programme Committee of the 7th Framework Research Programme on ICT. Jan has published his work in more than 160 refereed papers at internationally perceived conferences and journals. He is author and editor of 14 books, including the International Handbook on BPM published by Springer in 2010.

Robert Winter is Full Professor of business & information systems engineering at University of St. Gallen (HSG), director of HSG's Institute of Information Management and founding academic director of HSG's Executive Master of Business Engineering programme. He is a member of the scientific board of several institutions and authored/edited over 15 books as well as over 150 journal/conference articles in the fields of situational method engineering, information logistics management, enterprise architecture management, integration management, healthcare networking and corporate controlling systems.

Shuren Zhang is an Associate Professor of Information Management and Web Science at Hangzhou Dianzi University of China. He holds a PhD in Information system from the Renmin University of China. Shuren Zhang's research studies the collective behaviors in net community, discovers the mechanism of the emergent phenomena in cyber world, and examines the social interaction patterns in online-business.

Foreword

Many disciplines are born within the boundaries of other disciplines, or in strict connection with them, and even after developing a specific identity, they maintain important areas of overlapping. For example, medicine and chemistry are sister disciplines. They may study the very same object, such as a chemical compound, but with two different goals: chemistry studies the characteristics of a compound, and how to synthesize it; medicine studies the effects of this compound on the human organism. The study of the interactions between a drug and the human body may also be studied by psychology, or by evolutionary biology, or by other different disciplines. But this does not mean, of course, that medicine as a discipline has a shared identity with chemistry or with other sister disciplines. In other words, the identity of a discipline, and of a research community, is not defined by the inviolability of its boundaries, nor by monopolizing the objects of its study; rather the identity of a discipline results from the specificity of its purposes, and from the effectiveness of the research relationships established with all the other related disciplines.

The Information Systems (IS) research community is very young: it has not yet accumulated the disciplinary tradition of historical epistemic communities such as medicine, or chemistry. As a consequence, the identity of IS research is not consolidated yet, and the purpose, methods, and objects of study are still open for debate. In a first phase, the major threat to IS identity was that Computer Science had a clearer status and longer tradition. As a consequence, these two disciplines were sometimes considered as mother and daughter, instead of sisters: Computer Science was perceived as a "mother discipline" while IS was considered as its soft branch. Early IS researchers felt that this situation was very limiting in the same way as medicine would react if it were considered a mere branch of chemistry.

Major efforts were made, then, to differentiate IS research from Computer Science. Since the IS research community wanted to focus on ICT-aided "management of information" within organizations it appeared natural to seek reference theories not in mathematics and logic but in organizational theory and behaviour. Many IS groups around the world actively searched for a stronger link with organizational studies. This process was of great importance to contribute to build the current IS identity, because it strengthened the outsiders' perception of a specific purpose for the IS research activities, and (maybe even more importantly) started to legitimate IS research in the business and management academic communities.

Marco De Marco is among those in Europe who played a pivotal role in this affirmation process. When, in the 80's, the business academic community still equated IS studies with computer science, Marco started dedicating himself to supporting the affirmation and growth of the Italian IS research community.

A pioneer in European Union projects, Marco established links with other IS research communities which were rising throughout Europe, and encouraged other Italian IS academics to join these emerging networks.

Many other national communities, like the Italian one, were in fact struggling to have their work and role recognized in the broader academic community. The build-up of an international network of relationships was an essential step to legitimate the topics and methods of the emerging IS research and create an IS identity around the world.

Of the possible roads to take, Marco and a few others, choose to build a particular and privileged relationship between the IS community and organization study community. IS researchers wanted to study a key aspect of organizational life, namely the management of information. As a consequence, IS research outcomes could find a significant disciplinary space engaging in a friendly confrontation between the IS and the organization studies communities.

In the first years, until well into the 90's, the activation of such a disciplinary link was hard. Organization researchers, having a more established community, tended to consider IS studies as alien and technical, and integration took several years. Nevertheless, with a persistent and intense commitment, the IS community increased its dimension and its activities, and today we can observe a good level of cooperation and collaboration between IS and organizational academics. The most visible example is EGOS, the European Group of Organization Studies, where IS academics participate along with academics from all the other management disciplines. On the other side, in order to define and strengthen the IS community, acceptance of IS studies within organizational research may be, although very important, insufficient. Since Web 2.0 services are becoming the most used service on the internet, IS researchers have started focusing on the management of knowledge also outside the classic boundaries of organizations: in fact, ICTs have become a key element not only in organizations, but also in informal networks, within families, among citizens, in the whole society. As we write these lines, the very purpose of IS studies is going through a period of exciting, challenging evolution. IS research has the chance to capitalize on our theories and understandings of technology uses and its impacts act as an innovating factor beyond the context of organization and contribute to social studies at large.

As a consequence of this evolution, an opportunity to further extend the network of sister disciplines is emerging for IS. In addition to computer science on the one side, and to organizational studies on the other side, the complex, interdisciplinary nature of Information Systems requires establishing links also with human sciences, such as sociology and psychology and with design-oriented disciplines, such as engineering. The power and the material characteristics of the IT artefact embedded in social practices enable the emergence of sociomaterial assemblages whose study and understanding will be the key to understand the evolution of organizations and society at large for the time to come.

Some people consider this "multi-disciplinary growth" as a dangerous drift towards identity loss. But multi-disciplinary evolution may result in great opportunities if the IS community will be strong enough and mature to keep focused while continuously building up of networks of peer research relationships with sister disciplines. Marco is among those who actively participate in these recent, heated debates. If there was only one lesson to take away from Marco, it is that confrontation, pluralism, and integration are opportunities and not dangers.

After having been a pioneer of the "migration" of the IS community from the nest of Computer Science to the privileged relationship with organizational studies, he is now pioneering new disciplinary links and approaches developed outside the organizational studies traditions, such as the design-oriented approaches. There is no doubt that if such cutting-edge debates are being discussed in Italy it is because of Marco's persistence and attention to the changing context of IS research.

Marco has kept on working on these goals holding a series of institutional roles in the IS community. Marco was among the founders of ItAIS, the Italian Association of Information Systems, the Italian Chapter of the AIS. In his role as VP and President of ItAIS, he has carried out intense, visible and recognized work to promote the continuous growth of the European IS community and its integration in the international scenario. Thanks to Marco's work as AIS representative of Region 2 (Europe, Africa and Middle East) Italy was chosen to host ECIS 2003 and ECIS 2009, along with ICIS 2013. These results are important not only for the Italian IS community but for the European one at large. The commitment to his work has granted Marco the honor of receiving in 2010 the prestigious AIS Fellow Award.

All the IS Italian and international community is grateful for Marco's persistent work. This book is our tangible thanks.

Andrea Carugati and Cecilia Rossignoli
Århus and Verona, 15 December 2010

A Personal Note from the Editors

My destiny has taken me far from Italy. Today I live and work in Denmark and I have been outside of Italy since 1996. Finishing my Ph.D. in 2003 I was also quite sure that I would never be part of the Italian academic community. However, now, in 2010 I can only look back and see that a very large part of my connections and close friends are in fact from the Italian IS community. If this is the case now it is mostly because Marco De Marco in 2003, and relentlessly ever since, has helped me in being a part of this community and to thrive in it. As I have come to know Marco, I have appreciated his sense of strategy and his unsurpassed capacity of bringing people together. Together these two qualities are a powerful combination that Marco is able to juggle like a master. I feel privileged to have been part of the evolution of this community and to have seen my colleagues come to teach at very high international levels and publish competitively at international standards. Marco has planted the seeds and has nurtured the growth. This is among the best qualities a person can have and certainly one that I hope to learn myself. Dear Marco, a big thank you and my best wishes for the new ideas and challenges that you will feel like taking on in the future.

Andrea

I have known Marco since he supervised my Master's thesis at the University of Verona back in 1981. When Marco moved to the Catholic University in 1985 I decided to follow him and thereby I began my academic career. I feel that with Marco we have built many interesting and important initiatives. Together we built the Center for Research in Technology and Finance that has allowed us to come in contact with many European universities and research centers and to carry out important European framework projects. From these projects we have established a network of contacts in research in information systems. When I moved back to the University of Verona as Associate Professor, the Italian IS community was already consolidating. In 2003, in occasion of the ECIS conference in Naples, the first ECIS conference held in Italy, we founded the Italian chapter of the Association of Information Systems together with other prominent Italian academics. This was but the first occasion to internationalize our community, an occasion that brought us to host ECIS again in Italy in Verona in 2009, a fantastic event for a young research community. Thank you Marco for helping the Italian community in general and the Verona gang in particular to become open and strong. Marco, this book is the result of all your efforts, not ours. We have been merely the collecting instruments of something that was already formed.

Cecilia

Part I

IS Theory

The Eiderdown Project

Francesco Virili[1]

Abstract This chapter tells the story of the "Eiderdown project", a graphical two-dimensional map exploring the evolution of Organization and Information Systems, that Marco promoted and distributed with a group of friends, evolving it from a playful sense-making tool to a smart interdisciplinary means of connecting people and generating ideas. The first release of Eiderdown appeared as a gigantic white-background table, and was therefore named "Lenzuolo" (= bedsheet). After several additions, the bedsheet grew in content and size, earning the name of "Eiderdown" (= duvet, continental quilt). The story is structured in four sections: 1) the reasons and background of the project, the founding group and its first objectives; 2) the underlying structure and principles; 3) the evolution and the contributions collected over time; 4) the final outcome, its use and some paths for further evolution.

Background

I first came into contact with Marco at the Catholic University of Milan just after my first degree and I was impressed by how friendly and pleasant, but also smart and proactive at the international level he was with his group. His vision and contacts disclosed me new paths not only at the professional level (the doctorate in Germany, my introduction to the ECIS conferences and into the AIS community, the meeting with Andrea Pontiggia), but also in my personal life. In my view and experience Marco has a gifted form of altruism, a combination of empathy, vision, sensitivity, and immediate action that can change people's lives: he has been a "Lois Weisberg" [1; 10] not only for me, but also for many others.

In his genuine interest for helping and connecting people, fostering collaboration and supporting social initiatives, Marco conceived and actively patronized the Eiderdown project, transforming an effort of playful investigation into a smart interdisciplinary means of connecting people and generating ideas.

Over the years, while the IS academy was experiencing a convergence of Computer Science and Software Engineering with Organization and Management [2], Marco was acting not only as a central network gate connecting many individuals, but also as a bridge between different social worlds. When engineers and computer scientists were collaborating with social scientists, the complexity and sometimes confusion of different cultural legacies, different world views, different scientific references and even different languages had to be patiently managed, and Marco has always played a fundamental role to this aim. Also student and PhD education

[1] Universita' di Cassino, OrgLab, Dipartimento Impresa Ambiente e Management, Via S. Angelo, 03043 – Cassino (FR) – Italy. francesco.virili@eco.unicas.it

in this area has always needed tools not to get lost with so many different theories, dimensions and abstraction layers characterizing the interaction of organizational aspects and technical aspects of IT in organizations.

Initial Structure and Principles

"Let's start with a table! Would you give us a hand, Francesco?" When Marco and Maddalena Sorrentino involved me in this task I accepted with enthusiasm, but I have to confess now that I was looking at the "table approach" with a mix of curiosity and incredulity: their initial idea was to orderly enlist the main contributions from Organization and IS studies, to have the possibility to look at them together, side by side. Was an effective sense-making really possible with such a simple tool?

Since the very beginning, Marco insisted on two points: 1) we needed a bi-dimensional table map, a more complex analysis would not be useful at this initial point 2) the table map had to be printed out.

The first dimension to be mapped was the evolution of studies on Organization Theory. Organization Theory, while a relatively young discipline, in about one century of evolution has produced widely accepted schools of thought and recognized masters. In particular, we found that the historic, chronological approach typically adopted in Sociology of Organization (e.g. [3], [4]) could be used to facilitate further interdisciplinary comparison and mapping[2].

Therefore, the initial structure of the table was just a list of the most important organizational schools of thought, chronologically ordered. Given the fact that each recognized school is usually identified as being initiated with one or few masterpieces, we chronologically ordered them by the publishing dates of the initiating works. We dedicated separate columns to the name of each school, to the foundational references, and to a brief description of their contribution.

At this point, the resulting table was an ordered list of about twenty organizational schools and references spanning about one century with the top row located at the beginning of the XX century with the tayloristic school, and the bottom row ending the table at the beginning of the XXI century with contemporary postmodern theories.

On the IS side, as an underlying mapping principle we used a simple observation of facts: the organizational use of IT had to be preceded by the discovery, adoption and diffusion of IT. We had to dedicate a section of the table to identify the availability of enabling technologies, preceding their actual organizational adoption.

[2] An alternative approach often used in teaching Organization Theory and Design, (e.g. [5]) is the grouping of contributions and theories around the main contingency variables of organization design, like strategy, environment, dimensions, ... We left this and other alternatives to the pure chronological order to further multidimensional extensions of the initial project.

Therefore, the second dimension to be mapped was the chronological evolution of IT: we identified some of the main, widely recognized enabling technologies that have been characterizing the evolution of the IT industry throughout the last century, in parallel with the evolution of the organizational concepts and studies.

The first printouts of "the table" were already a nice discussion aid: even this early mapping was showing in a visual, straightforward way that the first Information Systems studies (not yet present in the table) should necessarily be lagging at least 50 years behind the first organizational studies, because the first commercial computer systems and the related enabling technologies started to appear only after the second world war.

The third dimension to be mapped was the progress of the IS studies, that we wanted to visualize side-by-side with the progress of the organizational studies. Here we had to take into account not only the relative youngness of IS studies, but also the absence of a widely accepted systematic account of the main schools of thought in the IS field[3]. Even a general agreement, on what may actually constitute the "core" foundational interest of IS research was actually lacking. In the wide range of subjects and topics taken into account by IS researchers, we had to make some selection, in order to limit the complexity of our first mapping steps.

In several occasions, seminars, formal and informal meetings and panels with IS researchers and students, Marco actively promoted an open debate on this issue: what could be regarded as the "core" of the IS studies. There is probably no simple and single answer to this issue; in any case, since the origins, a central tenet of IS research has been the study of the Information Systems Development Methodologies. The centrality of this subject was well backed both in the IS community and in the IS literature, therefore, we decided to adopt this view in our mapping exercise. We added to "the table" a set of columns including the progression of studies on IS development methodologies, classified according to the framework published in [7].

These three dimensions (Organizational Studies, Enabling Technologies, Information Systems Studies) were now populating "the table", and could be seen side-by-side in chronological progression.

Since the beginning, "the table" grew up so big that we started familiarly to call it "Lenzuolo" (bedsheet). And that was the official name of its first release.

First Release: "Lenzuolo"

The first drafts of the "Lenzuolo" (written in Italian) represented a playful, but meaningful, concept platform to exchange ideas on Organization and Information Systems theories and contributions.

[3] A noticeable exception may be the well known systematic analysis of the so-called "Scandinavian school" of Information Systems, appeared in [6].

Marco found several informal occasions to show the work in progress to Italian colleagues, and we received nice comments and encouragements.

The first printouts were already revealing patterns and connections. It was possible to draw lines connecting horizontally the three main colums of the "Lenzuolo" (Organization theories, Enabling technologies, IS development theories) evidencing common concepts and basic ideas. For example, a connection could be drawn between the first contributions in Organization (Taylorism) and the first IS Development theories (Structured approaches), both representing the first extensive application of a formalized rationality to, respectively, the organization of work and the development of information systems. Interestingly, a line drawn from the left (Organization theories columns) to the right (ISD theories) connecting Taylorism and Structured ISD approaches is strongly bent downwards. The table is organized chronologically: the beginning of the century is at the top rows, the end of the century at the bottom rows. Therefore, the tayloristic school is in the upper part of the table, while the ISD structured approach, proposed for the first time by Tom Demarco in 1979, is quite close to the lower end.

Similar connections may be drawn, for example, between the "Carnegie school of decision making" pioneered by Simon and March in the 50s, and the "Decision Support Systems" ISD approach, proposed by Keen and Scott-Morton and by Sprague and Carlsson around the early 80s; between the socio-technical schools of organization and the socio-technical approach of ISD; between the interactionist approaches in Organization and in ISD; between the Critical approach in Organization and the Trade-Unionist approach in ISD, and so on.

The steepness of the lines connecting Organization theories and IS development approaches from left to right shows that often new ideas in ISD had a previous correspondence in organizational schools, and that usually it needed quite a long time for an organizational school to influence and favour the generation of a new IS development approach.

These initial patterns could animate further discussion and analysis, and were actually looked at with interest from both the two worlds of Organization and IS development research. Several aspects were stimulating investigation and discussion. A primary issue was the reason of the time delay, that could be due to the late availability and diffusion of the enabling technologies, the late production and perception of organizational effects stemming from IT use, the time necessary to the diffusion of organizational concepts and ideas... Interestingly, this delay is progressively reducing: in the bottom part of the table, the connecting lines are less bent downwards than in the upper part, showing how at the end of the century the time for organizational ideas to migrate towards IS development ideas is sensibly reduced. This pattern may even now begin to revert the relationship, making recent IS findings influence new organizational patterns and ideas, as argued e.g. in [11].

In the preliminary discussions we also collected enthusiastic hints for new additions: several core ideas of the different school of thought in Organization and IS, could be better visualized using films and even novels. The idea was not entirely new, as several well known approaches had already been proposed using films to debate and discuss organizational ideas in research, practice and teaching. For example, in our country the monthly section "Fotogrammi" by Gianni Canova and Severino Salvemini in the journal "Economia & Management", have been proposing for years the organizational analysis of selected recent movies. Film projection and analysis is also sometimes used in management training [8] and also in University classrooms: for example, Roberto D'Anna (Università di Firenze) gave us nice suggestions on movies he had already selected and taken into account for teaching.

In our table, we felt we could use selected stories to illustrate the wider cultural and social context in which emerged new organizational ideas and schools of thought. Reminders to key scenes of well known movies could also effectively recall and visualize organizational concepts enriching our table and making it playful.

With his contagious enthusiasm, Marco opened our draft project not only to feedback and advice from various colleagues, but also to the occasional collaboration and contribution of several young researchers, that we called "tessitori" (weavers), including Franca Cantoni (Università Cattolica di Piacenza), Mauro Bello & Rita Bissola (Università Cattolica di Milano), Francesca Colarullo (Università di Cassino), Chiara Frigerio (Università Cattolica di Milano), Silvia Fiorelli (Università di Pisa), Vanessa Gemmo (Università Cattolica di Milano), Massimo Magni (Università Bocconi), Lapo Mola (Università di Verona).

The first Italian release of the "Lenzuolo" was presented at a poster session of the "4° Workshop dei docenti e ricercatori di Organizzazione Aziendale": it included a column with films and novels, and also a colum with what we called "cultural references", offering a wider panorama of economic, sociological, and philosophical master works that may have inspired or influenced the schools of thought in Organization and IS.

During the poster session we could experiment the effectiveness of a multimedia exploration: the printed version is very powerful and effective for an initial overview, while the pointers to films, books and papers help to give depth and richness to the first content layer.

Besides the color poster version, now populated with different types of references in different colours, we were able to build and present a first web site version, published as http://www.lenzuolo.net, in which the "Lenzuolo" sheet was accessible in html format, together with a brief presentation page and a "corredo" (trousseau) including the full bibliography, and further material to be used for teaching.

Besides the bibliography, the most relevant piece of the "corredo" is what we called "Lenzuolino" (small bedsheet). While the "Lenzuolo" is trying to display and connect the evolution of academic studies, the "Lenzuolino" is looking at the evolution of the actual applications of IT over time, focusing on the organizational role of IT, and its growth in wideness and depth over time. With informal interviews and meetings with experienced CIOs and IS managers, we identified seven "milestone technological architectures" in the last 50 years:

(50s) Electromechanical data processing systems
(60s) First generation mainframes: IBM S/360
(70s) Second generation mainframes + DBMS; minicomputers
(80s) Mainframes+RDBMS; workstations and Unix networks; single PCs
(90-96) Networked PCs with graphic interface; client/server applications
(97-03) Web systems and global networks; multi-tier client server.

In the "Lenzuolino" we tried to associate to each of the milestone architectures their typical area of application, together with the new organizational patterns and business models enabled by them.

Marco, Maddalena and I actually wrote a collection of teaching notes based on the Lenzuolino [12], and we have been using this material for several years for introductory courses in Information Systems and Organization.

Thanks to Cecilia Rossignoli and Lapo Mola, we also have an extended version of the "Lenzuolino", downloadable from the www.lenzuolo.net web site, including a connection of each milestone with further organizational concepts, metaphors and images [13].

Evolution: From Lenzuolo to Eiderdown

With the first release of the "Lenzuolo" we were actually surprised by its easy and friendly reception. Given the light and playful approach, without any pretence of rigorous scientific method, and particularly given the discretionary and possibly arguable simplification choices made in structuring and populating the table, I was expecting at least some degree of diffidence and criticism. Instead we received unanimous encouragements and also numerous enthusiastic suggestions. The few printouts we had prepared were immediately given out by Marco and we registered several further requests for new copies of the "Lenzuolo".

Marco was already looking forward to the next version: it would be in English, and it would include more content and direct links to videoclips, images and documents. A new project built over the "Lenzuolo", richer and, so to say, "fatter", just like a quilt over a bedsheet: what about naming it "Eiderdown"?

Marco was again actively involving volunteers around him, Maddalena and me.

A team composed by Valentina Albano (Università LUISS Roma), Katia Passerini (New Jersey Institute of Technology) and Elena Perondi (then Università di Milano) edited the first draft of Eiderdown in English.

Maddalena and Massimo Magni made a substantial further revision of the "Organizational Theories" column.

Anna Maria Morazzoni (Università di Milano Bicocca) with the support of Daniela Isari (then at Università Cattolica) proposed the addition of a column "Musical References", tracing down the evolution of contemporary music along the last century, including some of the masterpieces and also key events and technological breakdowns.

Andrea Carugati (then at IESEG School of Management, University of Lille) proposed the addition of a column "Philosophical References in Information Systems" based on a paper he had recently presented at ICIS [9] exploring the influences of philosophical schools on IS development theories and practices.

Substantial additions were included to the original multimedia content by an extended workgroup, with the participation, besides Maddalena, Francesco and Silvia, of Andrea Carugati, Angelo Gasparre (Università di Genova) and Elena Perondi. The group, working with periodical skype conference meetings, was able to select a few key scenes, to produce pictures, descriptions and finally upload on the Eiderdown web site a few clips, finding creative solutions to the problem of on line copyright violation.

The outcome of that effort was a new and bigger poster, full of pictures and colours, and a companion on line version including links to several clips and documents. From the lenzuolo.net web site it is possible to explore and download both the original "Lenzuolo" with its "corredo" and the new "Eiderdown" version.

Concluding Thoughts: What Eiderdown is For

Looking in retrospective at this project, I am really grateful to Marco and Maddalena for launching it and involving me. The singularity of this experience was that we made it just because we liked it, with no initial explicit research objective and organization. Marco made it possible personally covering the project expenses and recruiting enthusiastic volunteers who were glad to give a hand.

The posters and the web site have many limitations, both in the design and execution, but in their simplicity they can be appreciated by students as introductory material, giving a brief and playful overview of key ideas in Organization and IS in the last century. We used the project materials in introductory courses, both of Organization and Information Systems, and we found that they are far from perfect. The use of film clips could be much more extended, commented and technically improved (using e.g. youtube channels like in youtube.com/faracididattica). The IS column is limited to IS development theories and methods, with no mention of other streams of IS research. The connection between IS, IT and Organization is still to be characterized, and would benefit from the application of concept maps and other multidimensional graphic tools. The bibliography should be better connected with the references, possibly including online content were possible (e.g. papers and e-books) ...

But, besides the value of the project deliverables themselves, I discovered that a major outcome was in the positive contacts and relationships fostered at the national and international level by Marco, not only as the project sponsor, but also as the promoter of events, meetings, visits, occasions to meet and discuss, that have favoured the creation, and sustained the growth and education of an open, creative and mixed community or research around the themes of IS and Organization.

I do not remember exactly how many copies of Eiderdown were printed out, but I was told that if you go to visit Dave Avison at the ESSEC Business School in

Paris, or Guy Fitzgerald at the Brunel University in UK, or Richard Baskerville at the Georgia State University in US, or Jan Pries-Heje at the Roskilde University in Denmark, you may find a strange colourful poster hanging on the wall. Thank you Marco!

References

1. Gladwell, M. (1999). Six Degrees of Lois Weisberg, *The New Yorker*, January 11, 1999, http://www.gladwell.com/pdf/weisberg.pdf.
2. Pontiggia, A., Ciborra, C., Ferrari, D., Grauer, M. Kautz, K.-H., Martinez, M., and Sieber, S. (2003). Panel: *Teaching Information Systems Today: The Convergence Between IS and Organization Theory* In Proceedings of the Eleventh European Conference on Information Systems (Ciborra CU, Mercurio R, De Marco M, Martinez M, Carignani A eds.), Naples, Italy, 1571-1582, http://is2.lse.ac.uk/asp/aspecis/20030121.pdf.
3. Bonazzi, G. (1989). *Storia del pensiero organizzativo*. Franco Angeli (XIV edition 2008).
4. Adler, P. S. (2009) *The Oxford handbook of sociology and organization studies: classical foundation*. Oxford University Press, NY.
5. Daft, R. L. (2007). *Organization Theory and Design*. South-Western Cengage Learning, X edition.
6. Floyd, C., Mehl, W., Reisin, F., Schmidt, G., and Wolf, G. (1989). Out of scandinavia: alternative approaches to software design and system development. *Human-Computer Interaction* 4(4) (Dec. 1989), 253-350.
7. Iivari, J., Hirschheim, R., and Klein, H.K. (2001) A Dynamic Framework for Classifying Information Systems Development Methodologies and Approaches, *Journal of Management Information Systems*, 3(1), 179-218.
8. D'Incerti, D., Santoro, M. and Varchetta, G. (2007). *Nuovi schermi di formazione. I grandi temi del management attraverso il cinema*. Guerini e Associati.
9. Carugati, A. (2005). Information Systems Development as Inquiring Systems: Lessons from Philosophy, Theory, and Practice". ICIS 2005 Proceedings. http://aisel.aisnet.org/icis2005/25.
10. Virili, F. (2006). Non tutti i nodi di una rete sono uguali: Small worlds, effetti rete e accettazione tecnologica, *ticonzero*, 63/2006, 1-10.
11 Baskerville, R.L., and Myers, M.D. (2002). Information Systems as a Reference Discipline, *MIS Quarterly,* 26(1) 1-14.
12. De Marco, M., Sorrentino, M., and Virili, F. (2003). Organizzazioni e cambiamento tecnologico, CUESP, Milano.
13. Morgan, G. (1997). *Images of Organization*. SAGE, II edition.

Managing Technochange: Strategy Setting, Risk Assessment and Implementation[1]

Lapo Mola[2], Andrea Carugati[3], Cyrus Gibson[4]

Abstract In this paper we report the results of a multiple case study aimed at understanding the planning and execution of large IT-related business programs and projects. To distinguish the nature of these efforts from historically smaller systems development projects, Markus refers to the phenomenon of "technochange": *big, technology-driven, technology-dependent change seeking significant business benefit and requiring significant organizational change.* Analyzing the cases find a relation between strategic decisions, IT related project risk, learning style and execution style used to achieve the required business results. Based on the analysis the paper provides a three step framework and guidelines for setting the context, assessing the degree of risk of achieving business success, and executing. Depending on the level of risk, different learning styles are required that in turn call for advocating different approaches to program/project management, from "stop" to improvisational experimentation to big bang rapid implementation. The framework provides a practice based contingent approach to complex IT projects management.

We decided to present this contribution in the Marco De Marco tribute book as it represents in practice the way of thinking of Marco in terms of research development. Marco spent all his academic life, on one hand, in pushing young scholars to work and cooperate at international level and, on the other hand in involving Italian scholars working abroad to be active part of the Italian Information Systems community.

Introduction and Theoretical Framework

Research and practices have focused on IT related project execution techniques for a long time and have produced very promising results in specifying methodologies for the inclusion and involvement of people and organizational factors into technical change processes. The methodologies that have had the biggest impact can be briefly resumed by the English born tradition of socio-technical change (e.g [1; 2]) and the Scandinavian born tradition in participatory design (e.g. [3]). Despite the extreme value in IT project management of these techniques – and their derivates – there continue to be severe problems in getting business results from pervasive IT-

---

1 A previous version of this article was presented and published at itAIS 2008 the annual conference of the Italian Chapter of the Association for Information Systems with the title Patterns of Technochange Management in ERP Multisite Implementations [0] and won the best paper award.

2 University of Verona – Italy

3 ASB – Aarhus School of Business – Denmark

4 MIT Sloan School of Management – USA

related "technochanges". Technochange [4] refers to big, technology-driven, technology-dependent change seeking significant strategic benefits and requiring significant organizational change. From the management point of view these projects differ from smaller scale ones for their strategic dimension expressed in a need for alignment between technical and organizational changes and need for coordination across multiple projects active at the same time. The feeling is that while socio-technical and participatory techniques are apt to confined projects – this can be evinced from the settings from which these techniques evolved – for technochange projects other techniques should be used. At the same time looking at which IT projects are undertaken by both large and medium corporations today we see a predominance of large scale projects like ERP implementations, BRP initiatives, integrations initiatives connected with mergers, etc. Sometimes the failure is acute, visible and public, as reported in the press: e.g. Socrate project in France [5], Taurus project at the London Stock Exchange in UK [6], more often the failure is chronic and may drag on and drag down business performance undetected for years. The importance of new techniques for project management is further underlined by the monetary amounts concerning these projects. A survey of cost structures for large scale projects suggests that the hardware and software costs are less than 20% of the total costs of implementation, small in comparison to installation and testing (45%) and, most significantly, deployment or actually achieving effective use of technology (36%). Douplaga and Astani [7] in a survey conducted among companies of various size to discovered the major issues concerning ERP implementations, show that the major problem for organizations of all sizes was the lack of ERP training and education. Moreover, according to SAP, the leader vendor in ERP industry, it is possible establish an average ratio of 1 to 5 between the costs for the software and the costs needs for consultancy, customizations and training.

This study focus therefore on the knowledge and training issues in multisite ERP implementations and proposes a contingent approach to implementation strategies in accordance to the level of knowledge possessed by the company in the ERP technology.

Research Method

This work is based on two cases of multisite ERP implementations in two large American and European enterprises. The companies are manufacturers and have been operating for many decades. These companies were chosen because of their similarities (both manufacturers, multinationals, long tenure) and because they have been going through major successful technochange efforts in the recent past. The choice of the company with multiple sites fits the needs of this study because it can be expected that these companies have gathered experience with ERP implementation over time. Another reason to chose these companies is that the American one decided to carry out the ERP implementation completely on their own while the European one decided to carry out the ERP implementation using consultants. This is interesting because similar observations will increase the external validity of the results. The case studies are based on observation and interview to highlight the similarities in activities and processes in the implementations of the two technochange projects. We focus the study on the history of the implementations starting from the reasons and then following the sequence of events, tactics, and methods applied until the end of the two projects. This method follows the practice based research carried out by Levina [9]. The data has been analyzed in order to identify major decision, methods and processes chosen. The results of this part will be presented in the case studies below. Then the cases have been analyzed to highlight recursion of practices. Finally the practices have been arranged in a sequence taking also input from existing theory.

Case Study 1: Dow Corning Corporation

Dow Corning (DC) was established in 1943 specifically to explore the potential of silicones. Today DC is a global leader in silicon-based technology, offering more than 7,000 products and services with the majority of annual sales outside the United States. In 1995 DC was in serious trouble, after fifty years of growth, the $2.2 billion company was experiencing increasing global competition for its broad silicone-based product line. More pressing was the infamous breast implant situation since thousands of recipients were lining up for jury trials. With increasing pressure on earnings the CEO of DC led his operating committee through a strategic review. The business strategy that had evolved and served the company well was to be left intact but they hat to change the business processes and use IT as a significant enabler of change. Such a role for IT was new for DC that in that period was coming out of a large effort to create a global order entry system, a project called Goes – that resulted in a major technochange failure.

The executives assessed that the risk of success for IT-enabled operational change was very high. It was impossible for the analysts to get consensus among autonomous regional business units on systems requirements. While employees supported management in the current crisis situation, they had never experienced major changes. Management knew the DC culture was characterized by long job tenure and employee loyalty, but they had to make a case for transformational change. Management made two key decisions: the first was to appoint a new CIO in direct contact with the CEO; the second was the decision to accept the CIO recommendation to implement SAP R3 ERP.

The CIO called the change program "Project Pride". It unfolded in four distinct phases in 1996-1999. Each phase was characterized by different risks and DC management had to adapt different styles of project management. In phase one the CIO, in order to ensure employees would accept changes, decided not to use consultants, but to build capability and commitment having the work done in house. The CIO asked and received 40 of the best, most respected middle managers from operations around the world and made them the full-time implementation team. Few had IT experience, but they worked closely with IT. Employing a typical DC project management approach, consensus-oriented and with flexible milestones, the team began to learn SAP and to design work process changes to match SAP without modifying it.

Phase two of Project Pride began during the first year as the CIO reacted to what he saw as the limitations of the consensus-learning project style. While creative learning was certainly occurring, and the team of 40 became deeply committed to understanding SAP, little progress was made on redesigning processes. Employees in the field, aware of the executive pronouncements that big change was coming, were beginning to question the lack of firm milestones and signs of progress. The CIO took two important actions. First, he changed the project manager from one relatively comfortable with technology to a highly respected, result-oriented plant manager. Second, he tightened project planning to become more rigid: deadlines were set and expected to be met for a pilot implementation. At the same time he still left the Project Pride implementation team in charge of how they used their resources to meet the deadlines. This project approach led to a successful pilot implementation. The pilot was a full cutover to SAP for virtually all operations of a recently acquired autonomous business in Europe. The success of the pilot soon resonated throughout the DC culture as a symbol of top management determination and the capability of the project Pride team.

With the pilot done, the CIO recognized that he was in a new phase. There was a need for a change in project management to enable the worldwide implementation of SAP. The global scope and urgency of the project drove the risk and kept it high even though a climate of employee receptivity had been created. He modified the project style by strengthening the authoritative nature of his leadership and that of his lieutenants, while still permitting flexibility at the ground level. In the crucial period from 1997 into 1998, he led a relentless and unprecedented change effort at DC. He traveled extensively to spread the word and rally the project teams implementing SAP. He personally negotiated with and pressed his executive colleagues and old personal friends to adhere to their commitment to make changes. A key change came in 1998 when the CEO agreed to make project implementation one of the significant performance goals for the senior levels of line management. It was a strong statement of support for Project Pride.

At this point the fourth and final phase was underway. Although there were several pockets of reluctance, they were generally employees trying to maintain good customer relations and meet their operational goals: a positive form of resistance. The CIO and the teams picked up the pace and tightened and made rigid deadlines for site-specific sub-projects. Senior management stressed the new goals. Implementation time for sites went from 18 months after the pilot to 4 months in late 1998. In 1999 the installation of SAP was essentially completed. DC became the largest successful single-database installation of SAP R3 at that time, providing global integration for the company.

Case Study 2: Gruppo Manni HP

Gruppo Manni (GM) was established in the 1945 to recycle iron and steel. It was created by a single entrepreneur and developed its business by providing services to building yards becoming middleman between the steelworkers and final users. GM carries out industrial activities in steel-working division and in prefabricated steel elements, and components and structural systems for plants. They have a revenue of 492 m€/year and employ 800 employees in 8 operative companies and 15 production and distribution centers. In the 1996 the CEO became aware that the growth of the group, in value and volumes was not supported enough by the existing IT. High costs of maintenance, due to the high customization; functional bugs and architectural limits were some of the aspect that worried GM managers. In order to identify the weaknesses of the information systems a task force was created composed by the CIO, the project manager who developed the system in use and two external IT consultants. These employees founded together with GM a consulting company called Ratio with the specific purpose to aid the technochange initiative. A first assessment underlined the emergent needs of the group: centralization of the business decision processes common to the whole company; establishment of operational standard and common procedures among all the companies belonging to the group; optimization of marketing tools; integration with suppliers; real time connection among all the companies of the group; centralization and standardization of the IT infrastructure. The solution found for all these problems was to implement a group wide ERP which could cover all core and support processes. Ratio consultant decided, given the requirements identified to adopt a multisite ERP, called Diapason developed by Gruppo Formula. Ratio consultants decided for a gradual rollout per module and per site. They also went into a partnership with Gruppo Formula for the implementation project. Ratio personnel was involved in Formula's ERP implementation Project as observers in order to create a Ratio's internal group of consultants able to run a ERP implementation project from the both the technical and the managerial side. The initial phase while involving consultants had the same goal as in DC: learning first in the single site module by module and then move to multiple sites. They decided to implement the ERP system modules starting with finance followed by sales, manufacturing, and procurement. The original timetable of the gradual rollout project was as follow: September '97 Project start up; January 98 Finance in the Holding Go live; April '98 Controlling in the Holding GO live; January '99 Sale, Procurement and Manufacturing Go live in 2 Companies of the group as pilots; January '00 Procurement and Manufacturing Go live in all the company of GM. During 1998 in response to the successful implementation of the finance and controlling modules the CEO and CIO of GM asked for a profound change in the philosophy of the project. Rather than a gradual rollout, as originally planned, they asked for a "big bang" approach for the Sales, Manufacturing and Procurement modules in all sites. In January and February 1999 the tuning phase involved all personnel of GM.

Framework Development

The implementation of the global order entry system (Goes) and ERP (Pride) in the DC and the analysis and design in GM can be distilled to a cyclical process of strategy setting, risk assessment, and choice of appropriate execution style. All this activities appear, in the two companies to be centered on a relentless search to find in each situation the right learning style to decrease risk. This might not be evident at first glance but from the passage from risk assessment to execution there is an explicit or implicit effort to increase learning. The learning issue appears more clearly in phase one where the effort – learning ERP (SAP R3 for DC and Diapason for GM) with a limited use of external consultants – is explicit but returns in the other phases as well when the pilot projects are used to show – i.e. teach – the company ability to pull of these kinds of projects. This is a key element in multisite ERP implementations because after the first implementation there is the need to convince others to follow suit. In other words the top managers at DC and GM were intuitively mindful that strategic direction, risk and learning style and execution style where tightly coupled and their accurate choice was key to success. In each phase they implicitly or explicitly adjusted their strategy, conducted change risk assessments, used different learning styles to mitigate risks, and adjusted the method of project management to cope with remaining risk. The path followed by the projects in DC and MG can be seen in figure 1.

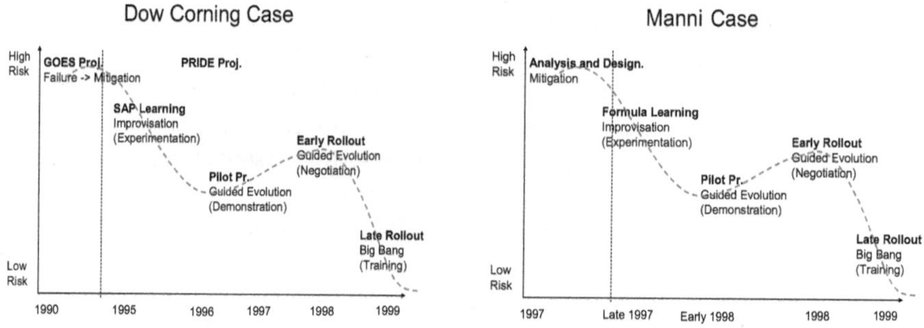

Figure 1: Risk profile and management/learning style adaptation at DC and GM

An interesting observation is that in the two companies they seemed to have grasped the concept that risk is not an absolute value. What is risky – or in other words difficult – can become straightforward when you know enough about the problem. By using different learning styles they were able to mitigate risks not by changing the nature of the problem but by changing their approach to it.

The second observation is that throughout the Pride project there was a continuous active participation of the highest levels of management. This seems to be necessary and mandatory for technochange processes. Top management involvement is necessary because of the large array of methods used. Only top management could accept the slow pace of the first phase of experimentation in the same way that only top management could change the reward structure to include project implementation in the performance goals for the senior levels of line management. Finally only top management could use the iron fist in the latest phase of the project when SAP was rolled out with a Big Bang style at record speed.

A third interesting point is to observe the wave pattern of the Pride project. Risk is not always decreasing because the nature of the problem changes. In 1998 the CIO had to engage in complex negotiations to assure the buy-in of the other sites in view of a smoother implementation later on. This part of the project – quite typical of technochange – is very different from before but could not be carried out without the knowledge previously created. The strong knowledge base obtained in phase one and two provided solid arguments that reasoned well with the local plant managers and line managers. In this delicate phase the CIO adopted a Top-down Coordination method of project management, with an authoritative style accompanying his traveling and convincing, but allowing for flexibility in timetables for particular projects.

Summarizing the observation of the DC case can be translated into a framework for the execution of technochange processes. The framework focus on the three macro activities: strategy setting, risk assessment and execution style, and conscious management of knowledge. The framework presents three phases, connected by guidelines for assessment and use. The three frameworks and guidelines are three steps in an iterative process for assessment and execution.

First, providing and understanding of the strategy, vision and context for programs and projects and checking progress of the program and project in their contexts over time. In this step initially the business case for the technochange program or project is created: covering the specific metrics of intended business success and the broad outline of the technical solution. We refer to these as the direct business technochange efforts: achieving cost savings, creating new revenue-producing service offerings, meeting a mandated requirement such as Y2K, or other business results. This first step also advocates separating these direct types of programs and projects from indirect efforts. Indirect programs or projects are those aimed at enhancing the capability of the enterprise. Indirect activities may include such goals as achieving an enterprise-wide IT architecture, changing the work culture, creating a learning organization, and the like. The business case in this step leads to a specification of the nature of the project in terms of its inherent difficulty, apart from the organization's capability to succeed with it. Second, conducting a diagnosis of the capability to carry out the particular technochange program defined in step one. Given the description and status of the program/project from step one, this step assesses how well leaders and stakeholders can build and install technology, make organizational changes, and address problems of alignment and coordination. The sequence in this step is a risk assessment of these capabilities, then a classification of the type of "learning" required to deal with the contextual level of risk, the approach to learning, and the nature of the execution. Taking inspiration from the DC and the GM cases and from Gibson [10], we offer and explain three styles of program and project management for execution. For high risk and experimental learning, an improvisational approach; for low risk and straightforward learning (such as traditional "training"), a "big bang" approach;

and for moderate risk and for demonstrative or negotiated learning, either an "evolutionary" or a "coordinated" approach.

Third, execution of the approach using appropriate techniques and mechanisms. For example, an improvisational approach will typically require mechanism to support intensive, focused, experimental learning by key individual stakeholders such as users of a new system or developers using a new technology. On the other hand a big bang approach could require mechanisms for widespread organizational communications and elaborate planning for coordinated cutover.

The three steps are repeated iteratively, with each cycle ending up with a review from the strategic level based on the success and issues with the previous execution phase. In technochange the reviews are an important component with new risk assessments as the effort progresses, and changes in the execution approach as required. The way in which evaluation takes place is shown in figure 2.

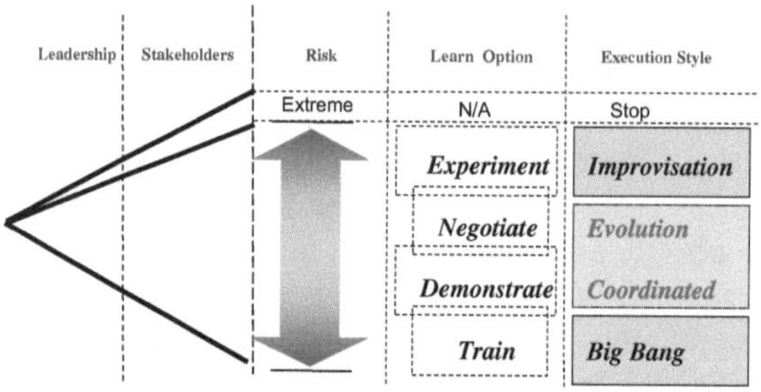

Figure 2: Framework for Technochange Execution

The diagnosis phase is carried out investigating the capability of the company leadership and of the other stakeholders. If both leadership and stakeholders have proven capabilities to carry out a given technochange process then the process is low risk and the learning required is of direct transfer of information – training like. If both leadership and stakeholders are incapable of carrying out such change then the risk is extreme and the options are either to redefine the problem differently or to engage in intensive learning of the experimental kind as carried out at DC in the first phase of Pride project. In case of mixed capability we end up in a grey zone where negotiation is required. We have put the leadership to the left giving it more importance in driving the risk factor because both in the DC and in the GM cases the type of decisions related to technochanges required first of all leadership understanding.

References

0. Carugati A, Gibson C., Mola L.(2010) Patterns of Technochange, Managing Multisite Implementations, in Atti di "itAIS 2008" , Information Systems: People, Organizations, Institutions, and Technologies, edited by D'Atri A., Saccà D. Springer Heidelberg.
1. Mumford E., 2003, Redesigning Human Systems, Idea Publishing Group
2. Checkland P., Scholes J., 1999, Soft Systems Methodology in Action, Wiley, Chichester.
3. Mathiassen L., 1999, http://www.cs.auc.dk/~larsm/rsd.html (visited in February 2003)
4. M.L. Markus, Technochange management: Using IT to drive organizational change. Journal of Information Technology. Volume 19, pp.4-20, (2004)
5. Mitev, N.,N., (1996) More than failure? The computerize reservation system at France railways Information Technology and People v.9 n.4 pp. 8-19
6. Drummond, H., (1998) Riding a Tiger: Some lessons of Taurus, Management Decision, v36, n.3 pp.141-146
7. Duplaga, E.A., & Astani, M. (2003) Implementing ERP in Manufacturing, Information System Management, v20 n.3, pp. 68-75.
8. Yin, R.,K., (1994) Case Study Research: Design and Methods, 2nd ed., Vol. 5 Thousand Oaks, CA: Sage Publications Inc.
9. Levina, N. (2005), Collaborating on Multiparty Information Systems Development Projects: A Collective Reflection in Action View, Information Systems Research, Vol. 16, No. 2, Pp. 109-130.
10. Gibson C, 2003, IT-enabled Business Change: An Approach to Understanding and Managing Risk , MISQ Executive, September 2003, Vol. 2, No. 2.

A New Taxonomy for Developing and Testing Theories

Pertti Järvinen[1]

I am pleased to contribute this essay in recognition of Marco De Marco's 35th year of his academic career. Marco, best wishes for your own continued good health and prosperity!

Abstract Colquitt and Zapata-Phelan [1] developed taxonomy for classifying empirical studies depending on whether a theory to be tested was nascent or mature. They also thought that one and the same theory to be tested could contain parts from both nascent and mature theories. In this paper we separated development of the theory to be tested from its empirical test. We found that development of the theory can be grounded on data or earlier theoretical concepts and their relationships. We also differentiated the first test of the new theory from its repetitive test. Based on those building blocks we succeeded to build a new taxonomy for theory building and testing. We shall also show how our taxonomy can be strengthened by formative validity and summative validity and can be extended by taking dissensus into account.

Introduction

Colquitt and Zapata-Phelan write that "it is difficult to overstate the importance of theory to the scientific endeavor. Theory allows scientists to understand and predict outcomes of interest, even if only probabilistically. Theory also allows scientists to describe and explain a process or sequence of events. Theory prevents scholars from being dazzled by the complexity of the empirical world by providing a linguistic tool organizing it." [1, p. 1281]. They created and used the taxonomy to examine trends in theoretical contributions over time, to see if the contributions offered by contemporary management articles differ from the contributions offered by management articles from decades past. Their analysis concerned Academy of Management Journal and its 50 years history and gave important information about trend in publication.

Colquitt and Zapata-Phelan continue as follows: "One way that empirical articles can make theoretical contributions is to *test theory*. The authors of empirical articles that follow the hypothetico-deductive model use theory to formulate hypotheses before testing those hypotheses with observations." (p. 1282)

Another way that empirical articles make a theoretical contribution is by *building theory*. Colquitt and Zapata-Phelan have found two ways to build theory:

[1] University of Tampere (pj@cs.uta.fi)

"Empirical articles that follow the inductive model begin with observations that the authors use to generate theory through inductive reasoning. … Of course, hypothetico-deductive empirical articles can also build theory, though typically in a different fashion. Early tests of a theory are typically concentrated on establishing the validity of the theory's core propositions. In subsequent tests, researchers begin exploring the mediators that explain those core relationships or the moderators that reflect the theory's boundary conditions. Eventually, in yet further tests they begin expanding the theory by incorporating antecedents or consequences that were not part of the original formulation." (p. 1282) In the former way (in the inductive approach) empirical articles can build theory, but the latter empirical articles contain 'early tests of a theory' as Colquitt and Zapata-Phelan themselves write.

The Colquitt and Zapata-Phelan's taxonomy (in Figure 1) is mainly based on two ways to test theory. What they call 'building theory' actually means that the empirical test concerns a theory just defined and first time tested. What they call 'testing theory means that that the empirical test concerns the theory is tested second, third, etc. time. Colquitt and Zapata-Phelan proposed that it is possible to consider the 'theory-building' and theory-testing axes of their taxonomy simultaneously, e.g. "*expanders* are articles that are relatively high in both theory building and theory testing. Like builders, expanders focus on constructs, relationships, or processes that have not been the subject of prior theorizing, but they conduct that examination while testing some existing theory." [1, p. 1286]. In the study classified by Colquitt and Zapata-Phelan as an expander, in its research model there are both the 'old' relationships received support in many earlier studies and the 'new' relationships not yet tested.

In Figure 1 the vertical axis describes theory-testing first time and the horizontal axis theory-testing second, third, etc. time. Hence, those two types of tests are independent and the axes can be orthogonal as in Figure 1. The real building new theory takes place before the 'early test of a theory' but Colquitt and Zapata-Phelan do not describe that theoretical development as a separate phase. This weakness is the main reason for us to build a new taxonomy for developing and testing theories.

In Figure 1 there are some minor shortages too. In the vertical axis the first class is "replications are attempts to cross-validate the findings of earlier studies" (p. 1284). To our mind, this category could belong to the theory testing axis. – Concerning the first class of theory testing Colquitt and Zapata-Phelan (p. 1285) defined "empirical articles that follow the inductive model do not include a priori hypotheses as a starting point, instead emphasizing the creation of propositions that can be tested in future studies". To our mind, this class describes an empirical way to build a theory, but it cannot be included into Figure 1 that concerns theory-testing only. This observation also supports our need to build a new taxonomy for developing and testing theories.

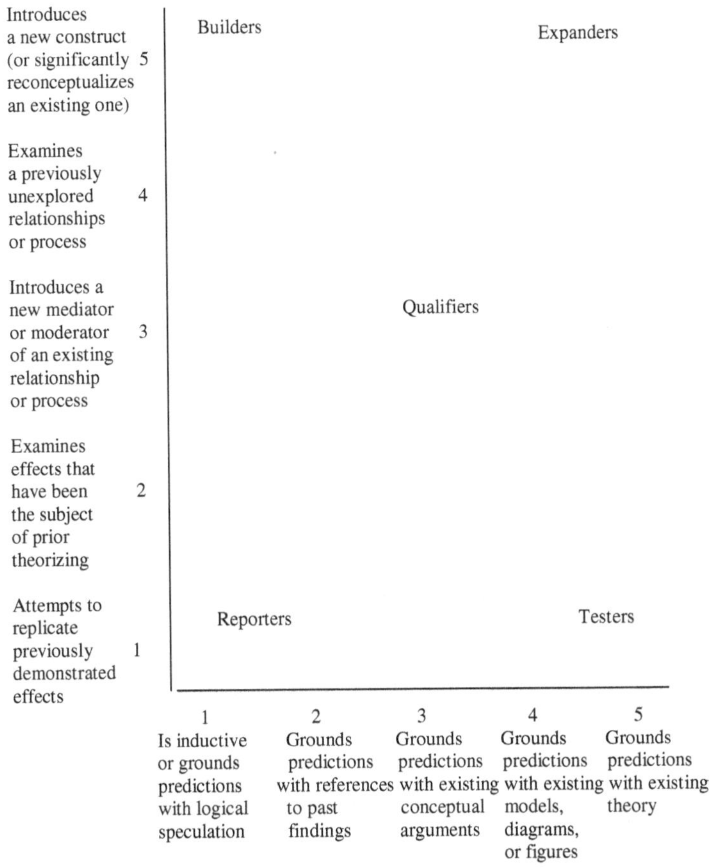

Figure 1: Colquitt and Zapata-Phelan's taxonomy of theoretical contributionsfor empirical articles

The rest of this paper is structured as follows: In the next section we present the building blocks or thinking devices of our taxonomy and develop our taxonomy. Thereafter we refer to the taxonomy introduced by Colquitt and Zapata-Phelan. We then analyze how we can allocate Colquitt and Zapata-Phelan's classes into our taxonomy. Finally we discuss the merits and limitations of our taxonomy and further research tasks.

A New Taxonomy

In this section we develop our taxonomy by using three differentiations: 'local/ emergent' vs. 'elite/ a priori' from Deetz [2], theoretical vs empirical (study), and original vs. repetitive (testing).

Deetz [2] used two dimensions in his classification of empirical studies. We here only use one of them. It "focuses on the origin of concepts and problem statements as part of the constitutive process in research. Differences among research orientations can be shown by contrasting 'local/emergent' research conceptions with 'elite/ a priori' ones." [2, p. 195] "The key questions this dimension addresses are where and how do research concepts arise. In the two extremes, either concepts are developed in relation with organizational members and transformed in the research process or they are brought to the research by the researcher and held static through the research process – concepts can be developed *with* or applied *to* the organizational members being studied." [2, p. 195].

The 'a priori' concepts brought by the researcher are used to form a tentative theory in the 'theoretical development' node and before empirical testing. Our tentative theory with some new concepts and/or new relationships is always nascent irrespective of whether it contains parts from the mature theory [cf. 3] The differentiation between the original test and repetitive test is based on how many times (one or more) the theory to be tested has received empirical evidence.

By combining those three differentiations we get our taxonomy (Figure 2).

In the 'theory creating' node, the new theory is grounded on the current data. In the 'original' node both the new theory from the 'theory creating' node and the tentative theory from the 'theoretical development' node are tested in a certain context and if that theory survives in this empirical test, its further testing can be continued in the 'repetitive' node. If that theory does not survive in the 'original' node, that theory must be corrected in the 'theoretical development' node and re-tested in another context and in the 'original' node. The 'repetitive' node thus is for re-testing the theory that already survived in the 'original' node. In the literature there are conflicting views on repetitive studies. On the one hand, Berthon et al. [4, p. 416] emphasize that "replications are an important component of scientific method in that they convert tentative belief to accepted knowledge", on the other hand, Colquitt and Zapata-Phelan [1, p. 1303] emphasize that "replications of previously published work and very incremental research rarely offer enough of a contribution to warrant publication". – If re-testing is successful, the repetitive testing of that theory in other contexts can be continued, but if re-testing fails, that theory must be corrected in the 'theoretical development' node and re-tested in another context and in the 'original' node.

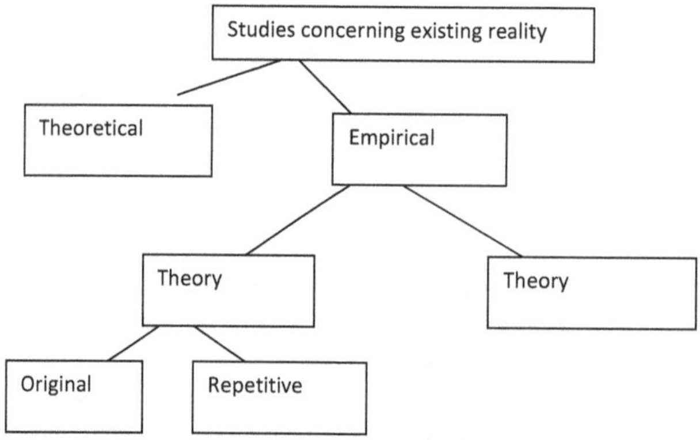

Figure 2: Our new taxonomy

The differentiation between the repetitive testing and the original testing resembles the recommended use of LISREL and PLS. Gefen et al. [5, p. 41] stated that "covariance-base SEM [LISREL] should be used as a confirmatory analysis method only. It needs to show that the hypotheses are plausible given the data. PLS, on the other hand, does not require strong theory and can be used as a theory-building method."

In order to familiarize our taxonomy let us assume a simple view on a theory as a combination of concepts and their relationships and let us assume that the first version of our simple theory is created either in the 'theory creating' node or in the 'theoretical development' node. Testing our simple theory means that all the relationships are tested and if the observations support our theory, the theory survives. If the test was performed in the 'original' node, the next tests of the same theory will be performed in the 'repetitive' node. But if some relationships are not supported, they can be dropped from our theory in the 'theoretical development' node, and the reduced theory will be tested again in the 'original' node.

The Taxonomy Introduced by Colquitt and Zapala-Phelan

The purpose of this section is to present the classes in the taxonomy introduced by Colquitt and Zapata-Phelan [1]. One of the three purposes of Colquitt and Zapata-Phelan's study was to "create a taxonomy that can be used to capture many of the facets of an empirical article's theoretical contribution. That taxonomy includes two dimensions: the extent to which an article builds new theory and the extent to which an article tests existing theory." [1, p. 1281] They continue as follows: "One way that empirical articles can make theoretical contributions is to test theory. The authors of empirical articles that follow the hypothetico-deductive model use theory to formulate hypotheses before testing those hypotheses with observations. ... Another way that empirical articles make a theoretical contribution is by building theory. Empirical articles that follow the inductive model begin with observations that the authors use to generate theory through inductive reasoning. ... Of course, hypothetico-deductive empirical articles can also build theory, though typically in a different fashion. Early tests of a theory are typically concentrated on establishing the validity of the theory's core propositions. In subsequent tests, researchers begin exploring the mediators that explain those core relationships or the moderators that reflect the theory's boundary conditions. Eventually, in yet further tests they begin expanding the theory by incorporating antecedents or consequences that were not part of the original formulation." [1, p. 1282].

Colquitt and Zapata-Phelan "introduce a taxonomy that combines the dual components of an empirical article's theoretical contribution: theory building and theory testing". ... The five levels of theory building are:

B1. Attempts to replicate previously demonstrated effects
B2. Examines effects that have been the subject of prior theorizing
B3. Introduces a new mediator or moderator of an existing relationship or process
B4. Examines a previously unexplored relationship or process
B5. Introduces a new construct (or significantly reconceptualizes an existing one)

> "The first two points on our theory building axis represent relatively low levels of theory building. Replications are attempts to cross-validate the findings of earlier empirical studies. In the operational replication a researcher attempts to duplicate all the details of another published study's methods, and in the constructive replication a researcher deliberately avoids imitation of the earlier study's methods to create a more stringent test of the replicability of the findings. Replications offer neither new concepts nor original relationships."

The next point on their theory building axis represents studies that examine effects that have been the subject of prior theorizing but not of prior empirical study. Like replications, these studies do not add to the ideas present in existing theory, nor do they introduce new relationships or constructs. However, they do open important new avenues for theory-driven research. A theoretical model is most useful for guiding research when the relationships it describes have not yet been tested.

The third point on their theory building axis represents a moderate level of theory building—articles that introduce a new substantive mediator or moderator of an existing relationship or process. These articles involve adding a new "what" (i.e., a construct or variable) to an existing theory in order to describe "how" a relationship or process unfolds or "where," "when," or "for whom" that relationship or process is likely to be manifested. Such articles represent a moderate level of theory building because they do clarify or supplement existing theory. However, adding one or two variables to an existing model may not fundamentally alter the core logic of an existing theory.

The next two points on their axis represent high levels of theory building. Articles that examine a previously unexplored relationship or process can serve as the foundation for brand new theory. The more a manuscript represents a radical departure from the extant literature, the more the field is impacted by the ideas presented within it.

Articles that introduce a completely new construct (or significantly reconceptualize an existing one) have the potential to be even more novel. The introduction of a new construct creates a radical departure from existing work by generating a number of new research directions that can shape future thinking. New constructs also represent an original and unique contribution on the part of authors, as opposed to new relationships between concepts already described, though not necessarily linked, in past research. Of course, a critical issue with such studies is whether the construct in question is *really new* or whether it represents 'old wine in new bottles'." [1, p. 1284]

The five levels of theory testing are:

T1. Is inductive
T2. Grounds predictions with references to past findings
T3. Grounds predictions with existing conceptual arguments
T4. Grounds predictions with existing models, diagrams, or figures
T5. Grounds predictions with existing theory

> "The first two points on our theory-testing axis represent low levels of theory testing. Empirical articles that follow the inductive model do not include a priori hypotheses as a starting point, instead emphasizing the creation of propositions that can be tested in future studies. Such articles may draw on existing theory to trigger research questions or guide the categorizing of observations [6-7]. The second point on their theory-testing axis represents empirical articles in which predictions are grounded with reference to past findings. These articles rely on the extant literature to ground a priori hypotheses. However, that grounding consists solely of lists of references to past findings, without explication of all the causal logic that might explain those findings. A paragraph reciting the findings of past studies can convince the reader that the same sort of relationships should be observed in the current article, though an understanding of why those relationships might exist would still be lacking [8].

Articles in which predictions are grounded in past conceptual arguments offer a moderate level of theory testing. Here authors attempt to explain why a given relationship or process should exist by describing the logic supplied by scholars in past research. However, those conceptual arguments have not been developed or refined enough to constitute true theory, nor do they paint a comprehensive picture of the phenomenon of interest. Nevertheless, describing some of the causal logic behind a given prediction supplies a critical ingredient that references to past findings do not [8]. A reader is able to understand the justification for a prediction while connecting that justification to the existing literature.

The next two points on our axis represent high levels of theory testing. Empirical articles in which predictions are grounded with existing models, diagrams, and figures come very close to testing actual theory [9]. Sutton and Staw [8] noted that diagrams or figures can explicitly delineate the causal connections among a set of variables, though the logical nuances behind the boxes and arrows is often lacking. Still, models, diagrams, and figures provide the symbolic representation of theory, and they often explicitly indicate the critical mediators and moderators that govern particular relationships or processes.

Finally, the furthest point on their axis represents articles that ground predictions with existing theory. In Sutton and Staw's [8] terms, true theory goes beyond models and diagrams by delving into the underlying processes that explain relationships, touching on neighboring concepts or broader social phenomena, and describing convincing and logically interconnected arguments. Although Sutton and Staw [8] focused on the degree to which an empirical article contained such discussion within its pages, Colquitt and Zapata-Phelan emphasized the degree to which such discussion could be found in existing descriptions of a theory. Those existing descriptions may be found in prior empirical articles, theoretical articles, or books and book chapters that provide the space needed to fully explicate a theory." [1, p. 1285]

Comparison Our Taxonomy With Colquitt and Zapata-Phelan's Taxonomy

Our first observation is that almost all the Colquitt and Zapata-Phelan's classes, B1, …, B5 and T2, …, T5 contain some kind pre-defined theory. This means that theories play a great role in their taxonomy. T1 is an exception and it is characterized as follows: "Empirical articles that follow the inductive model do not include a priori hypotheses as a starting point, instead emphasizing the creation of propositions that can be tested in future studies. Such articles may draw on existing theory to trigger research questions or guide the categorizing of observations." To our mind, T1 correspond our 'theory creating' node.

Classes B3, B4 and B5 belong to the theory building axe and their theory testing phase corresponds to our 'original' node. Respectively classes T4 and T5 belong to the theory testing axe and their theory testing phase corresponds to our 'repetitive' node. Hence, the high theoretical contribution level classes in the taxonomy introduced by Colquitt and Zapata-Phelan show similarities between their theory building and theory testing axes and our 'original' and 'repetitive' nodes, respectively.

The meaning of Class B3 is that a researcher added some moderator and/or mediator variables to the former theory before an empirical study. In our terminology, this means that a researcher added those moderator and/or mediator variables to the former theory in the 'theoretical development' node.

The meaning of Class B4 is that a researcher added one or more new relationships to the former theory before an empirical study. In our terminology, this means that a researcher added those new relationships to the former theory in the 'theoretical development' node.

The meaning of Class B5 is that instead of the former theory a researcher developed a quite a new theory before an empirical study. In our terminology, this means that instead of the former theory a researcher developed a quite a new theory in the 'theoretical development' node.

According to our terminology the meanings of Classes T2 and T3 first contain predictions that are first derived in the 'theoretical development' node and thereafter tested in the 'original' node.

The meanings of Class B1 and B2 refer to replication and to examination of prior theorizing and those classes therefore correspond in our terminology to 'repetitive' testing.

As summary we re-allocated all the classes introduced by Colquitt and Zapata-Phelan [1] into our terminology and in our taxonomy. We found both similarities and dissimilarities.

Discussion

Before evaluating the work above I would like to make two amendments, one strengthening and one enlargement, to our taxonomy. We can strengthen our taxonomy by referring to formative and summative validity developed Lee and Hubona [10]. They (p. 237) stated that "qualitative research is just as able as quantitative research to follow certain fundamental principles of logic in general and scientific reasoning in particular. Two such principles are the logic of modus ponens and the logic of modus tollens. In this essay, we frame different research approaches – positivist research, interpretive research, action research, and design research – in the forms of modus ponens and modus tollens".

Lee and Hubona [10, p. 246] "define formative validity as an attribute of the *process* by which a theory is *formed* or built (we will use the two terms, 'to form' and 'to build', synonymously). We [10] define summative validity as an attribute of the *sum result* or *product* of the process, namely, the theory. A theory achieves formative validity by following one or another accepted procedure in the process of its being formed. A theory, once formed, achieves summative validity by surviving an empirical test that uses the logic of modus tollens. Theory testing, we will show, involves comparing the theory's observational consequences with the observed evidence. Theory testing can lead to ether of two outcomes: if the evidence is consistent with the theory, then the theory has summative validity; if not, then the theory lacks summative validity."

Concerning the 'theory creating' node in our taxonomy Lee and Hubona [10, p. 246] give the following advice: "For a theory to have formative validity in grounded-theory research, the theory's variables or constructs must emerge from , or be 'grounded' in, the data rather than be taken entirely from a previously published theory and imposed on the current set of data." Concerning the 'original' and 'repetitive' nodes they give the following advice: "For a theory to have formative validity in statistical research, the process of building it must involve, among other things, data obtained through random or representative, rather than biased, sampling." [10, p. 246]. Concerning the 'theory development' node and the research process there Lee and Hubona do not give any advice how to achieve formative validity. A development of necessary requirements for formative validity in the 'theory development' node needs a new research project.

If the new candidate of a theory created either in the 'theory creating' node or developed in the 'theory development' node have formative validity, and if the candidate theory survives in empirical test, it has summative validity. If the test was performed in the 'original' node, the next tests of the same theory will be performed in the 'repetitive' node. But if some relationships are not supported, they can be dropped from our theory in the 'theoretical development' node, and the reduced theory will be tested again in the 'original' node. The 'repetitive' node is for re-testing the theory that already achieved summative validity. Failing to achieve summative validity in the 'repetitive' node might lead to falsify that theory [cf. 11] or to correct it in the 'theory development' node.

We can see that the results developed by Lee and Hubona [10] can supplement our taxonomy and this supplement clearly strengthens our taxonomy and gives some added value for it.

Lee and Hubona's [10, p. 246] rule: "For a theory to have formative validity in grounded-theory research, the theory's variables or constructs must emerge from, or be 'grounded' in, the data rather than be taken entirely from a previously published theory and imposed on the current set of data", gives a reason for a small but important side-result. Many researchers of interpretive studies [12-14] have recommended to use some earlier theories as *sensitizing device* [15, p. 326] in analysis of data and in development of a new theory grounded on those data. According to advice presented by Lee and Hubona the use of sensitizing device prevents to achieve formative validity of the theory.

Deetz [2] developed two dimensions, from which we used the first one in deriving our taxonomy. The second dimension could extend our taxonomy by taking care differentiation between consensus and dissensus. The second dimension focuses on the relation of research practices to the dominant social discourses within organization studied, the research community, and/or wider community. The research orientations can be contrasted in the extent to which they work within a dominant set of structurings of knowledge, social relations, and identities (a reproductive practice), called here a 'consensus' discourse, and the extent to which they work to disrupt these structurings (a productive practice), called here 'dissensus' discourse. I see these dimensions as analytic ideal types in Weber's sense mapping out two distinct continua. – The consensus pole draws attention to the way some research programs both seek order and treat order production as the dominant feature of natural and social systems. – The dissensus pole draws attention to research programs which consider struggle, conflict, and tensions to be the natural state.

The differentiation between consensus and dissensus would extend the 'theory creating' node in such a way that if consensus holds the output of the study will be one story, one new theory to be later tested. But if dissensus holds the output of the study will be two or more stories, two or more new theories to be later tested. Buchanan [16] gives a describing example. In the 'theory development' node dissensus correspondingly means two or more tentative theories to be later tested. In the testing phase, in the 'original' and 'repetitive' nodes the dissensus alternative must accordingly be taken into account.

Our taxonomy in Figure 2 shows that the theory testing and theory building axes introduced by Colquitt and Zapala-Phelan [1] are not two orthogonal axes. Our application of Deetz's [2] differentiation between 'local' and 'a'priori' views and our separation of the theoretical development from the empirical testing, both show that classification of empirical studies is more complex than two orthogonal axes.

During the comparison of two taxonomies we receive many examples about the possible alternatives of theoretical development, e.g. adding some moderator and/or mediator variables to the former theory, adding one or more new relationships to the former theory, substituting the former theory for a quite a new theory, and grounding predictions with reference to past findings or in past conceptual arguments.

Our taxonomy in the current form does not contain the priority order of classes as the Colquitt and Zapala-Phelan's taxonomy have. It is a clear weakness. We succeeded to relocate the classes described by Colquitt and Zapala-Phelan into our taxonomy. This means that Colquitt and Zapala-Phelan's analysis of empirical studies from the 50 years period in Academy of Management Journal is still valid.

In our taxonomy as also in the Colquitt and Zapala-Phelan's taxonomy there is such a limitation that empirical design research [17] is lacking. Consideration of Lee and Hubona's [10] formative validity showed that more research is still needed [cf. 18]. The same also concerns Deetz's [2] differentiation between consensus and dissensus.

Conclusions

We developed a new taxonomy for empirical studies analyzing what is a part of reality. It is more structured and based on both theoretical and empirical evidence than its best challenger, the Colquitt and Zapala-Phelan's [1] taxonomy. In the comparison process between these two taxonomies some mis-placements of classes in the Colquitt and Zapala-Phelan's taxonomy were also corrected. Some predicted amendments (Lee and Hubona's formative and summative validities, and Deetz's [2] differentiation between consensus and dissesus) to our taxonomy are promising but need still more research. The much used "sensitizing device" is misinterpreted as a key to interpretive studies and at the same time it prevents to achieve formative validity of the theory.

References

1. Colquitt, J.A., and Zapata-Phelan, C. P. (2007). Trends in theory building and theory testing: A five-decade study of the Academy of Management Journal. *Academy of Management Journal*, 50(6), 1281-1303.
2. Deetz, S. (1996). Describing differences in approaches to organization science: Rethinking Burrell and Morgan and their legacy. *Organization Science*, 7(2), 191-207.
3. Edmondson, A.C., and McManus, S.E. (2007). Methodological fit in management field research. *Academy of Management Review*, 32(4), 1155-1179.
4. Berthon, P., Pitt, L., Ewing, M., and Carr, C.L. (2002) Potential research space in MIS: A framework for envisioning and evaluating research replication, extension, and generation. *Information Systems Research*, 13(4), 416-427.
5. Gefen, D., Straub, D.W., and Boudreau, M.C. (2000). Structurational equation modeling and regression: Guidelines for research practice. *Communications of the Association of Information Systems*, 4(7), 1-76.
6. Glaser, B., and Strauss, A. (1967). *The discovery of grounded theory: Strategies of qualitative research*. London: Wiedenfeld and Nicholson.
7. Suddaby, R. (2006). From the editors: What grounded theory is not. *Academy of Management Journal*, 49(4), 633-642.

8. Sutton, R.I., and Staw, B.M. (1995). What theory is not. *Administrative Science Quarterly*, 40(3), 371-384.
9. Weick, K.E. (1995). What theory is not, theorizing is, *Administrative Science Quarterly*, 40(3), 385-390.
10. Lee, A. S. and Hubona, G. S. (2009). A scientific basis for rigor in Information Systems research. *MIS Quarterly*, 33(2), 237-262.
11. Lee, A.S. (1989). A scientific Methodology for MIS case studies. *MIS Quarterly*, 13(1), 33-50.
12. Walsham, G., and Sahay, S. (1999). GIS for District-Level Administration in India: Problems and Opportunities. *MIS Quarterly*, 23(1), 39-66.
13. Schultze, U. and Leidner D.E. (2002). Studying knowledge management in information systems research: Discourses and theoretical assumptions. *MIS Quarterly*, 26(3), 213-242.
14. Walsham, G. (2006). Doing interpretive research. *European Journal of Information Systems*, 15(3), 320-330.
15. Giddens, A. (1984). *The constitution of society*. Cambridge: Polity Press.
16. Buchanan, D.A. (2003). Getting the story straight: Illusions and delusions in the organizational change process. *Tamara Journal of Critical Postmodern Organization Science*, 2(4), 7-21.
17. Vaishnavi, V. and Kuechler, W. (2009). Design Research in Information Systems. Last updated August 16, 2009. URL: http://desrist.org/design-research-in-information-systems Accessed 26 April 2010.
18. Järvinen, P. (2004). *On research methods*. Tampere: Opinpajan kirja.

Thinking About Designing for Talking: Communication Support Systems

Dov Te'eni[1]

Abstract Supporting communication between people has become a major component of popular information systems for work and play. Once confined to office systems, nowadays communication support is pervasive; it is either the primary function of a system (such as email and social media) or an important complement to other functions (such as computing, data processing, e-commerce, medical treatment and decision making). Clearly, communication is prevalent in information systems. Knowledge about communication is therefore an important piece of a developer's kit box, or at least it should be. Unfortunately, it isn't, not in any systematic form. Information systems developers rely on their good judgment and on their own experience with email, instant messaging, tweets, video conferencing and others. I ask in this article – can we do better by building on theory?

Introduction

Information systems (IS) that support communication surround us almost constantly. As social creatures, we communicate perennially; many of us continually at work, at home and in between. It comes as no surprise that while using IS, whether for work or play, we need and want to communicate, and we usually can. Some systems are designed to enable communication as their primary function such as email systems and IM (instant messaging) or social media systems. Other systems include communication modules to complement their main functions. For example, decision support systems support communication between decision makers, e-commerce systems support communication with customers, and project management systems support communication between team members. And at home, calendar systems help coordinate meetings between friends and medical systems for self management support communication between doctors, patients and supporting family members. Whether as primary or secondary function of IS, communication support is pervasive in our daily work and play.

It is clear then that communication support is prevalent in IS development; it is not clear however how to design communication support effectively. In practice, information systems developers rely on their good judgment and on their own experience with email, IM, tweets, video conferencing and other communication systems. Indeed, there is much to learn from the huge success of popular communication tools such as email systems (Gmail) and IM (Yahoo! Messenger; Skype; Twitter) and from the more recent social media systems (Facebook, Linkedin).

---

[1] Faculty of Management, Tel-Aviv University, Tel Aviv, Israel

There is also much to learn from failing communication support systems. Google Wave[2] was expected to revolutionize communication support offering a sophisticated portfolio of synchronous and asynchronous communication tools. It was based on the idea that when we communicate, we rely on many different forms of communication so systems should support alternative communication behaviors. The idea sounds right but the product failed to attract a significant number of followers and was recently taken off the market; the lessons to be learnt are still being examined. We have good and bad experiences with such systems, but can the field of IS go beyond experience to offer a systematic basis for designing communication support systems?

Theories of Communication

The Google Wave experience could have demonstrated the power of adaptive communication theories, had Wave succeeded. Google Wave offers various communication tools so that users can use diverse combinations depending on their needs and preferences. Theories of adaptive communication suggest the same direction used by Google – that people adapt their communication behavior to a variety of personal and situational attributes. People adapt their communication style to the characteristics of their communication partners and the relationship between them. They also adapt to the physical, psychological, and cultural characteristics of the situation: people raise their voice in noisy situations, adopt a more formal language in a business meeting with unknown clients, explain at length when the communication partner lacks background knowledge and touch people to show empathy, but only when the norms allow touching. In other words, people make choices about the communication strategies they use, about the form of the messages and about the medium for transmitting the message.

Following the same line of thought, using an adaptable system such as Wave to communicate with a remote colleague, the communicator can adapt his behavior: when the situation is straightforward, the communicator can simply send an email to notify a supervisor the quantity of products sold that month; when the situation is complex, the communicator can combine showing pictures of a product and explaining vocally his concerns about the product; and when the situation is emotionally loaded, he can schedule a face-to-face meeting to fire an employee (although research findings show people often do the opposite, preferring to communicate bad news by email [1]).

A handful of communication theories have emerged in the past twenty years; they explain how people communicate effectively and, in particular, how people communicate effectively using IS. The early theories talk about the richness of media [2] and the social presence of media [3], claiming that certain media are

---

2 Google Wave is a novel communication package that was taken off the marketplace August 4 2010 (http://googleblog.blogspot.com/2010/08/update-on-google-wave.html – accessed August 31, 2010).

more suitable for certain situations, e.g., face-to-face provides the social presence needed for emotional conversations and lean media such as email is effective for simple, unambiguous messages.

More recent theories, refute, criticize and extend the earlier theories but generally adopt the idea that certain media fit certain conditions. I mention four significant enhancements. First, several researchers argue that constructs such as richness and social presence are in the eyes of the beholder; the medium is perceived, appropriated and used by individuals depending on the individual's characteristics and the situation [4]. Social information processing theory [5] claims richness may be constructed differently by different people, and channel expansion theory [6] adds that it depends also on the individual's experience and on the relationship between the communicating individuals, both of which evolve over time. Similarly, Yoo and Alavi [7] demonstrate how, for the same medium, social presence increases as the relationship between communicators tightens (Yoo and Alavi tested for two media: audio and video conferencing).

Second, communicators are proactive; rather than only choosing a suitable medium communicators appropriate the medium in creative ways and use it in ways the designer had not intended [4]. For instance, communicators using lean media such as email may nevertheless find ways to develop personal relationships, e.g., by using longer sentences, emoticons and more emotional content than usual [8-9]. Third, in contrast to the conduit metaphor, the receivers of the message are especially proactive in making sense of the message, independently or together with the sender as an interactive interpretation [10].

Fourth, recent articles have taken new perspectives, introducing new terms to highlight aspects of media and communication. Kock [11] talks of the 'naturalness' of face-to-face communication; any departure from the collocation, synchronous communication and non-verbal cues found in face-to-face communication requires extra cognitive effort that hampers the communication, at least initially. Dennis et al. [12] talk of media synchronicity and distinguish between the conveyance process and the convergence process of communication to predict what attributes of the medium should be used to improve communication performance. In sum, the last two decades have produced an abundance of theories that explain how communication processes and media attributes interact contingently to affect performance.

The Task

I noted above the prevalence of communication in a variety of tasks such as group decision making, purchasing, collaborative designing, team work and patient self management. Yet, the discussion above focused on the level of communication and media but not on the level of task for which the communication is needed. In order to link the levels of communication and task, theories of communication integrated higher level conceptualizations of task such as McGrath's [13] typology. McGrath defines four types of group activities inception, technical problem solving, conflict resolution and execution. For example, Dennis et al. [12] use McGrath's typology to analyze, according to the group activity, the need for conveyance and convergence communication processes and the appropriateness of certain media attributes.

Other theories at the level of task have been used to frame the communication process. Amongst them are social judgment [14], elaboration theory [15] and temporal sequences of decision making [16]. Generally, the higher level theory of tasks is integrated into a theory of communication in order to examine the impact of certain task characteristics on performance, recognizing that different communication patterns are more or less effective for certain types of tasks. In the next section, however, I look at the need to support adaptive communication concentrating only on the lower level of communication without regard to higher level treatment of task. In the last section, I return to the issue of task and relate it to adaptive communication.

A Model Linking Theory to Design

So far, we have looked at several theories that recognize the importance of adaptive communication behavior, i.e., in order to be effective, people fit the media they use and the way they communicate to the prevailing conditions. We have not yet seen a set of design implications emerging clearly from these theories. In this section I therefore present a model of organizational communication and link it to the design of communication support systems (CSS). The model is built on ideas taken from Habermas [17] and Searle [18]. It has three main factors: inputs, process, and impact (shown in Figure 1):

- **Inputs** to the communication process include task attributes, distance between communicators, and norms of communication;
- A communication cognitive-affective **process** that describes the choice of (1) communication strategies, (2) the message's form, and (3) the medium through which the message is transmitted; and
- The communication **impact** is both mutual understanding and relationship between communicators.

In addition to the inputs, process and impact, there is one more factor central to the model – the notion of communication complexity, which helps to explain the communicator's choices of communication strategies, message forms, and media. Communication complexity results from the use of limited resources to ensure successful communication under uncertain conditions. It grows as the demands on mental resources approach their capacity. The sources of complexity are cognitive, dynamic and affective [19]. When the message is difficult to understand, cognitive complexity grows; when the conditions in which you communicate keep changing, dynamic complexity grows; and when the topic is emotionally challenging, affective complexity grows. All three sources make for higher communication complexity. Moreover, when the communicator is inexperienced with the communication strategies or uses a new medium in place of a familiar one, communication complexity grows too.

Effective communication requires cognitive and affective effort to overcome the difficulties in sending, receiving and understanding the message; communication strategies are the means for overcoming the communication difficulties and reducing communication complexity. One such strategy is contextualization – the provision of background information that explains the message. For example, the core message may be a safety concern with a new toy sent from an engineer to a production manager; the contextual information could be the engineer's explanation why the product can injure young children, which is the main target population. The communication model explains how contextualization reduces communication complexity and makes it easier for the receiver of the message to understand and accept it. However, contextualization is effective only when needed [20] and can be counterproductive for receivers who easily understand the message.

How can this model inform better designs of CSS? According to the model, comprehensible and trustworthy communication is at once an act of building mutual understanding and relationships between the communicators [17]. Mutual understanding is necessary for agreement and task accomplishment, and relationship is necessary for gaining commitment between communicators. All too often, CSS ignore one or the other, e.g., ignoring relationships in communicating structured messages such as online purchasing. This discussion of communication impact results in the first design principle (see Table 1 – Principle #1).

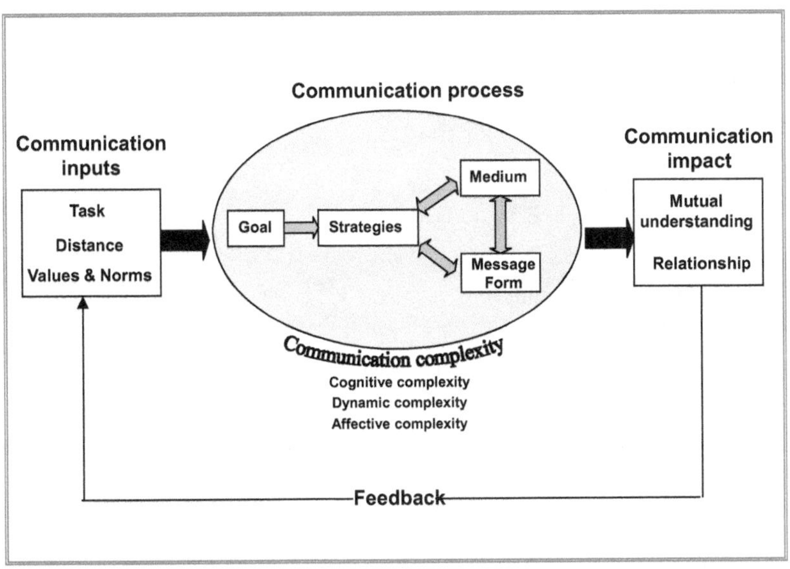

Figure 1: A model of communication (adapted from Te'eni [19])

Table 1: Principles of CSS design (adapted from Te'eni [21])

1	Design must simultaneously consider enhancing mutual understanding and promoting relationships between communicators
2	Design should support adaptive behavior, including the contingent use of alternative communication strategies, alternative message forms and alternative media.
3	Design should monitor complexity and alert communicators to a high propensity of communication breakdowns, including those related to dimensions of organizational structure.
4	Design should support multiple levels of communication and easy travel between levels.
5	Organizational memory should consist of speech act components, situations, norms and values.
6	Organizational memory should consist of associative information, accessible through multiple media, and represented in multiple forms, allowing for indeterminate and emergent views too

In a similar fashion, the other five principles have been developed [21]. The general functionality of CSS that is needed to implement these principles is shown in Figure 2; it includes functionality to support inputs, processes and impacts (of the model in Figure 1). The respective functions are labeled 1) Identify situation, 2) Support goals /strategies and Provide message, and 3) Feedback. All functions are enhanced by organizational memory (much like we humans use our memory to communicate).

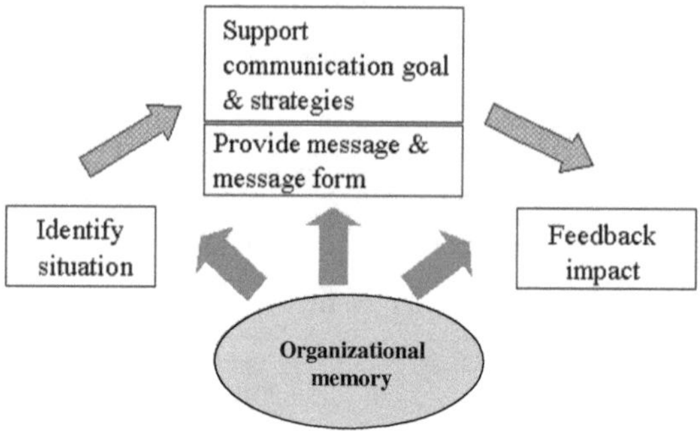

Figure 2: Functionality of communication support systems (from Te'eni [19])

Here is another example of CSS functionality – the need to contingently support communication strategies (Principle #2). Let's begin with the obvious. Increasingly, CSS allow both synchronous and asynchronous communication. In our terminology, adaptable systems support adaptive communication behavior. This is not to say that the system automatically changes from one mode to the other but it allows the user to change modes as she sees fit. More advanced systems may suggest which mode is more appropriate. Many e-learning systems, for example, provide asynchronous communication for teachers to deliver reading materials and students to submit assignments but also synchronous chats between teacher and student for urgent clarifications. Effective communicators may switch from email to instant messaging (IM) when they sense communication is ineffective and requires immediate explanations to understand a complex message. Systems should not only enable both modes but make it easy to switch from one to another, e.g., by listing previous emails that are relevant as part of the IM display. And this is what Google Wave offered. However, the greater functionality offered by the system increases communication complexity. The communicator needs to choose the appropriate strategy or medium and this may require effort that may become prohibitive when there are many options to choose from.

Let's take a more complicated example. We spoke of contextualization. CSS should allow the user to add to the core message contextual information, which can be retrieved from organizational memory. This idea was implemented in kMail [22]; the system builds links to relevant information automatically by parsing outgoing messages to detect information that elaborates the message. The challenge is to deliver context only when needed, in other words to support adaptive behavior when it is effective. As noted above, delivering contextual information when it is not needed maybe counterproductive [20]. To determine whether contextualization is needed, the system calculates differences in professional perspectives or differences in terminologies used by the particular pairs of communicators. When perspectives differ, contextualization is needed but not when perspectives are similar. Figure 3 depicts a message as it is sent (the screen on the left hand side) and after it is parsed and transformed into a contextualized message (the screen on the right hand side). In kMail, the different perspectives owned by different communicators are indexed so that people can see a message in light of alternative perspectives (labeled 'Personal' and 'Production Team' in the right hand column in Figure 3).

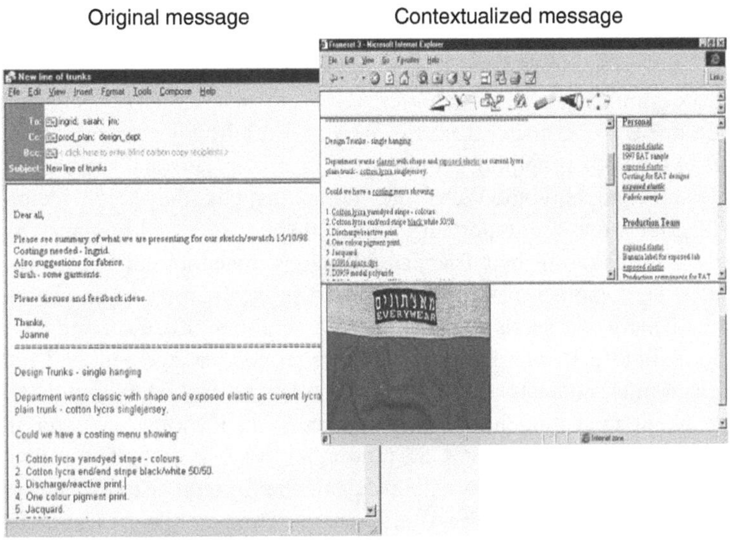

Figure 3: An original message before contextualization and its contextualized message (adapted from [22]).

Going Beyond

The previous section demonstrates how communications theory informs design. Looking at the CSS around us, there is room for improvement along the principles listed in Table 1. Bold trials such as Google Wave are needed but obviously some error was made, something that probably cannot be explained by the theories above. This section raises three aspects of CSS that go beyond the discussion so far: the role of task and domain of communication, the role of presentation and identity in communication and the human-computer interaction in CSS.

Most of the communication theories mentioned above allude to the central role of task and of the domain within which the communicators function. For instance, organizational norms dictate when and how empathy may be conveyed between employees of different ranks. In practice, dedicated or tailored systems often reflect the norms and practices of the particular domain or organization. But the theoretical link between communication theories and domain theories is weak or non-existent. In the field of health communication, research demonstrates how both task oriented communication and relational/affective communication affect health outcomes such as patient wellbeing. Unless the IS designer gets the integrated picture of communication and domain knowledge, it will be difficult to deal with tradeoffs between communication goals (e.g., understanding medical advice and increasing patient wellbeing) and to know what design leads to optimal communication. Metaphorically, the task/domain level directs and constrains the lower communication level. What is needed is a multi-level theory of communication fitting different domains.

The second aspect concerns a shift from the psychological/individual focus of the communication theories discussed to a more social/collective aspect of communication. Winograd and Flores' influential book 'Understanding computers and cognition' [23] argued that computers were more about communication than computation. Interestingly, they used Speech Act theory [18] to show how computers, like speech, create commitments and identities. Ten years later, Flores [24] claimed a new transition needs to be made, from the Web as establishing communication between parties to the Web as helping people create identities, personal and organizational. People spend hours on the Web – they do not just talk, they create identities, multiple identities, that are important to them; they are engaged in managing the impressions they make on their friends, colleagues, potential employers and others. It became clear, sometimes painfully, that the information users put on Facebook for the benefit of friends may end up in a corporate office ruining their prospects for a job. In effect, communication and impression management go hand in hand. Designers must understand not only the threats to privacy but why and how people go about managing impressions and creating identities in order to understand the design implications on CSS (and many other systems that reflect identities, e.g., corporate websites and online shops). The communication theories we reviewed are too narrow to address such issues. Broader theories such as 'Impression Management' [25] explain the goals of self presentation and the means of constructing it similar to the goals and strategies of communication (Figure 1).

Future work should examine how this theory can produce design implications to complement those emerging from the narrower view of communication.

The third aspect is that of designing the human-computer interface in CSS. Users need to use the keyboard and mouse, view information on the screen or listen to audio messages. This is the tool level of interaction, which has to be designed according to physical, cognitive and affective criteria. Returning to the levels metaphor, the tool level is below the communication level we have been discussing, and the levels are linked. The tool level should be transparent to the user so that she can concentrate on the task of communicating; when the user gets bogged down with the mechanics of the tool, communication suffers. Human-computer interaction research teaches us that the complexity of interface must be controlled. Furthermore, because communication occurs on several levels simultaneously, the tool should be consistent with the content of the message, e.g., synthetic voice that sounds happy when conveying sad news reduces message credibility. At the time of writing this paper, it is too early to conclude why Google Wave was abandoned. However, commentators and informal reports of the user blogs suggest that the system was too complex for the users (most of whom were experts and early adopters). The complexity of the human-computer interface, coupled with the higher communication complexity induced by multiple options for communication, were too high for the novice user to communicate effectively. It remains to be seen if new attempts in the same direction prove to be less complex. Facebook has just announced a new approach to designing communication – a portfolio of email, Facebook messages, Instant Messaging and perhaps voice[3]. Their idea is that the user communicates without worrying about the method used. Complexity is reduced by keeping a history of communication organized by contact (Facebook friend). Complexity may be further reduced by a system that automatically undertakes to choose or suggest the right method (e.g., email versus IM), relieving the user from the extra effort. Future research will have to address the human-computer interaction in conjunction with communication theory.

To conclude is a last example of communication support for patients self-managing their illness at home. A medical system that recommends treatments, medication and diets includes in the interface an embodied agent (an avatar) that represents the doctor giving advice. How should the agent be designed to improve communication between doctor and patient? A primary concern in this situation is the doctor's credibility; another concern is the patient's acceptance and motivation to adhere. The doctor's identity as it is projected by the agent is important to the doctor but also for his credibility as perceived by the patient. Vugt et al. [26], using social comparison theory, found that an image of a person similar to the user (patient in our example) enhances a positive attitude and greater likelihood of accepting the message. Similarity is not necessarily facial resemblance but can be achieved for example by similar gestures, which the system can adopt from viewing the patient's behavior. However, credibility and positive attitude may conflict.

[3] Facebook announcement, November 15th, 2010, http://www.facebook.com/FacebookLive – accessed November 16, 2010.

The normative behavior expected of a doctor may be violated if the embodied agent makes gestures copied from the patient. Thus the norms of medical context may dictate a particular appearance and tailored to the image the doctor wishes to manage. These are aspects of designing CSS that go beyond what can be learnt from the communication theories discussed.

I began with a claim that we should build on communication theory to inform and improve the design of CSS and demonstrated how it can be done with a given model of communication. The concluding section demonstrated the need to move even further beyond extant theories of communication used in IS literature if we are to build effective CSS for the new millennium.

Acknowledgment

Acknowledgement: I thank Michael Davern, Adi Katz and the editors of this volume for their insightful comments.

References

Sussman, S. W., and Sproul, L. (1999) Straight Talk: Delivering Bad News Through Electronic Communication. *Information Systems Research,* 10 (2), 150-166.

Daft, R. L., and Lengel, R. H. (1986) Organizational Information Requirements, Media Richness and Structural Design. *Management Science* 32(5), 554-571.

Short, J., Williams, E., and Christie, B. (1976) *The Social Psychology of Telecommunications,* New York: Wiley.

DeSanctis, G., and Poole, M. S. (1994) Capturing the Complexity in Advanced Technology Use: Adaptive Structuration Theory. *Organization Science,* (5(2), 121-147.

Fulk, J., Steinfield, C. W., Schmitz, J., and Power, J. G. (1987) A Social Information Processing Model of Media Use in Organizations. *Communication Research* 14(5), 529-552.

Carlson and Zmud (1999) Channel Expansion Theory and the Experintial Nature of Media Richness Perceptions. *Academy of Management Journal* 42(2), 153-170.

Yoo, Y., and Alavi, M. (2001) Media and Group Cohesion: Relative Influences on Social Presence, Task Participation, and Group Consensus. *MIS Quarterly,* 25(3), 371-390.

Markus, M. L. (1994) Electronic Mail as Medium of Managerial Choice. *Organization Science,* 5(4), 502-527.

Walther, J. B. (1992) Interpersonal Effects in Computer-Mediated Interaction. *Communication Research,* 19(1), 52-90.

Miranda, S. M., and Saunders, C. S. (2003) The Social Construction of Meaning: An Alternative Perspective on Information Sharing. *Information Systems Research* 14(1), 87-106

Kock, N. (2009) Information Systems Theorizing Based on Evolutionary Psychology: An Interdisciplinary Review and Theory Integration Framework. *MIS Quarterly,* 33(2).

Dennis et al (2008) Media, Tasks, and Communication Processes: A Theory of Media Synchronicity. *MIS Quarterly,* 32(3), 575-600.

McGrath, J. E. (1991) Time, Interaction, and Performance (TIP): A Theory of Groups. *Small Group Research* , 22(2), 147-174.

Bandura, A. (1986). *Social foundations of thought and action: A social cognitive theory.* Englewood Cliffs, NJ: Prentice Hall.

Petty, R. E., and Cacioppo, J. T. (1986) *Communication and Persuasion*, New York: Springer-Verlag.
Saunders, C., and Jones, J. W. (1990) Temporal Sequences in Information Acquisition for Decision-Making: A Focus on Source and Medium. *Academy of Management Review,*15(1), 29-46.
Habermas, J. (1984) *The Theory of Communicative Action: Reason and Rationalization of Society, Volume 1*, Beacon Press, Boston.
Searle, J.R. (1979) *Expression and Meaning*, Cambridge University Press, Cambridge
Te'eni, D. (2001) Review: A Cognitive-Affective Model of Organizational Communication for Designing IT. *MIS Quarterly,* 25(2) June, 251-312.
Katz, A., and Te'eni D. (2007) The contingent impact of contextualization on computer-mediated collaboration. *Organization Science*, 18(2), 261-279.
Te'eni, D. (2006) The language-action perspective as a basis for communication support systems. *Communication of ACM*, May, 49(5), 65-70.
Schwartz, D.G. and Te'eni, D. (2000) Tying Knowledge to Action with kMail. *IEEE Intelligent Systems*, 15(3) (May-June) 33-39.
Winograd, T. and Flores, F. (1986) *Understanding computers and cognition*, Ablex Publishing Corp., Norwood, NJ.
Flores, F. (1998) Information technology and the institution of identity. *Information Technology and People*, 11 (4), 351
Leary, M.R. and Kowalski, R.M. (1990) Impression management: A literature review and two-component model. *Psychological Bulletin*, 107 (1), 34-47.
Vugt, H. C., Bailenson, J., Hoorn, J., and Konijn, E. A. (2010) Effects of facial similarity on user responses to embodied agents. *ACM Trans. Comput.-Hum. Interact.* 17, 2 (May. 2010), 1-27

Evaluation and Control at the Core: How French Scholars Inform the Discourse

Frantz Rowe[1], **Duane Truex**[2]

Abstract Other disciplines now lay claim to research topics belonging to the domain of IS research, and the field itself is under challenge in academic institutions around the world. Thus having a clear conception of those concepts lying at the core of our field and which establish the legitimacy of Information Systems (IS) as an independent discipline is more important than ever before. This manuscript seeks to contribute a clearer understanding of what we mean by the central issues driving the field. But this manuscript takes a new twist by approaching this question from the point of view of a set of French IS scholars and social theorists. It advances the discourse by examining how French scholars, many of whom are not well known outside of French academic circles, may impact our reading of those issues considered to be most persistent and frequent in the IS literature.

Keywords: cores of the discipline, ontology, information system definition, evaluation, control, social theories, French scholars

Introduction

There has been substantial activity in print and in electronic sources over the issue of the core of our field. The issue has raised a passionate debate (c.f. CAIS vol. 12 and following) in which many voices contributed to the discourse. But the question of our 'core' as a field is not a new question. Twenty years ago Banville and Landry [1] questioned if the field might be *disciplined*, other scholars examined the development of distinctiveness in the field using various bibliometric analyses to see if IS as a field had made a break from our own reference disciplines [2-3]. Still other scholars considered if or how the field might fare with a diffuse pluralistic core wherein many flowers were allowed to bloom [4-5]. More recently, others have revisited the issue of whether we have become our own, unique, reference discipline [6-7]. Influential scholars and journal editors suggest that there is serious disagreement about the efficacy in the field and that the field is in crisis [8-11]. So, while there may not yet be a consensus as to the nature of the problem, there seems to be continuing concern that, at the core, there may be something amorphous and ill defined about our field.

[1] University of Nantes, France Institut d'Economie et Management de Nantes and Skema Business School, frantz.rowe@univ-nantes.fr

[2] Georgia State University, USA CIS Department dtruex@gsu.edu

Benbasat and Zmud [12] lament the ambiguity of the core or our field, and consequently argue that the field lacks a cognitive legitimacy. Their position is not unproblematic. Their paper seems to have encapsulated an opinion that is either taken at face value or, alternatively, is resisted as being but one particular view of the centrality of issues at the core of our discipline. Nevertheless their general notion is that identifying a core to the discipline helps explain that which is unique about the discipline thus differentiating it from reference fields and establishing its legitimacy. In a complementary view, Albert and Whetten [13] argue that to claim legitimacy as a separate field of endeavor a discipline must establish 1) the central character it is studying, 2) its distinctiveness, and 3) its temporal continuity. We return to these three points in section two. But first we address the question of why we should be concerned with establishing commonly accepted notions about the core of our discipline.

The current debate seems to have evolved into a question of 'whose' core as if there was but only one issue at the core. In this paper we do not posit a single core, rather we suggest that there may be a *'core set'* of issues. This enlivens the debate on the cognitive legitimacy of IS by examining the notion of the *central character of what we are studying* and in the process seeks to achieve higher cognitive legitimacy for the IS discipline itself. But this manuscript takes a new twist, that is, it approaches this question from the point of view that can be understood by an analysis of a set of French IS scholars and social theorists to see how they 'weigh-in' on the 'core issues' debate. The paper posits that a core set of issues is organized around the twin concepts of 'control' and 'evaluation' in the realm of IT-based solutions, information systems and the domains in which they are embedded. But first we acknowledge another motivation for this paper, that is, to broaden the IS research discourse. Most of the voices being cited in this discourse have been from the English-speaking world. But there is a changing demographic in our field; we are opening the doors to the discourse in other languages, literally. The Association of Information Systems (AIS), via its on-line publication the CAIS, is starting to offer full papers in French since july 2007 with other languages scheduled to come on-line. Accordingly we think it is a good time to see where French speaking IS theorists and social scientists might offer guidance on the issue of the 'core of our field', the main question to which we now return.

Clearly articulating the core issues embraced by a field is not a trivial exercise. This is because it both raises philosophical questions and presents political challenges typical when discussing any definitional issue. Postman [14] reasons that the knowledge of any discipline is defined by knowledge of the *language* of that discipline. This explains why definitional battles are prominent in many disciplines. Terminological development itself is a convoluted process. In our own field, this point is well illustrated by Robert Gray's historical review of the distinction between the commonly used and accepted terms 'data' and 'information' [15]. Thus if we claim that we are principally dealing with issues of control in the domain of IT and IS, then we can better tackle larger questions like "how do we conceptualize the IT artifact" [16-17] and more specifically "what are these 'objects' we are trying to control?"

The question is also non-trivial because defining an "information system" is an ontological issue where 'ontology' is the part of philosophy studying the relationship between essence and existence. That is, the question of being (existentialism) and the nature of being (essentialism) or simply being *as being*.[3] So in IS, as in other disciplines, we need to consider two different problems:

- The building *of an ontology* – a problem that has been taken very seriously by many researchers in data base management and in IS development [18]. The challenge is to *reduce the elements* of an objective reality to a limited number of notions, as general as possible (see for instance the two-layered ontology of Parsons and Wand [19] and to *describe the structure of the universe from these notions and their relationships.*
- the "*exploitation of being* – as contrasted with metaphysics or the questioning of the existence of being" [20 p. 358-359].

Using Sartre's ideas, in the realm of IS, we are dealing with the ontological or metaphysical problem that is the general question of the nature of reality as opposed to the ontic problem of describing a system of attributes.[4] In simpler terms, it is the difference between a *description of things* and the *nature of things*. For instance in the software design community some scholars define an ontology as a set of attributes describing an entity such as an organization or a system. For us, and for this discussion, the crux of the current discourse around what constitutes the core of the IS field is the struggle to understand IS in its intimate and deep nature (as is suggested in the 2nd problem) as opposed to its appearance or its attributes (as in the 1st problem above).

The balance of this paper proceeds as follows: Section two identifies the issues most frequently dealt with in the literature for the past twenty-five years and are posited to be 'core' issues. Section three provides three competing French views on the nature of an information system. Section four, examines how a French reading of this literature privileges the notion of evaluation and control, and is therefore consistent with a majority view in both the English and French literature. This is done through an analysis the way influential French scholars characterize the IS object or influence the characterization of the IS object. The fifth and final section summarizes and suggests a plan for further research including a program to examine how the core issues might be better understood.

---

3 But even raising this point is problematic at this moment in our history. This is because even though there exists a long and rich the discourse on ontologies within the IS literature, the term is now being used in very different ways within our own field. Take as an example the difference in use between the "design community", the requirements engineering community and the IS community. Thus it is necessary to briefly explain our use of the term as well as where within the ontology discourse we place ourselves.

4 "In an ontology things take ontic attributes. Consciousness, however, goes beyond the 'fact' of being to the 'sense' of being." (ibid., p.30). For Sartre, and other philosophers such as Husserl and Heidegger, it is a metaphysical problem of being.

A French Typology of Core Disciplinary Issues

Albert and Whetten [13] argue that, to claim legitimacy as a separate field of endeavor, a discipline must establish (1) the central character it is studying, (2) its distinctiveness, and (3) its temporal continuity. This manuscript will not allow a full treatment of each of these points. Points two and three have been well addressed in the current debate by Baskerville and Myers [7] and Hirschheim and Klein [10] as well as by others in the many articles in CAIS volume12 2003. However the first issue, that of the field's central character, is still being widely disputed and, we believe, would benefit with from considering a perspective characterized in a French scholarly setting.

One of the central claims to IS disciplinary distinctiveness is the focus upon the control and *evaluation* of IT in organizations, or what Benbasat and Zmud [12] call 'IT-enabled solutions.' While unpopular in some of the current debate, this claim is supported by a study examining 1,018 articles in major English and French publication venues from 1977-2001.[5] This study identifies six major problem areas addressed by the papers in these publication years and venues. Those areas are: 1) strategic management (*gestion stratégique)*, 2) economic and diverse issues (*économie, divers)*, 3) design (*conception*), 4) project management (*gestion des projects*), 5) evaluation (*evaluation)*, and 6) (roughly translated) appropriation and change management (*animation)* [21]. (c.f. figure 1 below) Their study illustrates how, for both English-speaking and French-speaking authors, the issue of 'evaluation' is an important focus and that a generalized notion of 'control' is the dominant theme of twenty-five years of research.

[5] Those venues included from the Anglophone world two relatively older venues—the MIS Quarterly and ICIS (1980 onward)--, and relative Francophone newcomers, two French journals—*Technologies de l'Information et Société* (TIS) (till 1996) and *Systèmes d'Information et Management* (from 1996) and two conferences—l'Association Information et Management (AIM) (from 1997), and les journées nationales des IAE (from 1984). In total the study compares 351 papers in French to 412 papers in English from 1987 to 2001. Authors justify their choice of publications by selecting the most recognized sources in the anglophone world and respectively in the Francophone world. They also acknowledge that this choice is far from giving a comprehensive view of the Anglophone production in IS.

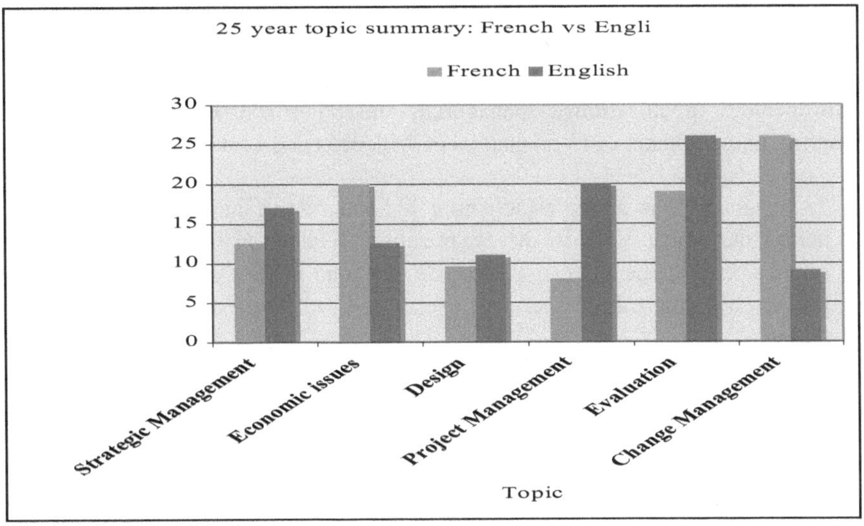

Figure 1: 25 years of topic areas in French vs English IS publications (reported in the Journal *Systèmes d'Information et Management cf.* [21])

> "One result stands clear: the theme of evaluation of information systems represents 25 % of the work. The more general theme of "control" (change management (15%), evaluation (25%), and personnel management (5% included in the diverse category)) dominates the field with 45 % far ahead of design and project management (28%) and strategic management (23%)." (p.10 translated).

For Desq, Fallery, Reix and Rodhain [21, p.31] control goes beyond management control of the IT function. It not only deals with control of performance of systems through evaluation, but also with measures of uses and organizational consequences through appropriation and change management, and control of human resources in the IS function. In other words, the theme of control goes beyond the evaluation of results and also encompasses the management of activities and of related resources (IT personnel) and behavior (appropriation and change management).

As shown in the French study, the theme of 'evaluation' has been a relatively stable construct over time. These findings are consistent with the typology worked out by Banker and Kauffman reviewing key themes appearing in fifty years of *Management Science* published articles on information systems [22]. However, the French study points out that in the past the issue of evaluation was analyzed at the individual level, but in recent years the notion has been applied more at the organizational or inter organizational level. The study also reveals how in the recent work, the dependent variables are more likely to address 'potentials' (e.g., competitive advantage, flexibility) than actual results.

In this manuscript we use the concepts of control and evaluation in a slightly broader sense. We view evaluation as a process that occurs at the various stages of information system (IS) evolution i.e., design, use, and impacts [23]. The later concern includes organizational, managerial, and other stakeholder impacts. For instance, in the domain of IS management Willcocks and Lester [24] say that

> "… evaluation is about establishing by quantitative and /or qualitative means the worth of IS to the organization. Evaluation brings in to play notions of costs, benefits, risk, and value. It also implies an organizational process by which these factors are accessed, whether formally or informally."

We adopt this definition because it identifies how evaluation is undertaken in any organizational setting as a matter of routine interfacing with an IS. The evaluation process is done in both formal and informal modes by managers as well as by other organizational stakeholders. So, given the embedded nature of IS artifacts in human organizational settings, the process of evaluation requires both managerial and technological tools and methods.

But IS design methods also incorporate procedures for managerial control and technical evaluation, taking into account goals, anticipating some of the impacts, and finally dealing with the specification methods for information needs [25]. So in the realm of system use, for example, control and evaluation occur for two main reasons: first, to anticipate or learn exactly how many people will really use the system, and secondly, to understand how (or if) users will appropriate it. The situated use of the IS often implies some measure of transformation from use as anticipated by the system's designer and builder's to that the use as employed at the user level. Thus, one other meaning of evaluation is concerned with diffusion and infusion issues [26]. This lag between conception and the adoption in organizational settings means that it is only *ex post* to system design, development and deployment, and typically much later after the appropriation of the IS in the organization, that researchers or managers can assess the net economic benefits of the system. In fact it has been suggested that it is only after competitors have made (or not made) similar investments, that we can assess the net economic benefits of the system. The context of evaluation is therefore not only organizational, but also includes the competitive structure of the industry in which the firm is located [23].

The importance of the issue of the notion of evaluation of our information systems and IT–enabled solutions, is also illustrated when examining the Editorial Policy of the French journal *Systèmes d'Information et Management.* This journal, arguably the most influential Francophone IS journal [27], states that, as an outlet for IS research, it contributes to three main objectives:

1. to *evaluate* the performance and characterize *information systems* both at the level of their genesis and the level of their use,
2. to analyze the actors *interpretation* processes in their activity of intelligence, communication, knowledge creation and integration,

3. to analyze IT appropriation processes and their effects on *coordination and socio-cultural norms.*

These three objectives define the set of core issues for the journal's Editorial Board and further underscores the sense that within the French IS scientific community the twin notions of control [21] and evaluation are central. Evaluation and control are linked concepts in large part because controlling requires having made and assessment (evaluation) and having an idea of what is 'good' or 'bad' within or without planning horizons, what meets or does not meet a specification and so on. So by control we are referring to the common notion of managing; keeping and activity within prescribed or planned norms or boundaries, rationalizing activities and processes, to regulate activities and exercise appropriate authority over an activity. But both concepts are culturally situated and are, of course, socially constructed.

As shown in the French study, evaluation is one of the core themes in IS and their concern is not typically French (cf. Figure 1)! However, if we consider the more general theme of control as also encompassing appropriation and change management, this emphasis on control may be more particularly French.

The preceding section illustrates the persistence, continuity and relative perceived importance of the twin concepts of evaluation and control as issues at the 'IS core' from a French reading of the IS literature. Of course this reading, like any other reading of texts is socially constructed. Next we turn our attention to how one might explain and understand why a 'French reading' might privilege the notions of control and evaluation. A French reading may privilege these notions because, for those controlling resources in business and government, control and evaluation of IS are universally invariant ***practical*** concerns; managers are looking ways to extract value from information systems in France [28] just as in the US [29]; but they might do it differently because of different social structures of control. A French reading also privileges evaluation and control because these notions are prominent in French history and culture and thus provide a context and background for French scientists. This context is reflected in the French social sciences as well as natural sciences and is especially strong in the French engineering tradition. Accordingly, if Banker and Kauffman [22] and others focusing on control and evaluation issues (i.e., [30]) are correct, then better understanding of the French viewpoint may help us better understand the importance or nature of these constructs themselves. It might also provide ideas as to alternative ways to address these issues in other contexts.

Six Conceptions Addressing the IS Core Within the French Scholarly Community

Within the community of French scholars, we can find at least six different conceptions that aid in addressing the core of the IS discipline. Those are: 1) rationalist and software engineering views; 2) general systems orientation embedded within a social-technical context; 3) the centrality of the social actor in interpreting information and the IS itself; 4) critical realist views of IS; 5) how human can circumvent all systems and 6) the interplay of control and agency. The first three of these represent competing views on the very nature of Information Systems. The three other streams help us understand how the French reading of the IS literature came to see the issues of evaluation and control as central to French psyche. We will discuss these six conceptions in turn.

Competing French View on the Nature of an Information System

The existence of the first three competing views contradicts the idea that there is a single "French" ontological view of an information system in contrast with say an "American" or "German" ontological view of an information system. Those views as expressed in the French IS literature are derived from:

- a rationalist and software engineering viewpoint wherein the nature of an information system is taken to be a formal code or an artifact that is fundamentally of a different nature than the socio-technical system it controls. These take form in cognitive modeling, formal theory development, methodologies and empirical studies.
- a general system theory conception wherein the nature of an information system is not seen to be different from that of the socio-technical system it is embedded in;
- a pluralist view wherein the nature of an IS is both human (via interpretation and negotiation), social (via social actors) and technical (through operating modes and IT) (c.f. [31]).

Conception One: Rationalist and Software Engineering Views: Rolland and Peaucelle

Their conceptualization arises from the discipline of computer science and the software engineering literature. For Peaucelle [32] the notion of an information system is implicitly restricted to formal systems, those dealing with data according to specified rules (id, p.8). He views an information system as a formal code and as the outcome of an intersubjective process, one which has a unique and collective fixed meaning that is justified by organizational routines. Both authors share the view that an information system is an artefact or artificial object. Consequently, their nature is different from that of organizations that can be considered either as socio-technical systems [32], or as natural objects [33].

By their insistence on a possible objective coding and fixed meaning, information systems appears as the tool of organizational rationalization. It aims at designating transactions and formal processes. It naturalizes the organization and derives from a realist ontology.

Conception Two: General System Theory View Embedded in Socio-technical System: LeMoigne

Le Moigne, is known in France as one who has adapted Von Bertralanffy's General Systems Theory [34] and for his strong criticisms of the analytical and Cartesian methods for designing information systems [35]. For LeMoigne an IS is first a system for preserving organizational memory and secondly is an intermediary regulation mechanism between the system of operations and the control system. But Le Moigne's view is that the goal of an information system can not solely be the control of a rational norm [36]. Rather, an IS is an organizational transformation that once in place allows the organization to see itself differently. Whereas systems design is concerned with the control of a system to achieve some presumed stable goal set, another concern deals with symbolic computation that incorporates an autopoetic learning process, self-actualizing its purpose by some learning process [37-38]. This idea is further developed by Le Moigne who sees the nature of an information systems as a kind of social engineering project.

There are however, other French IS theorists/researchers who build on these views, while at the same time incorporate complementary roots from within the social sciences.

Conception Three: The Nature of an IS as Both Human and Social: Reix and Rowe

Reix and Rowe, are both influenced by the French sociologists Bourdieu and Crozier, who move social actors front and center in social life. Thus Reix and Rowe [39] incorporate the notion that the social actor is constantly reinterpreting and playing with the meaning of the information in the system. They privilege the social actor in the information system rather than the technology. To them an information system is not just an abstract *objective* representation or the *fixed outcome* of social negotiation, but it *always* remains subject to interpretation, social games and conflict [40-41]. Adapting the definition first proposed by Reix and Rowe [39], Marciniak and Rowe [42 p.7] define an information system as … "a system of social actors who memorize and transform representations, via information technologies and operating modes ". This definition is both consistent with Le Moigne's idea of memory and transformation, but also with Peaucelle's idea of representation. In addition, with Robert Reix, Rowe argued that an information system can only be evaluated in context, which calls for an Heidegerrian ontology of an information system or a definition incorporating the idea of a recursively finalizing context [43].

We now turn our attention to an illustrative sample of four French sociologists–Crozier, Bourdieu, Latour and Foucault–to demonstrate how they have influenced IS scholars in France and abroad and to further illustrate how the notion of control is deeply embedded in the French psyche.

French Sociologists on the Topics of Control and Evaluation

In the French culture the issue of control has always been a central issue in scholarly and political discourse. The notion of rationalism, given full voice by the 16th century French philosopher Descartes, "…imbues understandings of technology and design" in which design is an attempt to control technical and natural artifacts [44, p. 18-25]. The importance of control and evaluation can be illustrated by the history of technical public decision making in France. For example, the decision to make the telephone widely available to the population was delayed because it was thought to be a subversive technology [45]. It is argued that the MINITEL system succeeded in France in part because it was a hierarchical and central system mimicking the uncertainty avoidance characteristic typical to the French. French banks readily accepted workflow systems because those systems reproduced managerial hierarchy and authority. But banks were suspicious of electronic mail systems because they were informal and difficult to control. Many French firms were quick to adopt ERP systems because they promised to provide better control over organizational resources and employees hence leading to better performance [46]. This tendency to prefer control and accept hierarchy can be better understood by examining the writings of four French sociologists Crozier, Bourdieu, Latour and Foucault.

Conception Four: Bourdieu's Critical Realism and Influence on IS Scholars

We see at least four ways Bourdieu expresses a French conception of control and evaluation that help in understanding IS. First, as a sociologist of practice, he clearly distinguishes between *opus operatum* and *modus operandi*, between prescription and activity. Second, he expressly argued against the ideas of philosophers of language (Ricoeur, Austin, Searle) arguing instead that language is rarely performative in itself; rather, it is the social status of the speaker that gives legitimacy and meaning to language propositions. Third, Bourdieu [40] sharply criticizes the reductionism of most quantitative surveys used for evaluation. In his own work, he adopts and advocates for mixed methods to investigate social phenomenon. Fourth, and most importantly, Bourdieu helps us think about control, power and domination. And in doing so, we can better theorize the practices of social actors.

For Bourdieu societal structures are socially defined and maintained. They have great persistence and are very difficult to change. As such, they have enormous influence over human behavior. One objective of Bourdieu's theoretical framework is to uncover the buried organizational structures and mechanisms that are used to ensure the reproduction of social order. His framework helps understand how changes arising from information technology may actually reinforce existing power structures and help perpetuate the social order. To Bourdieu, change (including technological change) is a self-regenerative mechanism required for the maintenance of stratified organizational hierarchies. So where, on the one hand, static structures can be figured out and conquered over time, on the other hand, changing structures keep actors off balance, and thus lead them to apply familiar strategies in unfamiliar contexts, reinforcing old structures, behaviors, rules and order. This reuse of learned dispositions (habitus) in new settings makes existing class positions self-sustaining.

Bourdieu gives voice to issues from deep within the French system of beliefs. He helps us see and better understand a French worldview and thus influencing French IS scholars as previously illustrated[6]. Bourdieu, has also influenced IS researchers outside of France and helped them examine the nature of those societal structures and the impact they have on the introduction and use of IS artifacts (here symbolic meaning) in societal settings. Shultze and Boland , [47] use Bourdieu to help understand the roles of information gatekeepers. Schultze [48] uses Van Maanen's [49] notion of confessional tales to frame the narratives in her ethnographic fieldwork in a way especially attuned to Bourdieu's call for reflexivity in intensive research. On the other hand, Kvasny's research program examining the digital divide in African American communities within the United States uses Bourdieu's concepts of capital, habitus and field as theories for understanding the IS practices of individuals, groups, and organizations. In particular, she is interested in how IT reproduces social inequality [50-52].

To these authors one advantage Bourdieu provides over that of other European critical social theorists such as Giddens and Habermas or over Postmodern theorists like Derrida is that Bourdieu's own empirical research offers some guidance as to how to go about using his theoretical framework. Bourdieu uses empirical work to develop theory, thus making his theory more convincing and easier to apply, whereas other social theorists have little to say about empirical research and methodology. Thus, Bourdieu combines an interest in the practical concerns of examining social order with the more cerebral act of theorizing about that order.

In another attempt to add further empirical work inspired by Bourdieu's theory in the domain of IS, Richardson [53] studied Customer Relationship Management (CRM) technology utilization. Richardson, in examining social relations around CRM system use, discovered the application of symbolic violence as a mode of domination and illustrated how the relationships between agencies and structures (social and technology enforced and supported) manifest and reinforce themselves in the logic of practice. While Bourdieu has been used on both sides of the Atlantic by IS scholars, it turns out that references to three other prominent French thinkers differ in their degree and domain of influence in our field. The first, Crozier, has been very influential in the work of French IS scholars. The second, Latour, has been very influential in IS research in Scandinavia and the UK. And the third, Foucault, has found proponents across the globe.

Conception Five: The Uncertainty Zone Enlarged by Social Actors: Crozier

Crozier [54] demonstrated that, even in bureaucracies, actors circumvent the rules and find some degree of leeway in any system. Crozier and Friedberg generalize this conduct and develop this notion showing how, in order to avoid domination, actors tend to increase their "uncertainty zone", i.e. their power to act as they want

[6] Unfortunately most of this work is published in French and is therefore not readily accessible to the English-speaking scholars.

which implies that their conduct is not totally constrained. They theorize that, "power resides in the degree of leeway that each partner has in a power relationship" [41, p.60].

Examining important differences between the conceptions of Crozier and Bourdieu, Caillé [55] points out how to Bourdieu, the social actor is more structurally constrained than with Crozier. Many French IS scholars cite Crozier, probably because his theory provides greater openness to human agency than do the post-structuralist theories of Bourdieu, Foucault, and Giddens. In the preface to Ballé and Peaucelle's "The Power of Data Processing" [56] Crozier acknowledges the emergent nature or organizational systems recognizing that this presents problems for IS developers and users. He says that the importance of an information system is not that an IS systems runs but that it always brings about change than can never be precisely anticipated. No matter what organizational rules are embedded in a system, social actors will always find a way to circumvent those restrictions; e.g., to maintain there zones of uncertainty and hence personal control. Crozier also suggests that high degrees of user participation in an IS project is not an ideal because in committing to being apart of a project users 1) lose the ability to distance themselves from the system and 2) restrict their ability to enlarge their uncertainty zone when organization emerges out from under the information system.

Conception Six: Control and Agency: Latour and Foucault

Space does not allow us to do justice to the complexity and breadth of thought from these two influential and provocative French scholars. The work of Latour and Foucault is more widely cited in the IS community outside of France than the work of Bourdieu and Cozier, hence we limit our discussion to a brief discussion of where Latour and Foucault have had impact on work in our field. The French sociologist and scholar of science and technology, Bruno Latour, has influenced IS research and thought on how IS are incorporated in complex networks or *collectives* of people and technologies [57- 59]. This is important as it helps understand the spread and diffusion of technology as well as the relative power relationship of humans and machines [60]. In giving voice to both human and nonhuman actants he deals with the issue of control but changes its focus from the exclusive domain of the human actor to a more shared domain of actants in a network. He has inspired others to illustrate how, in complex infrastructures, the notion of agency can be clouded such that it becomes more difficult to speak of control in traditional ways. Systems can escape the overt control of social actors because as members of the actor network they often treated as if they have agency and can subvert the will of human actors [61-64]. Latour's work on the sociology of translation provides insight into how designers and users can communicate the benefits and characteristics of a technology (c.f. the special issue on Actor network theory in *Information Technology and People, 2004).* It provides guidance as to how we may anticipate and evaluate the spread of any technology through a social network. This predictive power allows for better management and control of the processes of technological systems.

Foucault and Latour are similar in that both help us understand the ways that ideas are spread through social systems recharacterized as networks of actors. But Foucault is recognized as addressing the concepts of power and of control. But his conceptualization intertwines notions of knowledge, power and the self. To him power is not a construct dealing with domination of groups over other groups or individuals. Rather it deals with the socially constructed and largely self-regulated webs of relations and interactions in social organizations and settings or "… a multiplicity of force relations…" [65]. Thus power is an emergent construct. It is local and omnipresent and rooted in practice; networks of practice. Willcocks citing Deleuze says:

> "… that Foucault was one of the first to say we have been shifting from disciplinary societies to what Deleuze calls control societies. These no longer operate by, for example, physically confining people but though continuous control and instant communication enabled by developments in material technology. In this rendering, what has been called information society can also be read as control society. If this is correct, Foucault's power/knowledge, discourse, … remains as thoroughly applicable concepts, as Foucault intended them to be." [66, p. 259]

Because of his concerns for power and control Foucault is considered to be a French Critical Social Theorist who along with Habermas, Giddens and Bourdieu have shaped an Critical IS agenda examining power, control and emancipation issues in systems development, design and deployment. Recent special issues of the *Information Systems Journal* Exploring the Critical Agenda in IS Research (2005) and the *Database for Advances in Information Technology (2002, 2003)* are but two examples from a growing critical theoretic discourse in the IS literature.

Conclusion

In this paper, we posited that the issues of control and evaluation were two key constructs in a set of elements defining the core of the IS discipline. We framed the debate by highlighting the contribution of French scholars whose work has influenced the debate both from within the IS field and from the fields of sociology and science and technology studies. We have explored how a French reading of the IS literature sees the issues of evaluation and control as being the most frequently and persistently covered for a quarter of a century of published work. An examination of the work of three French IS scholars and four French sociologists has helped us to:

- To see how the concepts of control and evaluation remain a persistent concern in our field.
- To understand why the emphasis on control as encompassing appropriation and change management focused on behaviors is more typically French.

- To underline the major difference between a software engineering ontological view (realist) and that of a management and social scientist ontological view (be it constructivist, critical realist, pluralist or that of Latour). By definition, the latter assesses the relevance of an IS, as an artifact, with respect to its human and organizational context and not just with respect its capabilities and specifications for some tasks, i.e. from a logical viewpoint.
- To give some theoretical and methodological advice as to the study of the exercise of power and control.

It is also our position that given the increasing cultural, linguistic and geographical diversity in our field with IS scholars living in all corners of the globe, it is useful and appropriate to examine the perspectives and contributions made by non English-speaking scholars. We think that a similar endeavor by other IS communities and AIS chapters is necessary to nurture a healthy critique of the discipline. This will develop more easily as main languages areas are encouraged to exchange and publish in their own language. The fact that AMCIS 2010 accepts papers in Portuguese and Spanish is a first step in that direction.

References

1. Banville, C., and Landry, M. (1989) Can the Field of MIS Be Disciplined? *Communications of the ACM,* 32(January), 48-60.
2. Culnan, M.J. (1986) The Intellectual Development of Management Information Systems, 1972-1982: A Co-citation Analysis. *Management Science,* 32(2),156-172.
3. Culnan, M.J., and Swanson, E.B. (1986) Research in Management Information Systems, 1980-1984: Points of Work and Reference. *MIS Quarterly,* 10(3), 288-303.
4. Robey, D. (1996) Diversity in Information Systems Research: Threat, Promise, and Responsibility. *Information Systems Research,*7(4), 400-408.
5. Walsham, G. (2005) Agency Theory: Integration or a Thousand Flowers? *Scandinavian Journal of Information Systems,* 17(1), 153-158.
6. Alter, S. (2003) A General, Yet Useful theory of Information Systems. *Communications of the AIS,* 1(13).
7. Baskerville, R.L., and Myers, M.D. (2002) Information systems as a reference discipline. *MIS Quarterly* , 26(March), 1-14.
8. Dhar, V., Brynjolfsson, E., DeSanctis, G., Gurbaxani, V., Mendleson, H., and Severance, D. (2004) *Should the Core Information Systems Curriculum Be Structured Around a Fundamental Question?* ICIS 25 Capital Exchange: Crossing Boundaries and Transforming Institution through Information Systems, ICIS-AIS, Washington, D.C., 2004, pp. ICIS-AIS, Washington, DC, 1021-1023.
9. Karahanna, E., Davis, G., Mukhopadhyay, T., Watson, R., and Weber, R. (2003) *Embarking on Information Systems' Voyage to Self-Discovery: Identifying the Core of the Discipline.* ICIS 24 IT is Everywhere: Impacts on Life, Work and Learning Seattle, Washington, 998.
10. Hirschheim, R., and K.Klein, H. (2003) Crisis in the IS Field? A Critical Reflection on the State of the Discipline. *Journal of the Association for Information Systems,* 4(5), 237-293.
11. Weber, R. (2003) Editor's Comments. *MIS Quarterly,* 27(3), iii- xiii.
12. Benbasat, I., and Zmud, R. (2003) The Identity Crisis within the IS Discipline: Defining and Communicating the Discipline's Core Properties. *MIS Quarterly,* 27(2), 183-193.

13. Albert, S., and Whetten, D.A. (1985) Organizational Identity. *Research in Organizational Behavio,r* (7), 263-295.
14. Postman, N. (1988) *Conscientious Objections: Stirring up Trouble about Language, Technology and Education* Vintage Books, New York.
15. Gray, R. (2003) A Brief Historical Review of the Development of the Distinction Between Data and Information in the Information Systems Literature. *9th AMCIS 2003, AIS*, Tampa, Florida, 2843-2849.
16. Orlikowski, W.J., and Iacono, C.S. (2001) Research commentary: Desperately seeking the "IT" in IT research – A call to theorizing the IT artifact. *Information Systems Research,* 1(2), 121-134.
17. Sawyer, S., and Chen, T. (2002) Conceptualizing Information Technology in the Study of Information Systems:Trends and Issues," in: *Global and Organizational Discourse About Information Technology,* E. Wynn, E. Whitley, M. Myers and J. DeGross (eds.), Kluwer Academic Publishers, London, 109-131.
18. Hirschheim, R., Klein, H. K. and Lyytinen, K. (1995) *Information Systems Development and Data Modeling: Conceptual and Philosophical Foundations.* Cambridge: Cambridge University Press.
19. Parsons, J. and Wand, Y. (2000) Emancipating Instances from the Tyranny of Classes in Information Modelling. *ACM Transactions on Database Systems,* 25(2),
20. Sartre, J.P. (1943) *L'être et le Néant: Essai d'Ontologie Phénoménologique* Gallimard, Paris.
21. Desq, S., Fallery, B., Reix, R., and Rodhain, F. (2002) 25 ans de recherches en systèmes d'informations. *Systèmes d'Information et Management,* 7(3), 5-33.
22. Banker, R.D., and Kauffman, R.J. (2004) The Evolution of Research on Information Systems: A Fiftieth-Year Survey of the Literature in Management Science. *Management Science,* 50(3), 281-299.
23. Soh, C., and Markus L. (1985) How IT creates business value: a process theory synthesis "How IT creates business value: a process theory synthesis. *Sixteenth International Conference on Information Systems*, ICIS, Amsterdam: the Netherlands, 29-41.
24. Willcocks, L., and Lester, S. (1993) How Do Organizations Evaluate and Control Information Systems Investments? Recent UK Survey Evidence, in: *Human, Organizational, and Social Dimensions of Information System Development,* D. Avison, J.E. Kendall and J.I. DeGross (eds.), North-Holland, Amsterdam, 15-40.
25. Purao, S., M. Rossi and A. Bush, (2002) Towards an Understanding of the Use of Problem and Design Spaces During Object-Oriented System Development. *Information and Organization* 12(4).
26. Saga, V., and Zmud, R. (1994) The Nature and Determinants of Information Technology Acceptance, Routinization and Infusion, in: *Diffusion, Transfer and Implementation of Information Technology,* L. Levine (ed.), North-Holland, 67-86.
27. Rowe, F. (2006) The editorial view of Frantz Rowe, Editor in Chief: of *Systemes d'Information et Management.* Third in a series – On dissemination, national language and interacting with practitioners. *European Journal of Information Systems,* 15 (3), 244-248.
28. Kinsey/CIGREF, M. (2005) Relational Dynamics around Information Systems within Management Teams of Major French Companies.
29. Luftman, J. and McLean, E. R. (2004) Key Issues for IT Executives. *MIS Quarterly Executive,* 3 (2), 89-104.
30. Orlikowski, W. (1991) Integrated Information Environment or Matrix of Control? The Contradictory Implications of Information Technology. *Accounting Management and Information Technologies (now Information and Organizations),* (1) 1, 9-42.
31. Monod, E. (2002) Epistémologie de la Recherche en Systèmes d'Information, in: *Faire de la Recherche en Systèmes d'Information,* F. Rowe (ed.), Vuibert, Paris.
32. Peaucelle, J.L. (1981) *Les Systèmes d'Information: la Représentation* Presses Universitaires de France, Paris.
33. Rolland, C. (1986) Introduction à la conception des systèmes d'information et panorama des méthodes disponibles. *Revue Génie logiciel,* 4(June), 7-62.

34. LeMoigne, J.L. (1977) *La théorie du système général, théorie de la modélisation [The theory of general systems, theory of modeling]*.Presses Universitaires de France, Paris.
35. LeMoigne, J.L. (1996) La conception des systèmes d'information organisationnels: de l'ingénierie informatique à l'ingéniérie systémique, in: *Organisation intelligente et système d'information stratégique,*, J.A. Bartoli and J.L. LeMoigne (eds.), Economica, Paris, 25-52.
36. Dehaene, P. (1992) Organization, project and strategy as symbols. *CEMIT-CECOIA III Proceedings*, 243-247.
37. Von Foerster, H. (1984) Principles of Self-Organization In a Socio-Managerial Context, in: *Self-Organization and Management of Social Systems,* H. Ulrich and G.J.B. Probst (eds.), Springer-Verlag, Berlin, 22.
38. Simon, H.A. (1996) *The Sciences of the Artificial.* The MIT Press, Cambridge.
39. Reix, R., and Rowe, F. (2002) La recherche en systèmes d'information: de l'histoire au concept in: *Faire de la Recherche en Systèmes d'Information,* F. Rowe (ed.), Vuibert, Paris, 1-17.
40. Bourdieu, P. (1980) *The Logic of Practice.* Stanford University Press, Stanford, CA,.
41. Crozier, M., and Friedberg, E. (1977) *Actors and Systems: the Politics of Collective Action* Ginn and Co., Boston.
42. Marciniak, R., and Rowe, F. (2009) Systèmes d'information et dynamique des organizations. *Economica*, Paris.
43. Rowe, F. (2007) Systèmes d'information ; variations philosophiques sur une proposition de définition in: *Connaissance et Management, Ouvrage dédié a Robert Reix*, P.L. Dubois et Dupuy Y. (eds), Economica, Paris, 167-175.
44. Coyne, R. (1995) *Designing Information Technology in the Postmodern Age: From Method to Metapho.r* MIT Press, Cambridge, Mass.
45. Attali, J., and Stourdzé, Y. (1977) The birth of the telephone and economic crisis: the slow death of monologue in French society," in: *The Social Impact of the Telephone,* I.D.S. Pool (ed.), MIT Press, Cambridge, 97-111.
46. Besson, P., and Rowe, F. (2001) ERP Project Dynamics and Enacted Dialogue: Perceived Understanding, Perceived Leeway, and the Nature of Task-Related Conflicts. *DataBase* 32(4), 47-66.
47. Schultze, U., and Boland Jr., R.J.B. (2000) Knowledge management technology and the reproduction of knowledge work practices. *Journal of Strategic Information Systems,* (9), 193-212.
48. Schultze, U. (2001) Reflexive Ethnography in Information Systems Research, in: *Qualitative Research in IS: Issues and Trends,* E. Trauth (ed.), Idea Group, 78-103.
49. VanMaanen, J. (1988) *Tales from the Field: On Writing Ethnography* University of Chicago Press, Chicago.
50. Kvasny, L., and Keil, M. (2003) The Challenges of Redressing the Digital Divide: A Tale of Two Cities. *International Conference on Information Systems*, Barcelona, Spain, 817-828.
51. Kvasny, L., and Truex, D. (2000) Information Technology and the Cultural Reproduction of Social Order: A Research Program, in: *Organizational and Social Perspectives on Information Technology,* J.S. R. Baskerville, and J. DeGross (ed.), Kluwer Academic Publishers, New York, 277-294.
52. Kvasny, L., and Truex, D. (2001) Defining Away the Digital Divide: A Content Analysis of Institutional Influences on Popular Representations of Technology," in: *Realigning Research and Practice in Information Systems Development: The Social and Organizational Perspective,* B.F. Nancy Russo, Janice DeGross (ed.), Kluwer Academic Publishers, Boston, 399-414.
53. Richardson, H. (2003) CRM in Call Centres: The Logic of Practice, in: *Organizational Information Systems in the Context of Globalization,* M. Korpela, R. Montealegre and A. Poulymenakou (eds.), Kluwer Academic Publishers, London, 68-83.
54. Crozier, M. (1963). *Le phénomène bureaucratique, Paris:* Seuil.

55. Caillé (1981) La sociologie de l'intérêt est-elle intéressante? *Sociologie du travail,* 23(3), 257-274.
56. Ballé, C., and Peaucelle, J., L. (1973) *The Power of Data Processing.* Editions d'organisation, Paris,.
57. Monteiro, E., and Hanseth, O. (1996) Social Shaping of Information Infrastructure, in: *Information Technology and Changes in Organizational Work,* W.J. Orlikowski, G. Walsham, M. Jones and J.I. DeGross (eds.), Chapman and Hall, London,.
58. Monteiro, E. (2000). "Actor-Network Theory and Information Infrastructure," in: *From Control to Drift,* C. Cibbora (ed.), Oxford University Press, Oxford, 71-83.
59. Monteiro, E., and Hanseth, O. (1995) Social shaping of information infrastructure: on being specific about the technology, in: *Information Technology and Changes in Organizational Work,* W.J. Orlikoswki, G. Walsham, M.R. Jones and J.I. DeGross (eds.), Chapman & Hall, London, 325-343.
60. Latour, B. (1996) Social theory and the study of computerized work sites, in: *Information technology and changes in organizational work,* W.J. Orlikowski, G. Walsham, M.R. Jones and J.I. DeGross (eds.), Chapman & Hall, London, 295-307.
61. Rose, J., Jones, M., and Truex, D. (2003) *The Problem of Agency; How Humans Act, How Machines Act,* Action in Language, Organizations and Information Systems, Linköping University, Linköping, Sweden, 91-106.
62. Rose, J., Jones, M., and Truex, D. (2005a) Socio-Theoretic Accounts of IS: The Problem of Agency. *Scandinavian Journal of Information Systems* 17(1), 133-152.
63. Rose, J., Jones, M., and Truex, D. (2005b) The Problem of Agency Re-visited. *Scandinavian Journal of Information Systems* (17) 187-196.
64. Rose, J., and Truex, D. (2000) Machine agency as perceived autonomy: an action perspective, in: *IS 2000 The Social and Organizational Perspective on Research and Practice in Information Technology,* R. Baskerville, J. Stage and J.I. DeGross (eds.), Kluwer Academic Publishers, Aalborg, Denmark, 371-390.
65. Foucault, M., Faubion, J.D., and Hurley, R. (2000) *Power.* New Press, New York, p. 484.
66. Willcocks, L. (2004). Foucault, Power, Knowledge and Information Systems: Reconstructing the Present, in: *Social theory and philosophy for Information Systems,* J. Mingers and L. Willcocks (eds.), Wiley, Chichester, 238-296.

Beyond Darwin: The Potential of Recent Eco-Evolutionary Research for Organizational and Information Systems Studies

Francesca Ricciardi[1]

Abstract Theoretical studies that actually propose to use evolutionary paradigms in organizational/management studies are quite rare, as well as field studies explicitly adopting them. Moreover, these rare writings tend to refer to classical, "Darwin+Mendel+DNA" thought, surprisingly overlooking the last decades' advancements in evolutionary research, although these recent studies are progressively explaining complex phenomena, which Darwin's model did not encompass. This paper identifies three streams within recent evolutionary research, whose adoption may result in useful innovation for management, organizational and information system research. These streams of studies present evolutionary, ecological and social processes in an integrated fashion, providing strong frameworks to understand learning processes, procedure creation, flexibility, decision making, networks evolution, cooperation, and the role of relationships, moods and non-rational triggers in change processes. This paper suggests that deeper insights into these factors not only would let us better understand how organizations evolve, but would also give us hints for building organizations which are more compatible with human nature.

Introduction

Although the publication of Darwin's "The Origin of Species" sparked off the whole evolutionary revolution, Darwin's theories left many biological facts unexplained.

Since then, paramount efforts have been made by biologists to investigate those aspects of the evolutionary phenomena which still remained obscure, and these efforts have led to spectacular advancements in evolutionary theories. Generations of scientists have climbed higher and higher on the shoulders of Darwin and of his followers, and even if their names are often unknown, they have become able to see farther and farther than the giant who had started the investigation.

"Starting out with base pairs and their sequences, scholars of evolution have to consider – in the order of ascending biological complexity – alleles, quantitative allelic traits, physiological and morphological traits, life history traits, demographic rates, fitness, changes in genotype frequencies, population dynamics, trait substitution sequences, and population bifurcations, to eventually arrive at the levels of ecological communities and the biosphere. It would appear that no other field of contemporary science sports comparable ambitions." [1]. Today's evolutionary

[1] Catholic University, Milan, Italy, francesca.ricciardi@unicatt.it

thought, in other words, is vast and plural, and deals with a moltitude of issues (such as genetics, or network ecology) that Darwin could have no idea of.

Nevertheless, when other disciplines, and namely those in the areas of economic and social sciences, have approached the sciences of life in order to borrow frameworks and hints from evolutionary paradigm, they have often referred to Darwin's classical thought, and tended to overlook the important advancements of the last decades. Also organizational and management studies are affected by this "spyglass vision": when trying cross-fertilization with evolutionary studies, scholars tend to focus on Darwin and on the nineteenth century debates, and all the more recent advancements in biology and ecology (with the partial exception of genetics) remain substantially out of their fields of vision. As a consequence, evolutionary thought often appears to these scholars much more rigid, much more simplistic and much less effective in explaining (also organizational) phenomena, than it actually is today.

This paper is aimed at demonstrating the importance of taking into consideration the whole history of evolutionary thought. In this way, the scholar would be given the possibility to collect up-to-date ideas, frameworks and approaches that could effectively innovate and enhance Organizational, Management and Information System studies.

In the next paragraph we will briefly show, through a Literature Review, that there is not a critical mass of Organizational, Management and Information System scholars adopting and using the evolutionary paradigm yet, and that evolutionary-centred approaches have not attained a significant, regular presence in the mainstream journals of our disciplinary area. Furthermore, we will show that almost all the scholars that somehow cite evolutionary thought tend to refer to the classical "Darwin+Mendel" paradigm, overlooking any further development. In the following paragraphs, three issues within *recent* evolutionary research will be identified, that look particularly promising in order to provide organizational studies with reusable concepts and models. For each of these streams of studies, a synthetic description will be provided, and the advancement with respect to classical darwinism will be highlighted. Then, some hints about the potentialities for fertilizating Management, Organizational and Information Systems studies will be briefly illustrated. In the Conclusions, the results of the analysis of the four streams of studies mentioned above will be summarized, and some paths for further research will be outlined.

The Evolutionary Paradigm in Organizational and Management Studies

> "Substantial beachheads of Darwinism have been established in the many of the social sciences, most notably evolutionary psychology (EP). Yet the application of these ideas to the organizational sciences is a story of very limited engagement, mixed success, and some paradox. Darwinian precepts have entred thought and discourse more implicitly than explicitly, and it is

> rare for them to be acknowledged even within the research and writing of those areas of organizational sciences where they have clear relevance, such as in decision-making, gender issues, negotiation, and leadership." [2].

The reasons of such difficulties may be several. For example, there are ideological resistances: some people think that Darwinism, once introduced in social sciences, could be used as a tool to justify rough, pityless competition, or even refined, dictatorial social engineering. Other people (and among them many scholars, such as those belonging to post-structuralist, critical, interpretivist schools) think that social sciences and humanities should be protected against all the approaches coming from natural sciences, that are perceived as simplistic, mechanistic, deterministic, positivistic and completely unable to account for human self-awareness, free will and feelings, and for the complexity of social relationships. For a description (and fervent rebuttal) of those charges, see for example [3].

But there could be one more reason. In effect, management, information systems and organizational studies scholars have demonstrated a quite weak capacity to effectively exploit actual potentialities of evolutionary thought.

A special issue of the *Journal of Organizational Behavior* (n. 27, 2006), entirely dedicated to Darwinism as a new possible paradigm for organizational behavior, records that writings in which recognized organizational scholars have employed the evolutionary paradigm are very few. The issue cites Lawrence and Nohria [4], and Nicholson [5]. A specific field of studies that has generated a somehow larger debate is known as "organizational ecology" [6, 7, 8, 9]. These approaches focuses on a specific aspect of evolutionism, i.e. *selectionism*. Starting from Dawkins' [10] reasoning on the fact that any unit of replication (such as genes) undergoing processes of variation, selection and retention can evolve, these scholars have studied the evolution and struggle for existence of different forms of organization (e.g. political, religious, business organizations).

But, again, the articles collected in the Special Issue cited above tend to focus on traditional, classically Darwinian topics, such as competition, sexual selection, gender issues, or genetic-centred processes. Only two writings [11, 12] focus on issues that go beyond the traditional core of evolutionary studies, that was already established in the 1950s with the syntesis of Darwinism, Mendel works on hereditariness, and genetics.

The Editorial [2] identifies only one Case Study [13] linking a firm's success to its compliance with needs which were set by human eco-evolution: Johnson, in fact, states that a certain firm's spectacular success can be attributed to the founders' captivation with (and understanding of) some more recent outcomes of evolutionary studies, that were put in practice in designing the firm's organizational struture. According to Johnson, a key success factor for an organization is the adoption of forms and practices consistent with human nature and founded on those kinds of communities and networks of relationships that where selected through human eco-evolution, and where human beings are most effective.

To further assess the presence of Darwinism and evolutionary thought in Information Systems, Organizational and Management studies, a literature search was conducted on December 18th, 2009. The search was conducted on two of the most important and renowned on-line databases collecting studies in the economic and social areas: Business Source Premier and Econlit. To collect the major number of possible results, the query was very generic and simple: it was requested to select writings including the words "evolution" or "evolutionary" and "Darwin". The search yielded 161 writings, including the Special Issue of the Journal of Organizational Behavior and some other writings already cited above; but no further relevant writing in which evolutionary thought was adopted to address management / organizational / information systems issues was found.

The state of the art, then, is quite stagnant, and it would be unwise to attribute the whole situation only to the ideological resistances of the scholarly community against the "taking over" of natural sciences in a field that belongs to social sciences. After all, many frameworks coming from other non-humanistic disciplines, such as engineering and statistics, are widely accepted in our field, along with many tipically quantitative methods and positivistic epistemologies. This means that anti-natural-sciences ideology is not that powerful: should evolutionary paradigms prove effective, they could start to be accepted, in the same way they have already been successfully accepted in other fields, such as psychology. Clearly, an effort to enhance and update our community's understanding of evolutionary thought is advisable.

In the next paragraphs, we will outline some findings of the more recent advancement of evolutionary research, dating from the 1970s. These studies link classical variation-selection-retention approaches to an *ecological* understanding of evolutionary and co-evolutionary processes involving systems of growing complexity. They provide an elegant, integrated overview also on issues that are traditionally committed to social sciences: knowledge creation, tension between cooperation and conflict, feelings and moods in personal and social relationships, processes of social construction of networks and local environments that simultaneously serve and shape the needs of their occupants.

Procedures and Open Behaviors in Evolution Processes

To briefly describe this research stream, we will refer to the beginner and most important scholar of the studies on natural history of knowledge, i.e. Konrad Lorenz.

From an evolutionary point of view, knowledge stems from challenges; but challenges can have different characteristics as for crucial factors connected with *time*. There are, in fact, *long term challenges*: problems that tend to have similar features during time. And there are *short-term challenges*: problems whose characteristics tend to be different and specific each time, and that require *ad hoc* solutions. Long-term challenges are usually managed by long-term knowledge: that is, steady knowledge, stored in the form of automatic procedures and patterns. For example, mammals' knowledge about some ancestral risks can be stored in automatic (innate) procedures that cause adrenaline release if a snake appears. On the other hand, short-term challenges require intense learning activity to face the specific situation. For example, in case of ice on the road, the driver will stop listening to the radio and will concentrate on driving, because in this case it is unwise to rely on the "automatic pilot" of our standard driving habits. Thus, knowledge flows in parallel layers, from the more slowly changing to the more rapid, extemporaneous ones, like submarine streams. Long-term knowledge may be very difficult to change; in some cases, it is locked in the deepest layers, where only natural selection can affect it. But also habits and traditions, even if they are not written in the DNA, may be quite difficult to change, and this exposes to the risks of rigidity. That's why *healthy* systems feature a continuous stirring of the sea of knowledge: what has been learned tends to be transformed in unaware, automatic habit or procedure, to save energy and to achieve major efficiency (pattern/procedure making); but the *a priori* in deepest layers, in turn, tend to resurface and to be weighed against reality (pattern/procedure matching and testing; and, often, pattern/procedure *destroying*).

But what is the eco-evolutionary relationship between long-term knowledge, stored in the deeper layers, and short-term knowledge, that provides flexibility and improvisation capabilities on the surface of the "sea of knowledge"?

The more a program is open, i.e. the wider is the range of possibilities and solutions that it offers, the "wiser" it must be: to come to a flexible performance, an organism needs an amount of genetic information that is *greater* than what is needed for a "closed" procedure. So, the capability of usefully heeding extemporary information coming from the environment is made possible not by a decrease, but, on the contrary, by an *increase* of the "*a priori*" knowledge[2], rigidly embedded in DNA. This is a point that Lorenz, especially in [15], stresses particularly: flexibility is a superior performance, but it does not imply to eliminate the more archaic, rigid procedures; on the contrary, flexibility is *founded* on the long-term knowledge treasured by old procedures themselves, which stems from thousands of millenniums of attempts.

In the more evolved forms of knowledge, implying extemporary learning, curiosity, creativity and awareness, a further, great increase of the knowledge heritage embedded in DNA becomes necessary: surprisingly, *the price of (successful) flexibility is an increase, in the deeper layers, of (well-tested) rigidity.*

We will give here two examples of the possible solutions that evolutionary processes have provided to the puzzle "efficiency versus flexibility": blurred patterns, and procedure fragmentation.

Blurred patterns. Gooses can identify the shape of a predatory bird in the sky. This identification can be more or less selective (for example, gooses can be scared by a paper shape imitating the eagle, too), but it is always based on the manipulation of *patterns* that spot the essential, *architectural* characteristics of an object or a situation (for these "pattern matching" activities, Lorenz widely quotes [17]); and it is important to note that a characteristic is selected as "essential" and put in the pattern, only if it has proved to be relevant for surviving and health. Thus, Lorenz

[2] Lorenz often uses the expression "*a priori*" to indicate *innate knowledge*, explicitly referring to Kant.

says that even very simple animals can rely on abstracting performances. These *unaware* cognitive procedures, that Brunswik [18] called "ratiomorph", require an enormous computing power, which human *rational* thought is unable to touch. A goose, for example, *can* identify the danger represented by an eagle because the pattern of "eagle-like", although unaware, is available, embedded in the goose's cognitive equipment. This implies probabilistic computation, elimination of perceptive "noise", and many other highly sophisticated computing performances. It is an extraordinary amount of knowledge, that animals treasure in their nervous system since they're born, by direct order of the DNA: this is, according to Lorenz [15] *the "a priori" basis for every further buildup of information* (learning).

Also in organizations we can have knowledge layers with similar characteristics. A certain part of organizational knowledge tends to embed deeply in the very organization's structure, and to become very difficult to change. For example, in a certain industrial firm a surprising amount of knowledge can be implicitly embedded in the very factory's layout and geographical location, in the workforce tacit know-how, in hierarchical structures, or in legacy information systems. In case of sudden market crisis, complete changes in those deep layers (e.g. building a completely new fabric, creating a completely new hierarchical system or information system) may take years; and if this time is longer than the financial autonomy of the firm, the firm will die.

Thus, all organizational knowledge that is beyond the "change capacity threshold" is a sort of organizational DNA, from an eco-evolutionary point of view: it is a double-blade weapon, which ensures both fitness and fragility of the organization. Studying this embedded knowledge (and particularly the subsequent pattern matching and innate instruction activities) from an eco-evolutionary point of view could yield novel, interesting outcomes. In fact, let's concentrate on the selectivity of pattern matching processes. In changing and complex contexts, Lorenz demonstrated that a winning strategy is making *low-selectivity patterns available* for pattern matching, i.e. for identifying situations and triggering reactions. For example, gooses can be scared by a wide range of "eagle-like" shapes, not only by the precise shape of a certain eagle. These low-selectivity "triggering patterns" are only apparently rough: they are, instead, highly abstracting, and focus only on those characteristics of the object/ situation that have proved (by a long experience of previous challenges) really invariant and important for the goals. This can raise flexibility (in the meaning of "capability to face complexity") even dramatically, leaving wide space to further learning and fine-tuning. This need is being more and more felt in organizational studies: we cite, for example, Ciborra and Willcocks [19] who complain that "while the Artificial Intelligence specialist tries to embed into expert systems more and more sophisticated plans, never achieving the richness of the situation (the world), Suchman's recommendation is to keep plans vague and open to many possibilities".

Fragmented procedures. If the environment is variable and unpredictable, of course a single, rigid procedure will not be able to manage specific problems. Animals fitted to move on relatively uniform grounds (for example, runners of the prairies, like horses), have motor patterns that are too rigid to tackle difficult grounds, like steep rocky paths in the mountains. How can goats and ibexes, instead, succeed in this challenge? Not by renouncing motor procedures: on the contrary, by *breaking them into fragments*, each of them brief enough to allow extemporary assembling of innumerable, as Lorenz says, "motor melodies" [15, VI-7]. This solution implies that newborns are not immediately able to show perfect motor performances: they must train before, to "tailor" their motor sequences for their specific paths. After this, they will become extremely quick, just as if the whole movement was innate. These animals have a genetic heritage of motor sequences which is already broken in properly short fragments, and they also have a great, instinctive *desire of assembling* them: that's why they go on training, and repeating the *fluid, "perfect" procedure*, even when unnecessary. And that's why dancers, sportsmen and children can't help pursuing perfection in their movements – and feel such a deep pleasure, when they succeed.

This findings may help in integrating traditional, engineered procedure making with an authentic understanding of creativity and improvisation processes. But so far, those scholars who have most deeply perceived the need to go beyond the rigid and old-fashioned planning-and-procedures paradigms for management have also been fiercely against any paradigm coming from natural sciences, and prefer, for example, referring to philosophy or to sociology for cross-fertilization [20, 21].

Ecology of Knowledge. Imitation, Training, Trial-Error, Exploration, Tunnel Vision

To briefly describe the advancements of this research stream, that may be very fruitful for organizational studies, we will refer to two scholars: Konrad Lorenz again, and Paul Seabright.

According to Lorenz [14, 15, 16], evolution is a process of knowledge grasping, based on taking-the-form (*in-formatio*) of the environment that the evolving system is facing. A key strategy to do so is triggering *extemporary* learning activities based on a certain amount of a-priori, long term knowledge, that allows pattern matching and routes the creation of new knowledge.But what are these extemporary, learning activities, which result in the possibility of storing short-term knowledge not in the DNA, but in more flexible units of storing, such as the nervous system? In other words: apart from genetic evolution, how can we classify the other ways in which living systems can "take the fit form", in an eco-evolutionary sense?

Konrad Lorenz [15] lists the following[3]: *imitation, training, trial-error, exploration*. Another cross attitude which is always present in living systems' knowledge relationship with the environment is *tunnel vision,* whose major implications

[3] Lorenz also describes a more recent cross learning attitude, i.e. *pattern linking*. But pattern linking is related to the creation of language and to abstract planning/designing activities and it is a complex issue, which needs an ad-hoc writing; in this paper, we will restrict ourselves to the four, more ancient basic learning activities.

in organizational and economic disciplines has been studied by Paul Seabright [21].

Imitation. Some animals (apes, some birds, and humans) show an intense desire of imitating movements, sounds and expressions. Lorenz supposes that this attitude was selected because it allows animals to develop and train complex sensorial, vocal and motor patterns, and for "emotional tuning" in social and familiar contexts (for example, for identifying parents, or communicating a danger. In effect, imitation and self-imitation have also a great importance in communicating: e.g., dogs "say" they're thirsty by "meaningfully" putting their noses into their empty water basins, and then staring at their masters' eyes). Imitation is often the link between the individual and its group's *tradition* [15, VII and X]. Tradition creates procedures that not only give the individuals precise instruction about certain problems, but also fine-tune and address their trial-error and training activities (see below), partially overlapping the "innate instructors", i.e. the innate procedures that trigger and control learning activities in mammals and birds.

Training activities. Training is based on the assembling of fragmented a-priori procedures (see above, the example of goats and ibexes on rocky mountain paths). Successful training activities tend to create fluent movement and behaviors: e.g., after a proper training, we can become able to drive a car almost automatically, "without thinking about it". Sometimes these fluent movements can become as quick and efficient, but also almost as rigid, as the innate sequences. Let's try to think how difficult it would be fluently driving a car, if only the brake pedal was shifted to the right, replacing the accelerator.

Trial/error activities. If a procedure can be closed by identifying patterns of "success" or "failure", and not by a simple message of "end", many new possibilities of properly reacting to circumstances become available [16]. When trial/error learning leads to success (for example, a cat closed in an experimental cage finds a button that opens the cage), the new procedure developed in this way tends to supersede the innate instructor's flexibility, and to become a *habit* (when put in a similar cage, but with a different system of escaping, for example a door to be pulled by nails, the cat will disregard other attempts and will go on uselessly pushing the "old" button, and then it will quit trying to escape; but a "new" cat, not affected by the habit, will probably find the solution). In other words, *rewarded success fastens the achievement of similar successes, but decreases the capability of learning from one's own mistakes* [15]. Successfully learning is, then, a double-blade weapon, also for human beings: Lorenz quotes other researches and experiments [23, 24] suggesting that a human being, coping with a problem that requires a very simple, but *unusual* solution, can be unable of prevailing, even in 50% of cases, because of mental habits' tyranny. Procedures acquired by trial/error learning, thus, make us more efficient in the context in which learning has taken place, *but less* flexible in adapting ourselves to further changes.

Exploration and curiosity. Some animals have an innate urge to explore, even if (or rather: just *when*) they don't have immediate needs to meet. For example, a rat passing through all the shelters of its environment is not searching a den; it just wants to know if, "theoretically", the object of its analysis could become useful in the future. When they are not hungry, when they don't feel in danger, when they've had enough rest, these animals feel "bored" and start concentrating their attention and their experiments on their environment. The innate instincts managed by the genome trigger feelings of unease, that cause the animal to use its "free time" to explore; innate equipments also give the animal several procedures and patterns (see pattern matching and innate instructors, above) to compare with the objects of its attention; and feelings of pleasure and satisfaction are excited, when the exploring activity is successfully concluded. In other words, in order to trigger curiosity, the organism uses the same mechanisms of desire/satisfaction that all the animals have for food or sex, just addressing them to learning *in itself* [14, 15]. As a result, since there is no immediate need to meet, the result of this activity is not the creation of a habit, but the creation of mental *map*, that remains available for future needs (for example: escaping from a sudden danger).

Such animals are, as Lorenz says, "specialized in not being specialized" [15, chapt. VII, 6]. *Curious* animals are, in fact, the most cosmopolitan creatures: rats, ravens, and humans, are everywhere in the world. They can live in deserts, by the sea, in the woods, in the cities. Curiosity implies a certain degree of *freedom from external rewards*; this allows flexibility in *knowing*, which allows flexibility in *behaving*, and then in *living*.

Tunnel vision. All this new knowledge (traditions, fluencies, habits, maps) is stored in the deeper layers of the nervous systems, interacts with the Innate Instructors, sometimes superseding them, and becomes part of the pre-conditions for any further knowledge. This means that every time we watch the complexity of the world, we simply cannot have a "virgin eye": we focus on what our Innate Instructors, Traditions, Fluencies, Habits, Maps teach us to take into consideration, and we simply tend not to see all the other things that previous experiences have classified as "irrelevant". For example, when walking in a forest, we simply don't register the colors and shapes of all the leaves scattered on the ground; but if a boar suddenly appears, we will immediately collect an incredible amount of information from that corner of our vision field. This attitude is called "tunnel vision" [22] and has paramount eco-evolutionary implications.

These streams of research may provide management, organizational and information system research with a wide range of new frameworks to explore.

Within the well-established field of research that focuses on the Learning Organization [25], for example, a structured study of the whole range of basic learning activities (*imitation, training, trial-error, and exploration*) and of their consequences, which tend to embed in the deeper layers (*traditions, fluencies, habits and maps* respectively), could yield significant advancements.

As for tunnel vision, its importance for economic and organizational phenomena is effectively highlighted by Seabright [22]: "This morning I went out and bought a shirt. There is nothing very unusual in that: across the world, perhaps twenty million people did the same. What is more remarkable is that I, like most of these twenty million, had not informed anybody in advance of what I was intending to do. Yet the shirt I bought, although a simple item by the standards of modern technology, represents a triumph of international cooperation. The cotton comes from India, grown from seeds developed in the United States; the artificial fibre in the thread comes from Portugal and the material in the dyes from at least six other countries; the collar linings come from Brazil, and the machinery for the weaving, cutting and sewing from Germany; the shirt itself was made up in Malaysia. The project of making a shirt and delivering it to me in Toulouse has been a long time in the planning, since well before the morning two winters ago when an Indian farmer first led a pair of ploughing bullocks across his land on the red plains outside Coimbatore. Engineers in Cologne and chemists in Birmingham were involved in the preparation many years ago. Most remarkably of all, given the obstacles it has had to surmount to be made at all and the large number of people who have been involved along the way, it is a very stylish and attractive shirt (….) *In fact there is nobody in charge. The entire vast enterprise of supplying shirts in thousands and thousands of styles to millions and millions of people takes place without any over-all coordination at all.* The Indian farmer who planted the cotton was concerned only with the price this would subsequently fetch from a trader, the cost to him of all the materials and the effort he would have to put in to realize an adequate harvest. The managers of the German machinery firm worry about export orders and their relations with their suppliers and their workforce. The manufacturers of chemical dyes could not care less about the aesthetics of my shirt. (…) even the largest such company accounts for only a tiny fraction of the whole activity involved in the supply of shirts. Overall there is nobody in charge. We grumble sometimes about whether the system works as well as it could (I have to replace broken buttons on my shirts more often than seems reasonable). What is truly astonishing is that it works at all."

A deeper understanding of tunnel vision would be fundamental in organizational disciplines. Evolutionary paradigm is the only one that seems able to give us the tools to fully understand tunnel vision from an ecological point of view, and above all to understand under what conditions tunnel vision works and fails, and how it could/should be linked to (or superseded by) aware planning and design activities.

The most important drawback of tunnel vision, in fact, is the other side of its efficiency: what makes us focused, makes us also blind to what is outside our scope.

The study of rigidity caused by basic learning processes and by the "cross attitude" named tunnel vision looks particularly promising. For example, as we've seen above, every trial/error learning tends, to be efficient, to "punish" mistakes, and to reward successes. This tends to create habits, which can also become very difficult to change, afterwards. Of course, habits have excellent reasons to exist: they treasure a deep knowledge, and they let us save an enormous amount of energy. But, in some cases, habits and prejudices can become counter-productive. Success can make us stupid, and unable to wonder if what we call success is really a success, in a strategic perspective. Luckily, evolution has provided us with strong antibodies to prejudices and habits. Exploration, curiosity, boredom, serendipity, humor, pessimism, individualism, rebellion… these are all means to save us from our own habits [15]. Organizations and societies (and Information Systems) that totally repress these attitudes and behaviors are probably sewing the very straight-jacket that will kill them.

Communities, Groups and Networks Eco-evolution. Evolution of Cooperation

One of the traditional objections raised against the adoption of evolutionary paradigms in organizational studies is that organizational populations do not exhibit the levels of internal cohesion, isolation, and closure that are necessary for something like Darwinian evolution to occur. In other words, organizations are not "organisms" in a biological sense, and then they cannot be studied as such [44]. But this objection refers to classical Darwinian thought, and does not take into account the numerous recent studies on co-evolution.

The study of eco-evolutionary interactions inside communities, groups and networks (far beyond the selective relationship between the individual and the environment, that was at the core of classical Darwinian thought) is one of the most vital research streams within biology today [1, 26].

It would be difficult to summarize here all the studies that are being developed within this topic. We will confine ourselves to describing one of the most relevant emerging approaches: *Adaptive Dynamics*. For this approach, we will refer to the Evolution and Ecology Program of the IIASA. The International Institute for Applied Systems Analysis (IIASA) is an international research organization. It conducts inter-disciplinary scientific studies on environmental, economic, technological, and social issues in the context of human dimensions of global change[4].

One of the most important facts that the classical synthesis "Darwinian thought+genetics" was unable to explain is the issue of jump increases in biological complexity that result from the aggregation of individuals into mutual relationship-based wholes [27].

These and many more problems have a common source: *the interactions of individuals are bound to change the environments these individuals live in.* A new mathematical theory of the evolution of complex adaptive systems arises, closing the feedback loop in the evolutionary explanation. This is the general theoretical option that lies at the core of the emerging field of *adaptive dynamics*. The aim of adaptive dynamics studies is to elucidate the long-term effects of the interactions between ecological and evolutionary processes.

Another most recurrent criticisms against the adoption of Darwinian paradigms in organizational studies is that such paradigms are focused only on struggle and competition, and are unable to describe and explain the complex networks of cooperation, which are at the very base of organizations' existence. Also this criticism, however, is founded on an out-of-date, old-fashioned vision of evolutionary

[4] The following content of this paragraph is extracted, with minor changes and adaptations, from the IIASA website. (http://www.iiasa.ac.at/Research/ADN/).

research. Studies on cooperation as a crucial eco-evolutionary factor are becoming one of the most vital and successful streams in evolutionary research.

These studies are essential for understanding the rallying of diverse individuals around a common agenda. Such cooperation of units (each of them individually subjected to selective pressure) to form a higher-order unit (e.g. a pack, or an organization) offers a common thread for studying different adaptive processes, both in biological and cultural evolution.

Among the most relevant writing on this topic, we are citing here the most recent, which include useful references also to previous research [28, 29, 30, 31, 32, 33, 34, 35, 36, 37, 38].

There is a large and growing interest in studying organizations as communities (or parts of larger communities) and in focusing on the network of relationships as a key factor, or as the very essence, of organization viability. See, for example [25, 39, 40, 41, 42]. This research field would greatly benefit from adopting evolutionary paradigms, which promise to provide tools to understand those phenomena in their roots, and to give hints for a new, sustainable approach to global interactions among competing organizations.

So far, the movement is somehow one-way: it's the evolutionary studies community that is starting to take possession of topics related to networks, organizations and technological innovation (see for example [43]), while scholars of the management-organizational-information systems communities are in most cases still dedicating themselves to repeat that plans, designs, organizations and information systems are artificial systems, that cannot be described with the paradigms of natural systems (as if Descartes' error about separating our physical existence from "something else" had not been identified yers ago).

For example, the IIASA, already mentioned above, developed a long tradition in using tools from systems analysis for investigating conditions facilitating the evolution of cooperation. Such new approaches, all based on sound evolutionary paradigms, challenge the simplistic rationality assumption underlying much of classical game theory. As the IIALSA web site says, "recent research advances at IIASA have shed new light on the role of reputation for the evolution of indirect reciprocity, the importance of voluntary participation for sustaining high levels of cooperation, the joint evolutionary dynamics of cooperation and mobility, and on the effect of rewards and punishment in public goods games." It would be a pity if the management, organizational and information studies communities were left behind when it is becoming clear how evolutionary processes affect our subjects of interests.

Conclusions

One hundred and fifty years' research on evolutionary processes have led to a deep, sound and (more importantly) growing understanding of many complex phenomena, which are of great interest for management, organizational and information systems studies.

In this paper, we have advocated a major effort, on the part of our research communities, to better know and use evolutionary studies outcomes, and we have tried to explain why evolutionary thinking has not achieved lift-off in our field yet.

Then, we have identified three groups of topics that have been (and are being) successfully investigated by evolutionary studies in the last decades, and whose outcomes are, in our opinion, very promising in order to introduce innovation and advancement in our field.

Such outcomes would cast light on cutting-edge issues in management, organizational and information system studies, such as the relationships between (efficient) procedures and (flexible) improvisation, the processes of organizational learning, the effects, both positive and counter-productive, of rewards, habits and traditions, the relationships between top-down planning and self-organizing bottom-up phemomena, the dynamics within groups and communities, the relationships of trust and cooperation.

Not only in biological and ecological studies, but also in many other fields of studies, such as psychology, anthropology, sociology, or economics itself, the fact that our organizational behavior is strongly influenced by refined evolutionary processes is progressively becoming a commonly accepted idea. This paper aims at strongly encouraging our academic community not to stay behind, and to actively participate in this scientific adventure.

References

1. Dieckmann U., Doebeli M. (2005). "Pluralism in Evolutionary Theory". *Journal of Evolutionary Biology* 18:1209-1213 (2005).
2. Nicholson, N.; White, R. (2006). "Darwinism – a new paradigm for organizational behavior?". *Journal of Organizational Behavior*, 27, pp. 111-119.
3. Nicholson, N. (2005) "Objections to evolutionary psychology:reflections, implications and the leadership exemplar". *Human Relations,* 58 (3), 393-409.
4. Lawrence, P.; Nohria, N. (2002). *Driven. The four drives underlying human nature,* San Francicsco, Jossey-Bass.
5. Nicholson, N. (2000). *Executive Instinct: Managing the human animal in the information age,* New York, Crown Business.
6. Aldrich, H.E. (1999). *Organizations evolving.* Thousand Oaks, CA: Sage
7. Hannan, M.T.; Freeman, J. (1989). *Organizational Ecology.* Cambridge, Harvard University Press.
8. Nelson, R.R.; Winter, S.G. (1982). *An evolutionary theory of economic change.*, cambridge, the Belknap Press.
9. Baum, Joel A.C. (1999). "Organizational Ecology". In Clegg S.r.; Clegg S.; Hardy C., *Studying Organizations: theory and method*, Sage.
10. Dawkins, R. (1976). *The Selfish Gene.* New York, Oxford University Press.
11. Price, (2006). "Monitoring, reputation, and greenbeard reciprocity in a Shuar work team". *Journal of Organizational Behavior*, 27.
12. Pierce, White, (2006). "Resource context contestability and emergent social structure: an empirical investigation of an evolutionary theory". *Journal of Organizational Behavior*, 27.
13. Johnson, M. (2005). *Family, Village, Tribe: the story of the Flight Centre Ltd.* Melbourne, Random House.

14. Lorenz, K. (1966), *On Aggression*, Harcourt, Brace and World, New York.
15. Lorenz, K. (1973), *Behind the Mirror. A search for a natural history of human knowledge*, Harcourt Brace, New York.
16. Lorenz, K. (1996), Innate bases of learning. In Pribram, K. H., and King, J., eds., *Learning as Self-Organization*. Mahwah, New Jersey: Lawrence Erlbaum Associates, Publishers.
17. Campbell, D.T.,(1966). *Pattern matching as an essential in Distal Knowing*, Holt, Rinehard & Winston, New York.
18. Brunswik, E. (1957) "Scope and aspects of the Cognitive problems", in Bruner et al., *Contemporary approaches to Cognition*, Harvard University Press, Cambridge.
19. Ciborra, C. and Willcocks, L. (2006), "The mind or the heart? It depends on the (definition of) situation", *Journal of Information Technology* 21, 129–139.
20. Ciborra, C. (2002). *The Labyrinths of Information*. Oxford University Press.
21. Dreyfus, H.L. (1991). *Being-in-the-World*. The MIT Press, Cambridge Mass.
22. Seabright, P. (2004), *The company of strangers: a natural history of economic life*. Princeton University Press.
23. Maier N.R.F. (1929). "Reasoning in White Rats", in *Comp. Psycol. Monogr.*, 6, p. 29 Reydon,
24. Maier N.R.F. (1930), "Reasoning in Humans, I. On direction", in *J. comp. Psycol,* 10, pp. 115-43.
25. Brown, J.s.; Duguid, P. (1991). "Organizational learning and communities of practice. Toward a unified view of working, learning, and innovation". *Organization Science*, 2,1, pp. 40-57.
26. Jrgensen S.E. (ed.), (2008). *Encyclopedia of Ecology*, Elsevier.
27. Metz J.A.J., Mylius S.D., Diekmann O., (2008). "When Does Evolution Optimise?" *Evolutionary Ecology Research* 10:629-654
28. Brandt H., Ohtsuki H., Iwasa Y., Sigmund K. (2007). "A Survey on Indirect reciprocity". In Takeuchi Y., Iwasa Y., Sato K. (eds): *Mathematics for Ecology and Environmental Sciences*, Springer, Berlin Heidelberg, pp. 21-51.
29. Ferrière R. (1998). Help and You Shall be Helped". *Nature* 393:517-519 (1998).
30. Hauert C, Traulsen A, Brandt H, Nowak MA, Sigmund K. (2007). "The Emergence of Altruistic Punishment: Via Freedom to Enforcement". *Science* 613:1905-1907.
31. Henrich J., Bowles S., Boyd R.T., Hopfensitz A., Richerson P.J., Sigmund K., Smith E.A., Weissing F.J., Young H.P. (2003). "The cultural and genetic evolution of human cooperation". In Hammerstein P. (ed): *Genetic and Cultural Evolution of Cooperation*, MIT Press, Cambridge, UK, pp. 445-468.
32. Nowak M.A., Sigmund K. (2005). "Evolution of Indirect Reciprocity". *Nature* 437:1292-1298
33. Nowak M.A., Sigmund K. (2007). "How Populations Cohere: Five Rules for Cooperation". In May R.M., McLean A. (eds): *Theoretical Ecology: Principles and Applications*, Oxford UP, Oxford, pp. 7-16.
34. Sigmund K., Nowak M.A. (2001).: "Evolution – Tides of Tolerance". *Nature* 414:403 (2001).
35. Sigmund K., Nowak M.A. (1996). "The Natural History of Mutual Aid". In Stadler F. (ed): *Wissenschaft als Kultur*, Springer-Verlag, Vienna, pp. 259-272.
36. Sigmund K. (1998), "Complex Adaptive Systems and the Evolution of Reciprocation". *Ecosystems* 1:444-448.
37. Sigmund K. (2007). "Punish or Perish? Retaliation and Collaboration Among Humans". *Trends in Ecology and Evolution* 22:593-600.
38. Sigmund K.(2002). "The Economics of Fair Play". *Scientific American* 286:82-87.
39. Barney, J.B.; Hansen, M.H,.(1994). "Trustworthiness as a source of competitive advantage". *Strategic management Journal*, 15, pp. 175-190.
40. Conner K.R.;Prahalad C.K. (1996). "A resource-based theory of the firm: knowledge vs. opportunism". *Organizational Science*, 7, pp. 477-501.
41. Doney P.M; Cannon J.P. (1997). "An examination of the nature of trust in buyer-seller relationships". *Journal of Marketing*, 61, pp. 35-51.

42. Dyer J.H.; Singh H. (1998). "The relational view: cooperative strategies and sources of interorganizational competitive advantage". *The Academy of Management Review*, 23,4, oct. 1998, pp. 660-679.
43. Dercole F, Dieckmann U, Obersteiner M, Rinaldi S. (2008). "Adaptive Dynamics and Technological Change". *Technovation* 28:335-348.
44. Thomas A.C., Scholz, M. (2009). "Why Organizational Economy Is Not a Darwinian Research Program". *Philosophy of the Social Sciences*, Vol. 39, No. 3, 408-439.

Part II

Construction of the IT Artifact

Approaches to Developing Information Systems[1]

David Avison[2], **Guy Fitzgerald**[3]

Abstract Information systems development (ISD) is a core issue of information systems teaching, practice and research. In this chapter we provide a brief history of information systems development and then focus on ISD today, where speed-of-development issues have changed the scene greatly. We look at one approach, Dynamic Systems Development Method (DSDM), in particular as it strikes a good balance between speed and cost issues on the one hand and yet maintains many of the best practices of traditional ISD approaches.

A Brief History of Information Systems Development

In this section we examine some of the trends and issues related to information systems development until around 2000 (we discuss the current situation in the next section). It addresses methodologies for the development of business information systems, or what was called in the early days, data processing. As a result of analysing methodologies from a historical perspective, we have identified a number of specific periods or eras, which we argue have particular, identifiable, characteristics. Although described as eras, this does not mean that they are (or have been) experienced in exactly the same time period by every organisation or indeed every country. This will obviously vary. We break up our history into three eras: pre-methodology, early methodology, and methodology era.

Pre-methodology era Early computer applications, until around the 1970s and even early 1980s, were implemented without an explicit information systems development methodology. We thus characterise this as the pre-methodology era. In these early days, the emphasis of computer applications development was on programming. The two major skills required were that of the computer programmer, to ascertain requirements, and write, test and implement the programs, and the computer operator, to run them on the computer once implemented. The needs of the users were rarely well addressed with the consequence that the design was frequently inappropriate to the application. The focus of effort was on getting something working and overcoming the limitations of the technology, such as making an application run in restricted amounts of computer memory. A particular problem was that the developers were technically trained but rarely good communicators,

---

[1] An extended version of this chapter with a case study is provided in: Grant, K., Hackney, R. & Edgar, D. (2010) Strategic Information Systems Management, Andover: Cengage.

[2] ESSEC Business School, Paris, France, avison@essec.fr

[3] Brunel University, Uxbridge, UK, guy.fitzgerald@brunel.ac.uk

nor did they understand the needs of the business well. There was a distinct 'gap' between the technicians and the business users. The dominant 'methodology' was rule-of-thumb and based on experience. This typically led to poor control and management of projects. For example, estimating the date on which the system would be operational was difficult, and applications were frequently delivered late. The programmers were over-stretched, and spent a large proportion of their time correcting and enhancing the few applications that were operational. Most emphasis was necessarily placed on maintaining operational systems to get them right, rather than developing new ones. These problems led to a growing appreciation of the desirability for standards and a more disciplined approach to the development of information systems in organisations. It was also realised that having users and the business liaising directly with the implementers (programmers) was not the most effective approach. Thus the first information systems development methodologies were established.

Early methodology era As computers were used more and more and management was demanding more appropriate systems for their expensive outlay, it was felt that this rather ad hoc approach to development could not go on. There were four main changes:

1. There was a realisation that information systems needed to deliver value for money in a business context, with a calculation of the expected costs and proposed benefits.
2. There was a growing appreciation of that part of the development of the system that concerns analysis and design and therefore of the potential role of the systems analyst as a link to the business as well as that of the programmer.
3. There was a realisation that as organisations were growing in size and complexity, it was desirable to move away from one-off solutions to a particular problem and towards more integrated information systems.
4. There was an appreciation of the desirability of an accepted methodology for the development of information systems.

These changes led to the evolution of the Information Systems Development Life Cycle (ISDLC) as the approach to the development of information systems. This was an early methodology, although at the time it was not yet known as such. An information systems development methodology is defined by Avison and Fitzgerald [1] as: 'a recommended means to achieve the development, or part of the development, of information systems based on a set of rationales and an underlying philosophy that supports, justifies and makes coherent such a recommendation for a particular context. The recommended means usually includes the identification of phases, procedures, tasks, rules, techniques, guidelines, documentation and tools. They might also include recommendations concerning the management and organisation of the approach and the identification and training of the participants'.

The early-methodology era was characterised by an approach to building computer-based applications that focused on the identification of phases and stages that it was thought would help control and enable the better management of systems development and introduce some discipline. This approach is also commonly known as the *waterfall model*. It consisted of a number of stages of development that had to be followed sequentially. These stages typically consisted of feasibility study, systems investigation, analysis, design, and implementation, followed by review and maintenance, and this was the approach widely used in the late 1970s and early 1980s. Importantly, it is still a basis for many methodologies used today.

The feasibility study attempts to assess the costs and benefits of alternative proposals enabling management to make informed choices. From the potential solutions, one is chosen. Included in the study should be human and organisational costs and benefits as well as economic and technical ones. The systems investigation stage takes a detailed look at the functional requirements of the application, any constraints imposed, exceptional conditions and so on, using techniques such as observation, interviewing, questionnaires and searching through records and documentation. Armed with the facts about the application area, the systems analyst proceeds to the systems analysis phase and analyses the present system by asking such questions as: why do current problems exist, why were certain methods of work adopted, are there alternative methods, and what are the likely growth rates of data?

Through consideration of such factors, the analyst moves on to designing the new system. The design documentation set will contain details of input data and how the data is to be captured (entered in the system); outputs of the system (sometimes referred to as the deliverables); processes, many carried out by computer programs, involved in converting the inputs to the outputs; structure of the computer and manual files which might be referenced in the system; security and back-up provisions to be made; and systems testing and implementation plans.

Implementation of the design will include program writing, purchasing of new hardware, training of users, writing of user and operations documentation, and cutover to the new system. A major aspect of this phase is that of quality control. The manual procedures, along with the hardware and software, need to be tested to the satisfaction of users as well as analysts. The users need to be comfortable with the new methods. Once the application system is operational, there are bound to be some changes necessary due to errors or changes in requirements over time. These changes are made in the review and maintenance phase, when the lifecycle may start again. An important part of the lifecycle is the notion of iteration. If a problem is found at one stage, e.g. the design stage, then it may be necessary to iterate around the previous stage, e.g. analysis, or even further, until the problem is solved. For example, an inconsistency discovered in testing might only be resolved by returning to clarify the user requirements or by finding an error in analysis.

The ISDLC has a number of features to commend it. It has been well tried and tested. The use of documentation standards helps to ensure that proposals are complete and that they are communicated to users and computing staff. The approach also ensures that users are trained to use the system. There are controls and these, along with the division of the project into phases of manageable tasks with deliverables, help to avoid missed cutover dates and disappointments with regard to what is delivered. Unexpectedly high costs and lower benefits are also less likely. It enables a well-formed and standard training scheme to be given to analysts, thus ensuring continuity of standards and systems. The concept of iteration is also of benefit as it helps to ensure that problems are addressed at the correct place, however, in practice iteration was often ignored and errors not traced back to their source. It has been criticised for being somewhat inflexible, over complex and difficult to use, and it did not necessarily lead to applications that were accepted by the users. It has also been criticised for taking too long, over-focussing on analysis, and thwarting innovation. As a result a number of alternatives emerged.

Methodology era In this era the term methodology was probably used for the first time to describe these different approaches. These can be classified into a number of movements. The first are those methodologies designed to improve upon the traditional waterfall or ISDLC model by the inclusion of new techniques and tools along with improved training so as to reduce the potential impact of these problems. A second movement is the proposal of new methodology themes and methodologies that are somewhat different to the traditional waterfall model (and from each other). During the 1980s and 1990s, there have been many methodologies that reflect different views about information systems development.

Since the 1970s, there have been a number of developments in techniques and tools and many of these have been incorporated in the methodologies exemplifying the modern version of the waterfall model. Techniques incorporated include entity-relationship modelling, normalisation, data flow diagramming, structured English, action diagrams, structure diagrams and entity life cycles. Tools include project management software, data dictionary software, systems repositories, drawing tools and, the most sophisticated, computer-assisted software (or systems) engineering (CASE) tools. The data modelling techniques suggest that the waterfall models used the best process and data modelling techniques. The documentation has improved, thanks to the use of drawing and other tools, and it is more likely to be kept up to date and be more understandable to non-technical people. Further, tools can be used to develop prototypes, which can help to more quickly elicit and validate the user requirements, enable users to assess the proposed information system in a more tangible way, and thus speed up delivery of the operational system. The blended methodologies Merise [2] SSADM [3] and Yourdon Systems Method [4] could be said to be updated versions of the waterfall model. Although these improvements have brought the basic model up to date, many users have argued that the life cycle approach still remains inflexible and inhibits the most effective use of computer information systems.

As a reaction to this a number of alternative methodologies were proposed. To give some examples: Checkland's soft systems methodology [5] helps users understand the organisational situation and point to areas for organisational improvement through the use of information systems; Davenport's Business Innovation [6] uses business process re-engineering themes to attempt to ensure that IS development aligns with the business strategy; in participative approaches, the role of all users is stressed, and the role of the technologist may be subsumed by other stakeholders of the information system as illustrated well in Mumford's ETHICS methodology [7];

Rapid Application Development (RAD) [8] is an example of an approach that emphasises speed of development and developing prototypes, that is models of applications as a basis for the final product; structured approaches, for example, Yourdon [9] stress techniques, such as decision trees, decision tables, data flow diagrams, data structure diagrams, and structured English, which break up the complex tasks into its major tasks and then sub tasks (a process known as functional decomposition) and whereas structured analysis and design emphasises processes, data analysis concentrates on understanding and documenting data and involves the collection, validation and classification of the entities, attributes and relationships that exist in the area investigated and is an approach exemplified by Information Engineering [10].

In the 1990s there has been what we may call a second wave of methodologies. Object-oriented information systems development, in particular, has made a large impact on practice [11]. The basic concepts of the object-oriented approach, of objects and attributes, wholes and parts, and classes and parts are basic and simple to understand, and the approach unifies the information systems development process. Whereas in previous approaches data and processes were analysed and treated separately the object oriented approach combined them. An object, which might be a customer, would be described with its attributes, such as number, name, address, credit limit, etc. but also with its related processes, such as check balance, change address, increase credit-limit, etc. These processes or methods would be combined, or encapsulated, into the customer object. So, a system is made up of a series of discrete objects that interact together by the passing of messages from one object to another, which trigger the processes of the object. Thus Object-oriented modelling is concerned with representing objects, including their data and processes, and the interaction of objects, in a system. We also model hierarchies of objects (called classes), so we might have a high-level customer object that breaks down into various lower-level objects of customers, e.g. past customer, new customer, declined customer, etc. The object-oriented approach has the benefit of inheritance which means that anything defined in a higher level object can be inherited by the lower-level object, leading to ease of definition and consistency. It also facilitates the re-use of software code and therefore makes application development quicker and more robust. Indeed a great number of benefits are claimed for the object-oriented approach some of which have occurred but many of them are somewhat theoretical and have not been seen to the extent promised, in practice. Anyway, quite a number of object-oriented methodologies were proposed although many fewer were actually adopted than their proponents suggest.

We characterise the above as representing the methodology era because of the apparent proliferation of different types of methodologies, and their increasing maturity. Many attempts have been made to compare and contrast this diversity of methodologies. Avison & Fitzgerald [1], for example, compare methodologies on the basis of philosophy (paradigm, objectives, domain and target); model; techniques and tools; scope; outputs; and practice (background, user base, players, and product). In relation to the number of methodologies in existence, however, the characterisation of this as the methodology era does not mean that every organisation was using a methodology for systems development. Indeed, some were not using a methodology at all but most, it seems, were using some kind of in-house developed or tailored methodology, typically based upon or heavily influenced by one or more of the well-known methodologies, as described above.

However, many users of methodologies found the waterfall model and the alternative methodologies outlined above unsatisfactory. Most methodologies are designed for situations, which follow a stated, or more usually, an unstated 'ideal type'. The methodology provides a step-by-step prescription for addressing this ideal type, but unfortunately situations are all different and there is no such thing as an 'ideal type' in reality. Situations differ depending on, for example, their complexity and structuredness, type and rate of change in the organisation, the numbers of users affected, their skills, and those of the analysts. Further, most methodology users expect to follow a step-by-step, top-down approach to information systems development where they carry out a series of iterations through to project implementation. In reality, in any one project, this is rarely the case, as some phases might be omitted, others carried out in a different sequence, and yet others developed further than espoused by the methodology authors. Similarly, particular techniques and tools may be used differently or not used at all in different circumstances. There have been a number of responses to this challenge and it is these responses that bring us to more recent times and we discuss this in the next section.

Contemporary Information Systems Development

The current situation we characterise as the post-methodology era, in the sense that we now perceive systems development as having moved beyond the pure methodology era. Now it seems that although some organisations still use a methodology of some kind there is enough of a re-appraisal of the beneficial assumptions of methodologies, even a backlash against methodologies, together with a range and diversity of different approaches to internal systems development using methodologies, to justify the identification of a new era.

As we have seen methodologies were often seen as a panacea to the problems of traditional development approaches, and were often chosen and adopted for the wrong reasons. Some organisations simply wanted a better project control mechanism, others a better way of involving users, still others wanted to inject some rigour or discipline into the process. However, for many of these organisations, the adoption of a methodology was not the success its advocates expected. Indeed, it was very unlikely that methodologies would ever achieve some of the more overblown claims made by vendors and consultants. Some organisations found their chosen methodology not to be successful or appropriate for them and they have adopted a different one. For some this second option has been more useful, but others have found the new one not to be successful either. This has led some organisations to the rejection of methodologies in general. In the authors' experience this is not an isolated reaction, and there is something that might be described as a backlash against formalised information systems development methodologies.

This does not mean that methodologies have not been successful. It means that they have not solved all the problems that exist in connection with ISD. Many organisations are using methodologies effectively and successfully and conclude that, although not perfect, they are an improvement on their previous development approach, and that probably they could not handle their current systems development load without them.

Others adopt a more flexible contingency type approach to information systems development (as opposed to a more prescriptive approach), where a structure or framework is adopted but stages, phases, tools, techniques, and so on, are expected to be used or not (or used and adapted), depending on the situation. Those characteristics which will affect the choice of a particular combination of techniques, tools and methods for a particular situation could include the type of project, whether it is an operations-level system or a management information system, the size of the project, the importance of the project, the projected life of the project, the characteristics of the problem domain, the available skills and so on. Multiview [12] is such a contingency framework.

Another reaction to the perceived problems of using formalised methodologies, or plan driven methods, is the growth of agile development. Agile development aims to reduce the length of time that it takes to develop a system. It also attempts to addresses the problem of changing requirements as a result of learning during the process of development. This particular form of development has been termed 'timebox' development [8]. The system to be developed is divided up into a number of components that can be developed separately. The most important requirements and those with the largest potential benefit are developed first. Some argue that no single development phase should take more than 90 days, whilst others suggest even less, but whichever timebox length is chosen, the point is that it is refreshingly quick compared to traditional approaches which are usually around 18 months or upwards. The idea of this approach is to compartmentalise the development and deliver early and often (hence the term timeboxing). This provides the business and the users with a quick, but it is hoped, useful part of the system in a very short time scale. The system at this stage is probably quite limited in relation to the total requirements, but at least something has been delivered. This is radically different from the conventional delivery mode of most formalised methodologies which is a long development period of typically two to three years followed by the implementation of the complete system. The benefits of agile development is that users trade-off unnecessary (or at least initially unnecessary) requirements and wish-lists (that is, features that it would be 'nice to have' in an ideal world) for speed of development. It also has the benefit that if requirements change over that time (which typically they do), the total system has not been completed and the next timebox can accommodate the changes that become necessary as requirements change and evolve. It also has the advantage that the users become experienced with using and working with the system and learn what they really require from the early features that are implemented. Such an approach requires a radically different development culture from that required for formalised methodologies. The focus is on speed of delivery, the identification of the absolutely essential requirements, implementation as a learning process and the expectation that the requirements will change in the next timebox.

The agile approach is not just one methodology but is more of a general philosophy of development. A number of important agile proponents developed the Agile Manifesto which has become very influential in this context. The Manifesto has a number of principles including:

- Individuals and interactions are valued more than processes and tools
- Working software is valued more than comprehensive documentation
- Customer collaboration is valued more than contract negotiation
- Responding to change is valued more than following a plan.

The Agile Manifesto may be influential but is not necessarily particularly new, as Cockburn [13] states, "what is new about agile methods is not the practices they use, but their recognition of people as the primary drivers of project success, coupled with an intense focus on effectiveness and manoeuvrability".

Another reaction to the problems of the methodology era is to reject the use of a methodology altogether. A survey conducted in the UK [14] found that 57% of the sample were claiming to be using a methodology for systems development, but of these, only 11% were using a commercial development methodology unmodified, whereas 30% were using a commercial methodology adapted for in-house use, and 59% a methodology which they claimed to be unique to their organization, i.e. one that was internally developed and not based solely on a commercial methodology.

Some organisations have decided not to embark on any more major in-house system development activities but to buy-in all their requirements in the form of packages. This is regarded as a quick and relatively inexpensive way of implementing systems for organisations that have fairly standard requirements. Clearly packages of all kinds are available in the market place and do not have to be developed from scratch and they are also typically much cheaper than tailor-made systems. Although, of course, it should be remembered that the implementation costs are usually considerably greater than the price of the package, for example, the costs of training and accommodating the package in the business processes can be large. A degree of package modification and integration may be required which may be undertaken in-house. Clearly the purchasing (or licensing) of packages has been commonplace for some time, but the present era is characterised by some organisations preferring package solutions for virtually all their systems development needs. Only systems that are strategic or for which a suitable package is not available would be considered for development in-house. The package market is becoming increasingly sophisticated and more and more highly tailorable packages are becoming available. Enterprise resource planning (ERP) systems have become particularly popular as a type of package sold in modules that address the common functionality of many parts of the business and that are designed to integrate these different modules. A key for organisations seeking to utilise packages is ensuring that the correct trade-off is made between a standard package, which might mean changing some elements of the way the business currently operates to fit the package, and a package that can be modified or tailored to reflect the way they wish to operate. There are dangers in the utilisation of packages of becoming locked-in to a particular supplier and of not being in control of the features that are incorporated in the package, but many companies have taken this risk. There is also the fact that utilising a package means that the solution to a particular problem is also available for your competitor to purchase, i.e. there is no real competitive advantage available from a standard package compared to a tailor-made solution.

For others, the continuing problems of systems development and the backlash against methodologies has resulted in the outsourcing of systems development. In such cases the client organisation is probably not concerned about how the systems are developed. They are more interested in the end results and the effectiveness of the systems that are delivered. It is argued by some that this can actually be a cheaper approach because you are only paying for what you get and that the payment of real money (often coming directly from the business users) serves to 'focus the mind' and results in more accurate and realistic specifications, and expectations. This is different to buying-in packages or solutions, because normally the management and responsibility for the provision and development of appropriate systems is given over to the vendor. The client company has to develop skills in selecting the correct vendor, specifying requirements in detail, and writing and negotiating contracts, rather than thinking about and managing system development methodolgies. Outsourcing is an important element of systems development for many large organisations and its impact has been increased by the provision of many systems development activities offshore, i.e. in areas of the world where skilled labour rates are much cheaper than the US and Western Europe, e.g. India and increasingly China. Again outsourcing and offshore outsourcing has not been a panacea to the problems of successful systems development but it has proved popular.

Thus, in the post-methodology era, there are many different approaches to systems development taken, from outsourcing through to just buying packages. Many of these were driven by a backlash against internal development using traditional methodologies. As mentioned above one reaction against the traditional formalised methodology has been a move to agile development, and we look in more detail at one approach to agile (as you might expect, there are many!) in the next section.

Dynamic Systems Development Method (DSDM)

As outlined above, Agile methods are becoming increasingly important in systems development and so we will look at one such method in more detail and have chosen DSDM (Dynamic Systems Development Method). In the mid 1990s, and as a reaction to the perceived problems of traditional bureaucratic approaches to systems development, a more flexible and faster approach was evolved. DSDM came about from an independent and 'not for profit' consortium who defined a standard for rapidly developing applications. The Consortium, originating in the UK, includes IBM, the British Ministry of Defence, British Telecom and British

Airways, but now has an international mix of users. Rapid application development, mentioned earlier, is fundamental to DSDM. The DSDM approach not only addresses the developer's view of rapid systems development but also that of other stakeholders who are interested in effective information systems development, including for example, users quality assurance people, project managers, business managers, etc. It has nine principles as follows:

1. Active user involvement is imperative.
2. Teams must be empowered to make decisions. The four key variables of empowerment are: authority, resources, information and accountability.
3. Frequent delivery of products is essential.
4. Fitness for business purpose is the essential criterion for acceptance of deliverables.
5. Iterative and incremental development is necessary to converge on an accurate business solution.
6. All changes during development are reversible, i.e. you do not proceed further down a particular path if problems are encountered. Instead, you backtrack to the last safe or agreed point, and then start down a new path.
7. The high-level business requirements, once agreed, are frozen. This is essentially the scope of the project.
8. Testing is integrated throughout the life cycle, i.e. 'test as you go' rather than testing just at the end where it frequently gets squeezed.
9. A collaborative and co-operative approach between all stakeholders is essential.

Many of these principles are encompassed in the following characteristics of its practice:

Incremental development It is understood that not all the requirements can be identified and specified in advance. Some requirements will only emerge when the users see and experience the system in use, others may not emerge even then, particularly complex ones. Requirements are also never seen as complete but evolve and change over time with changing circumstances. So DSDM starts with a high-level, rather imprecise list of requirements, which are refined and changed during the process. The easy, obvious requirements and those providing most impact are used as the starting point for development.

Timeboxing The information system to be developed is divided up into a number of components or timeboxes that are developed separately. The most important requirements, and those with the largest potential benefit, are developed first and delivered as quickly as possible in the first timebox. The aim is to deliver quickly and often. This rapid delivery of the most important requirements also helps to build credibility and enthusiasm from the users and the business, indeed, all the stakeholders. The focus is on speed of delivery, the identification of the absolutely essential requirements, implementation as a learning vehicle, and the expectation that the requirements will change in the next timebox.

Pareto principle This is essentially the 80/20 rule and is thought to apply to requirements. The belief is that around 80% of an information system's functionality can be delivered with around 20% of the effort needed to complete 100% of the requirements. This means that it is the last, and probably most complex, 20% of requirements that take most of the effort and time. Thus the question is asked 'why do it?'. Instead, choose as much of the 80% to deliver as possible in the timebox. The rest, if it proves necessary, can be delivered in subsequent timeboxes (or not at all).

MoSCoW rule This is a form of prioritizing of requirements according to four categories:

M *'the Must Haves'*. Without these features the project is not viable (i.e. these are the minimum critical success factors fundamental to the project's success).
S *'the Should Haves'*. To gain maximum benefit these features will be delivered but the project's success does not rely on them.
C *'the Could Haves'*. If time and resources allow these features will be delivered but they can easily be left out without impacting on the project.
W *'the Won't Haves'*. These features will not be delivered. They can be left out and possibly, although not necessarily, be done in a later timebox.

The MoSCoW rules ensure that a critical examination is made of requirements and that no large 'wish lists' are made by users. All requirements have to be justified and categorized. Normally in a timebox all the 'must haves' and at least some of the 'should haves' and a few of the 'could haves' would be included. Of course, as has been mentioned, under pressure during the development the 'could haves' may well be dropped and even possibly the 'should haves' as well.

JAD workshops DSDM requires high levels of participation from all stakeholders in a project as a point of principle and achieves this partly through the JAD (Joint Application Development) workshop. This is a facilitated meeting designed to overcome the problems of traditional requirements gathering where users feel they have no real say on decision-making. A JAD workshop will help establish and agree the initial requirements, the length of the timebox, what should be included in the timebox and manage expectations and gain commitment from the stakeholders. Later workshops will firm up the detail.

Prototyping A prototype is a rough approximation of the application (or part of it) which can be used to test some designs and other features of the final product and gain user reaction at an early stage in the development process. Prototyping is an important part of DSDM and is used to help establish the user requirements and in some cases the prototype evolves to become the system itself. Prototyping helps speed up the process of eliciting requirements, and although speed is obviously important in DSDM, it also fits the DSDM view of evolving requirements and users not knowing exactly what they want until they see or experience using the system.

Extreme programming (XP) Version 4.2 of DSDM suggests a joint approach with another agile approach known as extreme programming (XP). Extreme Programming stresses the role of teamwork and open and honest communication between managers, customers and developers with concrete and rapid feedback. The customer must define their requirements in ***user stories;*** these are the things that the system needs to do for its users, and therefore replaces the requirements document. An ***architectural spike*** is an aid to figuring out answers to tough technical or design problems. This is usually a very simple program to explore the potential solutions; it builds a system, which only addresses the problem under examination and ignores all other concerns. ***Paired programming*** – two programmers per workstation – reduces the potential risk when a technical difficulty threatens to hold up the system's development. While one programmer is keying in the best way to perform a task, the other is 'thinking more strategically' about whether the whole approach will work, tests that may not work yet and ways of simplifying. Historically, as we have seen, there have been problems concerning speed of delivery in information systems practice and DSDM recognizes that the business often needs solutions faster than they can be delivered. It is recognized that deadlines are frequently set with no reference to the work involved, that is, the deadline is outside of the control of those tasked with the delivery of the project. In situations of tight deadlines it is tempting to introduce extra resources and people to a project. However, this frequently makes things worse as there is a considerable learning curve for new people joining a project and existing people are diverted to help bring the new people up to speed. Thus, if the deadline of a late-running project cannot be altered, the only thing left is to reduce functionality, i.e. take out some parts and leave them for a subsequent timebox. This is the solution that DSDM adopts.

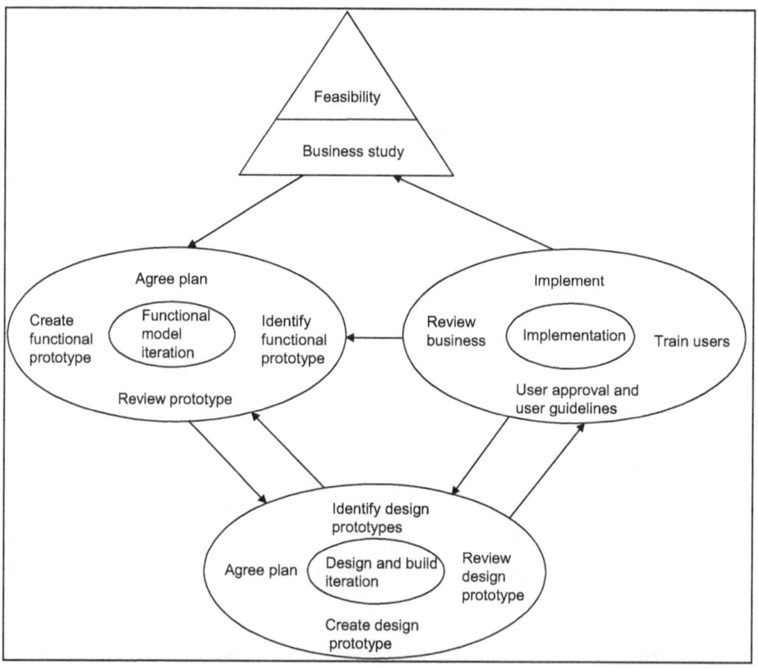

Figure 3.1: DSDM in overview

The phases and the main products that need to be produced in each phase together with the various pathways through the process are seen in Figure X. As can be seen, the feasibility and business studies are performed sequentially and before the rest of the phases because they define the scope and justification for the subsequent development activities. The arrows indicate the normal forward path through the phases, including iteration within each phase, though they also indicate the possible routes back for evolving and iterating the phases. In fact, the sequence that the last three phases are undertaken in or how they are overlapped is not defined but left to the needs of the project and the developers.

As can be seen there are five main phases in the DSDM development lifecycle:

1. **Feasibility study:** This includes the usual feasibility elements, for example, the cost/benefit case for undertaking a particular project, but also, and particularly important, it is concerned with determining whether DSDM is the correct approach for this project. DSDM recognises that not all projects are suitable for RAD and DSDM. This is concerned with the maturity and experience of the organisation with DSDM concepts. Further, where engineering, scientific or particularly computationally complex applications apply, the use of DSDM is not usually advised. Projects where all the requirements must be delivered at once may also not be suitable for DSDM. General business applications, especially where the details of the requirements are not clear but time is critical, are particularly suitable for DSDM. The feasibility study is 'a short, sharp exercise' taking no more than a few weeks. Thus it is not particularly detailed but highly focused on the risks and how to manage them. A key outcome is the agreement that the project is suitable and should proceed.

2. **Business study:** This is also supposed to be quick and is at a relatively high-level. It is about gaining understanding of the business processes involved, their rationales and their information needs. It also identifies the stakeholders and those that need to be involved. It is argued that traditional requirements gathering techniques, such as interviewing, take too long. Facilitated Joint application development (JAD) workshops are recommended involving all the stakeholders. The high level major functions are identified and prioritised as is the overall systems architecture definition and outline work plans. These plans include the Outline Prototyping Plan which defines all the prototypes to be included in the subsequent phases. These plans get refined at each phase as more information becomes available. DSDM advocates using 'what you know' and is not prescriptive concerning analysis and design techniques.

3. **Functional model iteration:** Here the high level functions and information requirements from the Business Study are refined. Standard analysis models are produced followed by the development of prototypes and then the software. This is described as a symbiotic process with feedback from prototypes serving to refine the models and then the prototypes moving towards first-cut software, which is then tested as much as is possible given its evolving nature.

4. **System design and build iteration:** This is where the system is built ready for delivery to the users. It should include at least the 'minimum usable subset' of requirements. Thus the 'must haves' and some of the 'should haves' will be delivered, but this depends on how the project has evolved during its development. Testing is not a major activity of this stage because of the on-going testing principle. However, some degree of testing will probably be needed as in some cases this will be the first time the whole system has been available together.

5. **Implementation:** This is the cut-over from the existing system or environment to the new. It includes training, development and completion of the user manuals and documentation. The term completion is used because, like testing, these should have been on-going activities throughout the process. Ideally, user documentation is produced by the users rather than the specialist developers. Finally a Project Review Document is produced which assesses whether all the requirements have been met or whether further iterations are required.

DSDM emphasises the key role of people in the process and is described as a 'user centred' approach. Overall there is a project manager, requiring all the skills of traditional project managers and more, as the focus is on speed! The project manager is responsible for project planning, monitoring, prioritisation, human resources, budgets, module definition, re-scoping, etc. The use of software project management and control tools are recommended. Some people see the use of such project control tools to be in conflict with the dynamic nature of DSDM, but most DSDM users argue that this is not the case. On the user side there are two key roles. The first is that of Ambassador User. This is someone (or more than one person) from the user community who understands and represents the needs of that community. The second is the Visionary User. This is the person that had the original idea or vision as to how the project might help in the business or organisation. As well as defining the original vision, they have a responsibility to make sure that the vision stays in focus and does not become diluted. In other contexts this might be described as the project champion. On the IT side, although they are crucial, there are in general no particular specialist roles, i.e. no distinction is made between different IT roles, such as analysts, designers, programmers, etc. Everyone has to have flexible skills and be capable of turning their hand to whatever is required at any particular time. Of course in practice particular skills may have to be imported at times, but the key IT team members are generalists and do not change. One exception to this is the specific role of Technical Coordinator, responsible for the technical architecture, technical quality and configuration management. A particular requirement for all is good communication skills. DSDM recommends small development teams composed of users and IT developers. A large project may have a number of teams working in parallel, but the minimum team size is two, as at least one person has to be from the IT side and one from the business or user side. The recommended maximum is six as it has been found that above this number the RAD process can prove difficult to sustain.

DSDM characterises many of the concepts of agile development and as mentioned above we believe it will be of increasing importance in the future. Of course, like any of the other approaches, it is not a panacea. It needs to be used flexibly and appropriately for organization and stakeholders. We believe, unlike some of the agile evangelists, that it should not be used on every project. We recommend a suitability analysis of the project prior to selection of the methodology. There are many projects, particularly where the requirements are known or knowable, where the more traditional approaches would be a more efficient method of development. Equally, where the project is safety or truly business critical then we would advocate a traditional approach where the risk is minimised. But for application areas where the requirements are complex, varied and difficult to ascertain, which is of course many in today's modern world, then agile would seem to be highly effective and appropriate.

To summarise, we believe that Information systems development (ISD) is a core issue of information systems teaching, practice and research. In this chapter we provide a brief history of information systems development and have then focused on ISD today. We have discussed the history of methodologies and identified a set of distinct 'eras' leading to the current 'post-methodology' era, with its variety of approaches and backlash against the past. We have discussed one important approach of this era, that of agile development, where the focus is on the speed of development. Different agile approaches abound but we have looked in detail at one agile approach, Dynamic Systems Development Method (DSDM), as an example of the general approach. As discussed, we believe that we are in what we term the 'post-methodology' era but that contemporary development can only be fully understood in relation to this history of methodologies and approaches. Such history teaches us that today's methods are only the latest stage in the ongoing evolution of development that addresses changing times, fashions, and circumstances. Thus, it would be a mistake to think, despite the current focus on agile, that this approach and indeed this era is likely to last forever. Our expectation would be that the next generation of ISD approaches are just over the horizon. What will they be? Who knows, but based on the history they will probably be an evolution of some existing methods, together with some specific techniques to address new circumstances, all wrapped up as a new package, with a fresh name. Whatever it is, it will be interesting and challenging, but we advise practitioners and academics not to be over concerned and view it through the lens of the historic evolution of ISD, which will make it more understandable and manageable.

References

1. Avison, D. and Fitzgerald, G. (2003) 'Where now for development methodologies?', *Communications of the ACM,* 46, 1, 78-82.
2. Quang, P.T. and Chartier-Kastler, C. (1991) *Merise in Practice.* Macmillan, Basingstoke.
3. Eva, M. (1994) *SSADM Version 4: A User's Guide*, 2nd edn, McGraw-Hill, Maidenhead.
4. Yourdon Inc. (1993) *Yourdon Systems Method: Model-driven Systems Development*, Yourdon Press, Englewood Cliffs.

5. Checkland P. and Scholes J. (1990). *Soft Systems Methodology in Action*. Chichester, Wiley.
6. Davenport, T. H. (1993) *Process Innovation*, Harvard Business School Press, Cambridge, Mass.
7. Mumford, E. (1995) *Effective Requirements Analysis and Systems Design: The ETHICS Method*, Macmillan, Basingstoke, UK.
8. Martin, J. (1991) *Rapid Application Development*, Prentice Hall, Englewood Cliffs, New Jersey.
9. Yourdon (1989) *Modern Structured Analysis*, Prentice Hall, Englewood Cliffs, New Jersey.
10. Martin, J. (1989) *Information Engineering*, Prentice Hall, Englewood Cliffs, New Jersey.
11. Booch, G. (1991) *Object-oriented Design with Applications*, Benjamin/Cummings, Redwood City, California.
12. Avison, D. E., Wood-Harper, A. T., Vidgen, R. T., and Wood, J. R. G. (1998) A further exploration into information systems development: The evolution of Multiview2, *Information Technology & People*, 11, 2, 124–139.
13. Cockburn, A. (2002) *Agile Software Development*, Pearson-Longman, Harlow, UK.
14. Fitzgerald, G., Philippides, A., and Probert, P. (1999) Information systems development, maintenance and enhancement: Findings from a UK study, *International Journal of Information Management*, 40,2, 319–329.

Problem Analysis for Situational Artefact Construction in Information Systems

Robert Winter[1]

Abstract The goal of Design Science Research in Information Systems is to construct artefacts that are useful solutions to certain classes of (Information System) design problems in organisations. An essential part of Design Science Research in Information Systems is therefore to delineate the addressed design problem class, to illustrate its importance and to understand the design problems within this class in sufficient detail so that solution artefacts can be purposefully and systematically constructed. Although most authors discuss the relevance of a design problem class, its boundaries are often not delineated systematically, and the issue of genericity vs. utility is not rigorously addressed. We therefore propose a field study-based technique which overcomes this deficit by not only clearly specifying a design problem class, but also by identifying relevant design situations within this class – an important prerequisite for situational artefact construction. The proposed technique is demonstrated using a situational artefact construction exemplar. In our discussion, we identify the need for additional research to incorporate economical considerations.

Introduction

Design Science Research is a research paradigm that has been, among other application domains, successfully deployed to Information Systems (IS). In the following, we will use DSR to abbreviate Design Science Research in Information Systems. At its core, DSR is about the rigorous construction of useful IS artefacts, i.e. constructs, models, methods, or instantiations [1]. Hevner et al. [2, table 1] generalize constructs, models, methods and instantiations as "technology-based solutions to important and relevant business problems." Design problems in organisations are generically defined as "the differences between a goal state and the current state of a system" [2, p. 85]. DSR is prescriptive because its results are intended to be means for specific ends.

Most authors recommend to start the DSR process with the identification of the important and relevant problem that is going to be addressed [3-10]. Eekels and Roozenburg call this first step "problem analysis" [5]; Takeda et al. "problem enumeration" [8]; Baskerville et al., Cole et al., and Offermann et al., "problem identification" [3; 4; 6]; Vaishnavi & Kuechler "awareness of the problem" [11]; Wieringa "implementation evaluation and problem investigation" [10]; and Peffers et al. "identification and motivation of a problem" [7].

[1] University of St. Gallen, St. Gallen, Switzerland, robert.winter@unisg.ch

An important issue is how to delineate such a design problem. Hevner et al. [2] as well as March & Smith [1] claim an DSR artefact to provide 'profit' or, more generally, 'utility' to the organisation applying it, usually by increasing revenue or by decreasing costs. A concrete methodological support how to identify a design problem, how to show its importance and relevance, and how to understand the design problem sufficiently to support subsequent solution design is however missing. Besides of being important and relevant, the design problem – and hence the proposed design solution (= DSR output artefact) – should be sufficiently general. For Hevner et al. [2, p. 87], generality is one of three quality criteria of an DSR artefact. Baskerville et al. [3, p. 1] demand a design research artefact to "represent [.] a general solution to a class of problems." In the following, we will therefore assume that DSR results are generic (and not specific) IS artefacts which are useful for solving a class of design problems. The two research goals of generality and utility are conflicting. In their research on reference modelling, Becker et al. designate this trade-off as *reference modelling dilemma*: "On the one hand, customers will choose a reference model that [...] provides the best fit to their individual requirements and therefore implies the least need for changes. On the other hand, a restriction of the generality of the model results in higher turn-over risks because of smaller sales markets" [12, pp. 28-29]. This dilemma is not only apparent in reference modelling, but also exists for other general solutions to classes of design problems (e.g. methods). In a very simple form, it can be formalized as

$$U * g = c$$

where U denotes an artefact's utility, g denotes its generality, and c is a constant. With increasing generality, the utility of a solution for solving a specific design problem decreases – and vice versa. As a solution to this dilemma for (reference) models, Becker et al. [12-13] propose adaptation mechanisms that instantiate a generic reference model according to the specific design problem at hand. We hold a larger view, i.e. refer to all four artefact types identified by March & Smith [1] and hence designate the extension of generic artefacts by adaptation mechanisms as *situational artefact construction* (SAC). In addition to situational reference modelling [e.g. 12], situational artefact construction has also been investigated for methods (situational method engineering, see e.g. [14]). Gregor & Jones [15] refer to the adaptability of DSR artefacts under the label of "artefact mutability".

As SAC allows the researcher to develop artefacts which are adaptable to different design problems within a problem class, a crucial decision during the construction phase is to delineate the range of addressed design problems (i.e. to specify the design problem class) and to understand the relevant design situations within this class. If a design problem class is understood as a set of design problems for which a generic DSR artefact provides useful solution, a design situation can be understood as a cluster of design problems which are similar with regard to certain properties. Depending on the degree of generality, a design problem class can be partitioned into few, very generic design situations or a larger number of (different) design situations of lesser generality. Based on a specified metric for certain problem properties (e.g. Euclidian distance), the similarity (or better:

dissimilarity) of two design problems within a class can be represented by an ultrametric distance. Ultrametric spaces are a special kind of metric spaces. Ultrametric distances have some nice mathematical properties: Triangles in ultrametric spaces are always isosceles or equilateral whereby the side in opposite of the two equal sides of an isosceles triangle (which is not an equilateral triangle) is always shorter than one of the two equal sides. Ultrametric distances can be nicely visualized by a graph whose vertical dimension is generality and whose horizontal (base) dimension is the set of design problems. The less similar two design problems are, the higher is the degree of generality of a solution that satisfies both – and vice versa.

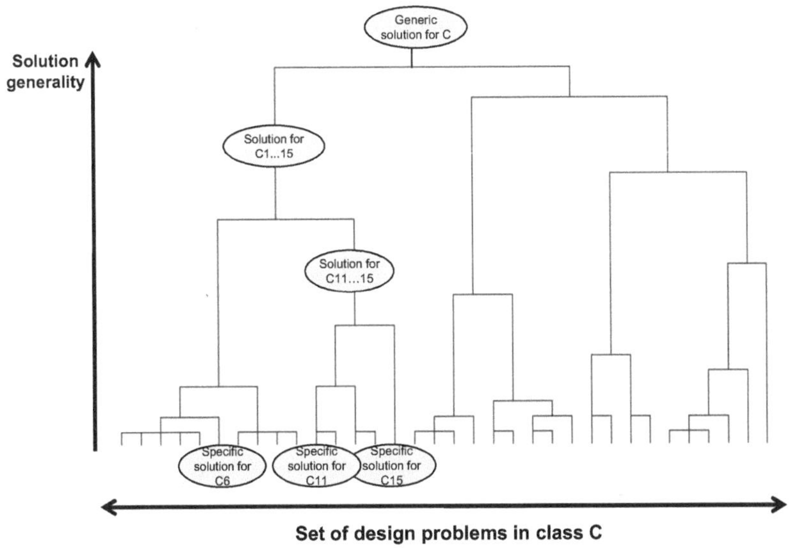

Figure 1: Visualization of ultrametric distances between design problems within a design problem class

Figure 1 depicts an idealized graphical visualization of ultrametric distances between design problems (C1...C33) within a design problem class C. The ultrametric distance between C11 and C15 is much smaller than that between C11 and C6 (i.e. C11 is more similar to C15 than to C6) because the common solution to C11...C15 is of lesser generality than a common solution to C1...C15. An ultrametric distance graph supports an intuitive understanding of how closely related (or how different) design problems in a class are. It also becomes intuitively clear that solution artefacts can be constructed on different levels of generality – the fewer artefacts are to be constructed, the higher their generality has to be. For the exemplary design problem class, whose ultrametric distances are illustrated by figure 1, nearly any number of solution artefacts between 1 (one "one size fits all" generic solution for *C*) and 33 (one specific solution for every single design problem *Cxx*) could be constructed. The important initial DSR process steps of "delineating the design problem" and "understanding the design problem class" thus require

(i) to identify relevant properties ("design factors") of the design problems,
(ii) to specify the property ranges that imply the addressed design problem class,
(ii) to define metrics for these properties that represent the similarity/dissimilarity of design problems within that class,
(iv) to calculate ultrametric distances based on these metrics and
(v) to use these ultrametric distances for specifying the desired generality level of the solution artefacts that are to be constructed in subsequent DSR steps.

After step (v), the design problem class has been sufficiently analyzed to allow for the systematic development of solution artefacts. For the exemplary design problem class illustrated in figure 2, we assume that the analysis yields a desired generality level of G_C. For G_C, the ultrametric distance graph yields four design situations and thus four solution artefacts need to be constructed (one for problems *C1...15*, one for problems *C16...24*, one for problems *C25...28* and one for problems *C29...33*).

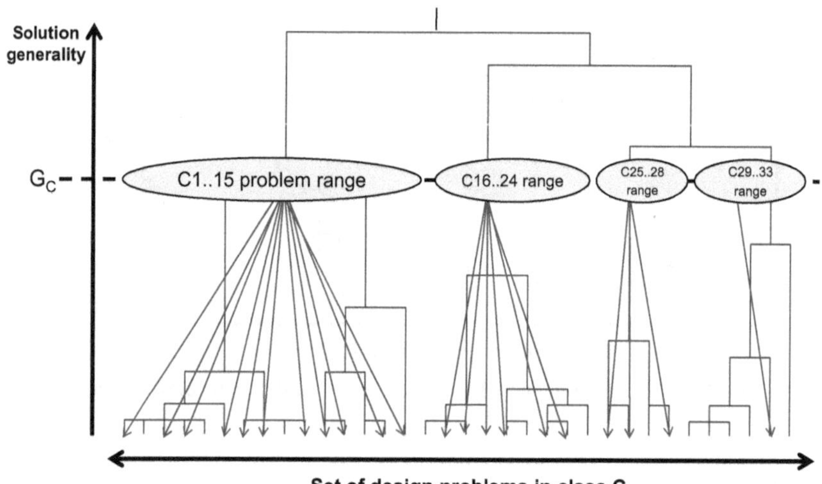

Figure 2: DSR problem class analysis as a genericity optimization problem

"Delineating the design problem" and "understanding the design problem class" clearly constitute an optimization problem. For a design problem class, the generality *g* needs to be determined that minimizes the sum of artefact construction and adaptation costs. Artefact construction costs are generally increasing exponentially with decreasing *g* due to the nature of the ultrametric distance graph (see figures 1 and 2); they are illustrated by the dotted line in figure 3. Artefact adaptation costs are generally increasing exponentially with growing *g* due to more complex and hence costly adaptations; they are illustrated by the solid line in figure 3. Using ultrametric distances allows to operationalize the above mentioned formula U * g = c.

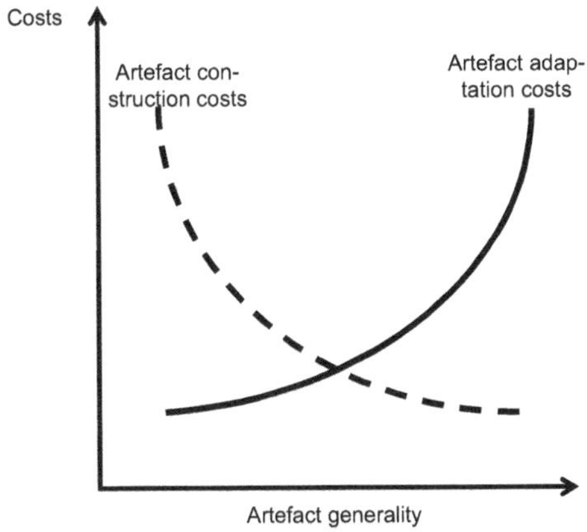

Figure 3: DSR problem class analysis as a genericity optimization problem

Since the early DSR steps "delineating the design problem" and "understanding the design problem class" need to create proper foundations for subsequent situational artefact design, we discuss the conceptual foundations of SAC in Section 2. In Section 3 we propose a field study based technique that (i) identifies relevant properties ("design factors") of the addressed design problems, (ii) specifies the design problem class, (iii) defines metrics for these properties, (iv) calculates ultrametric distances based on these metrics and (v) supports the determination of an appropriate level of artefact generality. The utility of the proposed technique is demonstrated using a situational artefact construction exemplar. The benefits and limitations of the proposed technique are discussed in the concluding Section 4. We will argue that 'technical' aspects like cluster homogeneity referring to certain contingency factors dominate, while economic aspects like construction and adaptation costs for generic design solutions are not sufficiently considered.

Conceptual Foundations of Situational Artefact Construction

In 1964, Fiedler [16] published a seminal paper on leadership effectiveness. Whilst preceding research in this field only investigates qualities of a successful leader, Fiedler was the first to consider situational factors, namely *affective leader-group relations*, the *task structure*, and the *leader's position power*. The consideration of such contingency factors has been developed into a contingency theory which builds upon two other organisational theories: the organic theory and the bureaucracy theory.

A good overview of the contingency theory is given by Donaldson [17]. "At the most abstract level, the contingency approach says that the effect of one variable on another depends upon some third variable" [17, p. 5]. In an organisational context, contingency theory "argues that success or failure of different organizational structures depends on contingency factors" [18, p. 29]. The three most important contingency factors in organisation theory are *size*, *task uncertainty*, and *task interdependence* [18, pp. 31-33]. The core proposition of contingency theory is that a fit between the contingency factors and the organisation of an enterprise leads to performance whilst a misfit leads to a lack of performance. This proposition has been investigated empirically in a plethora of studies. As not all of them support this proposition, Pfeffer [19], amongst others, heavily criticises contingency theory and questions its validity. Nevertheless, we agree with Donaldson that "overall, empirical studies show that fit positively affects performance, thereby supporting the central idea of contingency theory" [17, p. 242].

Contingency theory also supports the idea of constructing situational DSR artefacts: When constructing artefacts, situational factors should be considered. Nevertheless, although contingency theory enumerates some contingency factors, e.g. *size* or *task uncertainty*, it has not been proven empirically that contingency factors from organisation theory are also valid for DSR artefacts. Further "theory building" type research is needed to identify and validate appropriate contingency factors. While such contingency factors are not yet validated, DSR has either to wait or to intermediately use working hypotheses. In accordance with many other researchers who construct and evaluate situational artefacts, we vote for the second option.

A Field Study Based Technique for Delineating the Design Problem and Understanding the Design Problem Class

In the following, we present a technique that supports the initial DSR steps "delineating the design problem" and "understanding the design problem class".

Although Bucher and Klesse [20] developed their proposal for situational method engineering only, we believe that the procedure model can be extended for SAC in general. Bucher and Klesse distinguish four sequential process steps (cf. figure 4): Firstly, the artefact must be planned. For identifying potentially relevant contingency factors, a rough idea about the artefact (= the addressed class of design problems) must exist. Secondly, contingency factors are to be identified. Bucher et al. [14] propose to screen literature for potentially relevant contingency factors. As the list of contingency factor candidates might become long, they recommend sorting out those factors that lack an empirical or theoretical justification. Thirdly, they propose to conduct a field study in order to identify combinations of contingency factors that exist in reality. Such data help to aggregate "similar" design problems into design problem clusters. Finally, the artefact is constructed. Three options are distinguished: (i) to construct one artefact that fits all identified design problem clusters, (ii) to construct one artefact that fits only one design problem cluster (or few design problem clusters), or (iii) to construct a situational artefact that can be adapted to all or many of the problem clusters.

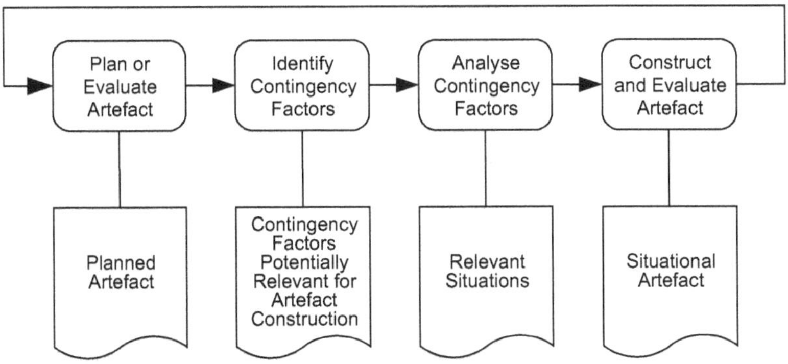

Figure 4: DSR problem class analysis as a genericity optimization problem

Our proposal is based on Bucher and Klesse [20], but differentiates more components and assumes that, in general, only adaptable artefacts on a certain level of generality are constructed:

(1) A rough idea about the delineation of the design problem class is developed (similar to step 1 in [20]). Results of this step are definitions, a description of the system under analysis and an idea about design goals for this class of design problems.
(2) A literature analysis is conducted in order to identify potential contingency factors for that class of design problems (similar to step 2 in [20]).
(3) A field study is conducted in order to analyze design problems of that class in practice. As a result, the list of potential contingency factor candidates is reduced to a smaller set of relevant "design factors" (similar to first component of step 3 in [20]). Design factors might be aggregates of several contingency factors that need to be semantically interpreted.
(4) The design problem class is redefined by specifying value ranges for the design factors (new).
(5) Those field study data of observations which still belong to the redefined design problem class, are used to calculate ultrametric distances between specific design problems. The calculation is based on certain 'similarity' metrics– usually the Euclidian distance with regard to the observed values of design factors (similar to second component of step 3 in [20]).
(6) A useful level of solution generality is determined. Usually clustering errors related to the number of clusters are used for this analysis.
(7) Using the desired solution generality, the resulting design situations are specified (similar to step 4 in [20]). The situations should not only be specified formally (by value ranges of the design factors), but also should be interpreted semantically ("design problem types").

By applying the proposed technique, sufficient foundations are created to allow for a systematic construction of adequately generic artefacts that solve the underlying design problem situations. According to contingency theory, it is assumed that all design problems within a situation can be solved by an appropriate solution artefact.

The proposed technique has been applied in many DSR exemplars, including the following:

- Leist [21, pp. 304-305] identifies eight enterprise modelling problem types. Based on that design problem analysis, she investigates which meta modelling approaches are best suited for which problem types.
- Baumöl [22] identifies four transformation project types. Based on that design problem analysis, she constructs project type specific recommendation which general and type specific transformation management instruments have been used in successful transformations.
- Klesse and Winter [23] identify four types of organizational designs for data warehouse service providers. Based on that design problem analysis, they give recommendations for consistent organizational designs and identify dynamic patterns (maturity).
- Aier, Winter and Riege [24] identify three types of enterprise architecture management approaches. Based on that design problem analysis, a situational method with problem type independent and problem type specific components is outlined.
- Bucher and Winter [25] identify four types of realizing Business Process Management (BPM) and five types of BPM transformations. Based on that design problem analysis, they construct a situational BPM method.
- Lahrmann and Stroh [26] identify three types of realizing information logistics in companies. Based on that design problem analysis, they derive guidelines and reference models for information logistics strategy design.

In the following, the Klesse and Winter [23] paper is used to illustrate the technique.

Step 1: Initial delineation of the design problem class

The aim of Klesse and Winter [23] is to provide situational solutions for organizing data warehouse service provision in companies. Their first step is to define the process of data warehousing and its sub-processes, the components of the data warehouse information system in large companies, and the organizational artefacts that are intended to be constructed. In addition, they define the design goal to devise those competencies to data warehouse service provision units that best match the respective positioning of such a unit in the respective company.

Step 2: Identification of potential contingency factors

Based on an analysis of the state-of-the-art of the data warehousing/business intelligence field, Klesse and Winter [23] assume that one reason for different organizational designs of data warehousing service providers is whether they maintain close service relationships to the respective company's business units or whether they consider themselves as separate from the business. Furthermore, it seems that data warehousing service providers can either produce all important services by themselves (highly integrated service delivery) or just integrate and customize services from other providers. As a consequence, the most important contingency factors to analyse are business integration and vertical integration. In addition, the usual contingency factors like company size, industry, and maturity with regard to data warehousing/business intelligence are considered as candidates.In order to analyse business integration and vertical integration, data warehouse IS components and data warehousing processes/sub-processes are conceptually mapped along the orthogonal dimensions "function" (development vs. operations vs. support vs. usage) and "object" (platform vs. integration infrastructure vs. applications). The resulting "competency map" (functions X objects) is related to the relevant roles (data warehousing service providers vs. business departments vs. internal IT vs. external service providers) in order to enumerate the potential competencies to look for in existing organizational solutions.

Step 3: Field study based analysis of design problems in practice

In order to obtain as many observations as possible from practice solutions for the design problem at hand, a questionnaire is designed and distributed using multiple channels (direct mailings to companies with data warehouse units, data warehousing practitioner conferences). Every data set (= filled out questionnaire) documents on practice solution. For the respective practice solution, the questionnaire documents the values of the contingency candidates like company size, industry, actual activities of the data warehouse service provider unit, relations between the data warehouse service provider unit with business units, etc.

In order to obtain an in-depth understanding of the data, an exploratory factor analysis (EFA) is performed [27, pp. 5-6]. Its purpose is to extract mutually independent factors which describe the activity shares of the relevant roles with regard to the data warehousing sub-processes. The principal components of the data set gained by this method can be interpreted as design factors.

Prior to the EFA, the adequacy of the data set is verified by means of two criteria. Variables are suitable for factor analysis, if and only if the anti-image of the variables is as low as possible. This means that off-diagonal elements of the anti-image covariance (AIC) matrix have to be as close as possible to zero. Dziuban and Shirkey [28] suggest to categorize a correlation matrix as unsuitable for factor analysis if the percentage of the off-diagonal elements unequal to zero (> 0.09) in the AIC matrix is 25 % or more. In Klesse and Winter's [23] data set, this criterion is about 12.5 %. The second criterion is the measure of sampling adequacy (MSA), as proposed by [29]. In literature, this criterion is regarded as the best available method to examine the correlation matrix [28, p. 360]. In the regarded case, the MSA is 0.789, which puts the data set at hand in the middling range [30]. Concluding, these findings prove the general suitability of the data set for factor analysis.

Principal components analysis is used as factor extraction method, as it has some additional desirable properties compared to principal axes analysis, and is probably the most frequently used EFA extraction method [27, p. 55]. In order to ascertain the desirable number of factors, the Kaiser-Guttmann criterion is applied.

The Kaiser-Guttmann criterion [31] suggests that the number of factors to be extracted should equal the number of factors with eigenvalues bigger than one. Therefore, three factors are extracted. The varimax factor rotation method with Kaiser normalization is used to clarify the nature of the underlying constructs. Varimax is the most common rotation of any kind, it is the default rotation in most statistical packages, and in about 85% of EFA applications varimax will yield a simple structure [27, p. 42]. Items are assigned to a factor if the factor loading adds up to at least 0.5 [30]. Table 1 exhibits the results of the exploratory factor analysis in Klesse and Winter [23].

The three identified factors consist of three to six items, respectively. According to the EFA, their data is reduced to three factors:

(1) Activity share of data warehouse IS support: The first factor encompasses the activity shares of development, business operations, and business support of the data warehouse integration infrastructure and the data warehouse applications.
(2) Activity share of data warehouse platform support: The second factor essentially contains the selection, setup, and configuration as well as the technical operations and support of the data warehouse platform.
(3) Activity share of data warehouse usage: The third factor covers the various types of use, i.e. the analysis-intensive processes and the performance of standard and special analyses.

The extraction of these factors suggests the conclusion that it is not the breakdown of functional processes that distinguishes the various data warehouse service providers, but their positioning along the components of the data warehouse IS. This means that data warehouse service providers can be differentiated by the activity shares of data warehouse IS support, data warehouse platform support, and data warehouse usage which they perform.

Table 1: Results of the Exploratory Factor Analysis from Klesse and Winter [23]

		Factor		
Activity shares		1	2	3
DW usage	Standard reporting	.117	.428	.708
	Special analyses	.252	-.054	.749
	Business processes	.126	-.119	.830
DW applications	IS planning/development	.886	.078	.218
	IS operations	.870	.202	-.076
	IS support	.824	.017	.291
DW integration infrastructure	IS planning/development	.773	.266	.284
	IS operations	.764	.368	.062
	IS support	.708	.327	.382
DW platform	IT development/ configuration	.300	.753	-.083
	IT operations	.140	.924	.034
	IT support	.183	.920	.088

Step 4: Refined specification of the design problem class

Based on the factor analysis of the questionnaires which yields a reduced set of aggregate design factors, the design problem class can be better specified. Instead of simply searching for situational solutions for organizing data warehouse service provision in companies, the design problem can be restated as (i) identifying organizational archetypes for data warehouse service providers in large companies (consistent solutions), (ii) devising which archetype is usually realized regarding the principal design factors "IS support", "platform support" and "usage" (contingencies). The more precise specification of the design problem class might require excluding certain questionnaires from further analyses of the data set because they do not match the refined criteria.

Step 5: Calculation of ultrametric distances

Based on the findings from the EFA, a cluster analysis of the extracted factors is performed in order to identify different data warehouse service provider models. In preparation for the cluster analysis, factor scores are calculated using the regression method [27, p. 44]. The k-means algorithm of SPSS 12 can be used as the clustering algorithm; this is a partitioning method which requires the number of clusters as input value. Euclidean distance is usually used as the distance measure. The starting partitions are determined at random. The individual cases (= observations) are then iteratively assigned to the appropriate clusters until the result is obtained where the variance between the elements of a cluster is as low as possible and the variance between the clusters is as high as possible. The cluster centres arise in each iteration from all the data sets assigned to a cluster.It should be noted that only certain clustering algorithms and certain similarity metrics create ultrametric distance data. Although other algorithms and other metrics can be used in principle in step 5, we recommend these algorithms and metrics.

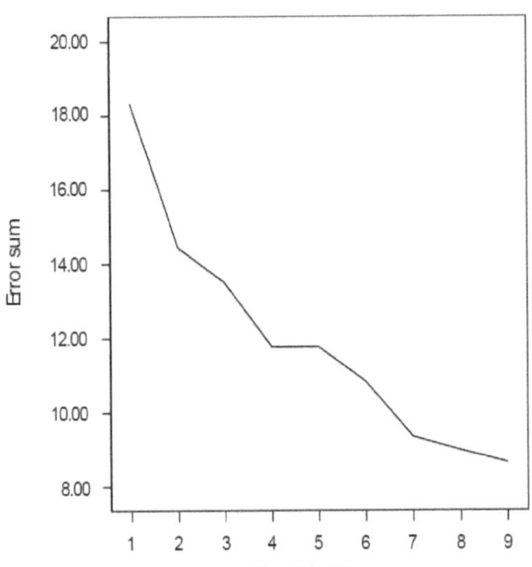

Figure 5: Clustering error vs number of clusters in Klesse and Winter [23]

Step 6: Determination of a useful level of generality

In order to determine the optimal number of clusters, several cluster analyses were carried out with a number from 1 to 9 clusters. They chose an upper limit of 9 to ensure representative clusters: with 68 data sets it is very unlikely that representative classifications will be obtained for more than 9 clusters. For each solution the error total which is obtained from the distances of all cases to their cluster centres is then calculated. On the basis of this error total, the elbow criterion is used [30]. This suggests giving preference to the solution up to which an increased number of clusters leads to an above-average improvement in the error total. If the error total is plotted against the number of clusters, this optimal point appears as an elbow in the error curve (figure 5). Elbows arise in the error curve for the 2-cluster, 4-cluster and 7-cluster solutions. As the 2-cluster solution does not produce adequate differentiation between service providers and as the 7-cluster solution produces too small clusters, a cluster number of 4 is the best candidate. Translated into the ultrametric distance graph (see figures 1, 2), this means that a G_c is chosen which yields 4 clusters (= generic solutions).A different decision rule was applied by Lahrmann and Stroh [26]: They selected a 3-cluster solution by (1) ranking the nodes of the tree according to their height, (2) determining the difference in height between two subsequent nodes, and (3) deciding for choosing the number of clusters where the nodes have the highest distance.

Step 7: Specification of design situations

Based on the *n*-cluster solution selected in step 6, the observations are grouped together in *n* different models which should be described with regards to the design factors identified in step 3.

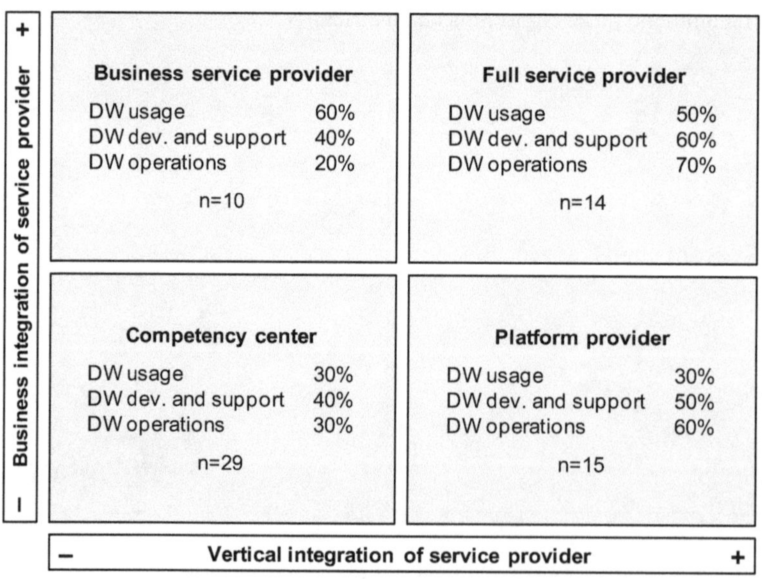

Figure 6: Design situations identified by Klesse and Winter [23]

Klesse and Winter's [23] design situations are illustrated by figure 6 and have been characterized as follows:

1. Full service provider: This service provider model shows a relatively strong involvement in the usage process: its activity share of the usage process is 50%, i.e., it assumes roughly half of the activities which arise in this area while the other half is performed by the business departments. It also plays a significant role in all tasks related to the data warehouse IS (activity share 60%; the remaining 40% is performed by internal IT, external providers or the business department). The platform is also managed by this model (activity share 70%; the remaining 30% is performed by internal IT or external providers). The full service provider performs the tasks of the data warehousing process itself and supports the business with analysis results.
2. Business service provider: This service provider model is very heavily involved in the usage process or performs the process itself (activity share 60%). This strong concentration on business services apparently explains why tasks related to the data warehouse IS are only performed in part (activity level 40%). Here, activities are shared with internal IT or with external service providers. Platform-related tasks are only supported to a limited extent (activity share 20%).
3. Platform provider: With this service provider model, unlike the business service provider, the focus is on the data warehouse IS (activity share 50%) and the platform (activity share 60%). The usage process is only partially supported (activity share 30%).
4. Competency centre: The competency centre is the most commonly found service provider model. Like the data warehouse platform provider, this model is only involved in support of the usage process (activity share 30%). At the same time, however, it does not perform all the tasks related to the data warehouse IS (activity share 40%) and platform (activity share 30%) on its own. These services are performed in collaboration with other IT departments or external providers.

In a rigorous and transparent way, the proposed technique has helped to delineate the design problem and to understand the design problem class. It yielded a useful number of design problem situations which are specified with regard to aggregate, statistically significant design factors. This allows to systematically construct appropriate problem-solving artefacts (like e.g. reference processes, reference responsibility lists for the illustrative example) in subsequent DSR stages.

Discussion: Economic Reasoning in Situational Artefact Construction

The strength of the field study-based technique is its capability to delineate the boundaries of a design problem class and to identify relevant design situations. Nevertheless, it does not explicitly consider economic reasoning. The applied clustering algorithm aims at maximizing intra-cluster homogeneity and inter-cluster heterogeneity. Although this is mainly a 'technical' procedure, we can show that the technique is not totally free of economic judgment.

Firstly, it is obvious that the costs for adapting a more generic solution artefact to a specific design problem are higher than those for adapting the more specific solution artefact. In general, we can state: The greater the dissimilarity within a design problem class for which a solution artefact has been constructed, the higher are the costs for adapting it to specific design problems within that class.

Secondly, as far as the construction costs are concerned, different interpretations are possible: In a first interpretation (I1), one might argue that the less general solution artefact is less detailed. Therefore, the costs for constructing it are less high. In a second interpretation (I2), one might argue that the construction of a general artefact is not as simple as assumed in interpretation (I1). For assuring the applicability of an artefact to a variety of design problems, all those design problems must be analysed. The researcher not only needs to have a precise knowledge of the diverse design problems within a class for constructing the solution artefact; he or she must also evaluate the artefact with respect to the different represented design problems. Both activities are very laborious. Therefore, the costs for constructing and evaluating a more general solution artefact are higher than those for constructing a more specific one. In a third interpretation (I3), one could argue that both effects mentioned in interpretation (I1) and (I2) balance so that the construction of a more general solution artefact generates approximately similar costs as the construction of a less general one.

In contrast to basic information concerning costs, the proposed technique provides less precise information concerning the economic importance of a design problem class. Assuming the field study to be representative, we can conclude that a design problem class with many elements is more important than a design problem class with only few elements. Nonetheless, this conclusion does not consider the economic importance of a design problem. It is possible that the solution of a certain design problem generates a high benefit for the organisation solving it, whereas the solution of a different design problem generates only little benefit to a different organisation solving it. The economic importance of a design problem class is not considered in the proposed technique.

If, for example, three design problem classes are identified by applying a clustering algorithm, it is possible that only one of them represents economically important design problems while the others represent economically unattractive design problems. In this case, from an economic point of view, it might be more useful to aggregate the two unattractive design problem classes into one more heterogeneous cluster (associated with a very general solution artefact) while splitting the economically attractive design problem class into two clusters (associated with two very specific solution artefacts). As a consequence, solutions with little generality (i.e. costly construction, but with little adaptation costs) are constructed for economically attractive design problems, while more general solutions (i.e. cheaper construction, but higher adaption costs) are provided for less important design problems.

Applying this idea to an ultrametric graph of a design problem class, the clusters would not be defined by choosing one specific G_c, but instead by choosing different G_{cx} for different design situations. The ultrametric distance between two design problem classes with economically more important design problems should be lower than that between two design problem classes with economically less attractive design problems. A respective design problem clustering solution is illustrated by Fig. 7.

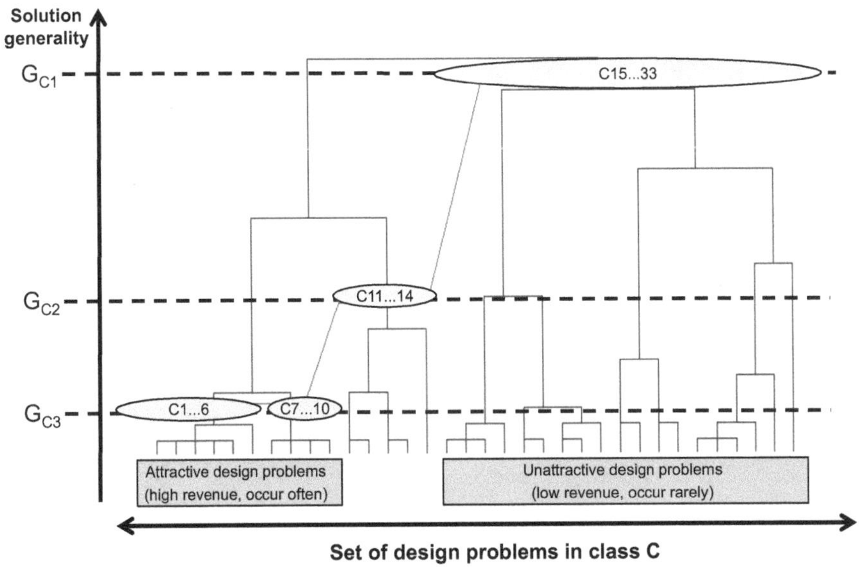

Figure 7: Illustrative situational solution design that considers economic aspects

For this example, we assume that the relatively similar design problem classes on the left side of Fig. 7 are of such a high economic value that they are worth to be addressed by less generic solutions, whilst the design problems on the right side are so unimportant that a more generic solution will be sufficient.

Further research should aim at solving this problem algorithmically. A good example of a solution of a similar problem is Weitzman's diversity theory [32]. Weitzman solves the problem how to maximize diversity preservation with a given budget and with given diversity measures and preservation costs, and exemplarily applies the theory to crane conservation [33]. He therefore also calculates an ultrametric tree describing the distances between the species. The application of the algorithm results in elasticities indicating the effect on diversity if effort is spent for saving a certain species.

We are encouraged by Weitzman's diversity theory that an analytic solution of the design situation specification problem as described above might be possible. Both problems, the economies of diversity and the economies of artefact situation, are very similar. The main difference between both problems is that the first one aims at maximizing diversity preservation with a given budget whilst the latter one aims at minimizing construction and adaptation costs for a given diversity among design problems. The economic optimisation problem of artefact situation can be defined as follows: With given economic attractiveness, construction costs, and adaption costs, the net benefit of artefact construction is to be maximised. The net benefit of a solution artefact is the difference between its gross benefit (i.e. the benefit accruing from the solution of design problems) and the costs for constructing and adapting the artefact.

Acknowledgement

The author wishes to thank Christian Fischer, University of St. Gallen, for fruitful discussions and co-authoring an earlier research report on this topic. Christian Fischer did also provide valuable feedback that helped to improve this paper.

References

1. March, S.T. and Smith, G.F.(1995). Design and Natural Science Research on Information Technology. *Decision Support Systems*, 15, 251-266.
2. Hevner, A.R., March, S.T., Park, J., and Ram, S.(2004).Design Science in Information Systems Research. *MIS Quarterly*, 28, 75-105.
3. Baskerville, R.L., Pries-Heje, J., and Venable, J.(2009).Soft design science methodology. In: *Proceedings of the 4th International Conference on Design Science Research in Information Systems and Technology* (DESRIST 2009). ACM, New York.
4. Cole, R., Purao, S., Rossi, M., and Sein, M.(2005). Being Proactive: Where Action Research Meets Design Research. In: Avison, D.E., Galletta, D.F. (eds.): *Proceedings of the International Conference on Information Systems*. Association for Information Systems.
5. Eekels, J., and Roozenburg, N.F.M.(1991). A methodological comparison of the structures of scientific research and engineering design: their similarities and differences. *Design Studies*, 12, 197-203.
6. Offermann, P., Levina, O., Schönherr, and M., Bub, U.(2009). Outline of a design science research process. *Proceedings of the 4th International Conference on Design Science Research in Information Systems and Technology* (DESRIST 2009). ACM, New York.
7. Peffers, K., Tuunanen, T., Rothenberger, M.A., and Chatterjee, S.(2007). A Design Science Research Methodology for Information Systems Research. *Journal of Management Information Systems*,24, 45-77.
8. Takeda, H., Veerkamp, P., Tomiyama, T., and Yoshikawa, H.(1990). Modeling design processes. *AI Magazine*, 11, 37-48.
9. Vaishnavi, V.K., Vandenberg, A., Zhang, Y., and Duraisamy, S.(2009). Towards design principles for effective context- and perspective-based web mining. DESRIST '09: *Proceedings of the 4th International Conference on Design Science Research in Information Systems and Technology*. ACM, New York.
10. Wieringa, R.J.(2009). Design Science as Nested Problem Solving. *Proceedings of the 4th International Conference on Design Science Research in Information Systems and Technology*. Association for Computing Machinery,12.
11. Vaishnavi, V.K.,and Kuechler, W.(2004). Design Research in Information Systems. Association for Information Systems.

12. Becker, J., Delfmann, P., and Knackstedt, R.(2007). Adaptive Reference Modeling: Integrating Configurative and Generic Adaptation Techniques for Information Models. In: Becker, J., Delfmann, P. (eds.): *Reference Modeling*. Physica, Heidelberg, 27-58.
13. Becker, J., Delfmann, P., Knackstedt, R., and Kuropka, D.(2002). Konfigurative Referenzmodellierung. In: Becker, J., Knackstedt, R. (eds.): *Wissensmanagement mit Referenzmodellen. Konzepte für die Anwendungssystem- und Organisationsgestaltung*. Physica, Heidelberg, 25-144
14. Bucher, T., Klesse, M., Kurpjuweit, S., and Winter, R.(2007). Situational Method Engineering – On the Differentiation of "Context" and "Project Type". In: Ralyté, J., Brinkkemper, S., Henderson-Sellers, B. (eds.): *Situational Method Engineering – Fundamentals and Experiences*, Vol. 244. Springer, Boston, 33-48.
15. Gregor, S.,and Jones, D.(2007). The Anatomy of a Design Theory. *Journal of the Association for Information Systems*, 8, 312-335.
16. Fiedler, F.E.(1964). A Contingency Model of Leadership Effectiveness. *Advances in Experimental Social Psychology*, 1,149-190.
17. Donaldson, L.(2001). The Contingency Theory of Organizations. Sage, Thousand Oaks.
18. Graubner, M.(2006). Task, firm size, and organizational structure in management consulting. An empirical analysis from a contingency perspective. DUV, Wiesbaden.
19. Pfeffer, J.(1997). New Directions for Organization Theory: Problems and Prospects. Oxford University Press, New York.
20. Bucher, T., Klesse, M.(2006). Contextual Method Engineering. University of St. Gallen, Institute of Information Management, St. Gallen.
21. Leist, S.(2004). Methoden zur Unternehmensmodellierung – Vergleich, Anwendungen und Diskussionen der Integrationspotenziale. Institut für Wirtschaftsinformatik Universität St. Gallen, St. Gallen.
22. Baumöl, U.(2005). Strategic Agility through Situational Method Construction. In: Reichwald, R., Huff, A.S. (eds.): *Proceedings of the European Academy of Management Annual Conference 2005*.
23. Klesse, M., and Winter, R. (2007). Organizational Forms of Data Warehousing: An Explorative Analysis. *Proceedings of the 40th Hawaii International Conference on System Sciences (HICSS-40)*. IEEE Computer Society, Los Alamitos.
24. Aier, S., Riege, C., and Winter, R.(2008). Classification of Enterprise Architecture Scenarios – An Exploratory Analysis. *Enterprise Modelling And Information Systems Architectures*, 3, 14–23.
25. Bucher, T., and Winter, R.(2009). Taxonomy of Business Process Management Approaches: An Empirical Foundation for the Engineering of Situational Methods to Support BPM. In: vom Brocke, J., Rosemann, M. (eds.): *Handbook on Business Process Management*. Springer.
26. Lahrmann, G., and Stroh, F.(2009). Towards a Classification of Information Logistics Scenarios – An Exploratory Analysis. In: Sprague, R.H. (ed.): *Proceedings of the 42nd Hawaii International Conference on System Sciences (HICSS-42)*. IEEE Computer Society, Los Alamitos.
27. Thompson, B.(2004). Exploratory and Confirmatory Factor Analysis: Understanding Concepts and Applications. American Psychological Association, Washington, DC.
28. Dziuban, C.D., and Shirkey, E.C.(1974). When is a Correlation Matrix Appropriate for Factor Analysis?. *Psychological Bulletin*, 81, 358-361.
29. Kaiser, H.F.(1970). An second-generation Little Jiffy. *Psychometrika*, 35, 401-415.
30. Härdle,W., and Simar, L.(2003). Applied Multivariate Statistical Analysis. Springer, Berlin.
31. Kaiser, H.F., and Dickman, K.W.(1959). Analytic Determination of Common Factors. *American Psychological Reports*, 14, 425-430.
32. Weitzman, M.L.(1992). On Diversity. *The Quarterly Journal Of Econimics*, 107, 363-405.
33. Weitzman, M.L.(1993). What to Preserve? An Application of Diversity Theory to Crane Conservation. *The Quarterly Journal Of Econimics*, 108, 157-183.

Regular Sparsity in OLAP System

Kalinka Kaloyanova[1], **Ina Naydenova**[2]

Abstract One of the primary challenges of storing multidimensional data is the degree of sparsity that is often encountered. Because the extremely sparse cubes are frequent phenomenon, OLAP engines offer different methods of increasing the performance of sparse cubes, but all of these methods do not take account of the sparsity nature and did not divide the sparsity into any types. Our experience leads us to a following division of the empty areas in the multidimensional cubes: (a) areas that are empty because of the semantics of the business (the semantics enforces lack of value) and (b) areas that are empty by a chance. To formally distinguish these types of sparsity, we introduce a new object ("regular sparsity map") which provides business analysts with the ability to define rules and place data constraints over the multidimensional cube. In this paper we present our regular sparsity map editor and discuss how it can be used for the purpose of data errors detection and selection of relevant dimension elements.

Introduction

Prior to the start of the Information Age in the late 20th century, businesses had to collect data from non-automated sources. Businesses then lacked the computing resources necessary to properly analyze the data, and as a result, companies often made business decisions primarily on the basis of intuition [1]. The modern technologies of computers and networks have made data collection and organization much easier. However, the captured data needs to be converted into information and knowledge to become useful. This puts a new class of problems related to the data integrity and correctness, results reliability, performance of the analytical query and others ([2],[3],[4]).

During the 1990s, a new type of data model – the multidimensional data model – has emerged that has taken over from the relational model when the objective is to analyze data, rather than to perform on-line transactions. Multidimensional models lie at the core of On Line Analytical Processing (OLAP) systems. Such systems provide fast answers for queries that aggregate large amounts of detail data to find overall trends, and they present the results in a multidimensional fashion, which renders a multidimensional data organization ideal for OLAP [5]. In a multidimensional data models, there is a set of numeric measures (facts) that are the objects of analysis. Each of the numeric measures depends on a set of dimensions,

[1] St. Kliment Ohridski University of Sofia, Faculty of Mathematics and Informatics, Sofia, Bulgaria, e-mail:kkaloyanova@fmi.uni-sofia.bg

[2] St. Kliment Ohridski University of Sofia, Faculty of Mathematics and Informatics, Sofia, Bulgaria, e-mail: naydenova@gmail.com

which provide the context for the measure. For example, the dimensions associated with a sale amount can be the store, product, and the date when the sale was made. The dimensions together are assumed to uniquely determine the measure. Thus, the multidimensional data views a measure as a value in the multidimensional space of dimensions. Often, dimensions are hierarchical; time of sale may be organized as a day-month-quarter-year hierarchy, product as a product-category-industry hierarchy [6]. In OLAP cube, cross product of dimensional members forms the intersections for measure data. But in reality most of the intersections will not have data. This leads to sparsity. The multidimensional cross relationships which exist in all OLAP applications and the fact that the input data is usually very sparse are the main reason most of the OLAP applications to suffer from data explosion consequences [7]. Because the extremely sparse cubes are frequent phenomenon, OLAP engines offer different methods of increasing the performance and reducing the size of the cubes. But all of these methods do not take account of the sparsity nature and did not divide the sparsity into any types.

In Naydenova [8] we introduce a new classification of multidimensional cube sparsity phenomena, define an object named "regular sparsity map" (RSM) and investigate the RSM applicability. The RSM saves information about empty domains of multidimensional cubes and provides analysts with the ability to define business rules and place data constraints over the multidimensional model. The map can be used at many stages of the business intelligence system life cycle (storage and performance consideration, user-interface improvements), but its primary function is to support the process of discovering inaccurate and inconsistent information.

We developed an editor for RSM creation and implement an algorithm that performs set operations between RSM and arbitrary multidimensional domains in the map space. We are going to briefly describe our implementation approach and discuss the data error and relevant dimension elements detection process. RSM can also be used for data storage and query optimization and also allows report enhancements. But these applications are not still implemented and they are out of the scope of this paper.

The Regular Sparsity Map

To explain what a regular sparsity map is, first of all we will introduce some definitions.

Multidimensional Data Model Definition

To define a regular sparsity map object we assume a simplified conceptual cube model that treats data in the form of n-dimensional cubes. The hierarchies between the various levels of aggregation in dimensions are of no interest to us.

- *Dimension* is a non-empty finite set;
- *Multidimensional space S* over dimensions $D_1, D_2, \dots, D_n$ (n>=1) is the Cartesian product $S = D_1 \times D_2 \times \dots \times D_n$. It contains n-tuples ($x_1$, x_2, x_n) where $x_1 \in D_1, x_2 \in D_2, \dots x_n \in D_n$
- *Rectangular domain* in multidimensional space S is a subset $M \subseteq S$, $M = A_1 \times A_2 \times \dots \times A_n$, where $A_1 \subseteq D_1$, $A_2 \subseteq D_2$, ..., $A_n \subseteq D_n$;
- Ø *is* a special value named "empty value";
- *Fact* F is a set, where $\emptyset \in F$;
- *Cube* is a function $C: S \rightarrow F$, where *S* is a multidimensional space, *F* is a fact;
- *Cell* in the cube $C: S \rightarrow F$ is a pair $c = (t, f)$, where $t \in S$, $C(t) = f$. The cell is *empty* if $f = \emptyset$ and *non-empty* otherwise;
- *Set of empty cells* in the cube $C: S \rightarrow F$ is the set $E(C) = \{t \in S \mid C(t) = \emptyset\}$, $E(C) \subseteq S$.

We might be building a cube for a supermarket, where one dimension (D1) is geography (individual stores), another one (D2) is time (months), another one (D3) is customers and the last one is products (D4). Measures in the observed fact (F) are the quantity sold and the revenue. If in "April 2008" customer "Andrew" bought "2 bars" of "chocolate" in store "Boyana" for "3 euro" then we have a non-empty cell (("Boyana", "April 2008", "Andrew", "chocolate"), ("2 bars", "3 euro")) in the cube. If in the same month he did not buy any "ice-cream" from this store, we have an empty cell (("Boyana", "April 2008", "Andrew", "ice-cream"), Ø).

Sparsity Definition

Many cells in an OLAP cube are not populated with data. The more empty cells found in a cube, the sparser the cube data is. This is measured by the density coefficient.

Density coefficient of cube C: S F is a ratio $\omega_C = \dfrac{|S| - |E(C)|}{|S|}$

If we have 60 stores, 500 products, 70 000 customers and 12 months in a year, our cube has a potential $60 \times 500 \times 70000 \times 12 = 25\,200\,000\,000$ cells, but we might only have 360 000 000 non-empty cells in our measure (40 000 customers shopping 12 months a year, buying average on 25 products at 30 stores) making our cube $(360\,000\,000/25\,200\,000\,000) \times 100 = 1.42\%$ dense.

Cube sparsity has many impacts on the storage size, loading and query performance in multidimensional databases. More information about the sparse data consequences and the relation between sparsity and exploding databases phenomenon can be found in Pendse [9].

Regular Sparsity Map Definition

A closer scrutiny reveals that there could be some difference between empty cells in terms of the causes provoking the cell's emptiness. We could not found proper classification of sparsity types neither in the literature nor in the current data warehouse and OLAP researches. In [10] sparsity patterns are classified as random, stripe, cluster and slice type in relation to their shape. Our experience in sparsity problems points at another kind of classification, so we divide the cube's sparsity into two types: random and regular sparsity. If one cell is empty because of the semantics of the modeled business area (the semantics enforces lack of value), then we witness "regular sparsity". If the cell is empty, but it is possible it had a value, "random sparsity" is what we have. In Naydenova and Kaloyanova [11] we investigate several forms of regular sparsity (irrelevant dimensions, segmentation of dimensions, dimension changes over time).

To formally distinguish regular from random sparsity, we introduce the following definition:

Regular sparsity map (RSM) of the cube C: S F is the set $R_C \subseteq E_C \subseteq S$

A regular sparsity map (or shortly map) R_C determines the cells which are empty because of regular sparsity (business rules, formal requirements, natural dependencies, etc.).

The set difference $E(C) \setminus R_C$ determines the cells which are empty because of random sparsity.

In the previous example we can observe random and regular sparsity. The store "Boyana" offers 3000 products. "Andrew" has bought only 50 of them. For the remaining 2950 products we have empty cells because of the random sparsity (in fact their value is zero). For the 7000 unavailable products we have empty cells because of the regular sparsity. If $Z \subset D_4$ is the list of available products in "Boyana" then $R_C = \{(d1, d2, d3, d4) \in S \mid d1 = \text{"Boyana"}, d4 \notin Z\}$.

RSM and Data Cleaning

In our experience the correctness of data is always a problem. Actually this is the problem which more often is an obstacle for the practical application of BI system. Usually, only after the data is loaded and the first results are obtained it is clear that there are defects in the data. The discovering and elimination of these defects is quite hard procedure because the input data is related with much dependence and passes through a number of transformations until it is presented to the multidimensional model. A second time data loading is often necessary and an execution of all the steps over again. The solution of this problem is the data to be verified on a possibly earlier stage of its processing.

The regular sparsity map describes constraints over the data in the term of multidimensional model, which is close to the concepts of the business analysts. At the same time it enables easy implementation of automatic data tests before receiving the results by the end users.

The development of a module for business constraints and dependence enforcement (BCE module) is a base application of the map information. The module can have the following functionalities:

- Validation of the regular sparsity map definition over a trusted data cube (cube without dirty data); this functionality is to be used immediately after the process of map construction, in order to check the correctness of the specified constraints;
- Errors detection and correction; after the validation of map definition, the constraints can be enforced over unverified data;

In our RSM Editor we implement error detection functionality. After the definition of a regular sparsity map the users can choose a trusted data cube and check the map definition correctness. Then they can choose another cube and see the conflicts – cube cells that have to be empty according to the RSM definition, but they are loaded with non-zero values.

According to the classification made by Rahm and Hong Hai Do [12], the major data quality problems can be divided to schema- and instance-related problems. The scheme level problems are related with poor schema design, scheme translation and integration, while Instance-level problems refer to errors and inconsistencies in the actual data contents which are not visible at the scheme level. We believe that the RSM can support the process of Instance Level inconsistent data detection. The Rahm et al. [12] discuss that in order to detect which kinds of errors and inconsistencies are to be removed a detailed data analysis is required. In addition to a manual inspection of the data or data samples, analysis programs should be used to gain metadata about the data properties and detect data quality problems. The constraints defined with a regular sparsity map are an additional source of metadata. Also the RSM based validation has the advantage that every modification in the RSM constraints immediately will be taken into account during the data cleaning process.

RSM and Relevant Dimension Elements Selection

The regular sparsity map enables the feature for automatic restriction of user choice of dimension filters or parameters. When a business analyst selects some dimension values, the values of the other dimensions can be restricted to the set of meaningful tuples.

Let us imagine that at a certain moment in time t_k all the supermarkets in our company stop offering product p_j. We have a new rule: "When time > t_k then services p_j". In the process of typical business intelligence slice and dice operation, the end user of the system can fix "Time" dimension to t_{k+1}. In fact, he or she is interested in a specific part of the entire cube. The application refers to the RSM

API, preprocesses the user request and returns a reduced sub-cube without the p_j layer.

Example

If we have a business rule "After January 2008, we don't offer travel insurance" and the user fixes the "Time" dimension to Feb 2008 the available choices of "Service" will be reduced to the available services over the month. The figure 1 illustrates the expected effect over the typical user interface of the BI tools. It demonstrates the available service choices without regular map filtering on the left side and reduced choices after the filtering on the right side.

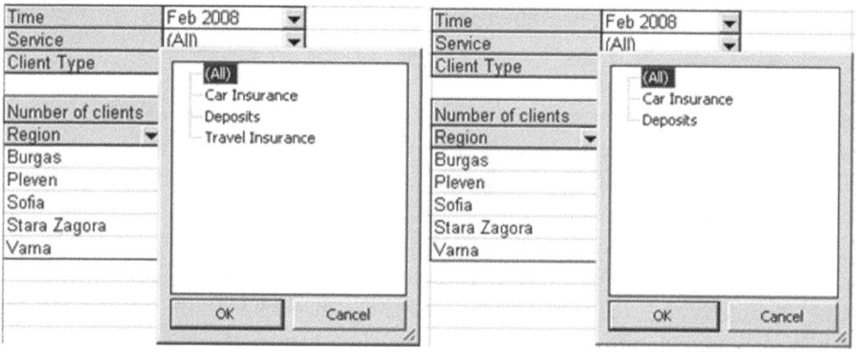

Figure 1: Automatic selection of relevant dimension elements.

Other RSM Applications

By virtue of RSM editor we are in the process of development of regular sparsity map applications related to query performance and storage optimization. In Naydenova and Kaloyanova [13] we have demonstrated a scheme for summary data preservation which can reduce a cube storage size several times. The reported results involve 6 cubes from a real-life data warehouse system. Depending on the data distribution, the percent of the cube size decrease varies between 32% and 96%.

The storage reducing scheme uses knowledge for a regular sparsity in a given cube. This gave us reasons to define special object that describes a regular sparsity and to investigate its applicability beyond storage compression techniques (to support an evaluation of a dimensions composite effectiveness, cube partitioning and others).

RSM Editor Implementation Approach

The RSM applications development is related to the question of how the map could be represented. The utilization of the regular sparsity map requires a proper model that is convenient and easy for use from:

- the people that will construct a map;
- the software that will use the map in different applications;

From the humans' point of view the regular sparsity map is a set of business rules. So in our editor the users define a map as a set of rules. Each rule describes a set of cells that should be empty.

The software that will use the map requires an algorithm that performs set operations between a regular sparsity map and a multidimensional domain. So the software for an extraction of the regular sparsity map information has to be able to answer the questions of the following type:

Let R_c is a regular sparsity map $R_c \subseteq E(C) \subseteq S$ of the cube $C: S \rightarrow F$, $S = D_1 \times D_2 \times ... \times D_n$ and Q is an input rectangle domain (question) $Q: Q \subseteq S$, $Q = A_1 \times A_2 \times ... \times A_n$, $A_1 \subseteq D_1, ..., A_n \subseteq D_n$,

We are interested in which cells of the domain $Q\{c = (t, f) \mid t \in Q, C(t) = f\}$ are empty because of the regular sparsity: $Q_E = Q \cap R_c$

We are also interested in which cells of the domain
$Q\{c = (t, f) \mid t \in Q, C(t) = f\}$ are potentially not empty: $Q_{NE} = Q \setminus R_c$

One solution is the regular sparsity model to store the set of tuples covered by the map (point-by-point approach). Then we can apply union or minus operation over tuples covered by the map and the tuples covered by the input domain I. Unfortunately, in real-life cases the number of empty cells in a map often exceeds 10^{13}. The performance of set operations depends on the cardinality of it arguments so this solution is unsatisfactory: in the case of 1.42% dense cube (the example above) it requires 24840000000 empty cells coordinates to be processed.

So our task is to find other representation of a regular sparsity map and a more efficient way to perform set operations with rectangular domains in a multidimensional space. You can see our idea of RSM representation and set operation algorithm in Naydenova et al. [14] but in our RSM editor implementation we do some modifications. We present a map as a union of empty rectangular domains, but they are not necessarily non-intersecting as is pointed in [14]. In our solution the input rectangular domain Q is spit to a set of rectangular sub-domains, each of which is entirely inside or outside the map.

This technique is used to detect non relevant dimension elements:

An input question Q is formed on the base of a user dimension selection. According to figure 1 the input question has the following form:

1. Time = February 2008, Region in (Burgas, Pleven, Sofia, Stara Zagora,Varna), Service in (Insurance, Deposits, Travel Insurance), Client Type = organization.
2. The dimension D_t, whose non-relevant elements are of interest to us, is specified as a target. According to figure 1 this is a Service dimension.
3. We apply the algorithms that split a question Q to a set of empty Q_E and potentially nonempty Q_{NE} rectangular domains.
4. The projection of the values of target dimension D_t in relation to all empty Q_E domains gives us the list of non-relevant dimension values.
5. In the simplified example from figure 1 we receive only one empty domain:
6. Time = February 2008, Region in (Burgas, Pleven, Sofia, Stara Zagora,Varna), Service= (Travel Insurance), Client Type = organization.
   So the "Travel Insurance" is a non-relevant value and we can remove it from the list of available services.

Conclusion and Further Work

The sparsity of OLAP cubes is a phenomenon in multidimensional data that every designer and database administrator must consider. Sparse data assist the data explosion problem in the pre-aggregation process and decreases the performance of OLAP. The current methods for overcoming of data explosion work mainly on physical level and don't take account of the nature of sparsity. We introduce a regular sparsity map in attempt to look at sparsity from another point of view – is there some useful information that sparsity can give us? With the help of an RSM editor and a map representation model we are going to implement others regular sparsity map applications. Also the BCE module can be improved with data correction functions, automatic generation of database constraints over the source data and others.

References

1. Mitchell, D. (2007). *Performance management*, eBook, Publisher Chandni Chowk, Delhi: Global Media.
2. Muller, H., and Freytag, J. (2003). *Problems, Methods, and Challenges in Comprehensive Data Cleansing*. Technical Report HUB-IB-164, Humboldt University Berlin, Germany.
3. Pedersen,T., Christian, S., Curtis,J.,and Dyreson, E. (1999). *Extending Practical Pre-Aggregation*. On-Line Analytical Processing, VLDB'99,663-674.
4. Pendse, N. (2007) *The Problems with OLAP*, DM Review Magazine March 2007.
5. Pedersen, T., and Jensen, Ch. (2005). *Multidimensional Databases*, The Industrial Information Technology Handbook by Richard Zurawski, pages 1-13, CRC Press.
6. Chaudhuri, S., and Dayal, U. (1997). *An Overview of Data Warehousing and OLAP Technology*. SIGMOD Record 26(1), 65-74.
7. Potgieter, J. (2003). OLAP Data Scalability. *DM Review Magazine*, October 2003. http://www.dmreview.com/dmdirect/20031031/7636-1.html
8. Naydenova, I. (2008). *Regular Sparsity Map*. ISGT'2010, Sofia, Bulgaria

9. Pendse,N.(2005).*Database explosion.* Business Application Research Center, http:// www.olapreport.com/DatabaseExplosion.htm
10. Kang, J.,Yong, H., and Masunaga, Y. (2002). Classification of Sparsity Patterns and Performance Evaluation in OLAP System, IEIC Technical Report, ISSN:0913-5685,vol.102, No.209, pp.61- 66, Japan.
11. Naydenova, I., and Kaloyanova, K. (2006). *Some Extensions to the Multidimensional Data Model.* Proceedings of the IEEE John Vincent Atanasoff 2006 International Symposium on Modern Computing, Bulgaria, 63 – 68.
12. Rahm, E., and Hong Hai, Do. (2000). *Data Cleaning: Problems and Current Approaches*, IEEE Data Engineering Bulletin, 23(4),3-13.
13. Naydenova, I., and Kaloyanova, K. (2007). *An Approach Of Non-Additive Measures Compression In Molap Environment*, Proceedings of the IADIS Multi Conference on Computer Science and Information Systems Lisbon, Portugal, July 2007, 394-399.
14. Naydenova, I., Kovacheva, Z., and Kaloyanova, K.(2009). A *Model of Regular Spasity Map Representation.* Scientifical Journal of Ovidius University of Constantza, Romania 17(3), 197–208.

Part III

ICT in Organizational Design and Change

Business Process Management (BPM): A Pathway for IT-Professionalism in Europe?

Jan vom Brocke[1]

Abstract According to recent studies, there is a dramatic demand for IT education in Europe: EMPIRICA estimates an average of half a million IT professionals needed in Europe within the upcoming years. In December 2009 the so-called eSKILLS initiative was launched in order to stimulate measures in all member states. From an academic perspective, this development seems to call for an extension of educational programs in the field of computer science and information systems on the one side. On the other, this trend also underlines the necessity to maybe rethink such programs in light of in how far they actually meet the current business requirements in Europe. This discussion lies at the core of the EU-project TRICE. In this paper, I will highlight and give reason for the importance of Business Process Management skills. The newly founded Master Program in Business Process Management at the University of Liechtenstein (MSc BPM) serves as an example for how such a program may be designed. A fruitful discussion may arise as to in how far process thinking may be set in relation to further pathways to IT professionalism in Europe.

Introduction

There is a dramatic need for IT professionalism in Europe. Already in 2007 it was estimated that there are 4.2 million ICT practitioners in the EU and that approximately 180 million people are using ICT at work [1]. Just in the years between 1998 – 2004, a study on the supply and demand of e-skills reported an increase in the estimated number of employees IT practitioners of about 48% [2]. Apart from ICT being the basis for most business transactions today, studies indicate that also 40% of the productivity in growth in Europe are induced by ICT [3]. According to the e-skills monitor of the EU, an estimate of half a million IT professionals is needed in Europe in the upcoming years [4]. However, these studies also indicate the demand for a particular kind of qualification, which we see in competencies on how to design and manage business processes. This focus is special in at least two directions: First, it is the focus on "technology in use" rather then an inventing new technology. No doubt, new technology will always play a vital economic role but to a large extend of our modern economy – and from a regular company's perspective – it is the efficient and effective use of technology in business processes that matters most. To this extend, IT professionalism neither calls for pure computer science nor for pure business administration but rather the linking bridge between

[1] University of Liechtenstein, Institute of Information Systems, Hilti Chair of Business Process Management, Fürst-Franz-Josef-Strasse – 9490 Vaduz (Liechtenstein), jan.vom.brocke@uni.li

both disciplines. Hence, people are needed that can understand both worlds, understand business related questions and IT-related solutions at the same time and who can intermediate between different people to be involved in solutions. This already indicates the second speciality: a second interlinkage between theory and practice. As a result, universities need to educate students not only to understand complex phenomena but also to act accordingly in practice. Apart from factual knowledge, this requires to a large extent methodological and social skills that re-needed in order to interact with people from different backgrounds on innovative IT-enabled solutions. A recent review of CIO's by Gartner [5] confirmed the significance of BPM. For the fifth year in a row, the study „Meeting the Challenge" confirmed competencies of improving business processes to be the priority number one among CIOs worldwide [5]. At the same time, very few companies actually succeed in managing their business processes right. Accordingly, Hammer resumes in his latest article that "despite its elegance and power, many organizations have experienced difficulties implementing processes and process management" [6]. However, very few study programs at our universities actually account for this demand. With this study, we want to characterize the concept of business process management as a means for IT professionalism. Against the background of a deeper understanding of BPM we would like to take a specific Master Program of BPM as an example, in order to show how BPM can be taught at our universities. We present a real fife program, introduced by the University of Liechtenstein in 2008 and discuss directions for future work in the field.

The Concept of Business Process Management

BPM can be characterised from different conceptual perspectives. To give a first impression, we would like to look at it as the missing link between IT and Business. A simple picture describing this role is given in fig. 1.

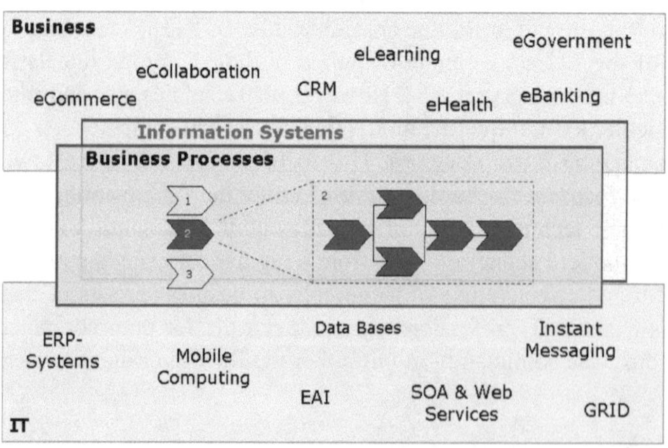

Figure 1: BPM as an Approach for IT Business Alignment

Without a doubt there are great achievements stemming from IT, such as integrated databases that have revolutionised information and process management in corporations worldwide. However, we can also learn from history about the effects of overestimating the economic potentials of IT. We did see this very clearly using the example of the new economy that led to one of the world's most serious economic crises. But still today, we see new technologies rocketing up very likely to be overestimated, such as Service-oriented Architectures, Software as a Service, Enterprise Mashups, or Cloud Computing. Actually, the development illustrated here, also founds empirical proof, looking for example at the Gartner Hype Cycle Analysis [7] that indicate a certain pattern of technology going through a certain "peak of inflated expectations" followed by a disillusion and then hopefully reaching a plateau of productivity. Business, at the same time, tends to underestimate the efforts related to making use of new technology in a sustainable manner. Very often, we see conventional disciplines such as "commerce", "banking", "government" relabelled to "eCommerce", "eBanking" and "eGovernment", with little substantially changed but the intention of making use of new technology, particularly the internet. What is needed is a linking layer that – to our belief – can well be provided by BPM. From this perspective, BPM is about a differentiated look on certain business areas enabling us to specifically choose IT devices, finding the most effective and efficient ways of integrating them, as well as identifying challenges and opportunities for business transformation. For example, in customer relationship management, different channels of customer interaction can be identified and detailed according to standard operating procedures. This puts us into the position of specifically choosing at what particular stage of the process and for what particular purpose, for example, mobile devices may be of use for the process. But what is the particular beauty of business process management? To our mind, this is the concept of process thinking, meaning to think in terms of specific work steps leading to a certain value for a customer. The beauty is that such work steps are literally everywhere. They even happen when they are not managed. So, from this perspective, you can not avoid processes. It is only a matter of identifying, managing and innovating them to the best service for the organisation. Figure 2 gives a rough picture of process thinking.

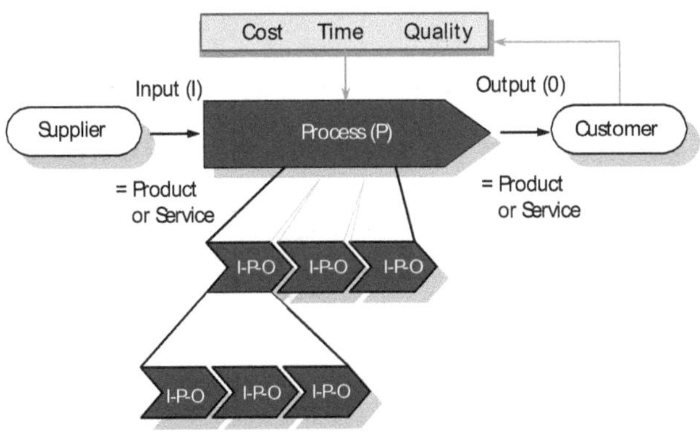

Figure 2: BPM and the "Process Pattern"

Processes can be perceived as transitions, transforming certain input-objects into output-objects such as products or services. Requirements for this transformation are derived from the customer perspective and, ideally, also specified as operational targets for the transformation, often structured by target dimensions such as time, cost and quality. The transformation itself is conducted by people following certain work steps and applying a certain technology aiming at a maximum of customer satisfaction. The particular beauty of process thinking now comes in as this pattern can be applied to various units of analysis. In particular, the pattern can be transferred both horizontally and vertically within a company. Horizontally, we see that units are acting as suppliers to customers and at the same time also act as customers towards their own suppliers. In this regard, requirements articulated by final customers are literally traced back in the entire value chain until the very first supplier. Looking at these entire value chains is very often referred to supply chain management. In particular, with today's requirements in mind in terms of sustainable businesses, such tracing back the working conditions and emissions not only within one company but within the entire value chain becomes of major importance. Apart from the requirements derived from the overall end-to-end process, they can be drilled down to each single sub-unit that itself can be perceived as a process. This brings in the concept of so-called internal customer-supplier-relationships that are essential for achieving business excellence in process-oriented organisations nowadays.

Indeed, establishing a process-oriented company turns out to be still a challenge for most companies [6]. Hence, profound competences are required leveraging the integrating power of BPM. Research on BPM maturity models helps to get an overview of the multifaceted discipline. In fig. 3, a model illustrating the six core elements of BPM [8] is displayed that has been derived from empirical studies on BPM maturity [9-13].

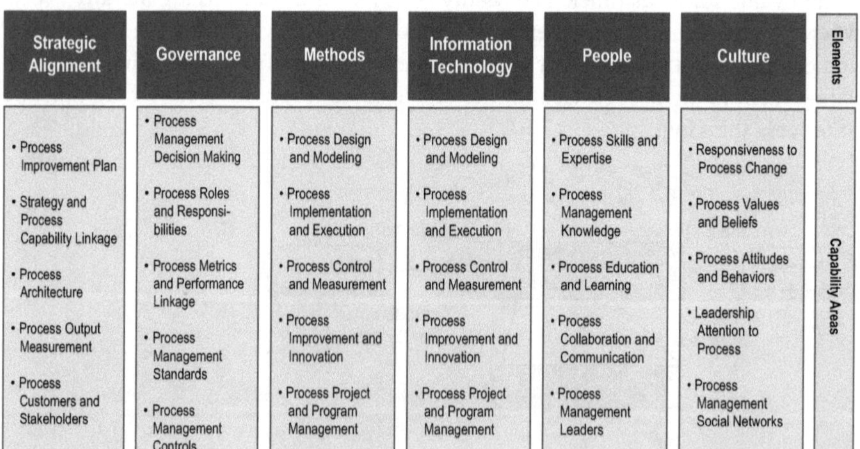

Figure 3: The Six Core Elements of BPM [8]

The model distinguishes six core elements critical to BPM. These are Strategic Alignment, Governance, Methods, Information Technology, People, and Culture.

- **Strategic Alignment:** BPM needs to be aligned with the overall strategy of an organisation. Strategic alignment (or synchronization) is defined as the tight linkage of organisational priorities and enterprise processes enabling continual and effective action to improve business performance. Processes have to be designed, executed, managed and measured according to strategic priorities and specific strategic situations (e.g. stage of a product lifecycle, position in a strategic portfolio). In return, specific process capabilities (e.g. competitive advantage in terms of time to execute or change a process) may offer opportunities to inform the strategy design leading to process-enabled strategies.
- **Governance:** BPM governance establishes appropriate and transparent accountability in terms of roles and responsibilities for different levels of BPM (portfolio, programme, project, operations). A further focus is on the design of decision-making and reward processes to guide process-related actions.
- **Methods:** Methods in the context of BPM are defined as the set of tools and techniques that support and enable activities along the process lifecycle and as part of enterprise-wide BPM initiatives. Examples are methods that facilitate process modelling or process analysis and process improvement techniques. Six Sigma is an example for a BPM approach that has a set of integrated BPM methods at its core.
- **Information Technology:** IT-based solutions are of significance for BPM initiatives. With a traditional focus on process analysis (e.g. statistical process control) and process modelling support, BPM-related IT solutions increasingly manifest themselves in the form of process-aware information systems PAIS. Process-awareness means that the software has an explicit understanding of the process that needs to be executed. Such process awareness could be the result of input in the form of process models or could be more implicitly reflected in the form of hard-coded processes.
- **People:** People as a core element of BPM is defined as individuals and groups who continually enhance and apply their process and process management skills and knowledge in order to improve business performance. Consequently, this factor captures the BPM capabilities that are reflected in the human capital of an organisation and its ecosystem.
- **Culture:** BPM culture incorporates the collective values and beliefs with regards to the process-centered organisation. Although commonly considered a 'soft-factor', comparative case studies clearly demonstrate the strong impact of culture on the success in BPM [9]. Culture is about creating a facilitating environment that complements the various BPM initiatives. However, it needs to be recognised that the impact of culture-related activities tends to have a much longer horizon than activities related to any of the other five factors [8].

A Curriculum for BPM-Education

BPM requires skills from various disciplines. Apart from Business and IT, the six building blocks of BPM show that also people- and culture-related skills are needed to leverage the integrating power of BPM. Looking at today's study programs at University, we rarely see such a wide coverage of relevant disciplines. The few programs considering BPM cover BPM in single courses or modules. In these programs BPM is mostly limited to modelling activities and languages of processes, such as BPMN (Business Process Modeling Notation), ARIS (Architecture of Integrated Information Systems) or UML (Unified Modelling Language) sometimes combined with technical issues of Workflow Management and customising of ERP-Systems (Enterprise Resource Planning). However, looking at the six core elements of BPM, we see that this covers merely one third of the capabilities needed to successfully implement BPM in a company. Going back to where we started in this article, we can also say that only looking into methods would actually not account for the characteristics of today's IT professionalism.

Due to the interdisciplinary nature of BPM, the competences required can hardly be covered sufficiently in one course or module of a study program neither in computer science, information systems nor business administration. On the contrary, there is a specific need to develop specifically shaped study programs for business process management. Such a program has been developed at the University of Liechtenstein. The program has been developed according to the Bologna Process and is accredited by internationally perceived institutions as a Master of Science in Business Process Management (MScBPM). In 2008 the first students from more than 15 member states of the EU entered the program, of which the first students will graduate in summer 2010. As part of the ERASMUS Mundus programs Lot 11 and Lot 14 also an increasing number of students from outside of Europe are now appointed to the program.

The curriculum of the program is displayed in fig. 4 and will be briefly illustrated in the following [14].

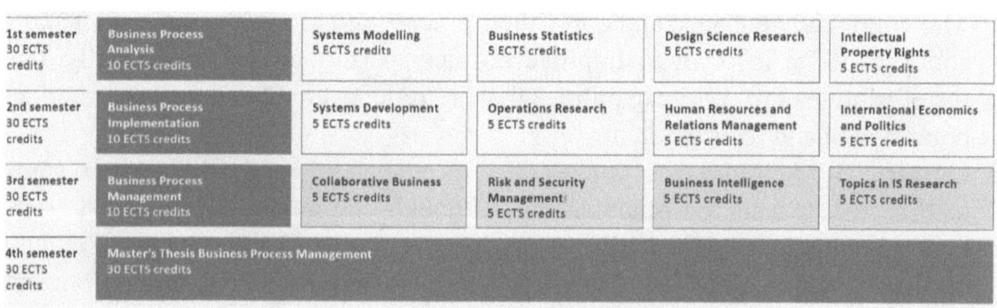

Figure 4: Curriculum of the MSc in BPM at the University of Liechtenstein

The program is structured by means of core modules, support modules and special interest models. Core modules represent essential steps in BPM, namely:

- **Business Process Analysis:** The program starts by delivering competences in analysing business problems according to a process-oriented way of thinking. Here, a wide variety of modelling techniques is subject to the course. Apart from standard methods for conventional business processes a focus lies on considering different context situations of process analysis [15]. Hence, both highly standardised and highly creative areas are differentiated, for example, calling for a special set of methods [16]. Also, in addition to teaching the method, emphasis lies on techniques and experiences on how to apply them in practice. This for example includes different techniques of inquiry.
- **Business Process Implementation:** For one thing, students know how to come up with to-be models for a specific business problem, they then learn how to implement these processes properly [17]. In terms of technical implementations, we use SAP as a role model for standard software products. Students can obtain an internationally perceived certificate from SAP (TERP10) on top of their diploma [18]. Business Process Implementation, however, does not only comprise technical implementation. Also organisational challenges of implementing new processes are subject to the module. Hence, apart from ERP Systems also Change Management plays an essential role [19].
- **Business Process Management:** Once processes are implemented, continuous activities for monitoring and measuring processes have to be tackled. Hence, in this module mechanisms of analysing the performance of processes lie in the focus. This comprises both the evaluation of running processes and the evaluation of potential process redesign [20]. While the former show a rather good coverage in management accounting, the latter is still highly under-researched. Here, we apply methods from investment accounting in order to evaluate the return on investment (ROI) of alternative process designs [21]. Apart from financial measures, we widen the scope towards sustainability thinking. Hence, we enable our students to also consider the ecological and social consequences of process management in order to prepare for sustainable business.

In parallel to the core modules, support modules provide in-depth knowledge on special skills required for different tasks in BPM such as analytical skills in maths (e. g. Operations Research), people-related business (e. g. Human Resource Management) or methodological skills in academic work (e. g. Design Science Research). In addition, also modules aiming at widening the scope are included here, such as international economics and politics, comprising courses in e. g. in intercultural communication. Apart from support modules also modules for special interest are included in positions for the third semester. These courses aim at focusing on special fields of interest currently of major interest in practice (e. g. Collaborative Business or Risk and Security Management). In order to capture most current issues, also a seminar on topics in IS research is included that is updated on a yearly basis.

As to the didactics, large amounts of the program are tought following principles of action learning. For this purpose students engage in practical projects by means of so-called project seminars that are also subject to research as part of the TRICE project. In these seminars, students are actively involved in practical work conducted at local organisations. In addition to projects in cooperation with large scale companies, such as the Hilti Corporation, also social work is conducted with the students. For instance, in the winter term 2009/10 a process analysis has been carried out together with 20 students helping a therapist school in Liechtenstein. These courses are essential for the students to learn how to apply their knowledge in a real life setting. In addition, these projects are highly appreciated by the industry and recognised by the local media and the government.

Conclusions and Future Work

To our practical experience, the Master Program in BPM proves successful. Students from the program enjoy a high reputation of employance. So far, there is an employability of 100% and students usually enter attractive positions in companies already during their studies. There are fellowship programs initiated by the local industry to financially support students to come abroad in order to enter the Master Program in BPM such as the Hilti Fellowhsip Program [22]. One may argue that BPM might be a trend. To our belief, however, BPM is rather a core competence that has been relevant in the past and that will remain (and increase) its relevance. Its core principles, subject to this educational program can well be traced back to a plethora of modern management approaches, such as Quality Management, Business Process Reengineering and Operations Management just to name a few. As IT becomes more and more a commodity, we can even expect competencies of flexibly combining solutions according to business process needs to be of growing and sustaining importance in the future. Another concern might be the broadness of the educational program. It is, therefore, recommendable, to our knowledge, to build BPM education on a profound first education, such as a bachelor program. This could either be a bachelor in information systems, business administration, computer science or engineering. Hence, the aim is a rather “T”-shaped education with the BPM program helping to both broaden the scope and also to integrate different subject areas as required in practice. So, finally, coming back to the overall theme of this article, we can conclude that BPM is indeed a pathway to IT professionalism. In addition, since products and services become more and more standardised, it may also be process leadership that might lead to competitive advantage and thus sustain profitable growth in Europe. That said, we can indeed imagine further pathways to IT professionalism in Europe which will be fascinating to further export in the future. To that extend, we hope that our perspective from BPM may well serve as a starting point for further discussion.

References

1. CEPIS (2007) *Thinking Ahead on e-Skills for the ICT Industry in Europe*, February 2007.
2. Rand Europe (2005) *The Supply and Demand of e-Skills in Europe*, September 2005.
3. EUCIP Programm (2008) *Competitiveness and Innovation Framework Programme* (CIP), http://ec.europa.eu/cip/, 30.05.2010.
4. Empirica (2009) *After the crisis, the e-skills gap is looming in Europe*, http://www.eskills-monitor.eu/, 30.05.2010.
5. Gartner, (2009). *Meeting the Challenge*: The 2009 CIO Agenda.
6. Hammer, M. (2010) What is Business Process Management?, in: *Handbook on Business Process Management: Introduction, Methods and Information Systems*(International Handbooks on Information Systems) (Vol. 1). Editors: J. vom Brocke, M. Rosemann, Berlin et al.: Springer, 2010.
7. Gartner (2010). *Gartner Hype Cycle Analysis*, http://www.gartner.com/it/docs/reports/asset_154296_2898.jsp, 30.05.2010.
8. vom Brocke, J., Petry, M., Sinnl, T., Kristensen, B. Ø., and Sonnenberg, C. (2010). Global Processes and Data. Learning from the Culture Journey at Hilti Corporation. In vom Brocke,J and Rosemann, M (Eds.), *Handbook on Business Process Management: Strategic Alignment, Governance, People and Culture* (International Handbooks on Information Systems) (Vol. 2,). Berlin: Springer, in print.
9. de Bruin, T. (2009) *Business Process Management: Theory on Progression and Maturity*. PhD Thesis, Queensland University of Technology, Brisbane, Australia.
10. Harmon, P. (2003) *Business process change: A Manager's Guide to Improving, Redesigning, and Automating Processes*. Amsterdam; Boston: Morgan Kaufmann.
11. Harmon, P. (2004) *Evaluating an Organisation's Business Process Maturity*, viewed 18th June 2007, http://www.bptrends.com/resources_publications.cfm
12. Curtis, B., Alden, J., & Weber, C.V. (2004) *The Use of Process Maturity Models in Business Process Management*. White Paper. Borland Software Corporation.
13. Rummler-Brache Group (2004) *Business Process Management in U.S. Firms Today*. A study commissioned by Rummler-Brache Group. March.
14. University of Liechtenstein (2010), Master of Science in Business Process Management, MScBPM, http://www.hochschule.li/GraduateSchool/MasterStudium/BusinessProcessEngineering/tabid/204/language/en-US/Default.aspx, 31.05.2010.
15. Recker, J., Rosemann, M., Indulska, M. and Green, P. (2009), Business Process Modeling: A Comparative Analysis. *Journal of the Association for Information Systems*, 10(4), 333-363.
16. Seidel, S. (2009) Toward a Theory of Managing Creativity-intensive Processes: A Creative Industries Study. *Information Systems and e-Business Management*, accepted for publication.
17. vom Brocke, J., Schenk, B., & Sonnenberg, C. (2009a). *Classification Criteria for Governing the Implementation Process of Service-oriented ERP Systems – An Analysis based on New Institutional Economics*. Paper presented at the Business-IT Alignment – Trends im Software und Servicemarkt Systems (AMCIS 2009), San Francisco, California.
18. SAP(2010),http://www.sap.com/services/education/catalog/globaltabbedcourse.epx?context=[[|TERP10|||095|G|]]|, 30.05.2010.
19. Aladwani, A. M. (2001) Change management strategies for successful ERP Implementation. *Business Process Management Journal* (BPMJ), 7(3), 266-275.
20. vom Brocke, J., Recker, J., & Mendling, J. (2009b) Value-oriented Process Modeling: Integrating Financial Perspectives into Business Process Re-design. *Business Process Management Journal* (BPMJ) in print, 16(2), 333-356.
21. vom Brocke, J., Sonnenberg, C., & Simons, A. (2009c). Value-oriented Information Systems Design: The Concept of Potentials Modeling and its Application to Service-oriented Architectures. *Business & Information Systems Engineering*, 1(3), 223-233

22. Hilti Fellowship (2010) Hilti Fellowship Program in Business Process Engineering, http://www.hilti.com/holcom/page/module/home/browse_main.jsf?lang=en&nodeId=-8468, 30.05.2010.

The Contextual Nature of Outsourcing Drivers

Tapio Reponen[1]

Abstract Outsourcing has been used throughout the history in different operations, resulting in multi-partner networks. Complexity has continuously grown in these demand-supply chains. Therefore, outsourcing is increasingly human interaction, where trust, collaboration and expertise are needed. The development to this stage has several different stages: from awareness through bandwagon effect to virtual organizations. The nature of the change is from cost savings through resource sharing to global survival. Many details in outsourcing processes may be on contract bases, but the overall development needs relationship management and trust. The drivers of outsourcing are increasingly the opportunities to achieve business goals, to execute strategies and to enhance innovations. Traditionally outsourcing has been focused on processes that been standardized and do not provide a competitive advantage to companies. With clear partnering arrangement, also more value-adding and varying processes can be outsourced. The paper studies this change and presents empirical evidence on the importance of close networking.

Stages of Outsourcing

The increasingly contextual nature of outsourcing will be discussed in this paper. The argumentation is based on experience gained from numerous empirical action research and case studies done in the department of Information Systems Science at Turku School of Economics. These practical examples have been complemented with an extensive survey in Finland [1].

Outsourcing is a historical concept, dating back to ancient Rome where tax collection was outsourced. In the area of information systems the first examples are from 1970's when software houses were established. The development speeded up in 1980's with conscious efforts to organize information management by service companies [2].E.g. we have examples in Finland of IT service companies, which were founded from earlier IT departments of global and national companies.

The first objectives were to outsource non-core business operations to cut the operational costs. The decision making was heavily cost-centered. The promises were that by outsourcing IT services the operating costs could be reduced by 20 to 30 per cent [3]. As we now know the promises were not totally met. The cost savings were very dependent on the service agreements made. The flexibility of using personnel is much higher in in-house operations than in buying services. Service operators charge for every action they are doing and the cost-efficiency was easily lost in "small" additional services.

[1] Vice-Rector University of Turku Finland (tapio.reponen@utu.fi)

Starting early 1990's a bandwagon effect strengthened [4]. The companies were increasingly outsourcing IT services in a variety of ways. This effect had connections to the core competence thinking, where recommendation was that every organization should concentrate on operations of their own key competencies. In IT sector this meant acquiring related skills, competencies and knowledge outside own organization.

From this strategic sourcing the development has continued towards "virtual organizations" where resources will be acquired from network partners. This may be called transformational outsourcing, where new business models are jointly developed using advanced ICT tools [5]. In the following we consider the changing role of outsourcing and illustrate that chance with some empirical examples.

The Concept of Outsourcing

Outsourcing is a multi-faceted concept which has several definitions. One very descriptive definition is the following:

Outsourcing: The transfer of activities and processes previously conducted internally to an external party [6]

Outsourcing is always a process of creating new relationships between partners. Levina and Su [7] have defined it in the following way

A Sourcing process: A set of organizational practices that facilitate discovering new supply opportunities, evaluating suppliers, developing supplier relationships, coordinating across suppliers, and changing levels of supplier commitment.

There is a clear change from outsourcing one function to global multisourcing strategy [7]:

- Beyond cost savings, firms increasingly outsource to create innovative IT applications and transform broken business processes
- Outsourcing relies on clients and suppliers investing knowledge and capital in the relationship, developing trust, and collaborating as partners.

The drivers of outsourcing have also changed [8]:

- The success of outsourcing is defined as the satisfaction with the intended benefits gained by service receiver as a result of outsourcing activity
- Benefits: cost drivers, user satisfaction, economic benefits, IS improvement, technological capabilities, business impact & business value
- Functional benefits: improvement of IT or MIS as a corporate function
- Technological benefits: to acquire, secure, and control IT capabilities
- Strategic benefits: to achieve business goals, to execute strategies, to enhance innovations

To summarize we could say that the nature of outsourcing has changed from cost savings through resource sharing to survival; from transaction cost theory to resource based view and to organizational theories; from domestic through internationalization to globalization; from efficient organization to focused organization and to virtual organizations, and from contract to relationship management and trust.

The strategic aspect of outsourcing is strengthening which means that value creation is the key criteria in decision making.

Value Creation Through Strategic Knowledge: Shared View Through Human Interaction

The nature of strategic knowledge is creative, the objective of which is to differentiate our operations from those of our competitors'. It is a combination of factual knowledge, practical knowledge, intuition, feelings, and faith, which all occur in consciousnesses of people involved [9-10]. Rauhala [11] and Pihlanto [12] state, that strategic knowledge is highly situational, organizational, and relational. Thus it depends on many contextual, organizational and personal factors.

Amazingly much of the strategic knowledge is, however, actually widely known within the organization, situating in parts and pieces in the minds of the personnel. Some key decisions are of course secretly made in closed circles, like within top management, but much of the decision information is generally available. E.g. the stock market analysts are able to present very detailed analyses on global companies, anticipating their strategic moves. This indicates that "strategic" information is more commonly known as the "transactional" information within the company [13].

Therefore, differentiating our operations from the competitors calls for intelligent use of ICT solutions in daily operations. Outsourcing should be considered from the perspective of how the solutions made add the operational competitiveness. Therefore shared knowledge in transaction networks is extremely important.

Koh, Ang and Straub [14]state, that many times, important terms and conditions are not explicitly incorporated in the legal contracts; parties rely, instead, on the spirit of the contract as embodied in a handshake. The psychological contract is an individual-level construct, and one may argue whether it is even applicable to an organizational level phenomenon such as IT outsourcing.

In Figure 1 there is an illustration on the many factors influencing human decision knowledge creation and decision making. These factors are relevant also in outsourcing processes. To build a trust between different partners is a process of mutual interaction and lengthy collaboration. We are able to reach the intensive level of outsourcing only through a process, where individuals find common interests through their personal consideration.

This indicates that the nature of outsourcing is changing from single objectives, like cost savings to human interaction in a network of partners. The rationale of outsourcings comes from strengthening the competitiveness of all actors in the network. In the following we illustrate with some empirical evidence this fact.

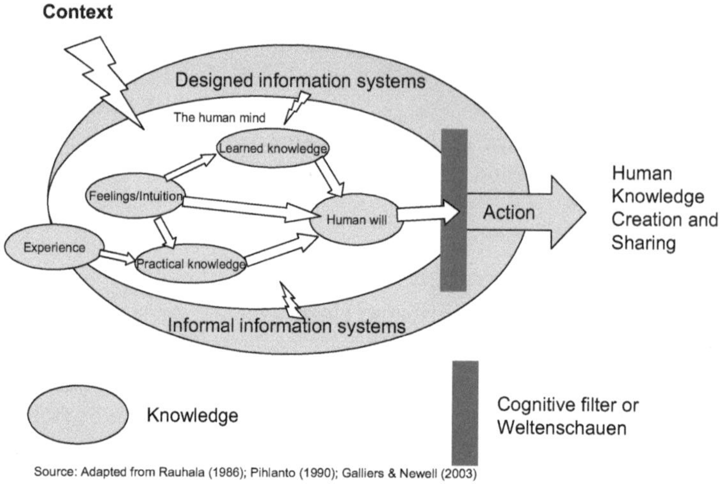

Figure 1: Human knowledge creation and sharing and the role of information systems

Empirical Examples

Hansaprint is a printing house in the Nordic region and a service company specialized in comprehensive marketing solutions. Hansaprint's services areas are: Printing services, multichannel services and marketing services. The company concentrates on developing printing and logistics solutions in the field of marketing communication that generate measurable benefits for its customers.

Hansaprint has refined its services and organization in order to meet its customers' marketing and communication needs. Increasingly, every marketing investment has to generate measurable results, driving constant improvement of the efficiency and impact of marketing. This is an example of modern outsourcing thinking from vendor's perspective.

In the interview with Mika Suortti, EVP, he presented the following thoughts:

> "Traditionally outsourcing has focused on processes that have been standardized and do not provide a competitive advantage to companies, for instance: IT platforms & hosting, Payroll and other finance/HR processes. With a clear partnering arrangement, also more value-adding and varying processes can be outsourced. The outsourcing partner has to have a deep understanding of both the customer's operations and the outsourced service. In the area of marketing communications services this means that the outsourcing company has to know the markets of its customers, and bring value to how they are spoken to."

Hansaprint has developed its services according to these lines. Instead of being a printing house, who prints magazines, manuals and marketing materials to fulfill orders they want to be a partner in marketing communication of their customers. This means a larger variety of services and deeper cooperation. Hansaprint is producing marketing materials to customers with their own call center solution. In this solution the customers need not to follow up the status of their materials, e.g. manuals, but they are delivered "automatically".

Another example is **STX Europe** (Earlier Aker Yards). It is one of the leading shipyards in the world to build modern cruising ships. The ships manufactured in Turku are mainly cruising on the Carribean sea. The company has developed over time from a shipyard to a network operator, linking thousands of subcontractors together. A modern cruiser is full of state-of-the-art IC-technology to meet all the high requirements of the customers. The ship has restaurants, swimming pools, ice-rink, gyms and several other services, which should operate smoothly.

One of their decision problems has been the IT governance at the network level. Centralization and decentralization are then the key questions. In the interviews the management has emphasized the following aspects:

> "Power and responsibility of IT and its development is now solely within the shipyard. Subcontractors have little or no interest on IT matters. We tried to organise an IT governance forum, but the time was not yet ready for that. Business applications are owned by the business units, who collaborate with subcontractors. Small IT department provides the IT platform. They are managed as a cost center, which serves only the shipyard departments."

> "We have been considering that is this sufficient, considering the role that IT has in ship building– or could have? Shouldn't the change in shipyards business governance be reflected in IT governance? Who has the incentive to innovate the systems – if benefits go to subcontractors?"

The shipyard has created a well-operating sub-contractor network, which is largely managed by the information systems. The coordination works, but among IT management there is an intuition that with a less conservative strategy of IT governance the benefits might even be higher. There is a desire for more interactive way of organizing IT.

Conclusions

In the following we present conclusions on the changing nature of outsourcing. This view is based on experience gained in different outsourcing processes at Turku School of Economics. The arguments are backed up with comments from interviews we have made recently:

Outsourcing is increasingly human interaction, where trust, collaboration and expertise are needed

> "Now we are with this one project in the situation where nothing seems to work. We should throw the vendors out. But then we have several other problems to solve" (CEO, ministry, 2008)

> "In the contract we have only minor sanctions. We should have some quality criterion. We should analyze that is it a definition error, software error, parametric error, or user error..." (CIO, Insurance Company, 2007)

Outsourcing has been used throughout the history, resulting in multi-partner networks

> "I have increasingly used the name portfolio manager of myself" (CIO, Manufacturing Company, 2007)

Complexity in these demand-supply chains is increasing

> "The challenge is that how to train our people in the thinking that although we have several suppliers, during the project we all are in the same boat" (CIO, Manufacturing Company, 2007)

Strategic partnership is often more problematic for the client than for the vendor

> "Although we have a hell of the problems with some vendor, we nicely wait and trust that we get the applications to work" (CIO, Ministry, 2008)

From our studies we may also draw some conclusions and recommendations for practical decision making. Firs one is that all organizations should design their own strategy on outsourcing. In the course of history there are a plenty of examples that outsourcing has been implemented according to the recommendations of outside consultants. Then the reason for outsourcing may be a "bandwagon effect" without thinking the real needs of own company. It is important to know, however, that outsourcing of problems is not possible, but you always have to solve them by yourself. Thus moving some operations outside the company is a feasible solution only after the operational problems have been solved. Another good advice is to collect experience from the market. You can find almost always similar cases to your situation, from which you can learn to avoid the same mistakes. One very typical one is that you let good ICT professionals move to some other organization, and consequently do not have the needed expertise to consider your information processes. For creating a deep partnership in the network long-term vendor relationships are needed. Of course realizing that in such a partnership the prices of the services tend to rise over time. You need control points to be sure of competitive pricing, but adding competitiveness calls for internalization of the problem area. A shared vision is needed to create new solutions. Contracts are important, but trust is the key for success. It is also important to react immediately to problem situations. The sooner you are able to stop poor development the smaller the damages are.

References

1. Salmela, H. and Spil, T. (2006) Strategic Information Systems Planning in Inter-Organizational Networks: Adapting SISP Approaches to Network Context. In Remenyi, Dan (ed.), *Proceedings of the 2nd European Conference on IS Management, Leadership and Governance*, July 2006, Paris, France

2. Reponen, T. (1998) Setting Up Outsourced Information Technology Service Companies. In *Strategic Sourcing of Information Systems*. Edited by L.P. Willcocks and M.C. Lacity. John Wiley & Sons Ltd, pp. 327-349
3. Reponen, T. (1993) *Outsourcing or Insourcing? International Conference on Information Systems* (ICIS), Orlando, Florida, December 5-8, 1993
4. Lacity, M. and Hirschheim, R. (1995), *Beyond the information systems outsourcing bandwagon*, Chichester, Wiley
5. Hätönen, J and Paju T. (2008) 30+ Years of Research and Practice of Outsourcing – Exploring the Past and Anticipating the Future (forthcoming)
6. Ellram, L.and Billington, C. (2001) Purchasing leverage considerations in the outsourcing decision.*European Journal of Purchasing & Supply Management*, 7(1), 15 – 27
7. Levina , N. and Su , N. (2008) Global Multisourcing Strategy: The Emergence of a Supplier Portfolio in Service Outsourcing. *Decision Sciences*, 39(3), 541-562.
8. Goo, J. H., Derrick, C. and Hart, P. (2008) A Path to Successful IT Outsourcing: Interaction Between Service-Level Agreements and Commitment, *Decision Science*
9. Nonaka, I. (1994). A dynamic theory of organizational knowledge creation. *Organization Science*, *5* (*1*), 14-37.
10. Bueno, E., and Salmador, M.P. (2003).Knowledge management in the emerging strategic business process: information, complexity and imagination. *Journal of Knowledge Management*, 7(2), 5 – 17
11. Rauhala, L. (1986). *Ihmiskäsitys ihmistyössä (The Conception of Human Being in Helping People),* Helsinki, Finland: Gaudeamus
12. Pihlanto, P (1990). *The Holistic Concept Of Man As A Framework For Management Accounting Research*, Turku, Finland: Turku School of Economics and Business Administration
13. Kerola , P, Reponen, T and Ruohonen, M(2003) On Interpretation of Strategic Knowledge Creation in a Longitudinal Action Research. In B Sundgren, P Mårtensson, M Mähring & K Nilsson (Eds.) *Exploring Patterns in Information Management: Concepts and Perspectives for Understanding IT-Related Change*, Stockholm, Sweden: Stockholm School of Economics
14. Koh,C, Ang , S. and and Straub, D.W. (2004) IT Outsourcing Success: A Psychologica'l Contract Perspective. *Information Systems Research*, 15(4), 356 – 373
15. Galliers, R.D. and Newell, S. (2003) Strategy as Data + Sense Making. In S. Cummings & D.C. Wilson (eds), Images of Strategy. Oxford, UK: Blackwell: 164-196

Information Models for Process Management – New Approaches to Old Challenges

Jörg Becker[1]

Abstract. Effective process management is an essential success factor for organizations. Especially the retail sector requires enterprises to implement lean and efficient processes to remain competitive. However, the implementation of an appropriate process management is a challenging and error-prone endeavor. As a major reason for this the lack of effective and comprehensible methods has been identified. Moreover, due to rising market dynamics, detailed knowledge of the internal business processes is crucial to develop competitive advantage. Market trends have to be identified and needs for action have to be established early to be prepared for market changes and to react accordingly. Therefore it is necessary that the company's processes are transparent and starting points can be identified quickly. This article aims to provide an approach of how a company can record its processes in a meaningful way to be able to improve them goal-oriented.

Process Management in Retail Markets

Managing business processes is a necessity for every organization. Since the early work of Adam Smith [1], this challenge has been discussed both among practitioners as well as in the research community. However, it was not until the fundamental contribution of Hammer and Champy [2] that an entire new paradigm for process management was created. The proposed radical focus on business processes led to new organizational structures and IT-related solutions. From an organizational point of view, new areas of responsibilities have been designed. The classical job enrichment and job enlargement have been applied along business processes. From an organizational perspective, by using new technological opportunities, flexibility, knowledge-sharing and development are supported. Furthermore – from an employees' perspective – the ways of working changed to a boundless cooperation [3]. As a consequence, process owners, process managers and more recently Chief Process Officers (CPO) have been established as an approach to appropriately acknowledge the requirements of process-oriented organizations.

Process management (PM) offers opportunities for savings by means of an efficient design of the internal business processes. This is especially relevant in retail markets since retail companies operate within market segments where prices are under heavy pressure by other market participants. Hence, optimization potential

[1] European Research Center for Information Systems, University of Münster, Germany, becker@ercis.uni-muenster.de

has to be identified within internal procedures and workflows. Even though process management is of great importance for retail markets, numerous process management projects fail due to a lack of structures and applicable methods. Frequently, critical deficiencies already occur during the basic analysis – the documentation of the organization's processes.

Initial Conditions and Related Work

A basic prerequisite for successful process management is accurate process documentation. During the documentation phase originated process models provide an indispensable foundation for significant analysis and well-founded decisions [4]. However, in practice there is often a lack of structured process recording. A multitude of different modeling methods and respective software tools are in use, ranging from traditional word processing or drawing programs (e.g. Microsoft Office Visio or Power Point) to specific process modeling tools [5-6]. Thus, the modeler has a very high degree of freedom during the modeling process, which often results in different models arising from the same fact.

Empirical studies show that conceptual models that have been constructed distributed by different modelers significantly differ with respect to identifiers and structure [7]. This implies the occurrence of defects like naming conflicts and structural conflicts [8-9] in the attempt to compare or merge models and model parts that address similar issues. Moreover, variations arise even if models are created by the same modeler at different points in time. This severely impedes the comparability of conceptual models. As a result, the analysis of such models – for example with purposes like integration or benchmarking – is generally very complex [10-11]. For a domain specific purpose a specialized language can reduce the variations in those models by limiting the freedom of choice during model creation (e.g. by using a semantic building block-based approach in the public sector) [12]. By using non-specialized software tools [13], there is a lack of clear specifications and goal-oriented guidelines [14-15] for the design of business processes in retail markets. This results in confusing or even misleading models.

The origins of the consideration of naming conflicts can be found in works of the 1980s and 1990s. At this time the integration of corporate databases was focused [8-9], [16-17]. In the context of database integration, typically clear identifiers are used for naming purposes. Hence, a semi-automatic solution for eliminating naming conflicts is possible. The requirements become more complicated and complex when using process models because whole sets of phrases are used [18].

The solution for structural conflicts is based on the graph theory. Moreover, the issue is also addressed in the modeling of data models and process models [19- 20]. Especially by comparing or integrating two or more models structural conflicts become obvious, even though the same facts were shown.

Another challenge is to make the results obtained accessible to the company's employees. This is necessary to ensure that all employees can work with the obtained data in a valuable way. Additionally, it enables employees to not only access the data but also actively participate in the process management of the company. Therefore, companies often utilize already existing corporate intranet structures to propagate process information.

While this offers a wide dissemination of the models in the company, in many cases a detailed document structure is missing. Decisions for storage locations for models are usually made by the subjective assessment of the modeler. For example, he or she has to decide independently whether the model is part of the purchase or the order management. In most cases the models are stored incorrectly due to time pressure or confusing structures and are therefore poorly accessible for the remaining employees. In addition, models are subject to constant revision and existing content is frequently changed or supplemented. If not adequately guided, these incremental changes will further nullify existing structures and thus impede quick access to process documents. If employees are required to work with these documents, this will inevitably lead to frustration and animosity towards process change. The readiness for participation, the essential foundation for process management, is being jeopardized in an early stage.

Another influence is the lack of integration of modeling and archiving of the models. Often, different systems are used in practice. Thus, the modeler is forced to create a model in a separate software program and make it available to other staff members through the intranet. This division into modeling and archiving systems leads to increasing effort for the application and the administration of the systems. The modeler has to register separately for both systems and gets different user rights and roles. This results in both delays in the workflow of the modeler as well as redundancies in the system administration that can be avoided through an adequate integration.

A New Approach: Bringing Semantics Into Reference Models

The previously described problems potentially lead to an inefficient implementation of a project and, thus, to the eventual failure of the company's process management efforts. The goal of this article is to introduce an approach that integrates a syntactic modeling language (as all the others are) with semantics, i.e. predefined content for specific industries/functional areas. As an example we show retail-specific content offering goal-oriented guidelines during modeling.

We structure the retail industry by using predefined reference models and defining four layers of hierarchy. Besides the use of reference models, also syntactic rules are adopted. The modeler obtains a pre-defined set of building blocks to generate phrases of the form "activity, business object" (e.g. 'store products', 'check invoice') while defining detailed processes. About 300 business objects and 50 activities are available. Hence, the modeler can choose the relevant activity and the relevant business object to generate the needed phrase for his purpose.

These predefined specifications address the Guidelines of Modeling (GoM) [21- 22] as an integrated part of the modeling language; previous weaknesses of purely syntactic modeling languages can be overcome. Thereby the modeler is provided with a manageable semantic modeling language. Additionally, not only the business objects and activities can be completed by the modeler, but also the reference models can be modified and adapted.

Four Layer Structure

The presented approach includes a four layer structure in which the retail-H (the framework) describes the first layer (see Figure 1). Each element of the framework provides a main process (layer 2), each element of the main process a detailed process (layer 3). The process building blocks (layer 4) provide a flexible design layer in order to deposit detailed information about the according parent detail process.

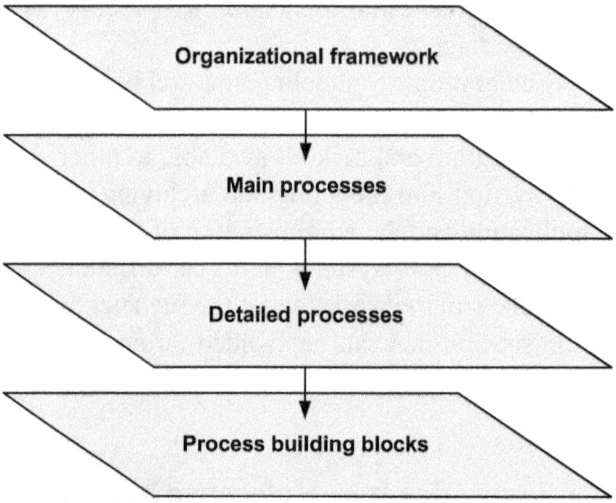

Figure 1: The four layers

Framework

The framework is a graphical means to describe the relevant elements and relations of an original. It does not rely on a pre-defined modeling language or meta model and aims to describe an area of discourse on a high abstraction level by adhering to a selected structuring principle. Thus, the purpose of this diagram type is to give an overview of the original, and when organizing the sub-ordinate detailing levels, to reveal their relations to other elements as well as the relations of the organizational frame [23].

In the context of retail markets, the organizational framework for trading companies, (retail-H-architecture) represents a well-founded and accepted navigation structure for processes in retail [24]. With its subordinated processes, it provides best-practices for the retail sector. Due to the architecture, a solid and proven framework for further implementation of processes is created which can be adjusted as needed by the respective trading company. The retail-H as a reference model represents the traditional commodity-related merchandise with the planning, logistical and technical areas of settlement and the related economic and administrative functions and business management responsibilities (see Figure 2).

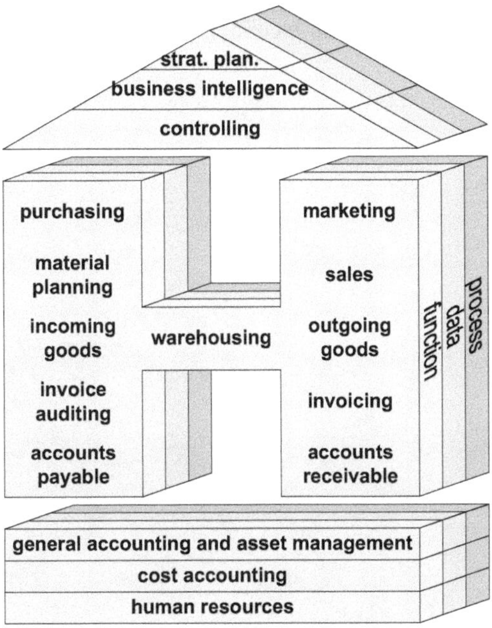

Figure 2: The organizational framework – the retail-H Source: Becker, Schütte [24]

This model was developed to divide and organize reference function, data and process models for retailing companies. The procurement and distribution areas, linked by the bridging function of the warehousing, are shown in the consecutive subtasks of purchasing, material planning, incoming goods, invoice auditing, and accounts payable, and, in an analog structure, in marketing, sales, outgoing goods, invoicing, and accounts receivable respectively. The left hand side contains the tasks with reference to suppliers, the right hand side the tasks with reference to customers. In addition, the operative-administrative and the management functions are mapped.

In addition to the characteristic of providing overviews, the organizational frame has other important functions: First, it creates a uniform basis for the terms and notations for all participants. The use of uniform terms and notations in the framework, i.e. an unambiguous vocabulary, lead to a clear and distinct understanding of the discussed processes and provides a likewise clear and distinct orientation in the organizational context. The framework enables the navigation to the level of the main processes.

Main Processes

Each element of the framework (the retail-H) forms a main process. Each main process is subclassified into detailed processes. The main process layer describes the important activities on a high level of granularity. Given the main process 'incoming goods', detailed processes might be 'plan incoming goods" or "receive goods", "accomplish main control", etc.

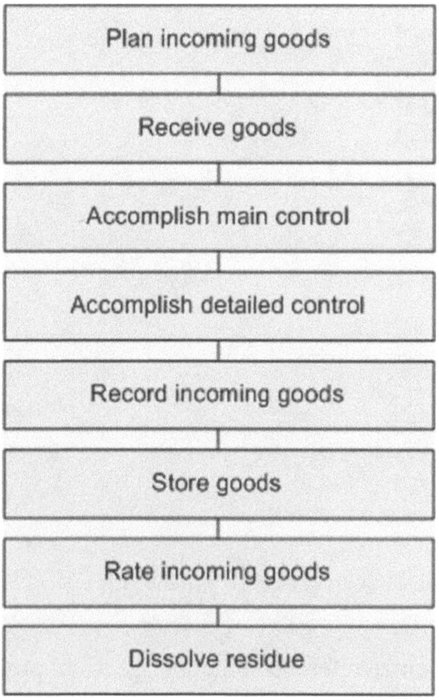

Figure 3: Main Process: Incoming Goods

In figure 3 the detailed processes of the main process 'incoming goods' are presented. It's about a gradual succession of processes that are carried out within this main process.

Detailed Processes

From the main processes layer the level of detailed processes is accessible, where the activities outlined in the corresponding main process are further refined.

On this level detailed process flows for each of the main processes are specified. The main advantage of this level concept is that it incorporates a complete organizational frame for retailers or companies of other lines of business. Decisions can be represented by branching the process flow.

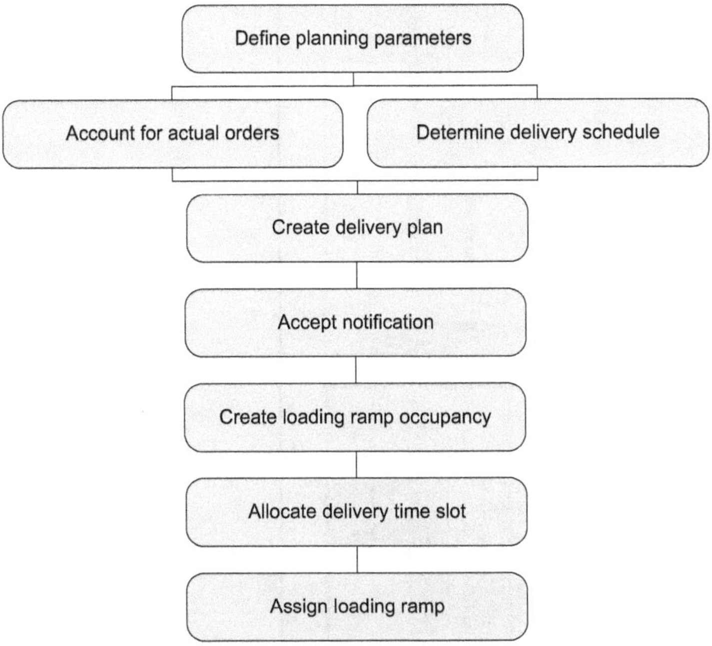

Figure 4: Detailed Process: Plan Incoming Goods

Figure 4 shows the process building blocks of the detailed process 'Plan incoming goods'. By following the sequential arrangement, there is a decision branch after the process of defining the planning parameters. By applying the prescribed steps, the user of the reference model is led step by step through the process for planning the incoming goods and can build his decisions on it.

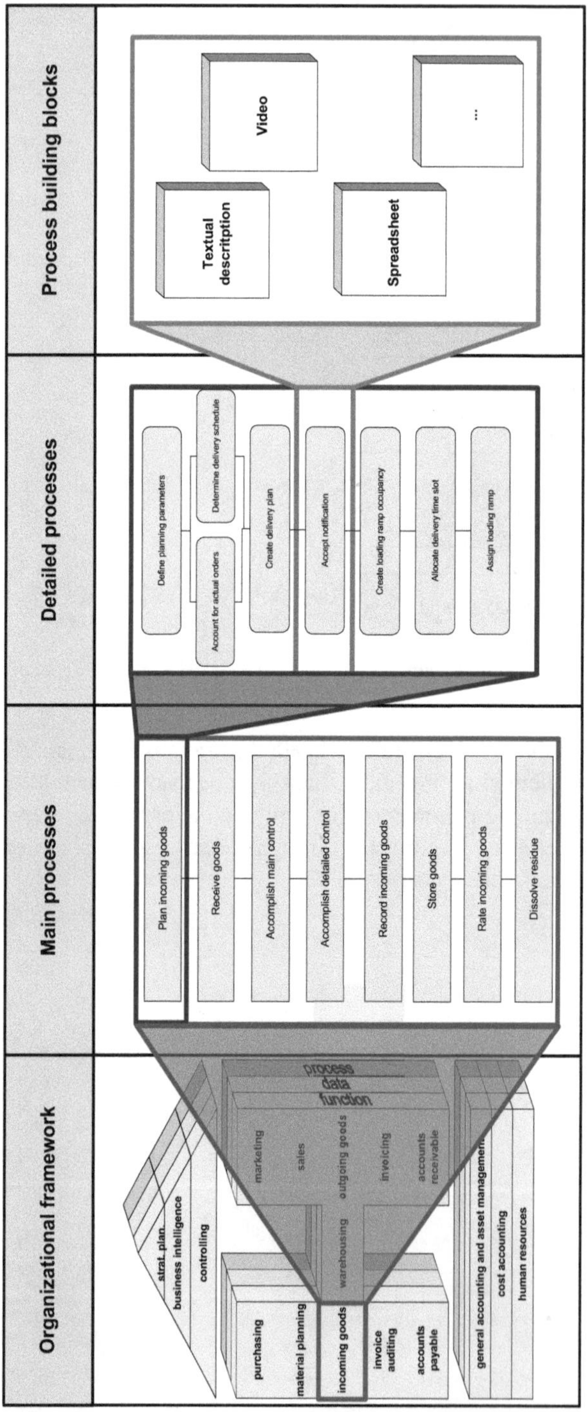

Figure 5: Navigation

Process Building Blocks

The process building blocks layer serves as a way to substantiate the detailed processes. Here, the individual process steps of a company are defined. A process building block is a container comprising different types of informational sources providing rich information for the task it intends to represent. Several types of documents are valid such as detailed process models, text documents, pictures, audio or video files.

Thus, the internal structure of a process building block is not predefined and will be instantiated according to the particular modeling or model usage objective. This principle is applicable to both analytic ("as-is-modeling") as well as synthetic ("to-be-modeling") documentation efforts.

Integration Beyond the Layers

Applying this concept of hierarchy of process models and navigation throughout all the layers (see figure 5) provides a sound foundation for continuous process management. The inherent structure guides the process management in a goal-oriented way. All modeling activities descend subsequently through the four levels of abstraction. In doing so, all model elements of a given level are derived from the model elements of the superordinate level. The elements of the framework lead to the elements of the main processes, the elements of the main processes to the elements of the detailed processes and so on. The models created in this fashion are consistent in terms of their level of detail and can therefore be compared to each other easily. This reduces the effort of navigating through the models, enabling the users to access the information they require quickly and intuitively.

References

1. Smith, A.(1937). The Wealth of Nations, 1776. Canaan ed.,New York: Modern Library.
2. Hammer, M.,and Champy, J.(1995) Business Reengineering. Die Radikalkur für das Unternehmen.; Frankfurt, New York; Campus-Verlag, 5. Aufl.
3. Imperatori, B., and De Marco, M.(2008). ICT and Changing Working Relationships: Rational or Normative Fashion? In D'Atri, A., De Marco, M., Casalino, N. (Eds) *Interdisciplinary Aspects of Information Systems Studies*, S. 105-114.
4. Bandara, W., Gable, G. G., and Rosemann, M. (2005). Factors and measures of business process modelling: Model building through a multiple case study. *European Journal of Information Systems*, 14 (4), 347–360.
5. Recker, J.(2010). Opportunities and constraints: the current struggle with BPMN. *Business Process Management Journal*, 16 (1), 181-201.
6. Davies, I., Green, P., Rosemann, M., and Gallo, S. (2004). Conceptual Modelling – What and Why in Current Practice. In: P. Atzeni, W. W. Chu, H. Lu, S. Zhou, & T. W. Ling, *Proceedings of the 23rd International Conference on Conceptual Modeling*, Lecture Notes in Computer Science (Vol. 3288, pp. 30-42). Shanghai, China: Springer.

7. Hadar, I.and Soffer, P.(2006). Variations in conceptual modeling: classification and ontological analysis. *Journal of the AIS*, 7 (8), 568-592.
8. Batini, C., Lenzerini, M., and Navathe, S. B.(1986). A Comparative Analysis of Methodologies for Database Schema Integration. *ACM Computing Surveys*, 18 (4), 323-364.
9. Lawrence, R., and Barker, K.(2001). Integrating Relational Database Schemas using a Standardized Dictionary. In: *Proceedings of the 2001 ACM symposium on Applied computing (SAC).* Las Vegas.
10. Phalp, K.and Shepperd, M.(2000). Quantitative analysis of static models of processes. *Journal of Systems and Software* 52 (2-3), 105-112.
11. Vergidis, K., Tiwari, A.,and Majeed, B.(2008). Business process analysis and optimization: beyond reengineering. *IEEE Transactions on Systems, Man, and Cybernetics* 38 (1), 69-82.
12. Becker, J., Breuker, D., Pfeiffer, D., and Räckers, M.(2009). Constructing Comparable Business Process Models with Domain Specific Languages – An Empirical Evaluation. In: *Proceedings of the 17th European Conference on Information Systems (ECIS).* Verona (Italy), 1-13.
13. Clegg, B., and Shaw, D. (2008). Using process-oriented holonic (PrOH) modelling to increase understanding of information systems. *Information Systems Journal*, 18 (5), 447-477.
14. Rosemann, M.(2006). Potential pitfalls of process modeling: part A. *Business Process Management Journal*, 12 (2), 249-254.
15. Rosemann, M.(2006). Potential pitfalls of process modeling: part B. *Business Process Management Journal*, 12 (3), 377-384.
16. Batini, C., and Lenzerini, M.(1984) A Methodology for Data Schema Integration in the Entity Relationship Model, in: *IEEE Transactions on Software Engineering*, 10 (6), 650-663.
17. Bhargava, H. K., Kimbrough, S. O.,and Krishnan, R.(1991) Unique Name Violations, a Problem for Model Integration or You Say Tomato, I Say Tomahto. *ORSA Journal on Computing*, 3 (2), 107-120.
18. Keller, G., Nüttgens, M., and Scheer, A.-W.(1992). Semantische Prozeßmodellierung auf der Grundlage „Ereignisgesteuerter Prozeßketten (EPK)“, in: A.-W. Scheer (Hrsg.), *Veröffentlichungen des Instituts für Wirtschaftsinformatik*, Heft 89, Saarbrücken.
19. Hars, A. (1994). *Reference Data Models: Foundations of Efficient Data Modeling.* [In German: Referenzdatenmodelle. Grundlagen effizienter Datenmodellierung]. Wiesbaden.
20. Mendling, J.(2007). Detection and Prediction of Errors in EPC Business Process Models. Doctoral Thesis, Vienna University of Economics and Business Administration.
21. Becker, J., Rosemann, M., Schütte, R.(1995). Grundsätze ordnungsmäßiger Modellierung (GoM), *Wirtschaftsinformatik*, 37 (5), 435-445.
22. Rosemann, M. (2003) Preparation of Process Modeling, In: Process Management – A Guide for the Design of Business Processes, Eds.: Becker, J., Kugeler, M., Rosemann, M., 41-78.
23. Meise, V.(2001). *Ordnungsrahmen zur prozessorientierten Organisationsgestaltung. Modelle für das Management komplexer Reorganisationsprojekte.* Hamburg 2001.
24. Becker, J., and Schütte, R.(2004). *Handelsinformationssysteme – Domänenorientierte Einführung in die Wirtschaftsinformatik.* Frankfurt am Main 2004.

Business Intelligence Systems, Uncertainty in Decision-Making and Effectiveness of Organizational Coordination

Antonella Ferrari[1]

Abstract. This work to the literature that deals with the effects of the adoption and use of information and communication technologies (ICT) on the enterprises. In the realm of all possible ICT solutions that can be adopted, our attention is focused on the study of Business Intelligence Systems (BIS) as support and decisional coordination tools. The strategic role of BISs in terms of improvement of performance and competitiveness is currently recognized by the management. However, these are primarily studied from a technological perspective and research on their organizational effects on the enterprises are limited. The purpose of this paper is to analyze BISs from an organizational perspective. A model will be proposed to study the relationship between a Business Intelligence system, the uncertainty related to decision-making processes and the effectiveness of organizational coordination.

Introduction

Currently, the emphasis on Business Intelligence systems mainly revolves around the potential pervasiveness allowed by the evolved technology used for their realization. This evolution mainly consists of the following two aspects: one aspect is relative to the data (the possibility to rapidly access numerous heterogeneous sources, the ability to analyze huge data quantities with tools that have different sophistication levels, the effective way to present the results of the data processing) while the other is relative to the user's friendliness which allows to enlarge the pool of users. Such pervasiveness makes the Business Intelligence systems potentially able to offer a support to the decision-making at all levels of the organization (from the strategic top to the operational staff).

ICT, and therefore Business Intelligence systems, as coordination technologies, that is, technologies aiming at the support and intermediation of processes of knowledge communication and decision-making among individuals that carry out tasks that are interdependent with each other, can be evaluated based on their contribution to the improvement of the existing coordination mechanisms and reduction of uncertainty in the decision-making processes. In literature, the studies on the relationship between ICT and coordination are many. However the researches carried out so far with regard to Business Intelligence systems have shown that we are dealing with relatively new phenomena that are primarily studied from a tech-

[1] Polytechnic Institute of Milan, Italy, antonella.ferrari@polimi.it

nological perspective. Research about their organizational effects on the enterprises is limited. The purpose of this paper is to analyze BIS from an organizational perspective. A model is proposed to study the relationship between a Business Intelligence system, the uncertainty related to decision-making processes and the effectiveness of the organizational coordination, based on the approach of Information Processing View (IPV).

Theoretical Framework

The fundamental role of information within the organizations is viewed as critical by many organizational theories. The use of information is typically examined in the context of decision-making processes. Data can be analyzed as information processing activities.

An approach that addresses information processing activities is the Information Processing View (IPV) proposed by Galbraith [1-2]. Information processing refers to the gathering, interpreting and synthesizing of information in the context of the organizational decision-making [3]. The interest in the Information Processing View is driven by the rapid diffusion of information processing technologies and the increasing information content of organizational tasks [4].

Organizations are open social systems which must commonly tolerate the uncertainty related to decision-making [5]. Facing this uncertainty the enterprises must facilitate the collection, gathering and processing of information as regards the functioning of the different organizational components, the quality of outputs, and the conditions in external, technological, and market domains [6]. The complexity and dynamics of the environmental uncertainty affects the complexity of the organizational management and functioning. Complex environmental conditions entail a larger quantity of information upon which decisions are made [7].

As the amount of activity interdependence that exists between the members of an organization is associated with the need for effective coordination and joint problem solving, activity interdependence is an important source of uncertainty [3]. When the type of interdependence becomes more complex, coordination and mutual problem solving demands increase [8]. According to Galbraith, a strong relationship exists between the concepts of uncertainty, information and the implementation methods of the organizational coordination [1-2]. Uncertainty directly contributes to increasing the information required by the players involved in the management of activities that are interdependent with each other. Information requirement is intended as the information complexity of the tasks to be carried out, as the difference between the information theoretically necessary to optimally carry out a given activity and the information actually available [9]. All conditions being equal, at a low level of uncertainty the information requirement may be absorbed by simple coordination forms, while a high uncertainty level can be dealt with using more articulated forms [10]. Galbraith [1-2] has proposed a theory (IPV), whereby an organization processes information in order to reduce the uncertainty related to decision-making, which is defined as the difference between the amount of information required to carry out decisional processes and the amount of information already owned by an organization. This difference is also commonly known as the "information gap" (Fig. 1).

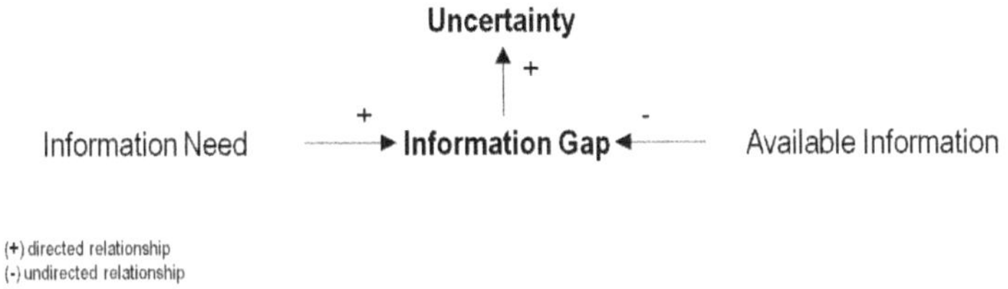

Figure 1: Relationship between "information gap" and uncertainty

The "information gap" depends in turn on two variables: the complexity level of the activity to be carried out and the ability of the player to deal with such complexity. Variety and variability of the problems to be solved and interdependence of activities define complexity. Complexity is the degree of variance of an event which can occur having different meanings. The goal of a BIS is to reduce the expected variance of an event. Variance depends either on the effective or potential differentiation of the events occurring at the same time, or on the possible different events during the time [11]. If the problems to be solved in the decision process are highly differentiated, more heterogeneous knowledge and information are required. Variety does not imply the inability to predict or preplan decision-making activities. Therefore standardization of behaviours and actions is not precluded, even though it is not viable when an activity is highly variable and unpredictable [12].

Hence, a simple activity is characterized by few problems, or exceptions, which are all of the same kind. A complex activity implies problems that are always new, different and oftentimes interdependent.

Therefore, the organizational players may have different information needs. Those who carry out repetitive activities that can be standardized are called to manage a limited amount of information. Others instead are called to carry out more complex activities and need therefore to be more able to manage the information.

Furthermore, the higher the interdependence between the various activities and the players that are responsible for their execution, the greater the information requirement. In order to reach a high level of ability to manage the interdependences it is necessary to develop an adequate ability to manage the related information flows [8].

In order to address a different degree of complexity and thus increase the levels of required information, a particular coordination mechanism or business process is adopted. If an activity is suitable and predictable, standardization mechanisms are preferable. If the variety and variability of the events are high and unpredictable, mechanisms that allow the gathering, processing and transmission of information, like mutual adjustment, are suitable. In order to reduce uncertainty, the more complex the activities, the greater the amount of required information and the higher must be the ability to manage this information [1-2].

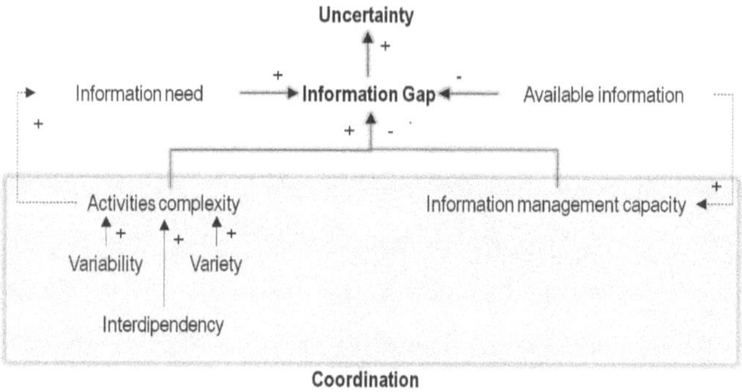

Figure 2: A reconsideration of the Information Processing View (IPV) model [2]

Therefore, in order to avoid a high degree of uncertainty, it is possible to (Fig. 2):

- Reduce the amount of required information to perform a specific activity (this implies a simplification of activities)
- Increase the amount of information available to improve the information processing capacity utilized for addressing complex activities.

The desired information processing capacity can be obtained with the creation of coordination mechanisms among members of the organization [1-2].

In addition, an organization may increase its ability to process information in the face of the increasing uncertainty related to decision-making processes investing in information technologies. The organizations increase the capacity of existing channels of communication, create new channels and introduce new decision mechanisms. The information is collected at the points of origin and directed at appropriate places in the hierarchy for decision-making purposes [1-2].

Business Intelligence Systems

In the works by Ghosthal and Kim [13] and Gilad and Gilad [14], Business Intelligence (BI) is intended as a managerial philosophy and as a tool used to help the organizations to manage and process information, with the aim of making increasingly more effective decisions. In 1989 the term BI has become popular thanks to the analysts of a famous consulting company in the ICT sector that used it to describe a number of concepts and methods to improve the *decision- making* business using support systems based on facts [15]. The evolution of the technologies available to develop the systems supporting the decisions and the studies relative to the information requirements that characterize the critical processes of the organizations have led to many changes and additions in the definition of the "Business Intelligence" term.

Some authors [16-17] deem that the term BI should include anything that concerns the use of information for the purpose of easing the decision-making processes and the management of future events. According to Thomsen [18], BI is a term that replaces Decision Support Systems (DSS), Executive Support Systems (EIS) and Management Information Systems (MIS). Arnott and Pervan [19] believe that the term BI is simply the present-day term for both DSS and EIS. A few authors [20, 21, 22] characterize BI as integrated infrastructures to support in real time all managerial levels. Davenport [23] stresses the fact that a BI includes a number of processes and technologies used to collect, analyze and distribute data for the purpose of making better decisions.

BI is also intended as the support function of the strategic top with the purpose of contributing to the qualitative improvement and increased speed of the decisional processes of the organizations which therefore may increase their competitiveness [24].

According to Moss and Atre [25] BI includes all those components that characterize an integrated infrastructure supporting the management of an enterprise.

Clark et *al.* [26] include BI systems within the Management Support Systems (MSS) (Fig. 3), intended as systems that support managerial *decision-making* activities [27].

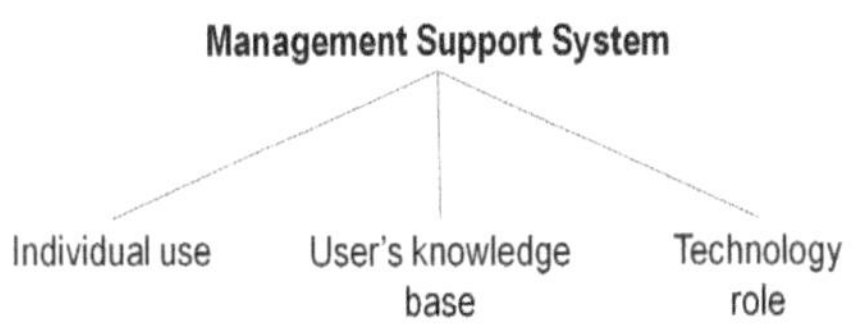

Figure 3: The three basic elements of a Business Intelligence System as a Management Support Systems

A relevant aspect is the individual use of the system linked in turn to the various *decision-making* needs.

A BIS also aims at improving the individual performance level. These systems aid users in managing huge amount of data to make decisions regarding the activities of the organization [28]. Even though these systems imply the use and analysis of the information aiming at improving the organizational action and *decision-making* processes [29], these are activated by the individuals, irrespective of the decisional, departmental or directional context [26]. BISs are implemented for analysis purposes to meet a variety of decisional needs [30, 19]. Clark et *al.* [26] consider the aspect linked to the "*user's knowledge base*", which is intended as "the experience and learning acquired with the operativeness supported thanks to the use of the BIS" [31]. This knowledge therefore consists of what the user knows as well as of the help that the system provides to him regarding its use [32].

One of the main functions of a BIS in fact is to provide a *system-based* guide aiming at supporting a better formulation of the problem and better solutions [33].

Recent developments within BISs are relative to sophisticated guided analysis functions (*guided analytics*). These ease users in the analysis of the data and in obtaining information. The ability of the user in making a decision is eased. In this respect it is fair to say that a Business Intelligence system contributes to increase the user's knowledge base [26].

A *knowledge base* constitutes the whole of the action/result relationships and is linked to the organizational learning [34-35], which is intended as the aggregation of individual learning acquired over time [34] and is related to the process of making better decisions through increased knowledge and comprehension of the phenomena.

In fact, it is possible to make better decisions using the existing competences as well as developing the ability to absorb and use new knowledge [36-37]. Using a BIS, each individual may make better decisions while the organizational learning process develops as the knowledge acquired by the individuals are shared, evaluated and integrated for the purpose of making decisions concerning the organization and its processes. The competences of individuals and organizations are therefore even more enhanced when the users are able to use and contextualize the support provided by the BISs in their organizational context and then reintegrate it in the BIS [26].

This is especially relevant regarding those systems designed to support the *decision-making* process at a managerial level and consequently the actions undertaken.

Choosing the most appropriate actions is not just the result of the use of the existing knowledge but also of the absorption and use of new knowledge [36-37].

A BIS may constitute the base and the support for this type of improvement [38-39].

The learning on the part of the individuals using a BIS allows to make better decisions. The organizational process of learning development resulting from this is shared, evaluated and integrated in view of the operativeness of the entire organization. In the light of the above it is fair to say that a BIS enables organizations to generate knowledge regarding their contexts, through the creation and extraction of the underlying knowledge bases [40]. The substantial part of this knowledge comes from the knowledge of the single users [40-41]. Individuals (*knowledgeable individuals*) have the information as well as the ability to integrate and structure the information within the context of their experience, competence and judgment [41]. Through the use of the system, this translates into an increase of their knowledge base [26]. Despite the effectiveness of a BIS – i.e., the ability to provide an effective support to decision-making processes – depends on many factors [42-45] technology continues to constitute a critical component [46, 47]. Special emphasis is placed on the need for an organization to be able to identify the right technological component as a prerequisite for the development of a BIS [48-50]. A careful choice of this component determines its success and acceptance by the users [51].

The Proposed Analysis Model

In the light of all the above considerations, in this paper a hypothetical model is proposed to evaluate the relationship between Business Intelligence systems, uncertainty inherent in the decisional processes and the effectiveness of coordination mechanisms. The model is based on the following hypotheses. As stated earlier, according to the IPV model proposed by Galbraith [1-2], the uncertainty inherent in *decision-making* processes depends on the information requirements, i.e., on the difference between the information theoretically necessary to make a decision in an optimal way and the information that is actually available.

Reduced uncertainty can translate into a reduced amount of necessary information (this implies simplified *decision-making* activities) or in increased amount of information available and improved ability to manage such information (this implies a better management of complex activities).

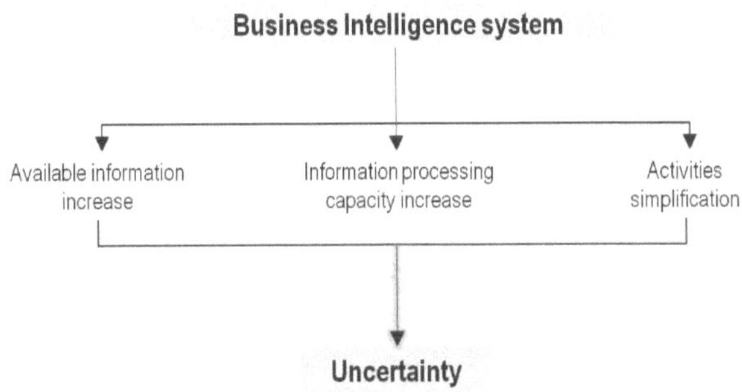

Figure 4: Business Intelligence System and uncertainty

A contribution to reduce uncertainty may be given by the information systems [1, 2]. More specifically Business Intelligence Systems, thanks to the largely described peculiarities may facilitate (Fig. 4):

- The increase of available information
- Increased ability to process such information
- Simplification of *decision-making* activities

Proposition 1: *BIS may increase the amount of available information*
A BI system usually relies upon a database that contains information coming from various sources of the organization, such as, ERP (Enterprise Resource Planning) systems, CRM (Customer Relationship Management) systems and Customer Service systems. Due to appropriate data extraction and transformation procedures using ETL (Extraction, Transformation and Loading) tools, the information contained in a BI environment would be valid from a qualitative standpoint – i.e., clear and univocally interpretable – and always updated. This is guaranteed by the technological performance of the system in terms of secure access to data, continuity of service, quick access time and even ability to adapt/satisfy future needs for data. In making available to the members of an organization the information necessary to carry out their activities, a BI system would guarantee a type of information transmission. This access to the information would enable the possibility to overcome the information fragmentation which existed prior to the BIS.

Data usability is facilitated thanks to the fact that users can use easily the system as its complexity is hidden from them and operates in a autonomous way.

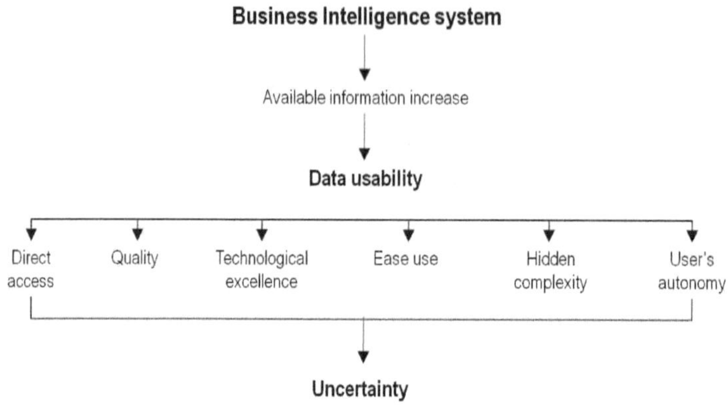

Figure 5: Available information and data usability

Proposition 2: *BIS may increase information processing capacity*
Information processing capacity could be associated to BIS features in facilitating transformation data into knowledge (Fig. 6). Multiple analysis tools are available to the user who can interactively navigate through the data, make analysis at his discretion and therefore enhance creativity. Effective information processing may be fostered and the organization members may improve the decision-making process as they reduce the time to make a decision and create conditions of increased certainty.

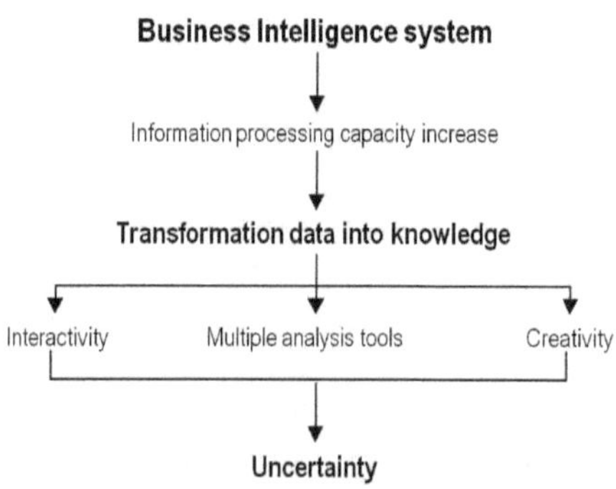

Figure 6: Information processing capacity and transformation of data in knowledge

Proposition 3: *BIS could reduce activities complexity (simplification of activities).*
Knowledge sharing and exchange could affect a reduction of activities complexity (Fig. 7). In addition to performing an informational function, BIS would promote communication among various positions and organizational units and, simultaneously, would become an environment that promotes stronger cooperation and exchange of knowledge, and in which individuals are motivated to share their knowledge and learn new information. In this sense, BIS would improve either the coordination of units with dependencies in terms of information flows, or the

coordination of units linked to one another by knowledge dependencies. Moreover, BIS may help control business process complexity, due to its variety and variability, facilitating coordination mechanisms like standardization of processes, standardization of capabilities and mutual adjustment.

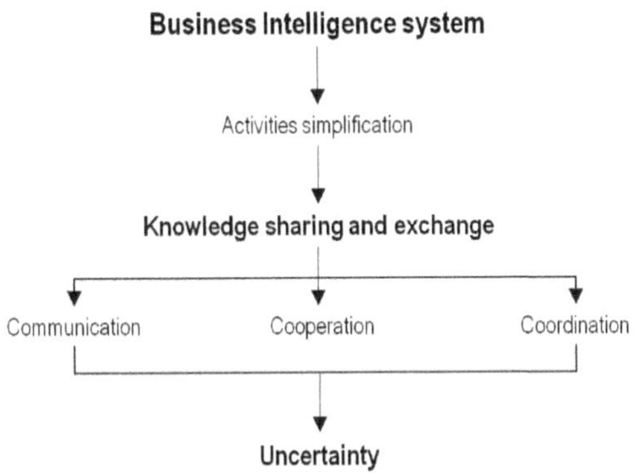

Figure 7: Complexity of activities and knowledge sharing and exchange

In the light of the above considerations, it is fair to say that a BI system (Fig. 8) contributes to making coordination more effective since it enables the decisional and collaboration processes[2].

Enabling of decisional processes practically translates in:

- Decisional decentralization and reduced centralization of information power
- Improved support to decision-making

Collaboration processes are enabled through:

- Improved internal communication and collaboration
- Greater exchange and sharing of knowledge.

---

[2] In this paper coordination is defined using the definition proposed by Malone and Crowston: "*Coordination is managing dependencies between activities*" which equals to say "coordination consists of managing the dependencies that exist among activities". This kind of management also relates to the concept of collaboration intended in a broad sense as the common work of several players within a given enterprise. Collaboration therefore may be interpreted as a different form of coordination [52].

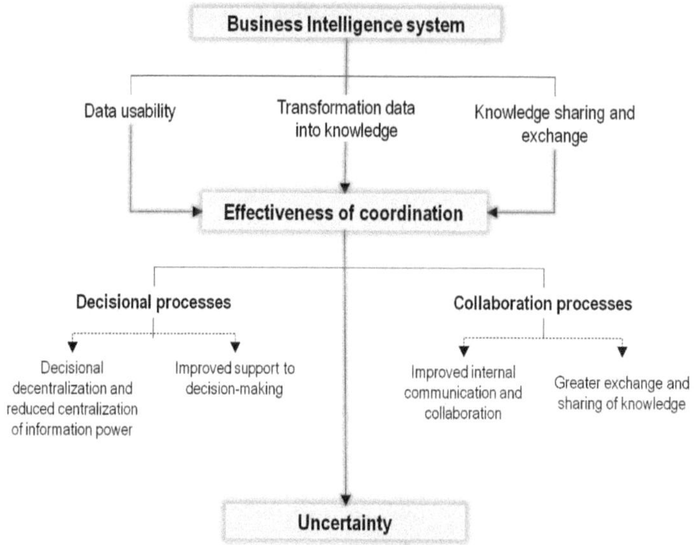

Figure 8: Potential effects of a Business Intelligence system on the effectiveness of coordination

Collaboration is a knowledge-based process and therefore is a process led by knowledge, that uses knowledge and provides a "rich" output of knowledge [53]. The ability to acquire, select, internalize and externalize knowledge are extremely important [54-55].

This is enabled by *computer-based* systems [56]. Therefore BI systems, as systems based on the use of a computer, should strengthen these abilities. In the exchange and diffusion of knowledge, coordination plays a critical role. As previously stated, many authors have dealt with this aspect, especially Nonaka and Takeuchi [57]. These authors have formulated a theory on the organizational knowledge and on the methods for its generation and sharing within the organization, since they consider it a resource of critical importance in the innovation processes of the enterprises. A real collaboration between the organizational players allows each of them to offer their contribution of knowledge, thus strengthen the ability of the entire organization to start a renovation process [58]. The improvement of coordination mechanisms in terms of effectiveness produces positive effects on the uncertainty, reducing it.

Conclusions

An empirical study will be conducted to verify the propositions of this analysis proposal.

The sample of enterprises would be selected on the following basis:

- Organizational structure (hierarchy, interdependences, coordination mechanisms, skills and competencies)
- Size (number of employees, as potential users of the BIS)
- Industry (complexity of activities, dynamics of the external environment)
- BIS pervasiveness, utilization methods and period of adoption.

It would also be critical to include variables concerning the attitude and behaviour of users since they always play a critical role in the success of a ICT-based system, such as Business Intelligence systems.

References

1. Galbraith, J. (1973. *Designing Complex Organizations*. Addison-Wesley, MA.
2. Galbraith, J. (1977). *Organizational Design*, Addison-Wesley. MA.
3. Tushman, M. L., and Nadler, D.A. (1978) Information Processing as an Integrating Concept in Organizational Design. *The Academy of Management Review*, 3(3), 613-624.
4. Choo, C. W.(1991) Towards an Information Model of Organizations. *The Canadian Journal of Information Science* 16 (3), 32-62.
5. Thompson, J.D. (1967*) Organizations in Action*, McHraw-Hill. New York (trad. it. L'azione organizzativa. Isedi, Torino, 1988).
6. Zaltman, G., Duncan, R., and Holbek, J. (1973).*Innovation and Organizations*. Wiley, New York.
7. Duncan, R. (1972) Characteristics of Organizational Environments and Perceived Environmental Uncertainty. *Administrative Science Quarterly*, 17, 313-327.
8. March, J.G., and Simon, H.A. (1958) *Organizations*. Chichester, Wiley (trad. it. Teoria dell'organizzazione, Edizioni di Comunità, Milano,1979).
9. Costa, G., and Gubitta, P. (2004) *Organizzazione Aziendale. Mercati, gerarchie e convenzioni*. Milano, McGraw-Hill.
10. Ferrando, P. (1997) L'incertezza e l'ambiguità, in Nacamulli R.C.D., Costa G. (a cura di). *Manuale di Organizzazione Aziendale*. UTET, Milano.
11. Rullani, E. (1984) La teoria dell'impresa: soggetti, sistemi, evoluzioni in Rispoli M. *L'impresa industriale*. Bologna, Il Mulino.
12. Martinez, M. (2004) *Organizzazione, informazioni e tecnologie*. Il Mulino, Bologna.
13. Ghosthal, S., and Kim, S.K. (1986) Building Effective Intelligence Systems For Competitive Advantage. *Sloan Management Review*, 28(1), 49-58.
14. Gilad, B., and Gilad, T. (1986) SMR Forum: Business Intelligence – The Quiet Revolution. *Sloan Management Review*, 27(4), 53-61.
15. Power, D.J. (2003) A Brief History of Decision Support Systems, *DSSResource.com*, World Wide Web, http:// DSSResource.com/history/dsshistory.html, version 2.8, May 31.
16. Halliman, C. (2000) *Business Intelligence Using Smart Techniques*. Information Uncover, Houston.
17. Kalakota, R.,and Robinson, M. (2000) *e-Business 2.0 – Roadmap for Success*. Addison-Wesley, Boston.
18. Thomsen, E. (2003) BI's Promised Land. *Intelligent Enterprise*, 6(4), 21-25.
19. Arnott, D., and Pervan, G. (2005) A Critical Analysis of Decision Support Systems Research. *Journal of Information Technology*, 20(2), 67-87.
20. Kemper, H., and Baars, H. (2006) Business Intelligence und Competitive Intelligence – IT-basierte Managementunterstüzung und marktwettbewerbsorientierte Anwendungen, in: Kemper H., Heilmann H., Baars H. (2006). *Business & Competitive Intelligence*. Heidelberg.

21. Negas, S., Gray, P. (2003) Business Intelligence. *Proceedings of the Ninth American Conference on Information Systems*. Tampa, Florida.
22. Eckerson, W.W. (2006) *Performance Dashboards*. John Wiley & Sons, Hoboken, NJ.
23. Davenport, T.D. (2006) Competing on Analytics. *Harward Business Review*. August.
24. Salonen, J.,and Pirttimaki, V. (2005) Outsourcing a Business Intelligence Function. *Frontiers of e-business research.*
25. Moss, L.T., and Atre, S. (2003).*Business Intelligence Roadmap: The Complete Project Lifecycle for Decision-Support Applications*. Addison-Wesley, Boston, MA.
26. Clark, D.T., Jones, M.C., and Armstrong, C.P. (2007) The dynamic structure of Management Support System: theory development, research focus, and direction. *MIS Quarterly*, 31(3), 579-615.
27. Scott Morton, M.S. (1984) *The State of the Art of Research. The Information Research Challenge*, Boston F.W., McFarlan (Ed). Harvard University Press, 13-41.
28. Watson, H.J., Fuller, C., and Ariyachandra, T. (2004). Data Warehouse Governance: Best Practices at Blue Cross and Blue Shield of North Carolina. *Decision Support Systems*, 38, 435-450.
29. Burton, B., Geishecker, L., Schelegel, K., Hostmann, K., Austin, B., Herschel, T., Soejarto, G., and Rayner A. (2006) *Business Focus Shifts from Tactical to Strategic*, Gartner Research, Stamford, CT, May 22. http://www.gartner.com.
30. Anderson-Lehaman, R., Watson, H.J., Wixom, B.H., and Hoffer, J.A. (2004) Continental Airlines Flies With Real-Time Business Intelligence. *MIS Quaterly Executive,*. 3(4), 163-176.
31. Hult, G.T.M. (2003) An Integration of Thoughts on Knowledge Management. *Decision Sciences*,24(2)
32. Sprague, R.H. Jr.,and Carlson, E.D. (1982) *Building Effective Decision Support Systems*. Englewood Cliffs, NJ, Prentice-Hall.
33. Barkhi, R., Rolland, E., Butler, J., and Fan, W. (2005) Decision Support Systems Induced Guidance for Model Formulation and Solution. *Decision Support Systems*, 40(2) 269-281.
34. Duncan, R., and Weiss, A. (1979) *Organizational Learning: Implications for Organizational Design*. Research in Organizational Behavior. Greenwich, B.M. Staw (Ed), JAI Press Inc. CT, 75-123.
35. Shrivastava, P.A. (1983) Typology of organizational learning systems. *Journal of Management Studies*, 20
36. March, J. G. (1991),. Exploration and Exploitation in Organizational Learning. *Organization Science*. 2(1), 71-87.
37. Stein, E.W., and Vandenbosch, B. (1996) Organizational Learning During Advanced Systems Development: Opportunities and Obstacles. *Journal of Management Information Systems*, 13(2), 115-136.
38. Kankanhalli, A., Tan, B.C.Y., and Wei, K.K. (2005) Contributing Knowledge to Electronic Knowledge Repositories: An Empirical Investigation. *MIS Quartely*, 29(1), 113-143.
39. Sharda, R., and Steiger, D.M. (1996) Inductive Model Analysis Systems: Enhancing Model Analysis in Decision Support Systems. *Information Systems Research*, 7(3), 328-341.
40. Gold, A.H., Malhotra, A., and Segars, A.H. (2001) Knowledge Management: An Organizational Capabilities Perspective. *Journal of Management Information Systems*, 18(1), 185-214.
41. Grover, V., and Davenport, T.D. (2001) General Perspectives on Knowledge Management: Fostering a Research Agenda. *Journal of Management Information Systems*, 18(1) 5-21.
42. Cooper, B., Watson, H.J., Wixom, B.H., and Goodhue, D.L. (2000) Data Warehousing Supports Corporate Strategy at First American Corporation. *MIS Quarterly*, 24(4), 547-567.

43. Massey, A.P., Montoya-Weiss, M.M., and O'Driscoll, T.M. (2002) Knowledge Management in Pursuit of Performance: Insights from Nortel Networks. *MIS Quartely*, 26(3), 269-289.
44. Scott, J., Globe, A.,and Schiffer, K. (2004). Jungles and Gardens: The Evolution of Knowledge Management at J. D. Edwards. *MIS Quarterly Executive*, 3(1), 37-52.
45. Wixom, B.H.,and Watson, H.J. (2001) An Empirical Investigation of the Factors Affecting Data Warehousing Success. *MIS Quarterly*, 25(1), 17-41.
46. Hinshaw, F. (2004) Data Warehouse Appliances Driving the Business Intelligence Revolution. *DM Review*, September, 30-34.
47. Rouibah, K.,and Ould-ali, S. (2002) PUZZLE: A Concept and Prototype for Linking Business Intelligence to Business Strategy. *Journal of Strategic Information Systems*, 11, 133-152.
48. Malhotra, A., Gosain, S.,and El Sawy, O.A. (2002) Absorptive Capacity Configurations in Supply Chains: Gearing for Partner-Enabled Market Knowledge Creation. *MIS Quarterly,*. 8(1), 145-187.
49. Zahra, S.A., and George, G. (2002) Absorptive Capacity: A Review, Reconceptualization, and Extension. *Academy of Management Review*, 27(2), 185-203.
50. Cohen, W., and Levinthal, D. (1990) Absorptive Capacity: A New Perspective on Learning and Innovation. *Administrative Science,* 35, 128-152.
51. Poon, P., and Wagner, C. (2001) Critical Success Factors Revisited: Success and Failure Cases of Information System for Senior Executives. *Decision Support Systems,* 30(4), 392-418.
52. Malone, T.W.,and Crowston, K. (1994) The Interdisciplinary Study of Coordination. *ACM Computing Surveys*, 26(1), 87-119.
53. Simonin, B.L. (1997) The importance of collaborative know-how: An empirical test of the learning organization. *Academy of Management Journal.* 40(5), 1150-1174.
54. Holsapple, C.W., and Joshi, K.D. (2002).Knowledge manipulation activities: Results of a Delphi study. *Information and Management*, 39(6), 477-490.
55. Hartono, E., and Holsapple, C. (2004) Theoretical foundations for collaborative commerce research and practice. *Information Systems and e-business Management*, 2, 1-30.
56. Tsui, E. (2003). Tracking the role and evolution of commercial knowledge management software. *Handbook on Knowledge Management*, 2, 5-27.
57. Nonaka, I., and Takeuchi, H. (1995) *The Knowledge-Creating Company: How Japanese Companies Create the Dynamics of Innovation*. Oxford University Press, New York.
58. Hoegl, M., Weinkauf, K., and Gemuenden, H.G. (2004) Inter-team Coordination, Project Commitment, and Teamwork in Multi-team R&D Projects: A Longitudinal Study. *Organization Science*, 1, 38-55.

A Study of E-services Adoption Factors

Ada Scupola[1], Hanne Westh Nicolajsen[2]

Abstract In this chapter we combine two subjects that are in our heart: e-services and diffusion of innovation. By drawing on earlier research on e-services, innovation, and technology adoption we investigate the factors that influence adoption of e-services in a specific academic library, Roskilde University Library (RUB). The conclusion of this research is that both external environmental factors and internal organizational factors are important factors in adoption of e-services at Roskilde University Library. However the study shows that external factors such as government intervention and technological development might have been having a more important role than other external factors and that top management might have more influence on radical e-services adoption than other factors in the organizational context.

Introduction

The academic *libraries* are facing numerous challenges mainly due to the advent of Internet and Web 2.0. As the academic libraries are going through a process of virtualization there is the need to redefine their role in the digital and physical environment. In order to do this, libraries need to leverage their strengths and innovate to create responsive and convenient services [1]. Brindley[2]suggests that in order for libraries to reposition themselves, they have among others to keep close to the library customers as well as invest more in innovation and digital activities. Central to this repositioning is investing into and adopting e-services. It becomes therefore important to look at the factors that influence the adoption of e-service in the research library. The research question addressed in this chapter is the following: Which factors influence the adoption of e-services in research libraries? To investigate the research question we draw on earlier research on e-services, innovation, and technology adoption and conduct a case study in a specific research library in Denmark. The chapter is structured as follows. The introduction presents the background and research question. The second section presents an in depth overview of e-service definitions and concepts. The third section provides the theoretical background, while the following section introduces the research method. The last two sections present the analysis and results as well as conclusions and limitations.

[1] Roskilde University ada@ruc.dk
[2] Ålborg University

E-Services: Definitions and Characteristics

Before going in depth with our study, we believe that it is important to explain and understand the concept of e-services, which is the object of the study in this chapter. There are many definitions of e-services [e.g. 3-4]. Some focus on the delivery and delivery infrastructure (digital networks) while others emphasize both the delivery process and the benefits or outcome of the service [5]. For example Scupola[3] states that, "*E-services are defined as services that are produced, provided and/or consumed through the use of ICT-networks such as Internet-based systems and mobile solutions [3]*". Rowley [6] defines e-services as "*deeds, efforts or performance whose delivery is mediated by information technology (including Web, information kiosks and mobile devices). Such e-service includes the service element of e-tailing, customer support and service, and service delivery.*" Furthermore, as illustrated and summarized in Table 1, some definitions emphasize the outcome and the benefits of e-services in addition to the delivery mode and delivery infrastructure of e-services [5]. However, what is in common to all these definitions is that e-services are characterized by the electronic delivery of the service (See Table 1).

Table 1: A summary of e-services definitions (Source: Scupola et al. [4])

Delivery and infrastructure view	Production, delivery and outcome view
Those services that can be delivered electronically [7]	Any asset that is made available via the Internet to drive revenue streams or create new efficiencies [8]
Provision of services over electronic networks [9-10]	An act or performance that creates and provides benefits for customers through a process that is stored as an algorithm and typically implemented by networked software [5]
Interactive services that are delivered on the Internet using advanced telecommunications, information, and multimedia technologies [11]	E-services as Internet-based applications that fulfill service needs by seamlessly bringing together distributed, specialized resources to enable complex (often real-time) transactions [12]
E-service is deeds, efforts or performance whose delivery is mediated by information technology (including Web, information kiosks and mobile devices). Such e-service includes the service element of e-tailing, customer support and service, and service delivery [6]	E-services are defined as services that are produced, provided and/or consumed through the use of ICT-networks such as Internet-based systems and mobile solutions [3]

Characteristics of e-Services

According to Scupola et al [4] there are a number of characteristics that distinguish goods from services, services from e-services as well as goods from e-services (see Table 2). Scupola et al [4] for example state that services are delivered by their immediate producers and are not anonymous in contrast to goods, which can be separated from the immediate producers and sold on an anonymous market. Therefore consumers will know who the immediate producers are (or will at least have the possibility to do so).

Table 2: Distinguishing features of goods, e-services and services

Goods	E-services	Services
Tangible	Intangible, but need tangible media	Intangible
Can be inventoried	Can be inventoried	Cannot be inventoried
Separable consumption	Separable consumption	Inseparable consumption
Can be patented	Can be copyrighted, patented	Cannot be patented
Homogeneous	Homogeneous	Heterogeneous
Easy to price	Hard to price	Hard to price
Can't be copied	Can be copied	Can't be copied
Can be shared	Can be shared	Can't be shared
Use equals consumption	Use does not equal consumption	Use equals consumption
Based on atoms	Based on bits	Based on atoms

Source: Charles F. Hofacker et al. [5]

Services are generally produced and consumed simultaneously and, therefore, require face-to-face contact between the producers and the consumers in the production/ consumption phase [9]. According to Scupola et al. [4] information and communication technologies (ICTs) affect all kinds of goods and services with respect to their transaction on the market (e-business). For example in the case of data, information and knowledge services (informational services such as newspapers, academic journals, books, etc.), it is the product itself, which is affected and transformed into e-services.

In addition Hofacker et al. [5]identify three prototypes of e-service:

(1) E-services as complements to existing offline services and goods. Examples can be online seat reservations offered by airlines and travel agencies
(2) E-services as substitutes for existing offline services. Examples can be e-newspapers or electronic versions of academic journals.
(3) Uniquely new core e-services such as online computer games.

Much of the theoretical literature on e-services focuses mainly on e-services that are substitutes or complements to offline goods or services. However, there are many studies investigating e-services that do not have an immediate commercial return, but are offered for example by government agencies or are e-services provided and co-produced by users such as wikis. Therefore, by taking a broad approach to e-services Scupola et al. [4] distinguish the following 4 main groups of e-services summarised in Table 3:

- Business-to-business (B-to-B): these play an important role in the trend towards supply chain integration and coordination as for example in the case of outsourced printing services and facilities.
- Business-to-consumer (B-to-C): these are mostly commercial e-services as for example e-banking [e.g. 13], e-newspapers and some types of portals.
- Government-to-business (G-to-B) or to consumer (G-to-C): these e-services are not commercial in nature and examples can be social security services provided online to remote areas, telemedicine or e-libraries.
- Consumer-to-consumer (C-to-C): this includes most of the literature on virtual worlds and online communities as for example wikis and online dating.

Table 3: A summary of E-service characteristics: (Source: Scupola et al. [4])

Types of e-services	B-to-B	B-to-C	G-to-B and G-to-C	C-to-C
Characteristics/ focus	Collaboration and relationship building	Selling to and retaining the customer	User/citizen empowerment, e-democracy, city/rural areas divide	Peer-to-peer value creation
Examples	Supply chain management in outsourced printing services and facilities, SaaS	E-retailing, e-customer relationship management, e-banking, e-newspapers, Web portals	Online tax returns, e-voting, e-libraries, telemedicine, remote social security services	Online auctions, consumer driven e-marketplaces, online gaming, online communities (newsgroups). Wikis

Theoretical Background

Having explained the concept of e-services as it is conceived in this paper, we present here our theoretical background. Rogers [14, p. 392] defines the innovation process in an organization as consisting of two broad activities: the initiation and the implementation stage. Each activity is then subdivided in a number of stages. Innovation adoption is determined by a number of factors and the role that these factors play might be different in the different stages of the innovation process [15]. According to Tornatsky and Fleischer [16] such factors can be distinguished into external to the organization, internal to the organization or related to the technology itself. By following Tornatsky and Fleischer [16], in this paper we distinguish the factors that influence e-services adoption mainly according to two categories: internal organizational factors and external environmental factors and thus propose the following model of e-services adoption factors in Fig 1:

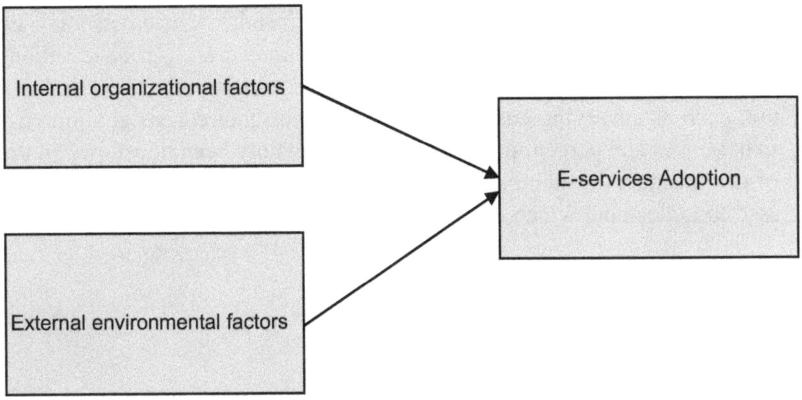

Figure 1: A model of factors influencing e-services adoption

Internal Organizational Factors

Earlier and recent innovation literature has focused on the organizational factors influencing innovation development and adoption [e.g. 14;16]. For example, much has been written about the important role of top management and employee involvement in the innovation process and innovation adoption [e.g. 16-17]. A number of studies emphasize the importance of the organisation and their employees in playing an active role for motivating users and converting user input to usable innovations [18-21]. Top management, through their beliefs and visions can offer guidelines to managers and employees about the opportunities and risks in developing or adopting technological innovations [22-23]. For example, in firms where top managers believe that e-services offer a strategic opportunity, their beliefs might serve as powerful signals to the rest of the firm's employees about the importance placed on e-services adoption and development. Innovation champions have also a key role in the innovation process. This is especially true for innovations that are costly, visible or radical [14].

External Environmental Factors

There are several factors belonging to the external environment that are influencing the adoption of e-services in academic libraries. The most important ones are technology development, technological trends from other industries, competitors, suppliers as well as the users/customers and their changing habits [e.g. 24-25]. For example Scupola and Nicolajsen [24] show how the competitor libraries have influenced the development and adoption of e-services at Roskilde University Library (RUB). Alam and Perry [26] also argue that customers may contribute with ideas by stating their needs, problems or solutions. They may also help in screening ideas by responding to concepts or alternative solutions with their thinking, dislikes, preferences etc. In order to contribute these insights, customers may be involved through face-to-face meetings, user visits or meetings, user observations [27] or click stream analysis [28]. Nambisan et al [29] further argues for indirect information such as surveying customer forums to gain indirect insights on customers' experiences and perceptions. While this has mainly been developed in the context of new product development (NDP), we argue here that such insights can also be used to understand which e-services to adopt or not in the research library context.

Research Method

The data used in this study are part of a larger case study [30]investigating innovation at Roskilde University Library that has been lasting over the last three years (e.g. Scupola and Nicolajsen[24,25]). The data consists of primary data collected through three years collaboration between the library and the authors and secondary data. The data collection includes qualitative explorative and semi-structured interviews, several meetings, workshops and presentations between the research team and the library employees and management as well as secondary data such as reports and other material on e-services adoption and development provided by the library personnel. This chapter is based on a small part of the collected data.

E-Services at Roskilde University Library (RUB)

Over the last few years RUB has gone through a digitalization process that has transformed many of the services offered as well as many of the articles and books collection into e-services. The e-services developed at RUB mainly take the form of substitutes of existing goods or services in line with Hofacker et al. [5] and can be classified as Government to business (G-to-B) or Government-to-consumer (G-to-C) e-services according to Scupola et al. [4]. E-services offered at RUB include access to electronic journals, access to electronic books, digital repository of the student projects, chat with a librarian, or a web-based system for the online registration of research and other activities of the faculty.

Analysis and Results

Internal Organizational Environment: Top Management and Employees

Similarly to general service innovations also in e-service adoption at RUB we found that the most important internal organizational factors are top management and core employees. Top management has an important role in the initiation stage especially by establishing the vision and setting the agenda for e-services adoption. As a top manager states:

> "Yes, in the big lines, what is under vision, that is top management. But there are a lot of other (ideas) that can come from the employees" (Top Manager, RUB)

A major source of inspiration and vision for top management is participation to international meetings, looking at competitors and, to a less extent, the customers. For example being in front of other competitors is a major drive for innovation and e-services adoption at RUB as the following statement shows:

> "You want to be a little bit better than your neighbour library" (Top Manager, RUB)

Employees also come up with many ideas about which e-services to adopt. The ideas can be solicited by top management or can come in a spontaneous way. In the latter case they are sent to the coordination board which meets every two weeks and has the purpose of screening all the suggestions and requests from the library employees and make a decision about what to do about them. Here top management can formally approve the adoption of the ideas or may decide that they are not worth to be pursued as the following shows:

> "... A new initiative or ending an initiative is put forward by a leader of a functional area to the coordination board. " (Leading librarian, RUB)

Some e-services innovations especially when pursued within the given frames (e.g. resource constraints) can be developed and adopted by employees without any further involvement of the management resulting in adoption of small and local solutions. However when further resources are needed or when the e-services are more profoundly changed the acceptance and support of management is required. This often implies a dialogue between top management and employees, the solution being to find a compromise.

Many of the new e-services being adopted are based on the appearance on the market of new technology of different kind. As a consequence the library needs to update the personnel IT competencies as a librarian states:

> "... We need bigger and more IT competencies... " (Leading librarian, RUB)

This is however not always an easy task as often when a decision to adopt new e-services is taken, there might be resistance among the employees due to the consequences that this decision might have for their ways of working.

External Environment: Government, Competitors, Technological Developments and Customers

We found 4 main factors belonging to the external environment that influence e-services adoption at RUB: government, competitors, technological development and users. The government has had a major influence on adoption and development of e-services through the policy program "IT Society for all" where the basis for the Danish information society were laid out. This program has affected many sectors in Denmark including the library sector and has laid the foundation for the library digitalization process. This government intervention has taken many forms including state support for the e-services development and adoption as well as enforcing collaboration between competitor libraries as for example the following statement shows:

> "The idea to chat has come from the DEFF project all together with the "library guard. "The library guard" is such a service where you chat and send emails. It was a project with the public libraries." (IT manager, RUB)

The technological development, also the one that is taking place in other industries and not only related to the library sector, is also affecting the development and adoption of e-services at RUB. For example one of the newer ideas of the management group is to develop a new e-service to allow customers to make reviews of books, articles, etc. This idea is inspired by the use of user forums in other industries such as Amazon.com who allows users to rate books and provides information on similar readings or the travel industry where customers rate for example hotels to inform other travellers as the following statement shows:

> "…We all know that when we book hotels then at the hotel web site there is a place where you may give stars and see stars given. Then we think can we turn this around and make something that makes sense in our world." (IT manager, RUB)"

Another example is provided by the chat function that RUB is using to communicate with the customers.

Our findings also show that customers are a factor in e-services adoption, but only to a limited extent and indirectly. In fact, the library can use the log data generated by the users during their use of e-services to make decisions regarding the adoption or non adoption of e-services. These log data can be used for example to run usage statistics of the e-services as the following statement shows:

> "... We make statistics on it, we try to see how many requests where there and what was the content…" (IT Manager, RUB)

Finally the IT manager states that making e-services in test-phase visible to the customers contributes both to get user feedback to improve the e-services and to test whether the e-service is of interest to the customer, thus providing useful information to the library regarding whether they should adopt the e-service on a permanent basis or not as the following statement shows:

> "We write to them (users) that we would like to get their feedback, then we get feedback that it is great and that we should make it more visible" (IT manager, RUB)

Discussion and Conclusions

This study is an exploratory study of factors that affect e-services adoption in research libraries. By drawing on data collected during a case study focusing on innovation practices at Roskilde University library, the study shows that there are two main groups of factors influencing e-services adoption at Roskilde University Library: the first group of factors belonging to the internal organizational environment, the second to the external environment. Within the internal organizational environment, top management and employees both have a role. Top management has the formal responsibility to approve the adoption of more radical e-services innovations while adoption of smaller changes can be done at employees and middle management level, without the approval of top management. This is especially the case when no extra resources are needed to adopt for example a slightly different version of an already existing e-service.

Within the external environment the major factors are the government and technological development. In fact, the Danish government has been the prime motor behind the digitalization process of the library e-services, which has been made possible also and especially due to the technological development in the fields of telecommunication and ICT. Competitors and library users are also important factors, however their influence is secondary to technological development and government influence. In fact, it has mainly been the government that through the Deff project has enforced some kind of "competitive" collaboration among the research libraries. Customers have had a more indirect role on the e-services adoption decision. Their e-services usage patterns and feedback provide information to the employees and to the top management on their needs and to what extent they as final users are interested to adopt an e-service or not.

The conclusion of this research is that both external environmental factors and internal organizational factors are important factors in adoption of e-services in research libraries. In the specific case of RUB, however, it might be concluded that external factors such as government intervention and technological development might have been having a more important role than other external factors and that top management might have more influence on radical e-services adoption than employees and middle management in the organizational context.

Finally, while this study provides some insights into e-services adoption factors, it also presents a number of limitations. For example the use of only one case study limits the generalization of the results. In addition the literature review could be expanded, a research model could be constructed and more formally tested in the case study. Finally, a quantitative survey of all the Danish academic libraries could be conducted to see if these preliminary results could be generalized also to other libraries.

References

1. Li, X. (2006) *Library* as incubating space for *innovations*: practices, trends and skill sets. *Library Management,* Bradford, 27(6-7), 370-378.
2. *Brindley*, L. (2006) Re-defining the library. *Library Hi Tech*, Bradford, 24(4), 484.
3. Scupola, A. (2008) E-Services: Definition, Characteristics and Taxonomy: Guest Editorial Preface, Special Issue on E-Services, *Journal of Electronic Commerce in Organization*, 6(2).
4. Scupola, A., Henten, A., Nicolajsen, H. (2009) E-services: Characteristics, Scope and Conceptual Strengths. *International Journal of E-Services and Mobile Applications*, 1(3).
5. Hofacker,C.F.,Goldsmith,R.E.,Bridges,E. and Swilley, E. (2007) E-Services: A Synthesis and Research Agenda. *Journal of Value Chain Management.*
6. Rowley, J. (2006) An analysis of the e-service literature: towards a research agenda. *Internet research* 16(3) , 339-359.
7. Javalgi, R. G., Martin, C. L., and Todd, P.R. (2004) The Export of E-Services in the Age of Technology Transformation: Challenges and Implications for International Service Providers. *Journal of Services Marketing*, 18 (7), 560-573.
8. Piccinelli, G., and Stammers, E. (2001) *From e-processes to e-networks: an e-service-oriented approach.* http://www.research.ibm.com/people/b/bth/OOWS2001/piccinelli.pdf
9. Rust, R. (2001) The rise of E-services. Editorial. *Journal of service research*, 3(1).
10. Rust, R. andKannan , P.K.(2003) E-service: a new *paradigm for business in t*he electronic environment. *Communnications of the ACM* ,46(6).
11. Boyer, K. Hallowell, R. and Roth, A.V. (2002).E-*services: operating strate*gy—a case study and a method f*or analyzing operational* benefits. *Journal of Operations Management*, 20(2).
12. Tiwana, A., and Balasubramaniam, R. (2001) E-services, problems, opportunities, and digital pla*tforms. 34th Hawaii International Conference on System Sciences. March 2001.*
13. ElissarToufaily, E., Daghfous N., and Toffoli, R., (2009), The adoption of "E-banking" by Lebanese banks: Succe*ss and critical factors, International Journal of E-Se*rvices and Mobile Applications, 1(1).
14. Rogers, E.M. (1995) *The Diffusion of Innovations*. 4th edition. Free Press, New York.
15. Zaltman,G., Duncan, R., and Holbeck, J. (1973) *Innovations and Organizations*, New York: Wiley and Sons.
16. Tornatzky, L. G.,and Fleischer, M. (1990) *The Processes of Technological Innovation*, Lexington Books
17. Jeyaraj, A., Rottman, J. And Lacity, M.J (2006) A review of the predictors, linkages, and biases in IT innovation adoption research. *Journal of Information Technology*, 21(1), 1-23.
18. Jeppesen, L.B. and Molin, M. (2003). Consumers as Co-developers: Learning and Innovation Outside the Firm. *Technology Analysis & Strategic Management,* 15(3), 363–383.
19. Magnusson, P. (2003) Benefits of involving users in service. *European Journal of Innovation Management,* 6 (4).

20. Matthing, J., Sandén, B. and Edvardsson, B. (2004) New service development: learning from and with customers. *International Journal of Service Industry Management*, 15(5),479-498.
21. Nambisan, S. (2002). Designing virtual customer environments for new product development: Toward a theory. *The Academy of Management review*, 27(33), 392-413.
22. Gallivan, M, J. (2001) Organizational adoption and assimilation of complex technological innovations: Development and Application of a New Framework. *Database for Advances of Information Systems*, 32 (3), 51-86
23. Chatterjee, D., Grewal, R., Sambaburthy,V (2002) Shaping up for e-commerce: Institutional Enablers of the organizational assimilation of web technologies. *MIS Quaterly*, 26(2), 65-90.
24. Scupola, A., Nicolajsen, H.W. (2010a) Open Innovation in Research Libraries-Myth or Reality? in A. D'Atri, M. De Marco, A. M. Braccini, F. Cabiddu (eds.), *Management of the Interconnected World*, ISBN: 978-3-7908-2403-2 Springer Physica-Verlag Berlin Heidelberg 2010, forthcoming.
25. Scupola, A., Nicolajsen, H.W. (2010b) Service *Innovation In Academic Libraries: Is There a Place for the Customers?* Library Management, Emerald, Vol. 31, No. 4/5 2010.
26. Alam, I. and Perry, C. (2002). A customer-oriented new service development process. *Journal of Services Marketing*, 16 (6), 515-534.
27. Alam, I. (2002) An exploratory investigation of user involvement in new service development. *Journal of the Academy of Marketing Science*, 30(3), 250-261.
28. Nicolajsen, H.W., Scupola, A., and Sørensen, F. (2010) Open innovation using blog. *Proceedings of IRIS33 Seminar*, Ålborg, 20-24th of August 2010 (Forthcoming).
29. Nambisan, S. And Nambisan, P (2008) How to Profit From a Better¿ Virtual Customer Environment. *MIT Sloan Management Review*, 49(3),53-61.
30. Yin, R.K., (1994) *Case Study Research Design and Methods*, Second Edition, Vol. 5, Sage Publications

Environment and Governance for Network Management

Toshie Ninomiya[1], Nobuyuki Ichikawa[2], Yusho Ishikawa[3]

Abstract Social infrastructure facilities in Japan are ageing, and appropriate maintenance is necessary for them to remain usable. We have addressed this issue by making use of Information Communication Technology (ICT) in collaboration with specialists in the fields of ICT and social infrastructure. First, we outline the environment and governance of projects with regard to Network Size, Structural Holes, Tie Strength, Centrality, Trust, Norms and Shared Vision. Next, we describe a successful project undertaken within the above framework performed in collaboration with the University of Tokyo, Metropolitan Expressway Co. Ltd. (MEX), Tokyo Electric Power Company (TEPCO), Tokyo Metro Co. Ltd. (METRO), East Japan Railway Company (JR-EAST), Hitachi Ltd. and Nippon Telegraph and Telephone Corporation (NTT). Project planning and member selection were performed in accordance with policies related to the environment and activities were undertaken based on policies related to governance. First, we analyse ways to expand new networks in the preparation phase. Then, we present the outcomes of the project with related environment and governance policies. Governance policies were developed in the second phase. As our achievements attracted political attention from key players in important organisations, our project acquired new resources, such as leading persons/organisations and extra funding in the second year.

Introduction

Social infrastructure in Japan has undergone a great deal of development over the past 60 years associated with economic development. However, the social infrastructure facilities are ageing, and require appropriate maintenance to remain usable [1]. Due to the lack of both engineers and funding in this field [2], large-scale innovation is required for the development of maintenance technologies and efficient use of social infrastructure facilities. We addressed these issues using Information Communication Technology (ICT) in collaboration with specialists in the fields of ICT and social infrastructure, as innovation is likely to emerge from mixed technologies in the fields of civil engineering and ICT. As innovation is based on social capital [3], i.e., resources between social network members, the purpose and outcomes of this project should include the expansion of social capital. To develop innovative maintenance technologies and efficient use of social infra-

[1] University of Tokyo, Tokyo, Japan, ninomiya@iii.u-tokyo.ac.jp
[2] University of Tokyo, Tokyo, Japan, n.ichikawa@iii.u-tokyo.ac.jp
[3] University of Tokyo, Tokyo, Japan, ishikawa@iii.u-tokyo.ac.jp

structure facilities, we discuss the environment and governance of a project involving a network of civil engineers and ICT specialists.

Framework

There have been many empirical studies of the relationship between social capital and innovation. Zheng [4] developed a framework in which the relationship is classified into three dimensions, i.e., 1) the structural dimension, 2) the relational dimension and 3) the cognitive dimension, as defined by Nahapiet and Ghoshal [5]. This classification framework has already been used in many studies, and Zheng [4] identified six sub-constructs belonging to these three dimensions based on a search of the relevant literature:

1. Structural Dimension
2. The structural dimension has four sub-constructs, i.e., Network Size, Structural Holes, Tie Strength and Centrality.
3. Relational Dimension
4. The relational dimension has two sub-constructs, i.e., Trust and Norms.
5. Cognitive Dimension
6. The cognitive dimension has one sub-construct, i.e., Shared Vision.

However, it is possible that the relational and cognitive dimensions are in a dimension [6]. Especially, norms in the relational dimension, which refer to shared expectations, are close to shared vision in the cognitive dimension [7]. For planning purposes in our project, the relational and cognitive dimensions were combined into one, which we call "Governance". Similarly, we refer to the structural dimension in our project as "Environment". It is important to set appropriate Environment and Governance for project management, which requires expansion of social capital to achieve innovation. Taking inspiration from the framework presented above, the environment of a project should be considered according to four factors to ensure the project leads to innovation: Network Size, Structural Holes, Tie Strength and Centrality.

The governance of a project should instead take three factors into account to ensure the project leads to innovation: Trust, Norms and Shared Vision.

Environment

As Environment consideration for our project, we established policies for Network Size, Structural Holes, Tie Strength and Centrality.

Network size is considered according to the total number of contacts between actors in the network. Direct contacts result in product innovation [8][9], contacts between upper management and key knowledge workers lead to the creation of knowledge [10] and frequent contact between teams in the network leads to high performance [11]. Therefore, we have Network Size policies that mandate regular high quality meetings, such as once a month meetings with core researchers and engineers, steering committees four times a year and frequent meetings between stakeholders and members of the top management team. In addition, extra meetings have also been held as necessary.

Structural holes refer to unique ties to other actors in discussion about which it is emphasised, such as scarcity value and superiority with knowledge quality [12][13][14]. In contrast, Structural Holes are not significant when knowledge heterogeneity is considered [15][16][17]. Thus, human capital could be complementary to social capital [18]. In cases in which the project has insufficient Structural Holes, it is desirable to have the participation of individuals and organisations with appropriate knowledge and expertise. Our project has several mechanisms in place to facilitate participation by new members with required knowledge and skills. Therefore, our project involves specialists in various areas.

Tie strength is considered based on combinations of the amount of time, emotional intensity, intimacy, reciprocal service, etc. [12][19]. As communication among actors is beneficial [20], appropriate clear steps, schedules and roles of each actor have been set up to promote tie strengthening.

Centrality is considered as an actor's position in the network. Thus, a high degree of Centrality means a higher position and more importance [21]. Although researchers in central positions can innovate with sufficient knowledge and information in the network, peripheral researchers in the network require external ties for innovation [16]. Our project has a social and political support mechanism for external ties to foster innovation in peripheral areas, because one of our purposes is to expand social capital to achieve innovation. Such considerations are extremely important to ensure that the project proceeds smoothly.

Governance

As Governance for our project, we established policies for Trust, Norms and Shared Vision. These policies are under constant development throughout the project.

Trust is defined as an actor's belief that actions of other people and their results will be appropriate from the viewpoint of the actor [22]. Trust keeps transaction costs low, facilitates communication and knowledge sharing, and leads to successful negotiation and collaboration [23][24][25][26][27]. Therefore, our project charter includes fair rules and management methods, especially with regard to our aims and duty related to confidentiality. In addition, when joining our project, all participants should accept the agreement established by all members.

Norms are expectations regarding appropriate or inappropriate attitudes and behaviours [28]. To establish Norms, we organised workshops with core members and meetings between individual stakeholders and the top management team. Collected information in these meetings was shared among core members to facilitate understanding of Norms associated with the project. We have collaborated effectively with other stakeholders, and Norms have been firmly established for all actors with a Shared Vision within a period of less than 6 months.

Shared Vision is a common mental model of the future state among actors [29] with resources such as shared representations, interpretations and systems of meaning in the network [5]. To develop a common mental model of the future state, we used various methods to determine their interests, analyse relationships between stakeholders, etc. Initially, it takes some time to build a consensus, but the project can proceed at a rapid pace once a Shared Vision and Norms have been established.

Four factors of Environment and three factors of Governance are shown in Tables 1 with definitions. We compared the required project situation (post-situation; objective situation) to the previous project situation (pre-situation). In addition, Table 1 presents the physical policies implemented to achieve innovation.

Table 1: Factors of Environment and Governance

Dimension	Factor	Definition	Pre-situation	Post-situation	Project Policy
Environment	Network Size	Total number of contacts between actors in the network	Contact within an organisation; regular meetings	Contact among organisations; extra meetings held if needed	High quality regular meetings and extra meetings if needed
	Structural Holes	Unique ties to other actors	Fixed actors	Flexible participants as required	Various specialists for effective knowledge resources
	Tie Strength	Nature of relational contact	Common goal, vertical division of labour	Common awareness and goals, horizontal specialisation	Appropriate clear steps, schedule, and role of each actor
	Centrality	Actor's position in the network	Solid centrality by plan	Fluid centrality by actors' interactions	Mechanism of social and political backing

Dimension	Factor	Definition	Pre-situation	Post-situation	Project Policy
Governance	Trust	Belief that actions of another person and their results will be appropriate from the view of an actor	Maximum achievement of each project, steady enforcement, following rules	Maximum achievement of common goals, respect and friendly rival relationships	Fair rules and management methods: Aim and confidentiality agreement by all participants
	Norms	Expectations about appropriate or inappropriate attitudes and behaviours	Maximum benefit for individuals and organisations	Maximum benefit for long-term win-win relationships, autonomous work, contribution to others	Reciprocal understanding: Correct and shared information by workshops and meetings
	Shared Vision	Facilitates communication in a group, such as shared representations and codes	Formation based on vision and goal, agreement of each role	Shared awareness of issue, joint planning of vision and goal through facilitation	Consensus building: Analysis of stakeholders' interests and relationships

Case Study

We embarked on a five-year project to achieve innovation in the infrastructure field in April 2009 named the "Research Initiative for Advanced Infrastructure with ICT". The aims of this project are as follows: 1) to achieve sophisticated management of infrastructure facilities with ICT; 2) to create new business opportunities with innovation in infrastructure utilising ICT; and 3) to develop an intelligent platform for practical research with a wide range of knowledge and experience. In the first year, seven groups participated in the project—the University of Tokyo, Metropolitan Expressway Co. Ltd. (MEX), Tokyo Electric Power Company (TEPCO), Tokyo Metro Co. Ltd. (METRO), East Japan Railway Company (JR-EAST), Hitachi Ltd. and Nippon Telegraph and Telephone Corporation (NTT). Prior to commencing this project, it was necessary to create a network for the project. Actors within the network should have a common (shared) vision of the project. Unfortunately, insufficient data are available regarding the preparation phase of this project, so we analysed the preparation phase of a new field within this project as a case study of creating a new network (Figure 1). Then, the research phase of this project is described as another case study of running a project.

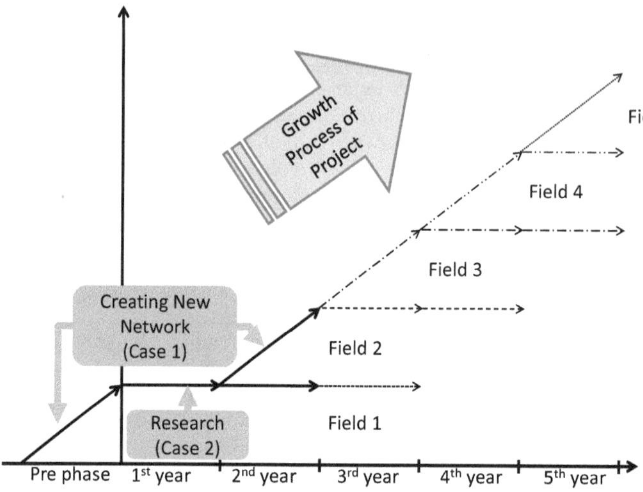

Figure 1: Project growth process

Case 1: Creating a New Network

In the project it was necessary to create a new network composed of various specialists, such as professors and practitioners of civil engineering, as well as executive officers in infrastructure, economics and communication, to expand the target fields of the project. The network should be of the appropriate size and must consist of appropriate actors with a common vision of the project before launch. Therefore, we examined how to expand a specialist network with new members from the viewpoint of network analysis in each event. The aims of this phase were to create a new specialist network and to put forward a proposal with the consensus of all actors. The points included in the analysis were as follows:

- Who should invite whom to the network?
- How should links be made between members?
- Over which links should information flow?

Sixty-three members—specialists from various organisations, such as universities, national ministries, local government agencies, foundations, corporations and others—participated in the network. The Network Size expanded gradually. Figure 2 shows the network through all events in the phase from 20 January to 3 June 2010. Circles indicate members, arrows indicate invitation to the network, dots indicate new links and lines indicate contact between members.

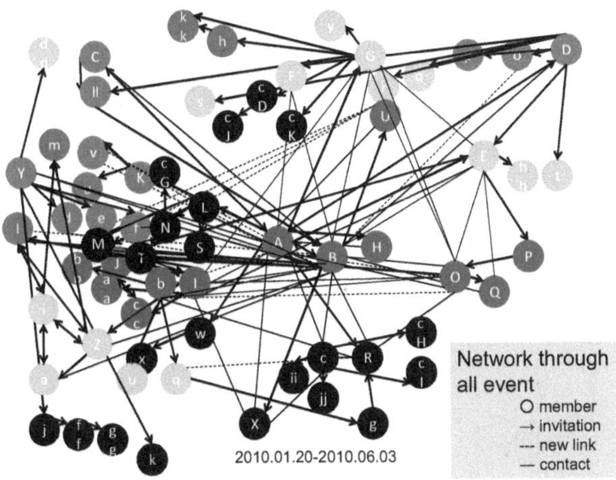

Figure 2: Network through all events

Who should invite whom to the network?
The Network Size expanded at each event due to member invitations. We analysed who invited whom to the network through all events in the phase. Table 2 shows a ranking list of the number of new member invitations. There was a tendency for people at higher positions in their organisations to invite new members. That is, each member has a supporter in his/her own organisation. Centrality of the network is strengthened by having supporters in positions higher than those of the members.

How should links be made between members?
Initially, there were no links between members. However, links were established between members in association with tasks and information flow. Table 2 shows a list of the number of links according to role in the network. The members in this list are those managing network activities. Links were established between members according to their own roles, i.e., each member had a clear role in the network.

Over which links should information flow?
Table 2 shows a list of the number of contacts with members. The members included in this list are group leaders. A tendency was observed for contact to occur with group leaders, i.e., the network has several sub-networks.

Table 2: Ranking list of the number of invitations, links and contacts

Rank	Invitation				Link				Contact			
	Member	Organisation	Position	Invitation	Member	Field	Role	Link	Member	Field	Role	Contact
1	A	U	Professor	9	B	O	M	19	B	O	M	150
2	Y	M	Chief	5	A	O	PL	10	A	O	PL	109
3	B	U	Researcher	3	O	3	WL	7	L	O	O	56
4	L	O	Officer	3	I	2	WL	5	I	2	WL	54
5	Z	F	Adviser	3	E	1	WL	4	G	4	WL	48
6	D	M	Director	2	G	4	WL	4	E	1	WL	46
7	E	F	S-Researcher	2	M	O	O	4	O	3	WL	45

<Organisation>U: University, M: Ministry, G: Local Gov., F: Foundation, O: Other
<Field> O: Office, 1: Working Group (WG) 1, 2: WG2, 3: WG3, 4: WG4
<Role>PL: Project Leader, M: Manager, WL: Working Group Leader, O: Other

In summary,to create a new network phase, we concentrated on establishing an appropriate Environment for innovative projects with regard to Network Size, Structural Holes, Tie Strength and Centrality. Sixty-three members joined the network in the phase of creating a new network phase. As the size of the network was too large, it was split into several sub-networks each of which had extra meetings.

The members were specialists from various organisations, including universities, national ministries, local government agencies, foundations, corporations and others.

Furthermore by assigning clear roles to all members we were able to increase the strength of the tie of the network. And finally, social and political backing came from supporters of all members within their own organisations hence enhancing the centrality of the network.

Case 2: Running a Project

The five-year project has a clear plan for each year. In the planning stages, important issues are extracted by searching related fields as well as discussion among members in the first year. In the second year, analyses of field issues are performed. In the third year, we will construct a framework for advanced facility management and new business. The fourth year will involve re-planning of practical research based on the results obtained in the third year. The final year will involve the development of information systems for each company and the construction of a feedback mechanism. In the first year, it was necessary to perform a current situation survey, needs and problem analyses, and policy design in social infrastructure related to ICT.

The first year of the project consisted of three periods. In the first period, the activity was based on the mechanism of social and political backing, i.e., Centrality. The kick-off meeting was held with an appropriately clear schedule and roles for each member (Tie Strength), as well as fair rules, management methods and consensus building (Trust and Shared Vision). A proposal was made to determine the present situation, classify and correct any existing problems and then evaluate measures through regular meetings, extra meetings and workshops related to the Network Size and Norms policies. The project has proceeded with all policies in place; Shared Vision is used throughout all processes in the project.

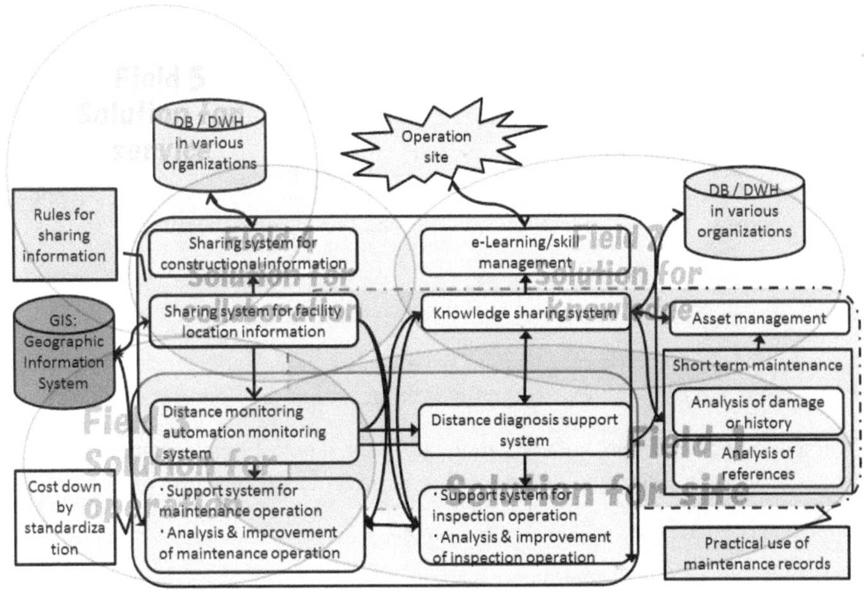

Figure 3: Relationships between systems

In the second period, we constructed a clear structure of the relationships between systems (Figure 3). The lower lines indicate systems for operation sites, and the upper lines indicate systems for sharing information. After achieving agreement among members, eight research plans with the eight main systems were made public, to obtain Centrality by the mechanism of social and political backing.

These included, at title of example an e-Learning/skill management system, a Knowledge sharing system, and a Distance diagnosis support system to obtain second opinions regarding inspections and plans in maintenance by highly skilled experts.

The agreement process was derived from fair rules, management methods and consensus building, i.e., Trust and Shared Vision. Our activities have obtained social and political approval based on public relations efforts regarding the project's outcomes. Following approval, the project developed some additional needs and issues. Therefore, we reconstructed the five research fields, including eight research plans that had already been established.

In the third period, the rules were established for new participants to cover the five new research fields. As the project needed extra knowledge and experience due to expansion of the research fields involved, new participants as human capital were complementary added to fill the identified structural holes Trust was maintained to develop fair rules of contract based on the consensus (i.e., the Shared Vision). Four participant styles were set as outlined below.

Core member
Core member can take part in all activities, such as management, publicity, main project field (Field 1), study activity, lecture meetings and interchange meetings.

Support member
Support members have the same rights as core members in most activities with the exception of decision-making authority.

Independent member
Independent members can take part only in specific fields (Fields 2, 3, 4, 5), which he/she chooses, and also in lecture meetings and interchange meetings.

Observer
Observers can enrol only in lecture meetings and interchange meetings.

We accepted new appropriate leading persons and organisations as well as extra funding for each of the five research fields at the end of the first year.

Over a period of one year, we used all the policies in both Environment and Governance. Especially, Trust and Shared Vision in governance appeared often as effective policies (Table 3).

Table 3: Effective policies in the three periods

Period	Activities/Outcomes	Effective Policies for Environment	Effective Policies for Governance
First (Apr–Sept 2009)	Start project Share 3 research aims (public) Search present situation Share 3 status & 3 environmental conditions Correct problems Share 133 problems	Tie Strength Centrality Network Size	Trust Shared Vision Norms
Second (Oct–Dec 2009)	Classify problems Share 8 problem areas & 33 measures Evaluate 33 measures Share 15 selected measures Build a structure of related systems Share 8 research themes (public) Public relations according to outcomes Correct additional issues Share 5 research fields	Centrality	Trust Shared Vision
Third (Jan–Mar 2010)	Establish rules for participation Share activity policy & 4 type participation styles Collect new members & extra budget	Structural Holes Tie Strength	Trust Shared Vision

Conclusions

Innovative projects have two phases—the first phase involves the creation of a new network to promote the project, while the second phase involves the outcomes of a project. Environment policies, such as Network Size, Structural Holes, Tie Strength and Centrality, are of primary importance in the first phase, while Governance policies, such as Trust and Shared Vision, are important in the second phase. A well-balanced project needs all of these policies. However, project movement is always dynamic, and it is therefore impossible to describe timetables with project policies. Therefore, we utilised checklists to manage the project to achieve innovation-

References

1. MLIT (2008). White paper on land, infrastructure, transport and tourism in Japan, 2008. English Outline Version is available from http://www.mlit.go.jp/common/000055283.pdf 15 August 2010.
2. MEXT: Ministry of Education, Culture, Sports, Science and Technology (2005). White paper on science and technology 2005: Japan's scientific and technological capabilities. English Version is available from http://www.mext.go.jp/english/news/2005/12/05121301.htm 15 August 2010.
3. Subramaniam, N. and Youndt, M.A. (2005). The influence of intellectual capital on the types of innovative capabilities, *Academy of Management Journal,* 48, 450-463
4. Zheng, W. (2008). A social capital perspective of innovation from individuals to nations: Where is empirical literature directing us? *International Journal of Management Reviews,,* Dec. 1-39
5. Nahapiet, J. and Ghoshal, S. (1998). Social capital, intellectual capital and the organizational advantage, *Academy of Management Review,* 23, 242-266
6. Tsai, W. and Ghoshal, S. (1991). Social capital and value creation: the role of intrafirm networks, *Academy of Management Journal,* 41, 464-476
7. O'Reilly, C. (1989). Corporations, culture and commitment: motivation and social control in organizations, *California Management Review,* 18, 9-25
8. Ahuja, G. (2000). Collaboration networks, structural holes and innovation: a longitudinal study, *Administrative Science Quarterly,* 45, 425-455
9. Shan, W., Walker, G. and Kogut, B. (1994). Interfirm cooperation and startup innovation in the biotechnology industry, *Strategic Management Journal,* 15, 387-394
10. Smith, K.G., Collins, C.J. and Clark, K.D. (2005). Existing knowledge, knowledge creation capability, and the rate of new product introduction in high-technology firms, *Academy of Management Journal,* 48, 346-357
11. Allen, T.J. (1977). Managing the flow of technology, Cambridge MA, MIT Press.
12. Granovetter, M.S. (1973). The strength of weak ties, *American Journal of Sociology,* 78, 1360
13. Burt, R.S. (1992). Structure Holes, Cambridge, Harvard University Press.
14. D.J. Brass, D.J. (1995). A social network perspective on human resource management, in Rowland, K.M. and Ferris, G.R. (eds) *Research in Personnel and Human resource Management,* Greenwich, JAI Press, 13, 39-79
15. Rodan, S. and Galunic, C. (2004). More than network structure: how knowledge heterogeneity influences managerial performance and innovativeness, *Strategic Management Journal,* 25,
16. Perry-Smith, J.E. (2006). Social yet creative: the role of social relationships in facilitating individual creativity, *Academy of Management Journal,* 49(1), 85-101

17. Fleming, L., Mingo, S. and Chen, D. (2007). Collaborative brokerage, generative creativity and creative success, *Administrative Science Quarterly,* 52, 443-475
18. Adler, P.S. and Kwon, S. (2002). Social capital: prospects for a new concept, *Academy of Management Review,* 27(1), 17-40
19. Coleman, J.S. (1988). Social capital in the creation of human capital, *American Journal of Sociology,* 94, 95-120
20. Reagans, R. and Zuckerman, E.W. (2001). Networks, diversity and productivity: the social capital of corporate R&D teams, *Organization Science,* 12, 502-517
21. Mehara, A., Dixon, A.L., Brass, D.J. and Robertson, B. (2006). The social network ties of group leaders: implications for group performance and leader reputation, *Organization Science,* 17(1)
22. Misztal, B. (1996). Trust in Modern Societies, Cambridge, Polity Press.
23. Williamson, O.E. (1975). Markets and Hierarchies, New York, Free Press.
24. Ross, W.H. and Wieland, C. (1996). Effects of interpersonal trust and time pressure on managerial mediation strategy in a simulated organizational dispute, *Journal of Applied Psychology,* 81
25. Brelade, S.B. and Hrman, C. (2000). Using human resources to put knowledge to work, *Knowledge Management Review,* 3(1), 26-29
26. DeLong, D.W. and Fahey, L. (2000). Diagnosing cultural barriers to knowledge management, *Academy of Management Executives,* 14(4), 113-127
27. J.D. Politis, J.D. (2003). The connection between trust and knowledge management: what are its implications for team performance, *Journal of Knowledge Management,* 7(5), 55-66
28. O'Reilly, C. (1898). Corporations, culture and commitment: motivation and social control in organizations, *California Management Review,* 18, 9-25
29. Pearce, C.L. and Ensley, M.D. (2004). A reciprocal and longitudinal investigation of the innovation success process: the central role of shared vision in product and process innovation teams, *Journal of Organizational Behavior,* 25, 259-278

Organisational Constraints on Information Systems Security

Maurizio Cavallari[1]

Abstract The present paper addresses an issue about the relationship between organisational structure and information systems security. Systems security is generally perceived as, and actually often constitutes, "restrictions" and "anti-ergonomics". The general research question we address in this research is the other way round: *What are the constraints of existing organisational structure and organisational processes that limit information systems security?* The general R.Q. is subdivided into three sub-questions regarding: 1) the relationship between ISS and organisational structure; 2) the conditions for effective implementation of ISS; 3) how the ISS implementation is hindered. The novelty of this research lies in answering all the mentioned sub-questions simultaneously. Conceptual analysis is utilised to interpret results, while socio-technical approach and the recent *"integrated social-technical theory"* are used as the main theoretical background. Research findings include organisational impacts on ISS and taxonomies of conditions and constraints that the organisation puts on Information Systems Security.

Introduction

In today's society security of information systems is one of the top priority areas in public as well as private organisations [1].

For an effective security plan to be established within an organisation, priorities must be based on investigation, assessment and implementation [2]. Aligning of information security policies and practices and applicable security technologies with business rules is a major issue in information systems security [3, 4].

A relevant part of research on IS security attributes the majority of security breaches to the human factor, which therefore is unanimously acknowledged as the weakest link in information systems security [5-10]. The nature of organisations demands a continuing, dynamic and real time information security system, and the "people" in the organisation are both the drivers and the destination of such ongoing security efforts [11]. Many authors state that from the information systems security governance perspective, it is advisable to have strong normative pressure in order to oblige individuals to abide by rules [12-14]. Social learning theory suggests that the influence of peer behaviour influences a person to do certain things under pressure, which they would not otherwise do [12, 13]. Behavioural regulation theory [14] adheres to the systems perspective of organisations, and

[1] Università Cattolica del Sacro Cuore di Milano – Italy

Gonzalez and Sawicka [5] have shown how to utilise this theory to create dynamic models of security compliance.

Common findings in research into the relationship between IS security and organisational issues, show that the implementation of efficient security measures within organisational structures limits action [4, 8, 14-18]. Security measures are largely oriented to restrict the availability of resources in adherence with security policy, authentication, protocols, procedures, restriction and control access to resources, data, information, distributed networks and the deployment of security technologies [19-27], all of which are an evident trade-off with labour efficiency, because their primary aim is to limit operations in order to render them compliant with the level of risk defined by security policies [17, 20, 23, 24].

Dhillon and Torkzadeh have pointed out that IS security must often cope with the organisational response to the restrictions brought by security measures and protocols [28]. Hagen highlights that IS security measures are often perceived by the user as a real and immediate obstacle (to be outmanoeuvred as far as possible) whose justification is the unclear (in the eye of the user) mitigation of a potential risk of uncertain nature [29-31].

In this research we address the opposite argument: is the organisation putting constraints on the implementation of appropriate IS security measures and actions and on the attainment of adequate levels of systems security? The study intends to verify whether the process of implementing information systems security faces, in retroaction, various organisational constraints. The aim of this research is to investigate what seems to be, normally, the dependent variable (i.e. the organisation, which has to adapt in order to adopt IS security measures), with respect to the retroaction towards what is often seen as the independent variable (IS security).

Overall R.Q.: *What are the constraints of existing organisational structure and organisational processes that limit information systems security?*

The quest to solve this issue can be divided into three research questions as follows:

- RQ1: How are issues regarding the information systems security related to the overall organisational structure?
- RQ2: What conditions are required for the effective implementation of information systems security within an organisational structure?
- RQ3: How is the process of effective implementation of information systems security hindered?

All these three research questions need to be answered in order. Firstly, this study will investigate the relationship between the information systems security and the overall organisational structure by analysing the security issues from a socio-technical perspective [32, 33] and then the impact of these issues on organisational structure on the basis of key findings from relevant research. Thereafter, it will move on to examine the conditions necessary for the effective implementation of information systems security within an organisational structure [14, 15, 29]. And finally it will focus on the hindrances to the process of effective implementation of IS security [34-36].

Much research into IS security focuses on different measures of digital security themselves, such as their pros and cons, technical specifications, products, costs and implementation plans [11, 24, 25, 27, 37] while others have tried to look into the issue of IS security from both angles, social and organisational, in order to examine how information systems security is integrated into the overall organisational process [cit. supra, 38-40].

The impact of IS security on IS development, which represents an interesting field of research for the scope of this study, has been investigated by De Marco, Avison, Siponen, Baskerville et al. [41-43]. However, there is a lack of study into the effective impact of an organisational structure on the implementation of IS security. Since IS security cannot be considered as a separate process from overall organisational processes and because of its impact on organisational structure and processes, it is quite evident that some organisational factors may hinder the process of effective implementation of information systems security.

Literature Review

It is first necessary to know what is actually meant by systems security and a review of different types of security measures and of literature regarding information systems and ISS needs to be made. This will help in furthering understanding regarding the relationship between IS security and organisational aspects.

System Security

A large number of definitions of system security are available [44]. Systems security can be defined as the process or system of undertaking specific measures to ensure the safety of electronic digital objects, flow, digital processing (programs), data (archives and DB) and networks [45]. Security procedures themselves are also identified as important aspects of IS security by many scholars [29, 46, 47]. Any sort of digital object can be stolen or hacked and thus personal, enterprise or confidential information stored in any digital form may be compromised [48]. Other scholars define information security as the process of protecting anything stored in electronic devices, in program routines, networks and in databases and, in general, as the ability of IS to provide accurate information and to prevent data spilling. [34, 49].

Three important mandates must be satisfied for information systems security implementations, according to Dhillon et al. [34, 46, 50]:

- The ISS implemented should allow the organisation to safeguard and monitor access to information stored in digital devices and across networks.
- It should facilitate the organisation to operate at the highest possible productivity level while enhancing performance level.

- It should also allow the organisation to bear an attack, absorb its impact and regain its functionality in its full form within a specific time frame.

According to other studies, ISS provisions should accomplish the following goals: integrity, confidentiality, availability and robustness [35, 37, 51].

Bishop and Booker argue that merely protecting the systems holding data about citizens, corporations, and government does not ensure, for itself, security [11, 44]. The whole infrastructure of networks, both public and private, that interconnect these systems must be preserved, or systems will no longer be able to communicate and to process appropriately [44]. Data integrity and data protection are, moreover, ambiguous concepts for themselves. Bishop points out that also the scope of the information held into the systems plays for the contextualised definition of "security". If secrecy would represent a priority, for instance, data integrity would rather mean that compromised digital information are deleted instead of discovered, while, other contexts, may play the opposite drive [37, 44].

Other interesting contributions from Ross Anderson offer a view on how information systems might reach acceptable security levels with the contribution not only of technologies but also of management strategies [52].

Certain security measures integrating technologies and organisational matters are often outlined in literature [35, 53]. These include security needs for data integration [34, 51] and the process of authentication and the identity of the user [35]. The mentioned studies highlight the different views of the security process, that of the user and that of the system administrator, which increase the chances of error and thus increase the gap related to the issues of security [35, 48, 53, 54] This last cited field of study leads us to understand how IS security is intimately related to processes and organisation rather than to technology alone or just security products [32-34, 38].

It must be noticed, however, that all these contributions emphasise a techno-centric view. The mentioned view has its appeal and brings an important contribution, but for the evident limit of that approach, which resides mainly in assigning to the people and the organisational structure a secondary importance, it is envisaged, with respect to the scope of this paper, an investigation about the social aspects of information systems security.

Information Systems Security Fundamentals

Thorough theoretical background can benefit information systems discipline and, as a consequence, IS security discipline. Contributions from Baskerville, Straub, Hevner, Beckhouse, Dzazali et al. [15, 18, 36, 47, 55] offer a reliable theoretical reference from which to concentrate the analysis into specific organisational matters.

Research into information systems borrows theories from other disciplines such as psychology, criminology, management and sociology. A review of information systems security governance research shows that theories from other disciplines inform research in this domain and help in better investigating issues and finding comprehensive solutions grounded in these theories. Theories such as general deterrence theory, theory of reasoned action, theory of planned behaviour, social bond theory, social learning theory, behavioural regulation theory and value theory, have been used by researchers in information systems security research [14]. Dzazali et al. propose a new theoretical perspective, called "the Integrated Social-Technical System Theory", in which researchers attempt to analyse and identify rather innovative underlying dimensions of information systems security [47].

Backhouse and Dhillon argue that structures of responsibility in organisations directly affect secure information systems and contribute to viewing security issues within an organisational perspective [15], while Mishra and Dhillon along with Gonzalez and Sawicka make an interesting contribution in framing IS security within a behavioural perspective, taking into account the human factor involved [5, 14]. Others point out how user interaction is the weakest link in IS security chain [56]. The human component in IS Security has recently gained a central role, and authors like Siponen et al. contribute with an insight view on organisational actions aimed at minimising user-related faults and propose a critical taxonomy of approaches [57]. Ghi and Baskerville, while revising the validity of information systems risk management taxonomies from older studies, argue that threat categories remain stable [58]. Findings in the same study show that human related faults, even though widely considered crucial for IS security, are nonetheless overlooked as a source of security risk [*ibidem*]. A theoretical framework based on the theory of contextualism is proposed by Karyda et al. in order to implement security policies successfully [59].

Other studies into combinations of organisational security measures, from the non-technological side of information security, show an inverse relationship between the implementation of organisational information security measures on the one hand and their assessed effectiveness on the other [29].

IS security has also been investigated as a "governance" matter since the early '80s as it has a significant impact on the general decision-making within organisations [60, 61]. Research in this field highlights a recurrent lack of organisational appropriateness of governance [18]. Interesting contributions point out how IS security arises mainly from top management organisational action rather then from technical specifications or enterprise security products or procedures [62, 63]. Thomson and von Solms offer an interesting viewpoint concerning the relationships that exists between corporate governance, information security and corporate culture; this contribution highlights the importance of the role of senior management [17].

Other fields of research look at the economic aspects of IS security, linking potential losses, security breaches and investments [64, 65]. Other studies discuss the economics of ISS in terms of the value of information [66-68].

A number of important contributions discuss the aspects of IS security within the discipline of information systems development [41-43, 69-71]. De Marco and Siponen argue that organisation of the information systems development does not pay sufficient attention to security aspects and that this constitutes the "original breach" after which security cannot be guaranteed [*41, 43*]. One suggestion is that it should be possible to eliminate such problems through better integration of security and software development practices, from a behavioural point of view [69, 72-74]. Methodologies and developers' attention would ensure *ab-initio* security to database design throughout the entire database software life cycle [75]. Cost-benefit analysis of resources utilised for ISS as a new paradigm for approaching the impact of ISS on budget is also approached [68, 76].

It appears very clear that the social aspects of information systems security are a central matter that often goes overlooked. Literature is abundant about the importance of the social aspects but empirical research also shows how much in the real world this does not comply with theories [42-45, 69, 70-74]. This paper is intended to investigate the most important organisational aspects, which are intimately related to ISS and its complete implementation.

Research Strategy and the Structure of the Research

The research has been conducted by sub-dividing the path into four consecutive steps, starting from the investigation of the relation between the IS security field of study and the overall organisational structure. The subsequent division into smaller focussed sub goals will discuss IS security as a discipline within the framework of socio-technical theory and the investigation of the impact on the organisation of IS security. After these steps it is possible to understand the conditions for an efficient implementation of IS security. Finally, the paper deals with the interpretation and the identification of organisational constraints on IS security implementation. Reciprocal retroaction between those aspects is also considered.

The key findings for R.Q. 1 will be descriptive as the question aims at finding the relationship between the two variables considered, while R.Q.2 and R.Q.3 will be presented in the form of a taxonomy based on the interpretation, the classification and the nucleation of the findings.

Relationship Between ISS and Organisational Structure

To discuss the relationship between IS security and the overall organisational structure, a twofold approach has been adopted.

Information Systems Security from the Socio-technological Perspective

Research into IS security have opined that IS security should be viewed from a socio-technological perspective. IS security systems can be characterized as a complicated blend of technological and social interactions, which are embedded in an organisational setting [77-83].

Thus we argue that it is not possible to ensure IS security if it is considered to be distinct from the overall organisational processes.

The socio-technical perspective offers an excellent framework for examining the phenomena that involve the interaction between the organisation and the security processes [32, 33]. The technological infrastructure of ISS has to be considered along with the social elements of organisational relationships, human behaviour, and the characteristics of organisational structures and work culture [34, 39, 40, 43, 57].

The performance of ISS depends on the interaction between these types of elements. This kind of concept of IS security is reflected in the creation of security models and architecture as an integral part of overall organisational architecture, not as a distinct concern. The aforementioned aspect is confirmed both from research which tends to focus on a narrow part of the organisational structure and processes, like role-based control over access to information, on the one hand, and from research focusing on a holistic treatment of the overall organisational process and related flows of information, on the other [36, 42, 43].

Organisational Impacts on Information Systems Security

From the research made we can state that the effectiveness of security measures can influence and be influenced by the organisational environment, depending on the implementation and level of acceptance by the organisation [84, 85]. Moreover, the characteristics of security systems can impact the ergonomics of the workplace and the entire organisation [86]. It has been shown that ISS processes are continuous and dynamic whereas organisations have their own established structure and pace.

The corresponding scenario is therefore: an existing organisation, on the one hand, with its stability and features (which often contribute to its competitive advantage) and, on the other, the highly changing environment of security [14, 36]. The difference between the "change rate capability" of the organisation [87, 88] and the fast changing realm of ISS constitutes a gap. Organisations have a limited response capability with respect to the needs of ISS implementation and governance [89]. We can conclude that the organisation has a definite impact on ISS due to insufficient flexibility in response to ISS governance. The most evident effect is that ISS implementation is constrained by the organisation's limited capability to adapt and shape itself to fast-changing security needs [90-94].

There is, however, no study to show how this impact varies across different organisational structures, work culture and organisational processes.

Conditions for the Effective Implementation of Information Systems Security – a Taxonomy

Before moving on to discussing possible constraints that may hinder effective implementation of IS security measures, the conditions for effective implementation should be highlighted. On the basis of the present research findings, the following taxonomy is identified as an appropriate reference for the implementation of ISS.

The taxonomy is limited to the specific aspects that impact on ISS from an organizational point of view and which, in the interpretation of the author, are most relevant to the research objectives.

- The members of the board of the organisation should be aware of how critical IS security is for their organisation.

- Instead of reviewing the performance of the security system only after a major incident takes place, the security governance should undertake regular reviews of the security system.
- An acceptable level of risk to the information system should be formalised and accepted. The risk level should be set on the basis of a comprehensive and periodical assessment.
- In order to form the basis for the organisation's policies and programs relating to security, the risk management plan should be aligned with the organisation's strategic goals.
- As regards duties, the Chief Information Security Officer (C.I.S.O.), who should report directly to the Chief Executive Officer (C.E.O.), should have responsibilities and rights, which are distinct from those of the Chief Information Officer (C.I.O.).
- Organisational policies should enforce the segregation of duties and define appropriate measures in order to reduce abuse.
- At a business unit level, responsibilities should also include information systems risk assessment.
- All employees of the organisation should be held accountable for complying with the policies and procedures of information systems security. [21-27, 46, 66, 95-99].

As widely acknowledged as these conditions may be, the findings of this research reveal a number of constraints that do not allow organisations to meet all the above mentioned conditions. From the very requirements for effective security implementation discussed above, it is now possible to examine the constraints of the organisation on ISS.

The Organisational Constraints on Information Systems Security – a Taxonomy

The findings of this research into the constraints on IS security by the organisation, can be summarised in the following taxonomy.

- Ever-present access to information and distributed systems: one of the most significant constraints on effectively implementing ISS is that in organisations most executives lack awareness of the highly connected nature of information systems. Accessibility of information and security are in trade off: risk increases with greater access [52]. This gives rise to conflicts between the area of management of ISS and the organisation [23-25].
- Organisation-wide nature of ISS: an effective IS security measure should protect and support all organisational processes. However, there is a lack of understanding of the full span and reach of ISS. Most notably, those who are responsible for implementing ISS often fail to make the whole organisation aware of the breadth of ISS and the needs and adaptations. [21-23, 97-99].

- Segregation of duties: ISS are generally misplaced within the realm of C.I.O. Even if a C.I.S.O is appointed, he has a tendency to report to the C.I.O. thus violating the segregation of duties, which will lead to inefficiencies. It has often been observed that C.I.O. and C.I.S.O. have conflicting demands in relation to ISS and the costs associated with it [45, 46].
- Priority: ISS are often given little priority and attention at senior management level and frequently the efforts relating to ISS are undercut by inappropriate organisational structure [66].
- Complicated international legal framework: organisational security requirements may flow from international, national and local rules and regulations as well as from global standards, policies and legal contracts. Security and privacy issues are becoming increasingly complicated and creating multiple layers of conflicting requirements which in turn are resulting in the development of inappropriate ISS implementations [22, 23, 100].
- Quantifying costs and benefits associated with ISS: since security is invisible, organisations very often have difficulty in addressing information security as budget items. As ISS is generally perceived by the top management of an organisation as means of disaster–recovery rather than as payoff-producing lower risk, justification of the investment in information security is a thorny issue [46, 62, 64, 96-97].
- Organisational security culture: achieving a particular state and level of security is not enough for ensuring that it will be sustained over the long run. Security can be seen as an ongoing process, which requires continuous improvement, assessment, monitoring, and execution. Continuous improvement requires attention and investment and security investments often come at the expense of other priorities in terms of accounting and economic opportunity. Organisations are reluctant to compromise on these opportunities in order to implement an effective security program [5, 7, 15, 16, 85, 87, 94, 101-103].

Conclusion

This study reveals that although ISS has become an important issue facing every organisation, it also represents a difficult challenge.

There is a retroaction coming from the organisational matters discussed within the paper, which constrains the implementation of appropriate ISS measures and plans. Security aspects are not treated as a priority in most of the organisations due to inappropriate organisational structure, the misallocation of duties and business processes that suffer from a lack of knowledge about information systems security and associated risks. All these act as organisational constraints on the implementation of effective ISS measures within the organisation.

Limitations

This study finds its limitations in its analytical study of the issue considered. Although conceptual analysis and the re-use of publicly available surveys and previous research findings are acceptable for research into IS [104, 105], no new empirical data has so far been gathered to support the analytical findings. This leaves a huge scope for further research.

Acknowledgements

I wish to express my sincere gratitude to Professor Marco De Marco for his guidance in my academic, professional and personal life since our friendship began in 1986.

References

1. The Economist (2010) Cyberwar: The threat from the internet. *The Economist*, July 1st 2010, (pp. 23-26). downloaded: http://www.economist.com/node/16481504 on July, 31th 2010.
2. Barr, J. G. (2010). Setting Security Priorities. *Faulkner Information Services*. downloaded: http://www.faulkner.com.ezproxy.piedmont.edu/products/faulknerlibrary/ on May, 3rd 2010.
3. Ertul, L., Braithwaite T. et al. (2010) *Enterprise Security Planning (ESP)*, downloaded: http://mgovernment.alfabes.com/resurces/euromgov2005/PDF/15_S036EL-S13.pdf on May, 24th 2010.
4. Zachman, J. A., (2004) *Primer for Enterprise Engineering and Manufacturing*. In The Zachman Framework for Enterprise Architecture e-book. downloaded: http://www.businessrulesgroup.org/BRWG_RFI/ZachmanBookRFIextract.pdf on June 4th 2010.
5. Gonzalez, J. & Sawicka, A. (2002) A Framework for Human Factors in Information Security. *WSEAS International Conference on Information Security*, Rio de Janeiro, Brazil.
6. Whitman, M. (2003). Enemy at the Gate: Threats to Information Security. *Communications of the ACM* (46:8) (pp 91-95).
7. Bottom, N. (2000). The human face of information loss. *Security Management* (44:6) (pp. 50-56).
8. Hitchings, J. (1995). Deficiencies of the Traditional Approach to Information Security and the Requirements for a New Methodology. *Computers & Security* (14) (pp. 377-383).
9. Magklaras, G. & Furnell, S. (2005). A preliminary model of end user sophistication for insider threat prediction in IT systems. *Computers & Security* (24) (pp. 371-380).
10. Schultz, E. (2002) A framework for understanding and predicting insider attacks, *Compsec 2002*. London UK, downloaded: www.itsec.gov.cn/docs/2009050716530 6643554.pdf on April, 13th 2010.
11. Booker, R. (2006) Re-engineering enterprise security, *Computers & Security* (25) (pp. 13-17). downloaded: http://www.elsevier.com/framework_products/promis_misc/450877_Re-engineering.pdf on April, 11th 2010.
12. Theoharidou, M. & Kokolakis, R. (2005) The insider threat to information systems and the effectiveness of ISO17799. *Computers & Security* (24) (pp 472-484).
13. Hollinger, R. (1993) Crime by computer: correlates of software piracy and unauthorized account access. *Security Journal* (4:1) (pp. 2-12).

14. Mishra S. & Dhillon G. (2006) Information Systems Security Governance Research: A Behavioral Perspective. *Proceedings of the 1st Annual Symposium on Information Assurance, academic track of the 9th Annual 2006 NYS Cyber Security Conference* (pp. 18-26). New York, USA.
15. Backhouse, J. & Dhillon, G. (1996) Structures of responsibility and security of information systems. *European Journal of Information Systems* (5) (pp. 2–9).
16. Siponen, M. (2000) Critical analysis of different approaches to minimizing user-related faults in information systems security: implications for research and practice. *Information Management & Computer Security* (8:5) (pp. 197-209).
17. Thomson K. & von Solms R. (2005) Information security obedience: a definition, *Computers & Security* (24:1) (pp.69-75).
18. Warkentin, M. & Johnston, A. C. (2006) IT governance and organizational design for security management, chapter 3. In Baskerville, R., Goodman S., and Straub, D. W. (Eds.). *Information Security Policies and Practices*. M.E. Sharpe.
19. Janczewski L. L. & Portougal V. (2000) "Need-to-know" principle and fuzzy security clearances modelling. *Information Management & Computer Security*, (8:5) (pp. 210-217).
20. IT Governance Institute (2006) Information security governance: Guidance for boards of directors and executive management, downloaded: www.isaca.org/Template.cfm?Setion=Home&Template=/ContentManagement/ContentDisplay.cfm&ContentID=24572 on March, 25th 2010.
21. Allen, J. (2005). Governing for Enterprise Security. *Software Engineering Institute*, Carnegie Mellon University. Pittsburgh, PA.
22. Allen, J. (2007). Why Leaders Should Care About Security. *CERT Podcast Series*. downloaded: http://www.cert.org/podcast/show/20061017allena.html on May, 2nd '10.
23. Allen, J. (2006). Security Is Not Just a Technical Issue. *Build Security*. Department of Homeland Security. downloaded: https://buildsecurityin.us-cert.gov/bsi/articles/best-practices/management/563-BSI.html on April, 13th 2010.
24. Barker, W. C. (2004). Guide for Mapping Types of Information and Information Systems to Security Categories. *NIST Special Publication 800-60 Volume I, Version 2*. In Gaithersburg, MD (Ed.) Computer Security Division, Information Technology Laboratory, National Institute of Standards and Technology.
25. Braithwaite, T. (2002). Securing E-Business Systems. *A Guide for Managers and Executives*. NY: John Wiley & Sons.
26. Business Software Alliance. (2003) Information Security Governance: Toward a Framework for Action. downloaded: www.bsa.org/usa/policy/index.cfm on May, 18th 2010.
27. Caralli, R. (2006) Sustaining Operational Resiliency: A Process Improvement Approach to Security Management. *CMU/SEI-2006-TN-009*. Software Engineering Institute, Carnegie Mellon University: Pittsburgh, PA downloaded: www.cert.org /archive/pdf/ sustainoperresil0604.pdf on April, 7th 2010.
28. Dhillon, G. & Torkzadeh, G. (2006) Value-focused assessment of information systems security in organizations. *Information Systems Journal* (16:3) (pp. 293–314).
29. Hagen, J.M., Albrechtsen, E. et al. (2008) Implementation and effectiveness of organizational information security measures. *Information Management & Computer Security* (16:4).
30. De Paula, R. et. al. (2005) In the eye of the beholder: A visualization-based approach to information systems security, *International Journal of Human-Computer Studies* (63:1-2) (pp. 5-24).
31. Vaast, E. (2007) Danger is in the eye of the beholders: Social representations of Information Systems security in healthcare. *The Journal of Strategic Information Systems* (16:2) (pp. 130-152).
32. Dhillon, G. & Backhouse, J. (2001). Current Directions in IS Security Research: Towards Socio-organizational Perspectives. *Information Systems Journal*, (11) (pp. 127-153).

33. Kling, R. & Lamb, R. (2000). IT and Organizational Change in Digital Economies: A Sociotechnical Approach, in B. B. Kahin (Ed.) *Understanding the Digital Economy. Data, Tools, and Research*. Cambridge, MA: The MIT Press.
34. Dhillon, G. (2007). *Principles of Information Systems Security: text and cases*. NY: John Wiley & Sons.
35. Layton, T.P. (2007) Information Security Design, Implementation, Measurement and Compliance. *Auerbach Publications, Taylor & Francis group*. Boca Raton, NY.
36. Straub, D., Goodman, S., & Baskerville, R. (2008). Framing of Information Security Policies and Practices. In *Information Security Policies, Processes, and Practices*. D. Straub, S. Goodman and R. Baskerville (eds.), Armonk, NY: M. E. Sharpe.
37. Clarkson, M. R. & Schneider, F. B. (2010) Quantification of Integrity, *23rd IEEE Computer Security Foundations Symposium* (pp. 28-43) downloaded: http://www.computer.org/portal/web/csdl/doi/10.1109/CSF.2010.10 on 1st August 2010.
38. Cresswell, A & Hassan, S. (2006) Organizational Impacts of Cyber Security Provisions: A Sociotechnical Framework, *40th Annual Hawaii International Conference on System Sciences HICSS'07* downloaded: http://www.computer.org/plugins/dl/pdf/proceedings/hicss/2007/2755/00/27550098b.pdf on February, 24th 2009.
39. Quigley, M. (2004) Information security and ethics: Social and organizational issues. *Hershey* IRM Press.
40. Orlikowski, W. J. & Barley, S. R. (2001) Technology and Institutions: technology and Research on Organizations Learn from Each Other? *MIS Quarterly* (25).
41. De Marco, M. (2004) *Le metodologie di sviluppo dei sistemi informativi*. Franco Angeli, Milano I.
42. Avison, D. & Wood-Harper, T. (2003) Bringing social and organisational issues into information systems development: the story of multiview. *Socio-technical and human cognition elements of information systems*. IGI Publishing Hershey, PA (pp. 5-21).
43. Siponen, M. & Baskerville, R (2001) A New Paradigm for Adding Security Into IS Development Methods. *Conference on Information Security Management & Small Systems Security* (pp. 99-112).
44. Bishop, M. (2003) What is computer security? *Security & Privacy, IEEE* (1:1) (pp.67-69). downloaded: http://nob.cs.ucdavis.edu/bishop/papers/2003-spcolv1n1/whatis.pdf on May, 17th 2001.
45. Allen, J. H. (2001) *The CERT Guide to System and Network Security Practices*. Boston, MA. Addison-Wesley.
46. Westby, J. R., (2004) *International Guide to Privacy*. Chicago, ABA Pub.
47. Dzazali, S., Ainin, S. et al. (2009) Employing the social-technical perspective in identifying security management systems in organisations. *International Journal of Business Information Systems* (4:4) (pp. 419-439).
48. Gordon, A. L., Loeb, P. M.,Lucyshyn, W. et al. (2005) CSI/FBI computer crime and security survey. *Computer Security Institute*. downloaded: http://i.cmpnet.com/gocsi/db_area/pdfs/fbi/FBI2005.pdf on November, 23rd 2007.
49. Barr, J. G. (2009). Security Convergence. *Faulkner Information Services*. downloaded: http://www.faulkner.com.ezproxy.piedmont.edu/products/faulknerlibrary/ on April, 3rd 2010.
50. Habiger, G. E. (2010). Cyberwarfare and Cyberterrorism: The need for a new US strategic approach. *White Paper 1:2010*. The Cyber Secure Institute. downloaded: http://cybersecureinstitute.org/docs/whitepapers/Habiger_2_1_10.pdf on May, 24th 2010.
51. Dhillon, G. & Moores, T. (2003) Internet privacy: interpreting key issues. *Advanced topics in information resources management*. Idea Group Publishing, Hershey, PA.
52. Anderson Ross, J. (2008) *Security Engineering: A Guide to Building Dependable Distributed Systems*, 2 edition, Wiley Publishing.
53. Schneier, B. (2000) *Secrets and Lies: Digital Security in a Networked World*. New York: John Wiley & Sons.
54. Neumann, G. & Strembeck, M. (2002) A scenario-driven role engineering process for functional RBAC roles. *Seventh ACM Symposium on Access control models and technologies*, Monterey, CA.

55. Hevner, A.R., March, S.T. et al. (2004) Design science in information systems research, *MIS Quarterly* (2).
56. Mitnick, K. (2003) Are you the weak link? *Harvard Business Review* (4).
57. Mikko T. Siponen (2000) Critical analysis of different approaches to minimizing user-related faults in information systems security: implications for research and practice. *Information Management & Computer Security* (8:5) (pp.197-209).
58. Ghi P. & Baskerville, R. (2005) A longitudinal study of information system threat categories: the enduring problem of human error. *ACM SIGMIS Database* (36:4) (pp. 68-79).
59. Karyda, M., Kiountouzis, E. et al. (2005) Information systems security policies: a contextual perspective. *Computers & Security* (24:3) (pp. 246-260).
60. Hambrick, D.C. & Mason, P. A. (1984) Upper echelons: The organization as a reflection of its top managers. *Academy of Management Review* (9:2) (pp. 193-206).
61. Hambrick, D.C. (2007) Upper-echelons theory: An update. *The Academy of Management Review* (32:2) (pp. 334-343).
62. Austin, R. D. & Darby, (2003) , The myth of secure computing, *Harvard Business Review* (6) downloaded: http://www.uncg.edu/bae/isom/tisec/docs/Myth.pdf on May, 4th 2010.
63. Johnston, A. C. & Hale, R. (2009) Improved security through information security governance, *Communications of the ACM* (52:1) (pp. 126-129).
64. Gordon, L.A. & Loeb, P. (2002) The economics of information security investment. *ACM Transactions on Information and System Security (TISSEC)* (5:4) (pp. 438–457).
65. Campbell, K., Gordon, L.A. et al. (2003) The economic cost of publicly announced information security breaches: empirical evidence from the stock market. *Journal of Computer Security*. IOS Press.
66. Taylor, P. (2004) A Wake Up Call to All Information Security and Audit Executives: Become Business-Relevant. *Information Systems Control Journal* (1:14)(pp.123-135).
67. Gordo, L. A. & Loeb, M. P. (2006) Budgeting Process for Information Security Expenditures. *Communications of the ACM* (49) (pp. 121-125).
68. Neubauer, T., Klemen, M. et al. (2005) Business Process-based Valuation of IT-Security. *Seventh international workshop on Economics-driven software engineering research EDSER*. St. Louis, Missouri.
69. Mouratidisa, H., Giorgini, P. et al. (2005) When security meets software engineering: a case of modelling secure information systems, *Information Systems* (30:8) (pp. 609-62).
70. Blanco, C., Fernandez-Medina, E. et al. (2008) How to implement multidimensional security into OLAP tools. *International Journal of Business Intelligence and Data Mining* (3:3) (pp. 255-276).
71. Vaidyanathan, G. & Mautone. S. (2009) Security in dynamic web content management systems applications. *Communications of the ACM* (52:12).
72. Fernández-Medina, E., Trujillo, J. et al. (2007) Developing secure data warehouses with a UML extension. *Information Systems* (32:6) (pp. 826-856).
73. Vela, B. & Fernández-Medina, E. (2006) Model driven development of secure XML databases, *ACM SIGMOD Database* (35:3) (pp. 22-27).
74. Soler, E., Trujillo, J. et al. (2008) Building a secure star schema in data warehouses by an extension of the relational package from CWM, *Computer Standards & Interfaces* (30:6) (pp. 341-350).
75. Fernández-Medina, E. & Mario Piattini (2005) Designing secure databases. *Information and Software Technology* (47:7) (pp. 463-477).
76. Gordon, L. & Loeb, M (2006). *Managing Cybersecurity Resources: A Cost-Benefit Analysis*. McGraw-Hill.
77. Järvinen, P. (1997) The new classification of research approaches. In: Zemanek H. (Eds): *The IFIP Pink Summary – 36 years of IFIP*. IFIP, Austria (pp. 124-131).
78. Järvinen, P. (2000) Research questions guiding selection of an appropriate research method. *Proceedings of the 8th European Conference on Information Systems (ECIS)*, Vienna, A.
79. Gadamer, H. G. (1989) *Truth and method*. 2nd rev. ed., Sheed and Ward, London, UK.

80. Mautner, T. (1996) *A dictionary of philosophy*. Blackwell Publishers Ltd, Oxford, UK.
81. Walsham, G. (1996) The emergence of interpretivism in IS research. *Information Systems Research* (6) (pp. 376-394).
82. Klein, H. K. & Myers, M. D. (1999) A set of principles for conducting and evaluating interpretive Field studies in information systems. *MIS Quarterly* (23) (pp. 67-94).
83. Klein, H. K. & Myers, M. D. (2001) A classification scheme for interpretive research in information systems. In: Trauth EM (Eds) *Qualitative Research in IS: Issues and Trends*. Idea Group Publishing, Hersney, PA (pp. 218-239).
84. Davis, F. (1989) Perceived usefulness, perceived ease of use, and user acceptance of information technology *MIS Quarterly*.
85. Conner, D. L. & Patterson, R.W. (1982) Building commitment to organizational Change. *Training and Development Journal*.
86. Carayon, P. & Smith, M. J. (2000) Work organization and ergonomics, *Applied Ergonomics* (31:6) (pp. 649-662).
87. Mullins, L. J. (2007) *Management and organisational behaviour*. FT Prentice Hall.
88. Gill, R. (2001) Change management--or change leadership? *Journal of Change Management* (3:4) (pp. 307-318).
89. Wright, P. & Snell, S. (1998) Toward a Unifying Framework for Exploring Fit and Flexibility in Strategic Human Resource Management. *The Academy of Management Review* (23:4) (pp. 756-772).
90. Volberda, H. (1996) Toward the Flexible Form: How to Remain Vital in Hyper-competitive Environments, *Organization Science*, (7:4) (pp. 359-374).
91. Hanseth, O., Monteiro, et al. (1996) Developing Information Infrastructure: The Tension between Standardisation and Flexibility. *Science, Technology and Human Values* (21:4) (pp. 407-426).
92. Hanseth, O., & Monteiro, E. (1997) Inscribing Behaviour in Information Infrastructure Standards. *Accounting, Management & Information Technology* (7:4) (pp. 183-211).
93. Hanseth, O. & Braa, K. (2001) Hunting for the Treasure at the End of the Rainbow. Standardisation Corporate IT Infrastructure. *Computer Supported Cooperative Work* (10:3-4) (pp. 261-292).
94. Monteiro, E. & and Hanseth, O. (1995) Social Shaping of Information Infrastructure: On Being Specific about the Technology. *Information Technology and Changes in Organisational Work*, in Orlikowski, W. J., Walsham, et al. (Eds). Chapman & Hall, London (pp. 325-343).
95. NASCIO. (2003) Enterprise Architecture Maturity Model. *National Association of State Chief Information Officers*. downloaded: www.nascio.org/publications/documents/nascio-eamm.pdf on July, 7th 2009.
96. Tolone, W., Ahn, T. et al. (2005) Access Control in Collaborative Systems. *ACM Computing Surveys* (37:1) (pp. 29-41.
97. Gordon, L. A., Loeb, M. P. et al. (2003) Sharing information on computer systems security: An economic analysis, *Journal of Accounting and Public Policy* (22) (pp. 461-485).
98. Harris, S. (2006) Introduction to Security Governance. *SearchSecurity.com*. downloaded: http://searchsecurity.techtarget.com/tip/0,289483,sid14_gci1210565,00.html on June, 11th 2010.
99. Smedinghoff, T. J. (2006) Where We're Headed-New Developments and Trends in the Law of Information Security. *Wildman Harrold News & Publications*. Downloaded: http://www.wildman.com/index.cfm?fa=news.pubArticle&aid=5072F372-BDB9-4A10-554DF441B19981D7 on June, 11th 2010.
100. Backhouse, J. & Dhillon, G. (2006) Circuits of power in creating de jure standards: shaping an international information systems security standard, *MIS Quarterly, special issue*.
101. OMB (2002) Circular No. A-11, Planning, Budgeting, Acquisition, and Management of Capital Assets (Part 7): Exhibit 300-Capital Asset Plan and Business Case. *US Office of Management and Budget*, Washington, DC.

102. Jakobs, K. (2000) Information Technology Standards and Standardization: A Global Perspective. *Idea Group Publishing*, Hershey, PA.
103. Straub, D.W. and Welke, R.J. (1998) Coping with systems risk: security planning models for management decision making. *MIS Quarterly*.
104. Lee, A. S. & Baskerville, R. L. (2003) Generalizing Generalizability in Information Systems Research. *Information Systems Research* (14:3) (pp. 221-243).
105. Siponen, M. (2002) Designing secure information systems and software, *published thesis*, University of Oulu, Finland (pp. 16-18) downloaded: http://herkules.oulu.fi/isbn9514267907/isbn9514267907.pdf on October, 26th 2008.

Part IV

ICT and Social Impact

Asymmetric 2-Mode Network in Social Computing and Decomposition Algorithm

Shuren Zhang[1], **Yu Chen**[2], **Meiqi Fang**[3]

Abstract In Social Network Service (SNS) using Web2.0 technologies, new social structures are constructed bottom-up. Such social emergence has recently drawn many interests. New social structures are characterized by the social relation formed from the gradual development among the users in the system. In this world, the optimization of the social structure and the organization of the information in Web2.0 communities can be improved with complex network decomposition, on-line social network analysis, and other methods. Such a cross field covering man-machine interaction design, complex network computing and social network analysis is known as social computing. An important step in social computing is to decompose various 2-Mode networks in a community. On the basis that the actions of subject nodes and object nodes during social computing were analyzed and found to be different extended investigation was conducted on the 2-Mode network decomposition algorithm in this study, concluding with the proposition of several 2-Mode network decomposition algorithms.

Introduction

In on-line network services, the records table of the user behavior can be treated as a 2-Mode network composed of two types of nodes: the user and the content, such as a user of an instant messaging software and the group he creates, a user in a social bookmark system and the objects he collects, or a flickr.com user and the tags he uses, etc. With analysis and computation being conducted on such 2-Mode network, the users' social relationship networks and their mutually indirect cooperation can be enhanced. On the other hand, the content correlation and structure inside the system supporting the network can be optimized [1], [2]. And finally, the swarm [3] intelligence can emerge at the system level. Here, the system computing object refers to the massive population with social attributes. The objective and structure of system computing are also optimized user-society cooperating relation and social structure, so the computing is also called as social computing.

With the rising of social software, Web2.0 and SNS, etc., studies about Social Computing have attracted increasing interests. Social computing does not only closely related to the social software, but also the analysis of the social network and the complex network computing in the information system [4].

---

[1] Alibaba Business College,Hangzhou Normal University, Hangzhou, China, 310036, Zhangshuren@gmail.com

[2] Information College, Renmin University, Beijing,China,100872 yuchen318@gmail.com

[3] Information College, Renmin University, Beijing,China,100872 , meiqif@gmail.com

The characteristics of the 2-Mode network in social computing studies are analyzed in this article. It is pointed out that no effective social computing could be carried out with conventional 2-Mode network algorithms without acknowledging the asymmetry of the cognitive subjects and the cognitive objects in the network. To address this problem , we propose few 2-Mode network decomposition algorithms based on the subjective cognition.

In the following we present the research background and the definition of 2-Mode network; part 2 introduces the 2-Mode network in social computing, related research status and existing problems; part 3 presents a few improved 2-Mode network decomposition algorithms based on the analysis of application scenarios in social computing and the last part is the conclusion.

2-Mode Network

The 2-Mode network refers to a network composed of two types of nodes, such as the reader and the library, the organizations that people take part in, the goods that people purchase and the information that people acquire. Such a network, which is different from the normal single-type nodes network, is known as a 2-Mode Network. 2-Mode Network is also known as Bipartite Network [5],[6].

Matjaz Zaversnik et al. defined a 2-Mode Network in the form of (U,V,R,w), where U and V were two node sets without intersected parts; $R \subseteq U \times V$ expressed the relationship between U and V; $w: R \to R$ was the weight, and it could be assumed that for all $(u,v) \in R$, $w(u,v) = 1$ if no weight was set [7].

A 2-Mode network can also be treated as a normal network (1-Mode) on the set of " $U + V$". The difference between the two networks lies in that the apexes of the 1-Mode network can be divided into two subsets with U and V, while the sides in the network can only exist between the nodes of two different subsets. This is also known as a Bipartite Network.

2-Mode Network in Social Computing and its Asymmetry

In systems related to social computing, the user's behavior is recorded and forms a bipartite user-behavioral objective group, such as a user and the bookmark he collects in social bookmark, a user and the classification tag he marks, etc., a user in wiki system and the entry he accesses/attends to, and a user in RSS social subscription system and the RSS he subscribes. In social computing, such bipartite groups can be treated as a 2-Mode network composed of the user information and the content about the recorded behavioral objective. In a social computing system, the system background should decompose this 2-Mode network (apart from displaying them directly) and divide it into two 1-Mode networks: the user correlation network and the content correlation network.

A general way of decomposing 2-Mode network to 1-Mode networks is to decompose (U,V,R,w) into (U,RR^T) and (V,R^TR) symmetrically [4]. Many studies on improved algorithms were also based on this principle of symmetric decomposition. However, the concepts of the two types of nodes are different in social computing. One type of the nodes is people (the user) who has the subjective cognition ability and becomes a potential social relationship network of the users after the decomposition. The formation of the actual social relationship network also depends on the cognitive judgments among the users. After content nodes are decomposed, a fixed content correlation network can be constructed in the system directly; alternatively, it can be subject to related users themselves to make judgments and choice before a fixed content correlation is eventually formed.

The asymmetry in 2-Mode network determines that the two types of nodes cannot be treated symmetrically with an equivalent method in decomposition.

At title of example, a 2-Mode network of user-volume formed in a volume loan/collection system is decomposed for finding the users with similar interests and the volumes with related contents. U represents the user set, and V represents the volume set. Each volume v_i has a different degree d_i which means that there are d_i users collect or read the volume v_i. In network decomposition, the crowd interest relationship network can be mined according to the volume collection. In general classification, identical collections are simply added up, but the difference in the interest differentiation abilities of the users brought by popular volumes or peculiar volumes is ignored. Compared with the interest correlation among the public who collects the same popular volumes, the interest correlation among a small reader group who collects one scarce volume is obviously much higher; in extreme conditions, all users collect one and the same volume, then the volume cannot be used to divide the user group into two different interest groups; among massive users, as long as two users collect the same volume, the interest correlation between them becomes the highest (a faithful friend is hard to find). Therefore, the degree of a volume node can be used as the differentiation degree factor for classifying user-interest groups for user clustering. However, the degree of a user node more likely represents the degree of participation in the community activities of the user when clustering the volumes. So the user degree (the number of collected books) cannot be used symmetrically as the differentiation degree factor for volume clustering analysis in the determination of the volume correlations.

Such asymmetry is not merely limited to the different actions of node degrees. In the next section we propose various improved decomposition algorithms and detailed illustrations.

2-Mode Decomposition Algorithms and Improvement

During the research practice, a large number of application scenarios were analyzed in detail [7]. On the basis of such analysis, three improved decomposition strategies are proposed for non-weight 2-Mode undirected networks: the key intermediate method, the cume betweenness method and the egocentric directional decomposition method; as to weighted networks, a general decomposition method based on cognitive weight for weighted 2-Mode network is put forward.

In a 2-Mode network, the nodes neither in U nor in V are connected directly with the same sibling nodes; instead, they are connected with the same sibling nodes indirectly through some other opposite sibling nodes. In the decomposition in 1-Mode networks, e.g., the generation of 1-Mode networks of set U, U-type nodes are objective relationship network nodes while the nodes in V are intermediate nodes. Whether they are connected with some intermediate nodes can be regarded as attribute characteristics of objective nodes, and the course of the establishment of the objective nodes correlation network actually is the course of analyzing the correlation of objective nodes in all the attributes of intermediate nodes. Such intermediate nodes are equivalent to the differentiation factors of objective nodes. The higher the degree of some intermediate nodes, the more popular the attribute characteristics connected to the intermediate nodes become in objective nodes, and the worse the capability of differentiating objective nodes becomes. The basic idea of the key intermediate method and the cume betweenness method is to highlight the differentiation factors with high discrimination and inhibit general differentiation factors. The nodes with higher degrees are more general with lower discrimination while the nodes with lower degrees (>=2) have higher discrimination. Besides, only the nodes with the degrees greater than or equal to 2 can connect two different objective nodes together. In other words, the nodes with the degrees smaller than 2 make no contribution in network decomposition and can be ignored. The nodes with the degrees of 2 are known as key intermediate nodes.

Definition 1: The decomposition method implemented merely based on key intermediate nodes with 2 degrees is known as the key intermediate method.

Specifically, the nodes with the degrees of 2 are picked out from the two sets, and those node pairs from another set, which are connected to these nodes, are connected to form two 1-Mode networks (both the two networks might not intercommunicate). Besides, the lower restriction can be accepted if the average degree of the intermediate nodes is very large, and all the nodes with the degrees smaller than or equal to k can be regarded as key intermediate nodes. This decomposition algorithm is known as the k key intermediate method.

For 2-Mode network $(U,V,R$, the side weights in sub-network U acquired through the k key intermediate decomposition are determined by (formula-1):

$$w_{u_i,u_j} = \begin{cases} 1 & ; \ \exists v_m : d_{v_m} <= k \text{且} \ (u_i, v_m), (u_j, v_m) \in R \\ 0 & ; \ other\ conditions \end{cases} \quad \text{(Formula-1)}$$

When k=2, it is the key intermediate decomposition method. The side weight in sub-network V can also be given symmetrically.

The key intermediate method is a practical network decomposition method. We can ignore those over-popularized intermediate nodes and rely on key intermediate nodes merely , so that the computation amount in analysis can be reduced greatly, then the nodes with the highest correlations can be found rapidly and effectively. This is very effective in improving the self-organization function of the users in the system, i.e., the function of classifying people according to their characteristics and achieving friend recommendation. All networks obtained with the key intermediate method involve peculiar common interest relationships, for the distinctive personality of a man is generally embodied in his interests that differ the most from those of the public. The focus of attentions is also generally upon the distinctive behavior. In the practice of the system implementation, a value of k can be determined according to the average degree of nodes and the degree distribution as well as a certain percentage, and the decomposition is conducted with the k key intermediate method. Besides, the assumption of the application of the k key intermediate method is: the probability of being selected for correlation of the key nodes in the system is basically the same as other nodes, but the key nodes are actually seldom being selected. Therefore, a key node must be an old node (with a sufficient probability to choose for correlations) of a dynamically growing network. A node which just enters the system may also exhibit a low-degree status while it is not ready to be connected with the other nodes.

The node degree corresponds to the number of the nodes in the opposite set which is connected to this node. Node v_i with the degree of d_{v_i} connects d_{v_i} U-type nodes, which consequently affect somewhat the paired connection among d_{v_i} nodes in network U in the decomposition results. The paired connection among d_{v_i} nodes forms $C^2_{d_{v_i}} = d_{v_i}! / 2(d_{v_i} - 2)!$ pairs of connection in total. With the weights being allocated to each connection pair averagely, the weight of each connection pair on v_i is $1/C^2_{d_{v_i}}$; for the key intermediate node defined above, the weight is $1/C^2_2 = 1$, which contributes the most; for v_j of all the nodes connected to U, the number of contributed correlation pairs is the largest, and the contributed weight is also the lowest, i.e., $1/C^2_m$ (m is the order of set U). With $L_{u_{k1},u_{k2}}$ denoting the set of V-type nodes, which connects u_{k1} and u_{k2} simultaneously, the weight accumulation of side (u_{k1}, u_{k2}) in the 1-Mode U network in the final decomposition result is as follows:

$$w_{u_{k1},u_{k2}} = \sum_{\forall v_i : v_i \in L_{u_{k1},u_{k2}}} 1/C^2_{d_{v_i}}; \qquad \text{(Formula-2)}$$

Where d_{v_i} is the degree of node v_i.

Definition 2: Different degrees of intermediate nodes result in different contributions to the correlations among the node sets that they are connected to. Based on this rule, the method, with which the contributions of intermediate nodes with different degrees to related correlations are differentiated in a quantitative manner and the side weights of a network generated from decomposition are obtained through accumulation, is known as the cume betweenness method.

In the cume betweenness method, the authority of different allocation is a monotonic decreasing function which is related to the intermediate degree. In 2, different sides are endowing with average values according to the number of the sides contributed by the degrees of intermediate nodes, which is known as the side-based allocation method. It also works if an appropriate decreasing function of intermediate node degree is chosen in practice:

$f(d_{v_i}) \propto \frac{\beta}{d_{v_i}^{\ \alpha}}$ ($\alpha, \beta > 0$) is used to substitute for $1/C_{d_{v_i}}^2$ in formula 2. If $f(d_{v_i}) = \frac{1}{d_{v_i}}$, then the method is known as a point-based allocation method.

After the 1-Mode weighted network is obtained, the system can use the weight sequence to find a node which has the highest correlation with certain node. In the implementation of the network clustering algorithm, the weighted network can be converted to a simplified non-weighted network by means of adding a threshold value for judgment filtering, so as to improve the computing efficiency, i.e., those correlation sides with the weights lower than a threshold value are removed while those correlation sides with the intensity higher enough to attract attentions are preserved. For instance, the weight value 1 contributed by key nodes is used as the judgment threshold for establishing correlations. Only when the cumulated weight value of the correlation between two nodes is greater than or equals to 1 can the side be preserved in the new 1-Mode network. Such simplification is necessary. From the perspective of Natural Dialectics, all things in the world are connected, but it is important to grasp principal contradictions and to analyze principal causes and effects in scientific research; in social network services, all people may have various direct and indirect correlations, but only those mutual influences of strong correlations deserve attentions; in the trust relationships among friends, only those relationships involving considerable trusts could recommend and transfer new friendships; on the Internet, many web pages have interior correlations, but only those with correlations reaching certain extent deserve mutual recommendation.

All the decomposition results from the above method are non directional networks, and the correlation of each adjacent pair is equivalent. In practical networks, however, the correlations of two nodes in an adjacent pair are not necessarily equivalent in different directions. Taking interpersonal relationships for example, user u_b may not necessarily treat u_a as his closest friend provided that user u_a regards user u_b as his closest friend. Taking the user relationship formed in volume collection for another example, all the collections of user u_a are collected by user u_b but these collections only takes a very small part in the whole collections of u_b, while most collections of u_b are the same as those of another user u_c. In this case, for user u_a, user u_b is the one with the largest interest intersections with his, but it is not vice versa. In consideration of the different basis on different standard nodes, a 2-Mode network can be decomposed into directional networks. The decomposition results from the decomposition method can be used to generate networks with different nodes as centers (if the nodes represent human, it is equivalent to the Ego Network obtained with the egocentric investigation method in social relationship network), so the method is known as the egocentric directional decomposition method. Here presents its definition and calculation formula:

Definition 3: If the adjacent nodes in one same pair have different degrees and different importance in all the relations of the opposite one, then the method, in which a 2-Mode network is decomposed into two 1-Mode networks with relation directivities according to the directivities of the relative degree ratio of adjacent nodes, is known as the directed decomposition method based on egocentrism.

The specific way of decomposition is to add a degree ratio between two of them as the correction factor in the generation of the correlation weight.

In the key intermediate method, the formula for determining the weight correlation after the addition of the correction factor is (formula-3):

$$w_{u_i \to u_j} = \begin{cases} d_{u_j} / d_{u_i} & ;\ \exists v_m : d_{v_m} <= k \text{ and} (u_i, v_m), (u_j, v_m) \in R \\ 0 & ;\text{Otherconditions} \end{cases} \quad \text{(Formula-3)}$$

In the above case, a threshold value p ($0<p<=1$) can also be set to simplify it to a non-weighted directional net. Let $w_{u_i \to u_j}{}' = 1$ when $w_{u_i \to u_j} >= p$. If $p = 0.8$, then a connection pointing at the opposite is established only when key intermediate nodes are connected and the ratio of opposite degree to the degree of itself is not less than 0.8 as well; in the case of collected volumes, the latter condition can be interpreted as that the other person can be regarded as a friend only when the total amount of his collections is not far beyond. In formula-3, the collection amount is used as the denominator, so the algorithm is used to differentiate the users with different total amounts of collections: there is a great possibility that a user with many collections has collection intersections with other users, so the system should be more strictly restricted in recommending neighbors (the larger the denominator, the fewer calculated weights will exceed the threshold value p);

The fewer collections of a user may be completely included by many other users, so the system restriction can be eased, and more recommendations can be given to him to help him extending his collections (the smaller the denominator, the more calculated weights will exceed the threshold value p). The more volumes being collected, the more strict and precise the system recommendation becomes; the fewer volumes being collected, the more choice recommended by the system, which promotes the collector to collect more contents faster.

In the cume betweenness method, the formula for determining the weight relation after the addition of correcting factors is (formula-4):

$$w_{u_i \to u_j} = \frac{d_{u_j}}{d_{u_i}} \times \sum_{\forall v_i : v_i \in L_{u_i, u_j}} 1 / C^2_{d_{v_i}} \quad \text{(Formula-4)}$$

Where d_{v_i} is the degree of node v_i, and $\frac{d_{u_j}}{d_{u_i}}$ is the degree ratio of u_i to u_j.

In the above analysis, the fact that the original 2-Mode network is a weighted network is not taken into account for the purpose of simplification, i.e., it is assumed that $w(u,v) = 1$ for all $(u,v) \in R$ in (U,V,R,w). In a practical information system, however, a 2-Mode network may sometimes have a weight. For instance, the correlation weight between a user and a tag in a social tag system can be used to represent the frequency of the user using the tag, and a tag with a high reference frequency indicates the user's favorites; the correlation weight between a resource and a tag represents the frequency of the resource referring to the tag, and a tag with a high reference frequency can do better in generalizing the class of a resource. The user can also evaluate the collected resources (or setting an importance indication). The evaluation can be used as the correlation weight between a user and a resource. The users' different evaluations of resources represent different (or even exactly opposite) cognitive relationships. Since different weights have different settings and different significances, different strategies are required in processing. Taking the above weights for instance, one is the calculated frequency (it can be statistics on V-type nodes based on U-type nodes or statistics on U-type nodes based on V-type nodes), and the other is subjective evaluation (it can be the evaluation of the nodes in set U on the nodes in set V, or the evaluation of the nodes in set V on the nodes in set U); taking tags (used as frequencies) for instance, a higher frequency (higher $w(u_i, v_j)$) suggests a closer correlation between u_i and v_j, and the significance of frequency on u_i should be considered in the generation of U-network through decomposition; in the generation of the V-network, the significance of the frequency on v_j should be considered.

The relative significance can be expressed by the relative weight ratio; $\overline{W_{u_i}}$ is used to represent the weighted average of all the correlation weights of v_j connecting to u_i; $\overline{W_{v_j}}$ is used to represent the weighted average of all the correlation weights of u_i connecting to v_j.

$$\overline{W_{u_i}} = \frac{\sum_{j=1}^{|V|} w(u_i, v_j)}{|V_{u_i}|};$$

$$\overline{W_{v_j}} = \frac{\sum_{i=1}^{|U|} w(u_i, v_j)}{|U_{v_i}|};$$

Where $|V_{u_i}|$ is the order of set $V_{u_i} = \{v_j \mid (u_i, v_j) \in R \text{ and } w(u_i, v_j) \neq 0\}$, i.e., the number of all the v_j having non-zero relationships with u_i. Note: Although the relationships with zero weights have been counted in the formula, they have no effects on the results and will not be averaged.

The relative weights are the ratios of $w(u_i, v_j)$ to $\overline{W_{u_i}}$ and $\overline{W_{v_j}}$, respectively. Thus, the weight is divided into two components with cognitions in different directions according to the significance, which represent the cognition of the importance of u_i to v_j and the cognition of the importance of v_j to u_i. Such cognitions are defined as cognitive weights and denoted by $W_{u_i \to v_j}$ and $W_{u_i \leftarrow v_j}$, where the arrows represent the directions that the cognitive subject pointing to the cognitive object.

Definition 4: According to the differences in the significances of the weights on the nodes at both ends of the 2-Mode network, the ratios of the weights in 2-Mode relationships to the weighted average weights for the nodes at both ends are calculated separately. Thus, two weights can be obtained for one same relationship to represent the mutual importance of the nodes. Such relative weights are known as the cognitive weights between the nodes at both sides of a relationship in a 2-Mode network. A cognitive weight has directivity, and a non directional weight can be decomposed into two directional cognitive weights.

The generation mode of the directivity of cognitive weights is different from that in the egocentric directed decomposition method, and has different significances as well. The cognitive weight is the correlation weight between two types of nodes while the weight in the egocentric directional decomposition method is the correlation weight between the nodes of the same type after decomposition.

In order to decompose a weighted 2-Mode network, two presumptions are required.

Presumption 1: The closer cognitive weights of the two nodes (u_a and u_b) in one same set in a 2-Mode network to that intermediate node v_i in another set, the greater the effect of the intermediate node in the transfer of the relationship between u_a and u_b becomes;

Presumption 2: In the comparison of the cognitive weights of two nodes (u_a and u_b) within the same set of a 2-Mode network relative to intermediate node v_i in another set with the average value of the cognitive weights of all other nodes relative to the intermediate node, when the average cognition value is deviated towards a direction, the intermediate node transfers positive relationships between u_a and u_b, and the weights of the positive relationships increase with the amplitude of the conjunct deviation; when the cognitive value deviates towards different directions, negative relationships are transferred and the absolute values of the negative correlation weights increase with the deviation (negative weights for negative relationships).

No more explanation is needed for presumption 1, for two subjects with similar cognitions of things are also close to each other. Presumption 2 is about whether the cognition deviates from the understandings of the public and whether opinions will contradict if the average public cognition is used as the reference system. If the cognitive difference emerges around the public average, then it represents different attitudes despite its slightness; if it emerges at one side of the public cognition, then at least the attitudes and preferences are similar despite the great difference. Therefore, the cognitive weight difference from the public average can be used to represent the cognition attitude. Besides, although the above descriptions are personated (cognitive subject, attitude and public, etc.), the described cognitive subject nodes are not necessarily limited to human.

Based on the above presumptions, a general decomposition method for weighted 2-Mode network based on cognitive weights is presented.

Definition 5: A 2-Mode weighted network is converted to two one-way 2-Mode networks based on cognitive weights (two 2-Mode networks serving as both cognitive subjects and objective items each other), then oriented decomposition is performed on the two one-way 2-Mode networks (only decomposed to cognitive subject networks, while objective item networks serve as cognitive subjects in another corresponding networks). For the Cognitive Subject Pair of each cognitive objective item, correlation weights are calculated according to the similarity in their cognitive weights and the deviation relative to the average cognitive degree (representing the cognition consistency in this objective item), then the total weight (general cognition consistency) for all conjunct cognitive objectives is calculated. Finally, calculation is made on each cognitive subject with a conjunct cognitive objective to obtain the correlation network of cognitive subjects. The method for decomposing 2-Mode weighted networks is known as a general one for decomposing 2-Mode weighted networks based on cognitive weights.

Taking the decomposition of the U-network for example, the steps of the algorithm are given as follows:

(1) For each u_i, $\overline{w_{u_i}}$ is calculated (mean correlation weight of all v_j that connect to u_i);

(2) The cognitive weights of u_i against each v_j connecting to u_i are calculated as $w_{u_i \to v_j} = w(u_i, v_j)/\overline{w_{u_i}}$; the cognitive weight network $(U, V, R, w_{u_i \to v_j})$ of U against V is obtained.

(3) For each $\overline{v_j}$, the average cognitive weight of all u_i connecting to v_j is solved and denoted as v_j; then, the different value of the cognitive weight of u_i against v_j with $\overline{v_j}$ is calculated as $(w_{u_i \to v_j} - \overline{v_j})/\overline{v_j}$ and denoted as $normal(w_{u_i \to v_j})$; the cognitive weight network of standardized U against V is obtained: $(U, V, R, normal(w_{u_i \to v_j}))$. In the step of the average value calculation above, all relationships with weights of zero are not involved in calculation. New zero-value will be produced from the results of this step, and the new zero-value suggests that the cognition of some objective item exhibits no preferences compared with the public cognition. Therefore, the objective item can not be used as the characteristics of cognitive nodes and is treated in the same way as other cognitive subjective nodes (nodes with original weights of zero) without relations with the objective items in decomposition.

(4) According to the standardized cognitive weight network, (U, RR^T, w_u) can be obtained with the general decomposition method.

In subsequent processing, the key intermediate decomposition method, the cume betweenness method and the directional decomposition method based on egocentric networks, etc., can be used again. Consequently, the 2-Mode weighted network decomposition method based on cognitive weights may become very complicated in practice.

Conclusions

It is our interest to advance the edge of information systems research by improving the users' social interaction experiences and to promote the optimization of the social network structures in on-line communities through the application of research based network analysis, social network analysis and other approaches in the design of Web2.0 system. However, the non-equivalence in the user nodes and content nodes in social computing is not taken into account in various conventional network clustering algorithms which, consequently, cannot be used in the system design of Web2.0 directly. Based on the actual application scenarios of Web2.0, several improved 2-Mode network decomposition algorithms were put forward, some of which have been applied in the design of some systems in practice [8]. The algorithms for social computing are somewhat different from general ones in terms of algorithm assessment criteria and testing methods. Due to the space limitations, this is not elaborated here.

References

1. Barry Wellman. For a Social network analysis of computer networks: A Socio-logical Perspective on Collaborative Work and Virtual Community. ACM SIGCPR/ SIGMIS 1996/04
2. Yang, C., H. Chen, et al. Dispositional Factors in the Use of Social Networking Sites: Findings and Implications for Social Computing Research. Intelligence and Security Informatics, Springer Berlin / Heidelberg. 5075: 392-400.
3. Ogawa, S., F.T. Piller. 2006. Reducing the Risks of New Product Development. MIT Sloan Management Review 47(2) 65-71.
4. White, D. R., J. Owen-Smith, et al. (2004). "Networks, Fields and Organizations: Micro-Dynamics, Scale and Cohesive Embeddings." Computational & Mathematical Organization Theory 10(1): 95-117.
5. Grujic, J.; Mitrovic, M.; Tadic, B. Mixing patterns and communities on bipartite graphs on web-based social interactions, Digital Signal Processing, 2009 16th International Conference DOI:10.1109/ICDSP.2009.5201238
6. Cormode, G., D. Srivastava, et al. "Anonymizing bipartite graph data using safe groupings." The VLDB Journal 19(1): 115-139.
7. Matjaz Zaversnik. Vladimir Batagelj, Andrej Mrvar. Analysis and visualization of 2-Mode network [EB/OL] http://www.math.uniklu.ac.at/stat/Tagungen/Ossiach/Zaversnik.pdf?q= Tagungen/Ossiach/Zaversnik.pdf.2011.3.
8. Zhang Shuren and Fang Meiqi. Social software and complex adaptability in-formation system paradigm. Memoir from the first session of national conference of China Association of Information System (CNAIS2005,In Chinese), Tsinghua University Press, 2005

The Meaning of Social Web: A Framework for Identifying Emerging Media Business Models

Soley Rasmussen[1]

Abstract In order to create a basis for future empirical inquiries, this paper presents a cross-disciplinary review of literature on Social Web and similar concepts by mapping them in a conceptual framework inspired by the Phaneroscopy and semiotics of the American philosopher C. S. Peirce. The relevance of the framework is demonstrated by an analysis of literature on blogs. The paper concludes by outlining the main challenges that the Social Web poses for traditional media companies, specifically newspapers.

> … l'autre appelle à venir et cela n'arrive qu'à plusieurs voix.
> Jacques Derrida

Introduction and Motivation

The Internet, the World Wide Web, and wireless communication are not media in the traditional sense. Thus, it does not make sense to compare the Internet to a newspaper in terms of 'audience'; we do not "read" or "watch" the Internet as we read newspapers or watch television, we *live* with it [1]. Therefore, Manual Castells calls the Internet 'the communication fabric of our lives' [1 p. 64].

While interpersonal (one-to-one and one-to-many communication), and mass communication characterized the early days of the Internet (e.g. e-mail and websites), today, long-standing dichotomies of interpersonal versus mass and non-mediated versus mediated communication are questioned, and established definitions of media and communication are changing [2]. In the diverse range of its applications, the Internet is evolving into a place of ever more complex social activity. To frame this, new concepts, such as mass self-communication (coined by Castells 2009 [1]), and many-to-many communication (adopted by e.g. Jensen 2010 [2]), are employed.

From the point of view of communication studies these concepts designate key characteristics of the contemporary Internet. Other research fields, as well as conventional wisdom, have invented other concepts to name the changed and changing "nature" of the Internet/Web, e.g. Web 2.0, Participatory Web, Social Computing, New Media, Social Media. However, none of these concepts are well-defined; they are often used as umbrella terms for a wide range of technologies (from RSS,

[1] Center for Applied ICT, Copenhagen Business School, sr.caict@cbs.dk

blogs, wikis and tags to new hardware platforms), a plethora of applications and service forms, and diverse social and cultural phenomena.

One of the notions often emphasized in the accounts of these concepts is that of the empowered user; readers, consumers, and customers, or rather "the people formerly known as the audience" [3], are becoming co-creators of software, content, artifacts, and services. One of the implications of this 'co-creation', 'prosumption' or 'peer-production' is that (more or less) self-organizing groups of individuals are gaining competitive advantages over firms (see e.g. Benkler 2006 [4]). There also seem to be general agreement that to remain competitive firms need to develop and adjust their business model [5]. However, research on business models in this area is still in its infancy; relatively little is known about how companies can create value by involving *prosumers*, or by 'harnessing collective intelligence' as a popular phrase says [6].

In this paper I employ the term 'Social Web'. Although a justification for my choice of the term will be offered, it is not the intention of the paper to argue for the strengths of one term over the other. It is, however, my intention to provide an account of the *use* of this and similar concepts, i.e. concepts that combine a word that has cultural connotations, such as 'Social', with a word that has technological connotations, such as 'Web'. What do people mean by them? Why do they employ them? What underlying phenomena do these concepts signify? And what are the implications of these phenomena for traditional media companies, newspapers in particular, and their business models?

Methodology

This paper will not provide comprehensive answers to all these questions, but it will suggest a framework within which such questions can be answered. It will also present an overview of what key concepts are employed in the literature discussing the Social Web, and give an example of how the framework can be used to identify "white spaces", i.e. blanks in our knowledge of this phenomenon and its implications. The main contribution of this paper is the development of a conceptual framework inspired by the semiotics and phenomenology (phaneroscopy) of the American philosopher, C. S. Peirce (1839-1914). This will be presented in the section 'Theoria'. In the next section, 'Reading', the framework will be used to identify key concepts employed by the authors of about 150 key articles, chosen from a sample of almost 1100 papers that were identified to be of potential interest in this context. At the end of this section the framework will be used to identify what is said and not said about the phenomenon blogs in these papers. The final section 'Discussion and Outlook' will discuss implications for future research in this area, and relate the readings to recent literature on business models, by outlining the main challenges for traditional media companies.

If one could simply enter 'Web 2.0', 'Social Media', or 'Social Web' into Google, ISI Web of Knowledge, or one of the specialized research databases, and find comprehensible answers to such questions as the ones closing the introduction of this paper, the content of this paper would certainly be a lot of fuss about nothing. However, the Internet is a moving target. Neither developers, nor users, nor researchers can predict the future of the Internet, not even in the short term [2]. While new concepts can be considered *signs to think with* [7], the vast number of new concepts and the conceptual inflation of old ones could be a sign of an emerging (scientific) revolution. Another sign of such revolutions is a tendency to involve philosophers [8]. Although I have no intention of discussing whether or not the Social Web (phenomenon or concept) is a sign of revolution, I do sense a need to turn to the philosophers for guidance, because both the object of study and the methods for studying apparently are changing rapidly, and fundamentally, in this field. When both measured and scale is changing, the American philosopher E. A. Singer said that a "sweeping-in" process is needed [9].

One of the original contributions of C. S. Peirce is his work on methods of inquiry and the addition of the third logical category; abduction. Apart from deduction and induction, Peirce insisted on the existence of abductive reasoning, and on a particular sequentiality of the inquiry process: abduction-deduction-induction. While it is beyond the scope of this paper to discuss the concept of abduction and this sequentiality, in this context abduction can be understood as the logic of the 'best guess', and the sequentiality as a sweeping-in process (for an introduction to abduction, Peircean logic, and "how-to" see e.g. [10-13]). As the following sections will reveal, developing the kind of conceptual framework that will be introduced in this paper, searching for research literature, as well as for meaning in the realm of the Social Web, involves a substantial amount of guessing; abduction is the art of choosing among these guesses.

Theoria

In the following, the structure and content of a diagram of the Meaning of Social Web is presented (fig. 1). I employ the notion 'Meaning of Social Web' to refer to the symbolic, self-evident imaginations of a person or a group of people about (Internet/WWW) technology and all the possible ways it can be utilized. In this I am inspired by Jette Hansen-Møller's 'Meaning of Landscape' [14], and the typology for analyzing the imaginations and intentions of different stakeholders that she has developed for the field of landscape planning. The diagram should be thought of as a conceptual framework; an open "system" of signs or metaphors to think *with* before, while and after collecting "data".

PHENOMENA MODALITIES	CULTURE	SOCIAL WEB	TECHNOLOGY
POTENTIALITIES	~~SENSE~~	AFFORDANCE	~~TECHNOLOGY~~
ACTUALITIES	EXPERIENCE	DRIFT	OBJECT
HABITS	ARGUMENT	SYMBOL	PATTERN

Figure 1: The Meaning of Social Web. Diagram of the three modalities of Culture, Social Web and Technology and their relations.

The core of the diagram is the vertical column, termed Social Web. Hansen-Møller uses the term 'Landscape' to refer to one of many possible stations on the continuum from Culture to *Nature* [14 p. 86]. I use the term 'Social Web' in a similar way; as one point of reference among many on the continuum from Culture to *Technology*. Web 2.0, Social Media, Social Computing etc. could be other such points.

The typology developed by Hansen-Møller is based on the Peirce. With a clear reference to Peirce, one of the most influential contemporary semiotists, Umberto Eco, describes semiotics in this way:

"Semiotics is concerned with everything that can be *taken* as a sign. A sign is everything which can be taken as significantly substituting for something else. This something else does not necessarily have to exist or to actually be somewhere at the moment in which a sign stands for it" [15 p. 7, Eco's italics].

My primary motivation for adopting a semiotics perspective in this specific context is the sense that concepts such as 'Social Web' (i.e. concepts which combine signs that have cultural connotations with signs that have technological connotations) are surrounded by a certain "fuzziness", as the extensive literature review to be presented in the later sections of this paper will also reveal. At the same time, I am interested in the relations between these concepts, and the phenomena they are intended to designate. This implies an interest in the (implicit) assumptions held by the people who use the signs. Hakken, Teli and D'Andrea [16] note that the term 'Social Computing' only makes sense, if 'computing' a priori is taken not to be social. I believe the same could be said of 'Social Web', 'Social Technology' etc., and, consequently, that there is a need for a conceptual meta-perspective on signs and the relations between them, if one wishes to be able to make sense of what is said and written in this field. And in particular, I believe, if one wishes to be able to introduce sensible accounts of the practical implications of "new" phenomena in a business context. Semiotics, and Peircian semiotics in particular, offer us a sphere of inquiry and a meta-analytical conceptual framework for the study of signs and sign complexes. Thus, as a background for introducing the diagram of the Meaning of Social Web in more detail, a brief introduction to Peircean semiotics will be presented in the following.

There are two main strands of (philosophical) semiotics: A "European" grounded in the work of Saussure who introduced the binary relationship sign-object (signifier and signified), and the pragmatic strand founded on Peircean semiotics and Peirce's phenomenology, which he called phaneroscopy to distinguish it from the phenomenology of Hegel and Husserl [17 p. 49]. While Saussure collapses the object and interpreter into a single signified, a model that denies any possible differences between an object and our perception of it, Peirce introduces a distinction: To Peirce 'A sign, or *representamen*, is something which stands to somebody for something in some respect or capacity' [18, 2.288], i.e. Peirce introduces a triadic relationship: Representamen (something), Interpretant (somebody), and Object-relation (something else in some respect or capacity). As it is somewhat confusing to say that there are three elements of a sign, one of which is the sign, to capture the idea it is important to note that in Peirce's terminology it is not the sign as a whole that signifies; only the *signifying element* does so, e.g. it is not the color or material of a chair that signifies the chair, but rather its shape (therefore shape is the element of the sign responsible for signification as representamen).

Peirce also distinguishes between three different modalities of signification; a sign presents itself in three different modes. Peirce defines these categories as a "table of conceptions drawn from the logical analysis of thought and regarded as applicable to being" [18, 1.300]. At the level of firstness signfication takes place by virtue of qualities; at the level of secondness by virtue of existential or physical facts, and at the level of thirdness by virtue of conventions and laws [19]. Combining these three modalities with the triad Representamen – Object-relation – Interpretant results in nine sign-classes, out of which the triad Icon-Index-Symbol is the most well-known.

Hansen-Møller adopts a rectangular structure based on W. Nöth [20], and I have adopted this structure (fig. 2) as the foundation for the diagram of the Meaning of Social Web that is introduced in the beginning of this section (fig. 1).

	INTERPRETANT	OBJECT-RELATION	REPRESENTAMEN
FIRSTNESS	RHEME	ICON	QUALISIGN
SECONDNESS	DICISIGN	INDEX	SINSIGN
THIRDNESS	DELOME	SYMBOL	LEGISIGN

Figure 2: C. S. Peirce's nine sign-classes.

As mentioned in the introduction of this section, the core of the diagram of the Meaning of Social Web (fig. 1) is the vertical column, termed 'Social Web'. It was also mentioned that I use 'Social Web' to refer to one of many possible stations on the continuum from Culture to Technology on the horizontal scale.

First, it should be noted that I adopt the notion of culture from Clifford Geertz's 'symbolic anthropology'. In his famous 'Thick Description: Toward an Interpretive Theory of Culture', Geertz closes in on a definition [21 p. 5]:

"Man is an animal suspended in webs of significances he himself has spun, I take culture to be those webs, and the analysis of it to be therefore not an experimental science in search of laws, but interpretive one in search of meaning."

This notion of culture corresponds with Peirce's 'mental phenomena' that he divides into the modalities 'feeling', 'action of opposition' and 'synthetic thought' [18, 1.350]. I employ the terms Sense, Experience, and Argument to characterize its modalities, as will be explained below. All though Geertz would surely have objected to any attempt to frame *culture* in a diagram (see e.g. [21 p. 11]), my intention behind the diagram is not inconsistent with Geetz. Like Geertz, I wish to avoid any general theory (or philosophy) of meaning or culture. By means of the diagram I simply intent to be explicit (or as explicit as I can manage in condensed "writing") about the conceptual framework that would otherwise be nested implicitly in the *readings* and conclusions to be presented in the following sections of the paper. To quote Geertz himself: "I have a conceptual framework – you have to have that." [22].

Second, the term Technology in the diagram should not be understood in opposition to Culture. However, questions concerning the "nature" of the relation(-s) between Culture and Technology, or between 'nature', 'human' and 'artificial', are by no means easy to clarify. On the one hand, one could argue that technology is 'practical implementations of intelligence', as the French philosopher Frederick Ferré [23] writes. On the other hand – and following the line of thinking of another French philosopher, Jacques Derrida – the reflex of thinking that places technology *after* the human could be questioned. To Derrida technology is *the* determining question of humanity, of the 'human', of becoming human, but – at the same time – he encourages us to think beyond the dichotomies living-dead, biological-technical, essential-artificial, and consider the *complication* or *co-implication* of the 'natural' and 'artificial'. To Derrida questions concerning technology would always have to exceed the 'human' in the narrow sense of the term, and he insists on an infinite differentiation of the field of technology on one side of the human, and of 'nature' on the other side of the human [24].

I adopt a Derridean notion of technology for the purpose of developing the diagram of the Meaning of Social Web. All though Geertz's interpretive anthropology did not move in the direction of deconstruction, but toward the hermeneutics of Ricoeur and the linguistic philosophy of Wittgenstein, this notion of Technology could be considered consistent with Geertz's thinking, as he, like Derrida, rejected any idea of a humanity prior to language, symbolization, and culture [23]. At the same time, the thinking of both Geertz and Derrida could be considered consistent with that of Peirce; Geertz's thinking most certainly, as he explicitly places symbolic anthropology within the tradition of Peirce (see e.g. [22]), but also Derrida acknowledged that Peirce, and especially his concept of secondness, "goes very far in the direction that I have called the deconstruction of the trancendental signified [...] The thing itself is a sign." [17 p. 49], [25].

Peirce considered matter to be *effete* mind [18, 6.24], i.e. *mind* frozen into a 'regular routine' [18, 6.277], [14], and much like Derrida, he considered the artificial and the natural, mind and matter to be '*termini* of a single *continuum*' [14]. Following this line of thinking, I tentatively employ the term, 'Social Web' to signify a Peircean/Derridean co-implication of culture and technology; i.e. I do not wish to make claims about the chronology of the phenomena and their interrelations, but I do wish to emphasize that the very notion 'Social Web' is a combination of two different words with connotations to two different phenomena, culture and technology, respectively (though not necessarily exclusively), and, therefore, the undertaking of interpreting what is meant by the term, is very likely to be an undertaking of interpreting what is meant by culture and/or technology.

As Peirce's nine sign-classes (on a conceptual level) could be said to exhaust all possible signs, the diagram of the Meaning of Social Web could be considered a (tentative) conceptual "map" of all possible ways of thinking about the co-implication of culture and technology in the area of the contemporary Internet, and thus, in contemporary Internet (and Internet-related) research. As a conceptual framework the diagram should be thought of as an open "system" of signs or metaphors to think with before, while and after collecting "data"; it is *not* a theoretical account of *something* or *anything*. As I will show in the section 'Reading' the term 'Social Web' could be considered to have *emerged* from the IS and media- and communication literature (or my interpretation of it). However, at this point it should be considered my *best guess* of an initial designation of a space in the diagram that would otherwise have been left blank; namely the space carved out by the '2.0' in 'Web 2.0', the "new" in 'new media', 'new technology', 'new practices' etc. Besides being a conceptual framework for guiding the (my) search for the meaning of the Social Web, my intention with the diagram is also to facilitate the identification of (new/other) white spaces in the literature. The hypotheses behind this being that were there no white spaces in that vast landscape of literature, there would be no need for any of concepts that I choose to represent with the symbol 'Social Web'. Finally, the diagram forms a basis for future empirical studies, and could be used as a "guide" to analyze interview transcripts. Hansen-Møller develops her diagram 'Meaning of Landscape' for this purpose, and exemplifies its use. To this end Peirce's combination of the nine sign-classes into 10 sign-classes is employed, see Hansen-Møller 2004 [14].

In the following the content of the nine spaces of the diagram Meaning of Social Web will be presented. While the (any) 3x3 matrix in itself is nothing more than a syntax; a structure, the nine spaces could be considered the semantics of this structure. Finally, the choices of some content over other (within this structure, and in the analysis in the following section of the paper) are pragmatic choices; purposive interpretation *is* pragmatic.

Potentialities

As mentioned, to Peirce a sign presents itself in three different modes. Therefore, the vertical scale of the diagram is divided into Potentialities, Actualities, and Habits. These are considered different modalities of the phenomena on the horizontal scale (i.e. Culture, Social Web, Technology). Potentialities involve unanalyzed, instantaneous, immediate feeling; direct 'suchness' dependent on nothing beyond itself for its comprehension. Potentialities are monadic and qualitative [14].

Sense | The term Sence substitutes the Peircean Rheme in fig. 1. A Rheme is a sign of qualitative possibility, which for its Interpretant is understood as representing a specific kind of possible object [18, 2.250]. Hansen-Møller defines it as the 'personal modality' of Culture [14]. It could be considered the individual (psychological) modality [18, 1.350], or, using a term from Heidegger, the modality of *Befindlichkeit.* Peirce used the notion 'feeling'. Thus, *moods* and *affections* (emphasized in e.g. Claudio Ciborra's work in the Information Systems field [26], [27], which is indeed inspired by Heidegger [26 p. 159], [28]) are potentialities; i.e. at the level of firstness the sign presents itself as a mood, an affection. Sense is crossed out in line with Heidegger's crossing out of the term Sein (Being), indicating that we speak about Sense in a mode from before language was corrupted [14].

Affordance | The relationship between Sense and Technology (see below) I designate Affordance to indicate a familiarity with Gibson's original use of the term [29]. The Peircean Icon refers to the Object that it denotes merely by virtue of characteristics of its own, and which it possesses, whether or not such object actually exists [18, 2.247]. It has no dynamic connection with the object it represents; its qualities simply resemble those of that object, and excite analogous sensations in the mind [18, 2.299], [14]. Thus, Affordance refers to the innumerable qualitatively different combinations of the potentialities of Sense and Technology; a phenomenon considered manifest (therefore the term is not crossed out), and as such perceivable by others, but only from the outside, i.e. at the level of secondness [14]. In line with Peirce's notion of firstness, Gibson refers to affordances as "possibilities or opportunities" [29 p. 18]. Following Gibson's original definition, Affordance refers to *the actionable properties between an actor and the world* (summarized by Don Norman [30 p. 1]), and could be considered *the psychology of everyday things* as Norman frames it [31]. Ciborra refers to Norman, and explain that (visible and invisible) "affordances capture those fundamental properties that seem to tell of what things can do for us" [26 p. 90]. Affordances can also be understood as examples (on the level of firstness) of the Derridean *co-implication* of Culture and Technology discussed above.

Technology | As mentioned, in Peirce's terminology it is not the sign as a whole that signifies; only the *signifying element* does so. To explain what I mean by the term Technology, I return to the example of the chair; the shape is the signifying element (representamen) of the chair, while the color or material is not. At the level of firstness, however, all possible qualities are at play; i.e. shape, color, material etc. Peirce used termed 'Quali-sign' for the first sign of the Representamen to express the possibilities of sign-giving, before they are embodied [18, CP 2.244]. Therefore, the term Technology refers to potential qualities of technology that are not yet realized into objects. The term is crossed out in correspondence with the term Sense, and could be considered to represent all the potential, un-embodied *fundamental properties* of technology that Affordances capture, once they are embodied.

Actualities

To Peirce the level of secondness involves the dynamic idea of 'otherness', of a dyadic consciousness as action and reaction to stimulus. Thus, Actualities refer to something that actually takes place; they are existential or physical. It is through actualities we face, and deal with, reality and acquire experience [12], [14], [19].

The notion 'other' is central to understand what is at stake at this level. Peirce referred to the "the real" as "that which insists upon forcing its way to recognition as something other than the mind's creation" [18, 1.325]. All though paralleling Peirce's and Derrida's notion of 'other' might be stretching it too far, I suggest that we understand Actualities through the lens of Derrida. As mentioned, Derrida considered Peirce's ideas about secondness close to his own ideas about deconstruction. To Derrida 'the other' means the wholly, radically other; a key to understand his thinking. The epigraph in the beginning of this paper reveals some resemblances to Peirce's 'other':

"The other is what is never inventable and will never have waited for your invention. The call of the other is a call to come, and that only happens in multiple voices." [32 p. 343]

The quote is from the closing passage of Derrida's essay 'Psyché: Invention le l'autre'. Hillis Miller refers to this passage to illustrate that the other is possibly a "multitudinous murmurous cacophony"; a murmur "that calls [something] to come in many overlapping and incompatible voices" [33 p. 3]. I adopt this notion of 'other', and therefore a notion of Actualities as the modality of the discursive and dialectic coming into being of the "new".

Experience | At the level of secondness Peirce termed the semiotic Interpretant Dicisign; a sign of actual existence coming into being through the assertion or denial of the emotional and intentional qualities of the Rheme (Sense) and the laws of the Argument (see below) [18, 2.251]. Peirce makes a distinction between perception and action. Perception makes us conceive that other things also exist by virtue of their relationships with each other. Experience is the result of our interaction with the *other*; our surroundings make us think or act differently than usually, and they 'urge' us to act upon them and modify them. Peirce uses the notion 'action of opposition' [18, 1.325, 1.336], [14]. Hansen-Møller defines Experience as the 'social modality' of Culture, but it could perhaps also be thought of as the "swamp of everyday life" to use a phrase of Ciborra's, see below.

Drift | The Peircean Index is determined by its 'dynamic object', by virtue of being in a real relation to it. It serves to identify its object and assure us of its existence and presence [18, 4.447, 8.335], [14]. Adopting Ciborra's concept 'drift' to designate the ongoing mutual exchanges between Experience and Object (see below), I wish to emphasize that here we talk about technology in use:

"Drifting denotes the dynamics of an encounter, of pasting up a hybrid composed of technology, organizations, people, and artefacts. Drifting is a way to capture the unfolding of the intrinsic openness of such an encounter. The fluid territory on which such an encounter takes place is the swamp of everyday life in organizations [...]. Drift is the outcome of the match between two agents: technology-possessing affordances; and humans in their various roles of sponsor, user, and designer." [26 p. 90f].

Object | At first sight it might seem more in line with Ciborra's use of Drift to identify the second level of the representamen as Affordance, instead of Object. However, the Peircean Sinsign should be understood as an actually existent thing or event; 'sin' means 'being only once' as in single, simple. The Object can only exist through its qualitative relationship to its 'dynamic object' – the factual combination of form, texture etc.; it serves as a sign through its actual embodiment [18, 2.245], [14]. As I employ the term Affordance to signify the potentialities of *use* (much like Ciborra's use of the concept), the term is too "narrow" at the place of the sinsign, as *all* embodied qualities, i.e. all existential facts [19], are sinsigns, i.e. both the shape and color of the chair are sinsigns, but only the shape is an Affordance. Another example is that an assemblage of screen, keyboard and power-supply is a sign-vehicle for 'computer', but not necessarily for 'computing'.

Habits

As mentioned, to Peirce mind is *effete* mind. Peirce considered physical laws to be derived from the psychical, and therefore the law of mind to be the "great law of the universe" [34 p. 133]. To Peirce this law is habit:

"Logical analysis applied to mental phenomena shows that there is but one law of mind, namely, that ideas tend to spread continuously and to affect certain others, which stand to them in a peculiar relation of affectability. In this spreading they lose intensity, and especially the power of affecting others, but gain generality and become welded with other ideas. ... This tendency is nothing other than the tendency to form habits." [18, 6.104, 6.612]

Habits embody continuity and refer to all kinds of intellectual activities, e.g. logical thinking, mental growth and communication. They are future oriented and enable us to predict the becoming [14]. Despite the name, the law of mind is not to be thought of as fixed and deterministic. On the contrary, mind only exercises "gentle forces" which make it more likely to act in one way than another [34]: "There always remains a certain amount of arbitrary spontaneity in its actions, without which it would be dead" [18, 6.148].

Argument | Peirce used different terms for the Interpretant at the level of thirdness, i.e. the level of 'synthetic thought' [18, 1.350]; Delome was one of them, Argument another. In the diagram Meaning of Social Web Argument is maintained to signal the link with argumentation and reasoning. Contrary to other phenomenologists, e.g. Husserl, Peirce did not believe that an argument could be reduced to a matter of feeling (Sense). To Peirce it is our ability to understand a sign in terms of its place in some pattern of reasoning or system of signs that enable us to derive information from it (qua reasoning) [19], [43]. If there were no Arguments, there would be no Symbols (see below). Hansen-Møller identifies Argument as the 'cultural modality' of the Interpretant; it embraces the habit of questioning the statements and actions of others – according to conventions, i.e. generally accepted regulations [14].

Symbol | The Peircean Symbol is perhaps the best known of Peirce's concepts, and it is also maintained in the diagram. Words, for example, are Symbols, and so are broad speech acts like assertion and judgment [19]. A Symbol refers to the Object that it denotes by virtue of law (convention) which operates to cause the Symbol to be interpreted as referring to that Object; Symbols do not denote a particular thing, but a kind of thing. Symbols grow out of other signs, they serve to make thought and conduct rational, and enable us to predict the future [18, 2.292, 2.249, 4.448], [14]. The terms discussed in this paper, 'Web 2.0', 'Social Media', 'Social Web' could be considered to be Symbols, e.g. 'Web 2.0' is a Symbol that refers to a new and improved version of the Web, because the convention (of the packaged software industry) tells us that '2.0' mean "new and improved". However, the arbitrariness of the assertion between Object and Symbol is also what gives Symbols the ability to deceive and lie.

Pattern | Peirce considered all conventional signs to be Legisigns, but not conversely. The crucial signifying element of a Legisign is primarily due to convention, habit or law; Legisigns signify by virtue of the conventions surrounding their use, e.g. traffic lights are signs of priority, and Peirce thought of them as general types established by men [18, 2.246], [14], [19]. By employing Pattern, and not e.g. Law, I follow Hansen-Møller, who places the laws of nature here, arguing that Peirce believed in a tendency of nature to create habits or stable patterns, within matter as well as within mind, over time (see also the quote above about the law of mind). Therefore, Technology at the level of thirdness is taken to be the patterns that we can sometimes observe in technological development, e.g. Moore's law, Hype-cycles, or evolutionary patterns [35]. These patterns might not be comparable to the laws of nature and mind, but they could be thought of as general types established by men (/women).

Reading

In the following the results of a search for literature to sweep-in potential meanings of Social Web will be presented. This search identified 143 relevant articles out of 1078 potential articles in 13 (top-) outlets; 4 IS journals: Information Systems Research, Journal of Management Information Systems, Journal of the AIS, MIS Quarterly; 2 IS Conference proceedings: Proceedings of the International Conference for Information Systems, Proceedings of the Americas Conference for Information Systems; 3 Media Management journals: Journal of Media Economics, International Journal of Media Management, Journal of Media Business Studies, 3 Media- and Communications journals: Global Media and Communication, Journal of Communication, New Media & Society, and one Newspaper research journal: Newspaper Research Journal.

The main search terms I have employed are: 'Web 2.0', 'Social Media', and 'New Media'. Identifying and choosing among search terms must, by nature, rely on guessing, i.e. abductive reasoning. My guesses are based on my prior experience reading and researching within this field, on the experiences I have from spending substantial amounts of time in a large Danish media company, Jyllands-Posten, as part of that research (listening to the everyday language of media practitioners), and of my experiences as a user of the Internet, and its plethora of applications and services. However, as there are many concepts in circulation, the three main search terms does not cover all potentially relevant material within the

13 journals. Therefore, I also conducted systematic searches with combinations of relevant words, e.g. 'Media' AND 'Internet' or 'Social' AND 'Technology'. The table in Appendix I lists all these search terms, and provides an overview of the results of the searches for each of the journals (including how many relevant articles I identified per journal). The primary criterion for relevance I employed was whether a relevant term (i.e. a term with connotations to both Culture and Technology) was included in 1) keywords, 2) abstract, 3) full text. If I found the paper relevant, I identified key concepts of the article (one article could include more than one key concept, and several articles could include the same concept), and noted the definitions, explanations etc. given by the authors. This identification was also an abductive process.

Then, as a first step in the process of analyzing the content of the articles, the key concepts were categorized in terms of their connotations to Culture, Technology, and Social Web. In total 90 key concepts were identified, and fig. 3 presents the aggregate result of their categorization (for a fuller list of key concepts, and the number of articles that employ them per journal, see Appendix II). To qualify my choices of search terms, I used Google to get an indication of the relevance of each term. The number of links for the three main search terms were: "Social Media": 41.900.000, "Web 2.0": 40.400.000, "New Media": 20.000.000. This method was also employed as an indicator of the relevance of each of the key concepts within each of the three categories (sign-classes), as explained in Appendix II. While both 'Web 2.0' and 'New Media' can be identified in many of the 143 articles (Web 2.0: 43, New Media: 17), only one article included 'Social Media'. However, based on the number of Google links, I chose to employ 'Social Web' as the common denominator, as 'Social Media' and 'Web 2.0' are in fact the most common concepts in the middle category (in terms of Google links, see Appendix II). 'Social Web' covers the three most frequent concepts in the sample, if 'Media' is taken to be implicit in the term, and 'Social' to be implicit in 'New Media'.

CULTURE	SOCIAL WEB	TECHNOLOGY
Peer Community Social Network User generated Production Producer Developer Product Content Consumer User Support Recommendation Endorsement Communication Empowerment Interactivity Knowledge	Primary key concepts: SOCIAL MEDIA - WEB 2.0 - NEW MEDIA Social + TECH (e.g. social software, social computing) Social Network + TECH (e.g. social networking site) Collaboration + TECH (e.g. collaboration software, collaboration engineering) Computer-mediated + CULTURE (e.g. computer-mediated communication) Virtual + CULTURE (e.g. virtually community) Online + CULTURE (e.g. online community, online content) TECH + Communication (e.g. digital communication) TECH + Community (e.g. online community, internet localization) TECH + Knowledge (e.g. online knowledge contribution) TECH + Networks of Practice (e.g. electronic NoP, opensourcing) CULTURE + TECH + Services (e.g. personalized information technology services)	Web-based Technologies, New Media Technologies, New Communication Technologies, Social Media Platform, Digital Media, Online Media, Multimedia, Digital/Electronic Network, Open Source Software, Many-to-Many Communication setting, Computer-mediated Communication Technologies, Ubiquitous computing, Web 3.0

Figure 3: Categorization: The most frequent concepts related with Social Web

Out of the 90 key concepts, four were not included in the initial categorization: 'Blog', 'wiki', 'wikipedia', and 'instant messaging', as they neither have (apparent) connotations to Culture, Technology, nor Social Web, and, at the same time, could be said to have connotations to all three categories. In the following blog is chosen as an example for analysis for four reasons: 1) In the literature 'blog' is frequently associated with the concepts in the middle column, e.g. with 'Web 2.0' or 'New Media'; 2) 'Blog' is in fact *the* most frequent term in the sample (in terms of

~~SENSE~~ Weblogs in the form of online diaries first appeared in the early 1990s as pioneers documented their personal lives ... present[-ed] their thoughts, activities or interpretations of events [37]. Blogging is becoming increasingly popular as a global phenomenon [38].	AFFORDANCE [P]rivate individuals use media technologies to create and share personal expressions through digital networks [39], establishing social relationships and networks with others through various links including citations, blogrolls, comments, and trackbacks [40]. [A] Web log or blog [is defined] as a Web-based form of communication ..., some [blogs] function as more personal online diaries [41]. [I]t is difficult to get a snapshot of the blogosphere with enough blogs over a long enough period to capture the real situation [38]	~~TECHNOLOGY~~
EXPERIENCE [Today] 50 million Internet users visit blogs [42]. The blog is one of the most familiar social media to Web users. Its social nature suggests that blogging is not only about writing and publishing bloggers' experience and thoughts, but also about establishing social relationships and networks [40]. Millions of web users engage in the online activities such as blogging, online forums, or online review systems to interact with people and to capture attention ... users compete for the scarce resource, attention, when participating in the online Web 2.0 activities [43]. [T]he emergence of a new type of actor ... [imply] field-level changes and outline areas for further research on technology discourse, new media, and knowledge entrepreneurship [44].	DRIFT Individual blog traffic and blogosphere structure are of interest to academia and practice [38]. In a many-to-many communication setting ... individuals may be strongly tempted to free-ride on others' contributions, which would eventually lead to the collapse of the community [45]. This analysis ... showed that the blogs contained a small number of postings and failed to create much interaction between bloggers and readers [37]. [T]he use of blogs as a source of news ... [impact] other media such as television and newspapers [42]. [B]log was defined as a type of Web site produced by a ... media outlet in which commentaries or opinions from both local ... journalists and audience members are displayed in a diary fashion [41]. [We] examine the reason why media managers implemented blogging at their media outlet [46].	OBJECT [D]igitalization, ... media technologies, personal media (e.g. mobile phones, email, instant messenger, blogs and photo-sharing services) [39]. A typical blog combines text, images, and links to other blogs, Web pages, and other media related to its topic [41]. Researchers tend to agree that blogs are user-generated, frequently updated Web pages containing text, pictures and video [37].
ARGUMENT We examine ... entries collected by a technology news aggregator website ... [B]loggers position themselves [thro-ugh specific discursive practices] as knowledge entrepreneurs within the blogging discourse community and within the wider discourse ... As they attempt to establish claims to legitimacy and influence in this discourse, individual bloggers contribute to the construction of ... bloggers as a collective actor and challenge the positions of established actors [44].	SYMBOL As with any social phenomenon, the very term blog took on a life of its own ... [M]any people use it [blog] to refer to a wide variety of Internet activities [37]. The word blog can also be used as a verb to describe the process of writing a blog, and users are typically known as bloggers [41]. Blogs may be classified by subject (e.g. politics, entertainment, travel, music) or by the individual content producer. Researchers and historians differentiate between two blog styles filter and journal [37].	PATTERN [C]haos theory finds underlying order in this apparent random and complex phenomenon. Key concepts of chaos theory ... construct an interpretive framework to illustrate blog system behavior dynamics ... Blog systems tend to be nonlinear, dynamic, and deterministic, as well as sensitive to initial conditions [38].

Figure 4: Illustration of the Meaning of Social Web – Example: Blog

Google links = 2.570.000.000); 3) Many online newspapers have blogs, but no business model for them [36], 4) Most people are familiar with blogs.

Thus, the diagram of the Meaning of Social Web is used to analyze and illustrate what is said about blogs in the literature reviewed for this paper. The key concepts from the categorization (fig. 3) have been used to guide the analysis; in terms of what to look for in the papers, and is indicators of where to place it in the diagram. The result is a new diagram (fig 4.). The nine spaces present "raw" text, i.e. text from the articles, composed into (more or less) coherent narratives. Therefore, the reader is also encouraged to read in a creative way, i.e. purposefully contribute to the pragmatic layer of meaning on top of the syntax and semantics.

Discussion and Outlook: The Dark Side of Knowledge

The analysis of the literature on blogs can tell us something about what white space there are in our understanding of the phenomenon. For example, the fact that Technology is blank, or that Pattern contain text from only one article (that primarily refers to blog systems as cultural systems) could point at a need for future research to address the fundamental technological properties of blogs (and blog systems). At the same time, this, and other missing pieces in the diagram (e.g. affective aspects of blog use in Sense, deep studies of blog Affordances, or the of the role of Symbols in our understanding of blogs), indicate that there are indeed blanks in our knowledge of the *phenomenon* Social Web (at least when we look at it through the lens of these 13 outlets from a Peircean standpoint).

One way to address the white spaces is to adopt perspectives from related fields, e.g. computer science or science and technology studies (STS). By integrating evolutionary perspectives (see e.g. De Marco, Fiocca, and Ricciardi [47], Williams and Steward [48-49]) the "*dark side* of artifacts, i.e. their embedded knowledge" [47 p. 156, original emphasis], as well as the fact that ICT supplier offerings are "*unfinished* technology" [49 p. 1, original emphasis] is brought to our attention. And so is the role of social learning; Williams and Steward explicitly state resemblance between their use of 'domestication' and Ciborra's use of 'bricolage', and the resulting *drift* in the use of technology [48 p. 139]. This calls our attention to the space in the middle of the diagram (fig. 4). It may not be a white space, but still there seem to be blanks.

As mentioned, I employ Drift, to signal an emphasis on technology *in use*. To Ciborra, Drift is the result of a process where "[a]rtefacts and people become the springboard for new actions [...] the disclosure of dispositions (hidden affordances) keep the everyday world moving, and makes *bricolage* and improvization into the sources of innovation." [26 p. 91, Ciborra's italics]. Therefore, Drift is a key to answer questions like "What are the implications of these phenomena for traditional media companies, newspapers in particular, and their business models?"

In the final remarks, I will focus the attention on two main implications for traditional media; both are major challenges for newspapers companies.

First, returning to the diagram on blogs (fig. 4), and taking a closer look at the article behind the last bit of text in Drift (Sheffer and Schultz 2009 [46]), suggests some "serious management issues related to blogging". These authors find that media managers, on the one hand, like the idea of blogging, seem to have made efforts to implement it in their content offerings, and that most managers see it as a way to increase advertising revenues. On the other hand, however, the addition of blogging increases the workload of journalists, but managers do not seem willing to compensate them with additional pay or training. Sheffer and Schultz conclude that this indicate either uncertainty or unwillingness on the part of media managers, and that "such an approach does not bode well for the successful implementation of blogging [...], nor does it suggest that managers should be successful in regards to implementation of any number of new media technologies." [46 p. 15f].

Second, as mentioned in the introduction, there is general agreement that to remain competitive firms need to develop and adjust their business model, but much uncertainty about the economic value of the Social Web. The journal Long Range Planning recently published a special issue on business models [5]. According to the editorial of this special issue, the topic of business models "... is of exceptional importance to managers. The choice of business model is typically seen as a key component of organisational success. This special issue is [...] creating legitimacy for the concept and inviting scholars to make it centre stage in future academic research." [5 p. 143]. One of the articles [6] focuses on the implications of the Web 2.0 for creating value on the Internet. The authors identify four headings for factors of importance for business models: 1) social networking; 2) interaction; 3) personalisation/customisation; 4) user-added value, and discuss how Internet business models can adapt to the challenges of the Web 2.0. The authors emphasize that their findings "lend further support to the concept of 'open innovation'", by arguing: "in the realm of Web 2.0 firms need to "possess strong sensing capabilities [...]. This implies that the entire firm, and not just the top management, needs to be involved in constant environmental scanning. In fact, not only organization-internal resources can contribute to an improved understanding of technological changes, but the firm's customers are becoming an increasingly important source of information about these changes." [6 p. 287]. As the authors note, there are very few academic articles on business models in this area [6 p. 286]. Their article, and the special issue as a whole, suggests that traditional media companies face major challenges, *because* of the Social Web phenomenon, but, at the same time, it suggests opportunities for strategic development of business models, also for traditional media companies.

However, for Social Web to become a source of innovation and value creation for newspapers there seem to be some dilemmas involved. Some are managerial, and some of more fundamental nature. The conceptual framework suggested in this paper points at white spaces in our knowledge of the phenomena that 'Social Web' and similar concepts designate. Of course, only a glimpse of literature has been presented, and a 3x3 matrix is still a matrix, but were there no such blanks in our understanding of these phenomena, much of the speculation about emerging business models would probably be obsolete, and questions concerning of the future of newspapers and other so-called traditional media either answered or irrelevant.

APPENDIX I: OVERVIEW OF SEARCH TERMS / JOURNALS

Journal	Information Systems						Media Man/Bus			Media- and Comm.				
Search term	ISR[A]	JMIS[A]	JAIS[A]	MISQ[A]	ICIS[B]	AMCIS[B]	JME[A]	JMM[C]	JMBS[D]	GMC[C]	JC[C]	NMS[E]	NPR[C]	*Checked art./term*
web 2.0 (FT)	1	9	5	9			2	3		1	1	30	2	*63*
web 2.0 (AB)					5	21			0			6		*32*
web 2.0 (KW)					8	18								*26*
social media (FT)	0	2	1	2			0	1		1	1	10	1	*19*
social media (AB)					3	1			0					*4*
new media (FT)	2	12	0	11			21	39		0	94	393**	89**	*179*
media (AB)	4	8	1	6	49		50**	60**		33**	122**	116**	43**	*68*
new media (AB)					1	1	21	8	3	1	2	35	5	*77*
media AND internet (AB)							3	6		4	11	50	5	*79*
media AND web (AB)							0	2		1	2	16	4	*25*
media AND online (AB)							1	4	1	2	4	33	4	*49*
media AND digital (AB)							1	3	1	2	3	25	2	*37*
social (AB)	18	21	18	24	98*		6	7		19	54	122***	9	*176*
social (KW)					0							49		*49*
social AND media (AB)					18									*18*
social AND technology (AB)					30									*30*
social AND computing (AB)					3									*3*
communities (AB)	16	12	10	13	21		0	2		8	11	40	11	*144*
Relevant articles/journal	**15**	**12**	**12**	**17**	**21**	**24**	**0**	**8**	**5**	**3**	**4**	**15**	**7**	**143**
(checked articles)****	41	64	35	65	138	41	55	72	5	39	183	294	43	1078

FT= full text, AB= abstract, KW = keyword.

ISR - Information Systems Research, JMIS - Journal of Management Information Systems, JAIS - Journal of the AIS, MISQ - MIS Quarterly, ICIS - Proceedings of the International Conference for Information Systems, AMCIS - Proceedings of the Americas Conference for Information Systems, JME Journal of Media Economics, JJM - International Journal of Media Management, JMBS - Journal of Media Business Studies, GMC - Global Media and Communication, JC - Journal of Communication, NMS - New Media & Society, NRJ - Newspaper Research Journal

A Database: Business Source Complete. Year: 2005-2010. Method: Check for relevance: 1) title, 2) keywords/subject, 3) abstract, 5) full paper.

B Database: AIS e-library. Year: 2007-2009. Method: No 'full text' search, because of too many non-relevant results. Check for relevance: 1) title, 2) keywords/subject, 3) abstract, 5) full paper.

C Database: Communication & Mass Media Complete. Year: 2005-2010. Method: Check for relevance: 1) title, 2) keywords/subject, 3) abstract, 5) full paper.

D Source: www.jombs.com. Year: 2005-2010. Method: "Manual" 1) title, 2) keywords/subject, 3) abstract.

E Database: Sage. Year: 2005-2010. Method: Check for relevance: 1) title, 2) keywords/subject, 3) abstract, 5) full paper.

* Because this set is so large, more specific searches are conducted: 'social' (keyword), and 'social AND ...'.

**Because these are media- and communication journals, this is too many results, and more specific searches are conducted.

***Because New Media and Society is a media- and communication journal, with a clear social focus, this is too many results, and a more specific search is conducted: 'social' (keyword).

****For 'new media' (full text), 'new media' (abstract), 'social' (abstract) the marked numbers are not included in the total.

APPENDIX II: CATEGORIZATION OF KEY CONCEPTS IN THREE CLASSES

Journal / **Key concepts** (total: 90*)	ISR	JMIS	JAIS	MISQ	ICIS	AMCIS	JME	JMM	JMBS	GMC	JC	NMS	NRJ	Total**	Google ***
INTERPRATANT: CULTURE (total: 19)															
social networking (social network)	2			1	4									7	76.300.000
peer production	1	2						1						4	78.800
user generated content				1	2									3	4.480.000
Interactivity (interactive)												1	1	2	5.000.000
user community						1								1	6.700.000
(communities of) free software developers										1				1	4.870.000
peer support				1										1	1.680.000
consumer-generated product	1													1	395.000
peer networking			1											1	217.000
user participation					1									1	184.000
OBJECT -RELATION: SOCIAL WEB (MEDIA) (total: 44)															
web 2.0		3	5	5	5	16		3		1		5		**43**	**40.400.000**
new media				1	1	1		4	3			6	1	**17**	**20.000.000**
online community	2		3		2									7	19.000.000
virtual community (communities)	1				2						1			5	890.000
digital divide	1		1											2	2.700.000
enterprise 2.0						2								2	2.520.000
social software (applications)			2											2	1.560.000
social computing			1		1									2	650.000
online product recommendation	1		1											2	59.000
social media					1									**1**	**41.900.000**
REPRESENTAMEN: TECHNOLOGY (total: 23)															
open source software		1			1	1								3	10.500.000
digital network	2													2	3.040.000
electronic network			1		1									2	369.000
multimedia		1												1	300.000.000
online media									1					1	6.130.000
web-based technologies			1											1	2.110.000
web 3.0								1						1	1.360.000
new media technologies							1							1	1.330.000
cross-media (formats)													1	1	1.160.000
new communication technologies										1				1	795.000

*The total number of (distinctly) different key concepts in the 143 relevant articles is 90. This table lists the 10 most frequent concepts for each of the three categories.

** Total = frequency of the search term. Priority: 1) The most frequent concepts in the articles, 2) The number of Google-links when the frequency = 1

*** Date for Google search: June 9, 2010. Method: "term", 1) Search on search term, 2) Search on similar spelling etc. (e.g. singular/plural) 3), 4) The term with the largest number of links is noted.

Journal / **Key concepts**	ISR	JMIS	JAIS	MISQ	ICIS	AMCIS	JME	JMM	JMBS	GMC	JC	NMS	NRJ	Total	Google
NOT INCLUDED IN FIRST ROUND CLASSIFICATION (total: 4)															
Blog (noun/verb)		1			1			2					2	6	2.570.000.000
Wiki		1		2		1								4	368.000.000
Wikipedia		1												1	271.000.000
Instant Messaging (noun/verd)			1											1	19.400.000

References

1. Castells, M. (2009) *Communication power.* Oxford University Press
2. Jensen, K. B. (2010) New Media, Old Methods – Internet Methodologies and the Online/ Offline Divide. *The Handbook of Internet Studies*, Blackwell (in press).
3. Rosen, J. (2006) The People Formerly Known as the Audience. Blog post, permalink: http://journalism.nyu.edu/pubzone/weblogs/pressthink/2006/06/27/ppl_frmr.html
4. Benkler, Y. (2006) *The Wealth of Networks.* Yale University Press
5. Baden-Fuller, C. et al. (eds.) (2010) Special Issue: Business Models. *Long Range Planning*, 43(2-3)
6. Wirtz, B. W., Schilke, O. and Ullrich, S. (2010) Strategic Development of Business Models: Implications of the Web 2.0 for Creating Value on the Internet. *Long Range Planning, Special issue on Business Models*, 43(2-3), 272-290.
7. Sällström, P. (1991) *Tecken att tänka med* [Signs to think with]. Carlssons bokförlag
8. Khun, T. (1962) *The Structure of Scientific Revolutions.* University Of Chicago Press; 3rd ed. 1996
9. Singer, E. A. (1959) *Experience and Reflection*, University of Pennsylvania Press
10. Paavola, S. (2006) *On the origin of ideas – An abductivist Approach to Discovery*, Philosophical Studies from University of Hensinki 15, University of Helsinki
11. Patokorpi, E. (2006) *Role of abductive reasoning in digital interaction*, doctoral dissertation, Åbo Akademi University, Åbo Akademis Tryckeri.
12. Shank, G. and Cunningham, D.J. (1996) Modelling the six modes of Peircean abduction for educational purposes. In: M. Gasser (ed.), *Proceedings of the 1996 Midwest Artificial Intelligence and Cognitive Science Conference.* Indiana, USA
13. Stanford Encyclopedia of Philosophy (2009) *Charles Sanders Peirce.* Available online: http://plato.stanford.edu/entries/peirce/#dia
14. Hansen-Møller, J. (2006) The Meaning of Landscape: A Diagram for Analysing the Relationship between Culture and Nature, based on C. S. Peirce's Semiotics. *Studies in Environmental Aesthetics and Semiotics* 2006 (5) s. 85-108
15. Eco, U. (1979) *A theory of semiotics.* Indiana University Press
16. Hakken, D., Teli, M. and D'Andrea, V. (2009) *Intercalating the Social and the Technical: A Key Step in Coordinating Future Software Development.* Unpublished manuscript
17. Derrida J. 1976 (1967). *Of Grammatology.* Transl. GC Spivak. Baltimore: Johns Hopkins Univ. Press
18. Peirce, C. S. – *Collected Papers of Charles Sanders Peirce*, 8 vols. Eds. Charles Hartshorne, Paul Weiss, Arthur Burks. Cambridge: Harvard University Press, 1931–1958. Charlottesville: Past Masters CD-Rom Databases
19. Stanford Encyclopedia of Philosophy (2006) *Peirce's Theory of Signs.* Available online: http://plato.stanford.edu/entries/peirce-semiotics/
20. Nöth, W. (2000) *Handbuch der Semiotik* 2. [*Semiotic Manual*, 2.] Stuttgart: J. B. Metzler
21. Geertz, C. (1973) Thick Description: Toward an Interpretive Theory of Culture". In: *The Interpretation of Cultures: Selected Essays.* Basic Books
22. Geertz, C. (2002) I don't do systems. An interview with Clifford Geertz (with Arun Micheelsen), In: *Method & Theory in the Study of Religion. Journal of the North American Association for the Study of Religion* (Leiden/NED: Koninklijke Brill NV), vol. 14 no. 1 (1 March 2002), pp. 2-20
23. Ferré, F. (1988) *Philosophy of technology.* Prentice-Hall
24. Johnson, C. (2008) Derrida and Technology. In: Glendinning, S. and Eaglestone, R. (ed.) *Derrida's Legacies.* Routledge
25. Morris, R. C. (2007) Legacies of Derrida: Anthropology. *Annual Review of Anthropology*, 36, 355-389
26. Ciborra, C. (2002) *The Labyrinths of Informatio.* Oxford University Press
27. Ciborra, C. and Willcocks, L. (2006) The mind or the heart? It depends on the (definition of) situation. *Journal of Information Technology,* 21(3), 129-139.

28. Depaoli, P. (2008) Interdisciplinarity and Its Research: The Influence of Martin Heidegger from 'Being and Time' to 'The Question Concerning Technology'. In: D'Arti, A., De Marco, M. and Casalino, N. *Interdisciplinary Aspects of Information Systems Studies.* Physica-Verlag HD
29. Gibson, J. J. (1986) *The Ecological Approach To Visual Perception.* Lawrence Erlbaum Associates (originally published in 1979)
30. Norman, D. A. (2007) *Affordances and Design.* Available online: http://jnd.org/dn.mss/affordances_and_design.html
31. Norman, D. A. (1988) *The psychology of everyday things.* Basic Books
32. Derrida, J. (1989): *Psyche: Invention of the Other.* In: Attride, D. (red.): Acts of Literature. Routhledge (1992)
33. Hillis Miller, J. (2001) *Others.* Princeton University Press
34. Potter, V. G. (1997) *Charles S. Peirce on norms & ideals.* Fordham University Press
35. Spivack, N. (2008) *The Semantic Web.* Video: Bonnier GRID 2008 conference, Stockholm, Online:http://link.brightcove.com/services/player/bcpid1803302824?bclid
36. Rasmussen, S. (2009) The Value of Online Newspapers Web 2.0 Adoption. *Proceedings of IADIS International Conference WWW/Internet 2009*, p. 125-132. IADIS Press
37. Dailey, L. et al. (2008) Newspaper Political Blogs Generate Little Interaction. *Newspaper research Journal*, 29(4), 53-65.
38. Gou, X. et al. (2009) Chaos Theory as a Lens for Interpreting Blogging. *Journal of Management Information Systems,* 26(1).
39. Lüders, M. (2008) Conceptualizing personal media. *New Media & Society*, 10(5), 683-702.
40. Jiang, T. and Wang, X. (2009) How Do Bloggers Comment: An Empirical Analysis of the Commenting Network of a Blogging Community. **ICIS 2009 Proceedings**. Paper 99.
41. Schultz, B. and Sheffer, M. (2008) Blogging from the Labor Perspective: Lessons for Media Managers. *International Journal on Media Management*, 10(1), 1 – 9.
42. Hargrove, T. and Stemple, G. (2007) Use of Blogs as a Source of News Presents Little Threat to Mainline News Media. *Newspaper Research Journal* , 28(1), 99-102.
43. Shen, W. (2009) Competing for Attention in Online Reviews. *AMCIS 2009 Doctoral Consortium.* Paper 2.
44. Vaast and Davidson (2008) New Actors and New Media in Technology Discourse: An Investigation of Tech Blogging. *Proceedings of ICIS 2008.* Paper 162
45. Sohn, D. and Leckenby, J. D. (2007) A Structural Solution to Communication Dilemmas in a Virtual Community. *Journal of Communication*, 57(3), 435 449.
46. Sheffer, M. and Schultz, B. (2009) Blogging from the Management Perspective: A Follow-Up Study. *The International Journal on Media Management*, 11: 9–17
47. De Marco, M., Fiocca, R., and Ricciardi, F. (2010) The Ecology of Learning-by-Building: Bridging Design Science and Natural History of Knowledge, In: Winter, R., Zhao, J.L., and Aier, S. (Eds.): *DESRIST 2010, LNCS 6105*, pp. 154–166. Springer-Verlag, Berlin
48. Williams, R., Stewart, J., Slack, R. (2005) *Experimenting with Information and Communication Technologies: Social Learning in Technological Innovation.* Edward Elgar Publ
49. Stewart, J. and Williams, R. (2005) The Wrong Trousers? Beyond the Design Fallacy: Social Learning and the User, In: Rohracher, H. (ed.) *User involvement in innovation processes. Strategies and limitations from a socio-technical perspective.* Profil-Verlag, Munich

Digital Natives in a Knowledge Economy: will a New Kind of Leadership Emerge?

Alessio Maria Braccini[1], **Antonio Marturano**[2], **Alessandro D'Atri**[3]

Abstract The aim of this paper is to understand whether digital natives will need a different approach to leadership development. The authors discuss that in knowledge economies learning approaches based on extrinsic and explicit knowledge (knowing that) are more important than traditional learning methods based on the idea that knowledge has a value per se and it is transferred in a tacit way (knowing how). In conclusion, authors do acknowledge the importance of extrinsic and explicit knowledge in digital natives learning; but they stress that, if they wish to become leaders, digital natives still have not only to turn their explicit knowledge into implicit (internalization) in order to intuitively use what they are learning, but also they need to learn more about social skills.

Keywords: Digital natives, knowledge economy, leadership, knowing how and knowing that, digital immigrants.

Introduction

The aim of this paper is to answer to the question whether the shift to a knowledge economy will change the way in which leadership is usually practiced in business organizations. Knowledge economy indeed puts its emphasis on management of intangible assets than management of material goods.

In the first section we will analyse the significance of such shift for leadership and we will argue that "knowledge" in knowledge economy became a kind of commodity and therefore it has an extrinsic value; for this reason it should be accessible virtually in the most explicit way. In the second section we will show how people that have been born in the digital era deal with knowledge they get basically from Information and Communication Technologies (ICT) which at the same time shape their minds. Digital native knowledge processes, are quite different from the past popular theoretical-based learning; digital natives rely more on explicit knowledge. In the fourth section we will show that in digital natives, knowledge management processes play a relevant role in this stage of decision making. In the fifth section we will follow Nonaka showing how knowledge is usually transformed among individuals by means of four knowledge transformation processes: externalization, internalization, socialization, and combination. In the

[1] CERSI LUISS Guido Carli Rome, Italy, abraccini@luiss.it

[2] CERSI LUISS Guido Carli Rome, Italy, marturano@btinternet.com

[3] CERSI LUISS Guido Carli Rome, Italy datri@luiss.it

sixth section we will see with the help of Chinese's art of contextualizing such transformation processes allow for a holistic understanding of phenomena; such methodology helps firms themselves to face the need to become learning organisations, continuously adapting management to change.

In the conclusions we will acknowledge the importance of extrinsic and explicit knowledge in digital natives learning; but, if they wish to become leaders, digital natives still have to turn their explicit knowledge into an implicit one (internalization) in order to intuitively (or emotionally) use what they are learning, together with a deeper understanding about social skills.

From Material Production to Knowledge Economy: A Change in Leadership Paradigms

It is generally agreed that we entered into a knowledge economy. Knowledge economy is a term that refers either to an *economy of knowledge* focused on the production and management of knowledge in the frame of economic constraints, or to a *knowledge-based economy.* In the second meaning, more frequently used, it refers to the use of knowledge technologies (such as knowledge engineering and knowledge management) to produce economic benefits as well as job creation. Although not yet well distinguished in the mainstream literature, "knowledge" in the first case is a *product*, in the second case it is a *tool*. However is in the very nature of knowledge to be ambiguously a product and a tool; in fact, knowledge produces new knowledge which can be used the same times as a tool to produce material goods. A typical example is electricity: knowledge about electricity created new knowledge on electricity too (*knowledge as product*) that leads to the invention of lamps (*knowledge as tool*) which is in turn an interesting subject of knowledge.

Furthermore, according to J.F. Lyotard [1]

> "We may thus expect a thorough exteriorisation of knowledge with respect to the "knower," at whatever point he or she may occupy in the knowledge process. The old principle that the acquisition of knowledge is indissociable from the training (*Bildung*) of minds, or even of individuals, is becoming obsolete and will become ever more so. The relationships of the suppliers and users of knowledge to the knowledge they supply and use is now tending, and will increasingly tend, to assume the form already taken by the relationship of commodity producers and consumers to the commodities they produce and consume – that is, the form of value. Knowledge is and will be produced in order to be sold; it is and will be consumed in order to be valorised in a new production: in both cases, the goal is exchange".

Lyotard – in other words – seems to suggests that economy knowledge should be not focused on the idea that knowledge is a process or tools; rather it should be focused on the idea that knowledge as such has not anymore a pure *intrinsic* value (a value *per se*, as traditionally it did – Lyotard says "knowledge ceases to be an end in itself, it loses its "use-value."), but rather an *extrinsic* value. Indeed, according to Lyotard, "it is not hard to visualise learning circulating along the same lines as money…". Knowledge economies – in other words – realize a *commodification* of knowledge: a modification of relationships, formerly untainted by commerce, into commercial relationships. Knowledge did not have an economic value. The raise of knowledge economy has assigned to knowledge a value and hence market values have replaced other traditional social values (i.e. its intrinsic value).

Knowledge as a Commodity

A peculiar characteristic of intrinsic knowledge is the fact that – especially for professional learning – it was transferred from a master to some disciples. Such learning was based on the transfer of specific skills a disciple needed to be, in some ways, internalized. Often steps to understand how to paint, how to build an artfully craft, were not explicit but tacitly passed from a master to a disciple. If we look at the Renaissance, we have examples of master painters able to transfer only some basic skills to their scholars whose have to reinterpret art in their own way. Famous Perugino student Raphael (Raffaello Sanzio) did not work for the monumental Sistine Chapel in the Vatican, but he learnt and improved his predecessor's way to reproduce light in paintings which was unsurpassed during the while Renaissance. Raphael is indeed one of the big names in the history of western painting, while Perugino plays a marginal role (which is an example of the tacit-tacit knowledge transfer described by Nonaka and Takeuchi, [2]).

On the contrary, when knowledge is treated and exchanged as a commodity, some implications arise due to its nature. Usually in an exchange something is given away and something is received. In economics this exchange mechanism is at the very foundation of the market economy. Commodities are exchanged on markets, and during the exchange their value is measured with the price, by means of money.

Knowledge by itself is a quite different kind of commodity, and its peculiarities appear evident in the exchange. When knowledge is exchanged it is never given away. In order to clarify with an example, let us think about the situation where two persons, A and B, exchange two commodities *a* and *b*, respectively owned by individual A and B. After the exchange A does no longer posses *a*, he now possess *b*. At the same time, B no longer possesses *b*, but now possesses *a*. This is also known as the *quid pro quo* principle.

Anyhow, if the two commodities *a* and *b* are pieces of knowledge, after the exchange A possesses both *a* and *b*. The same is also true for B. Thence, when knowledge is exchanged is not given away, and knowledge does not fall under the *quid pro quo* principle. When knowledge is exchanged, from the point of view of the individual exchanging it, is not lost, it is rather increased. Doing so, knowledge looses its scarcity and, by loosing scarcity, it also looses its exchange value. Interpreted under this point of view it might seem that knowledge is of no value. Indeed knowledge might have value even if it becomes less and less scarce in exchange. This is so because many forms of knowledge exchange are not based on a market economy principle, where value is a direct consequence of scarcity, but they are rather based on a gift economy principle, where value is a direct consequence of abundance.

We are not digital natives and therefore we still have in mind a reminiscence of the distinction between knowledge as having a value per se and knowledge as having an extrinsic value. The next step is to understand whether this distinction still hold for digital natives.

Digital Natives as Protagonists of Knowledge-oriented Economies

Penetration and pervasiveness of Information and Communication Technologies (ICT) affect every aspect of human life, starting from childhood to maturity. In 2001, discussing the adequateness of the current scholar systems of the United States of America, Mark Prensky introduced for the first time the concepts of "Digital Natives" and "Digital Immigrants" [3-4].

For the first time Prensky noticed that the generation of pupils that were attending schools by that time has one relevant difference from the previous generations. These pupils were all born in the digital era. They were born and grew up in a world where Information and Communication Technologies were already there.

These students have spent their entire lives surrounded by, and using, computers, videogames, digital music players, video cams, cell phones, and all the other toys and tools of the digital age [3]. According to Prenski, average college graduates have spent less than 5,000 hours of their lives reading, but over 10,000 hours playing videogames, and 20,000 hours watching TV.

These habits and behaviours contributed to develop in them new learning and information processing capabilities that have been largely ignored by the traditional learning system [4]. Anyhow, these characteristics allow them, as a matter of fact, to think and process information in a fundamental different way from their predecessors.

In his paper(s), Prenski depicts the identikit of digital natives as follows. Digital natives are used to receive information really fast. They like to parallel process and multi-task instead of doing things in strict sequences. They prefer graphics representations before the text, rather than the opposite. Instead of reading books from the first to the last page, they prefer to walk through documents in random access: in other words, they prefer hypertexts to books. Being used to mobile phones, social networks and the like, they work better when networked. They thrive on instant gratification and frequent rewards. Finally, they prefer games to serious works.

All these characteristics can be noticed in digital natives. But the difference among digital natives and digital immigrants is more broad. These habits are just the exterior signs of something that is more deep and profound. Being surrounded by technologies for their entire lives, Digital Natives started to be acquainted and familiar to them pretty soon, in a way that could have altered how their brain work.

It is therefore not only because Digital Natives are used to technologies that they are capable of processing information in a different way from their predecessors, but it is because they are different from their predecessors. They have thinking and learning patterns profoundly different from those of the Digital Immigrants [3]. Their brain reorganized itself in consequence of the stimuli received by the intense use of ICT. This claim is something more than an affirmation of a researcher, but it is also supported by recent findings of the neurobiology science [4].

Prenski describes the characteristics of Digital Natives to support his hypothesis that education and training systems are not adequate to properly educate these students. Those who were graduates and students in 2000, will be no longer students in the next years, but they will be next managers, decision makers, and leaders. Their characteristics, their information processing skills, and their different thinking patterns, will anyhow stay (or will even strengthen).

Digital Natives and Decision Making

Learning does not only happen in childhood and jouth. It rather goes with everyone for the entire working carrier, possibly for the entire life. The characteristics that, according to Prenski, Digital Natives show, will not only alter the way they learn in schools and colleges. These characteristics will stay in their lives as permanent marks and will modify their learning habits during their whole lives, both as individuals and as members of organisations.

Learning plays an important role in human activities. Organisation theory posits that organisations live and act thank to the actions of people that compose them. The actions that compose organisational behaviours are normally divided into three processes, called the fundamental organisational processes. These processes are: sense making, decision making, and knowing [5-6].

In individual and in organizational contexts human actions does not happen detached from the environment. Every action taken by an individual takes inputs and gives feedback to the environment where the individual acts. With the sense making processes, each actor tries to give proper meaning to the events and the environment that surrounds him in order to take a decision.

Once meaning of events and environments has been identified, action takes places. With the decision making process, individuals take decisions, and therefore perform actions. Decisions may be taken in different ways. Basically there are four kinds of decision making processes: standard, political, incremental, and anarchical. Each one of these kinds of decision making processes requires an information processing activity to generate proper understanding on the problem in order to take the decision. This intelligence activity happens with respects of the limits of the bounded rationality principle [7].

If possible, to reduce computational uncertainty, standard rules and procedures are used to take the decision. If such a strategy is viable, this decision making process is called *standard*. If it is the behavioural uncertainty that has to be addressed, in the place of computational uncertainty, decisions are taken trying to puts generate consensus and mediate conflicts among interested actors. This happens in *political* decision making processes. If the problem to be addressed is very complex, and the decision to be taken is equal so, the decision is taken step by step with a set of smaller decisions taken on a trial and error basis. This is the case of *incremental* decision processes. Finally, if both the decisions and the solutions are already available in a *garbage can* of problems and solutions, the decision might be taken by chance when a problem and a solution are, randomly, matched. These kinds of decision making processes are called anarchical.

Finally, when the decision is taken, a knowing process is normally executed to generate new knowledge. The information gathering and processing activity that supports decision making processes does not automatically generate knowledge. To generate knowledge out of information, a learning process is necessary [8]. Knowing processes are thence those processes that are executed after a decision has been taken to generate new knowledge out of information gathered. Besides learning processes, also knowledge management processes play a relevant role in this stage of decision making. The ability of an individual to successfully perform, and therefore to successfully take decisions, in the environment, also depends on his stock of knowledge and on his capacity to activate knowledge processes when the environment requires them [9].

Cognitive Processes in Digital Natives Learning Processes

Knowledge is a blurred concept whose definition engaged philosophers for thousand years [10]. Usually knowledge is considered as the result of aggregation of one or more pieces of information, which in turn are formed by one or more data [11].

Traditionally, knowledge can be also divided into two main groups: tacit knowledge and explicit knowledge [12]. Knowledge is explicit if it can be shared among individuals by means of a physical support. Such a support can have the form of a book, a movie, a picture, a conversation, or other. Thence, if it is explicit, knowledge can be codified in some languages.

Explicit knowledge is not all the knowledge that individuals possess. As Polanyi says: "we can know more than we can tell". There is also the tacit knowledge. Tacit knowledge is that form of knowledge that encompasses all the thinks individuals know but find difficulties in transmitting to others or making them explicit. Intuition, ability, competence, and similar, are all forms of tacit knowledge.

Knowledge is usually transformed among individuals by means of four knowledge transformation processes: externalization, internalization, socialization, and combination [13]. In an externalization process and individual transforms his tacit knowledge in explicit knowledge, if possible, using a language and a support to store it. The opposite process is instead called internalization, when one individual transform his explicit knowledge into tacit knowledge. Externalization and internalization processes may involve only one individual or more but, in any case, they involve an exchange from one form of knowledge (tacit or explicit) into the other (respectively, explicit or tacit). When two (or more) individuals exchange the same form of knowledge, and thence do not transform it, then the socialization and combination processes are necessary. With the knowledge socialization process, two (or more) individuals exchange their tacit knowledge. With the knowledge combination process, instead, two (or more) individuals exchange their explicit knowledge.

Knowledge processes, to be effective, do not only require individuals, but they also require a physical place where they will take place. Nonaka and Konno [14] introduce the concept of *Ba* to indicate a shared space among all individuals involved, where knowledge transformation processes might take place. According to them, there are four kinds of Ba called respectively: Originating Ba, Interacting Ba, Exercising Ba, and Cyber Ba. Each one of these forms of Ba supports one of the previously described knowledge transformation processes.

The Originating Ba represents a face-to-face space where individuals share feelings, emotions, experiences, and mental models. The Originating Ba supports the knowledge socialization processes. The Originating Ba is the primary Ba from which knowledge creation processes begins. The Interacting Ba is close to the Originating Ba, but it is more consciously constructed. In this case the interaction always happens face to face, but among people with the right mix of specific knowledge and capabilities like those forming project teams, taskforces, or cross-functional teams. In this Ba, individuals share their mental models, but also reflect and analyze their own. The Interacting Ba supports the externalization process. In the Cyber Ba, instead, the interaction happens through a virtual world instead in a real space and time context. In this form of Ba, collaborative environments utilizing information and communication technologies support knowledge combination processes. In this Ba individuals combine their existing information and knowledge with new explicit knowledge generating and systematizing new explicit knowledge. Finally the Exercising Ba supports the internalization phase facilitating the conversion of explicit knowledge to tacit knowledge. In this form of Ba, focused training with senior mentors and colleagues form the basis for continuous exercises that stress certain patterns and working out of such patterns.

Learning Models and the Role of Information Technologies Between East and West

Knowledge learning is traditionally based on knowledge transfer (from a teacher to, usually, many students) and linear ways of learning. Such linear paradigm reflects the way in which we advance in our reasoning. The german philosopher Immanuel Kant (1787: A48-49/B66), in particular, showed how the linear notions of time, space and causality were not empirical constructs but rather forms of sensibilities that are a priori necessary (immanent) conditions for any possible human experience: they are tools, so to speak, through which we make order among different kind of tangible experiences. Kant claimed that the human subject would not have the kind of experience that it has were these *a priori* forms (or tacit forms of knowledge) not in some way constitutive of him as a human subject. For instance, he would not experience the world as an orderly, rule-governed place unless time, space and causality were operative in his cognitive faculties.

On the contrary, the chinese tradition, "sought the understanding of order through the artful disposition of things, a participatory process which does not presume that there are essential features, or antecedent-determining principles, serving as transcendent sources of order [such as time, space and causality in western tradition]. The *art of contextualizing* seeks to understand and appreciate the manner in which particular things present-to-hand are, or may be, most harmoniously correlated. Classical chinese thinkers located the energy of transformation and change within a world that is *ziran*, autogenerative or literally 'so-of-itself', and found the more or less harmonious interrelations among the particular things around them to be the natural condition of things, requiring no appeal to an ordering principle or agency for explanation" [15].

While information technologies may be moving the border between tacit and codified knowledge, they are also increasing the importance of acquiring a range of skills or types of knowledge. In the emerging information society, a large and growing proportion of the labour force is engaged in handling information as opposed to more tangible factors of production. Computer literacy and access to network facilities tend to become more important than literacy in the traditional sense. Although the knowledge-based economy is affected by the increasing use of information technologies, it is not synonymous with the information society. The knowledge economy is characterised by the need for continuous learning of both codified information and the competencies to use this information.

As access to information becomes easier and less expensive, the skills and competencies relating to the selection and efficient use of information become more crucial. Tacit knowledge in the form of skills needed to handle codified knowledge is more important than ever in labour markets. Codified knowledge might be considered as the material to be transformed, and tacit knowledge, particularly know-how, as the tool for handling this material. Capabilities for selecting relevant and disregarding irrelevant information, recognising patterns in information, interpreting and decoding information as well as learning new and forgetting old skills are in increasing demand. The accumulation of tacit knowledge needed to derive maximum benefit from knowledge codified through information technologies can only be done through learning or contextualizing. Without investments oriented towards both codified and tacit skill development, informational constraints may be a significant factor degrading the allocative efficiency of market economies. Workers will require both formal education and the ability to acquire and apply new theoretical and analytical knowledge; they will increasingly be paid for their codified and tacit knowledge skills rather than for manual work. Long life education will be the centre of the knowledge-based economy, and learning the tool of individual and organisational advancement.

This process of learning is more than just acquiring formal education. In a knowledge-based economy "*learning-by-doing*" is paramount. A fundamental aspect of learning is the transformation of tacit into codified knowledge and the movement back to practice where new kinds of tacit knowledge are developed (the chinese *art of contextualizing*). Training and learning in non-formal settings, increasingly possible due to information technologies, are more common. Firms themselves face the need to become learning organisations, continuously adapting management, organisation and skills to accommodate new technologies. They are also joined in networks, where interactive learning involving producers and users in experimentation and exchange of information is the driver of innovation [16].

Conclusions: Which Leadership for Digital Natives?

We have seen that digital natives learning is strongly based on *know that*, or *learning by doing*, that is on what Nonaka calls the "externalization" process. However an effective leadership is characterized by intuitive application of knowledge to a particular organizational dilemma or problem, which in turn is not just an application of job knowledge but rather a mix of abilities mainly job knowledge and social skills.

A recent study conducted by Gary Small at the UCLA's Memory and Aging Research Center, Semel Institute for Neuroscience and Human Behavior, (Small is UCLA's Parlow-Solomon Chair on Aging) [17] claims that the Internet is indeed changing the way human brains operate, but at the same time it is making *digital natives* anti-social and have an increased tendency to suffer from ADD (Atention Deficit Disorder). According to Small, digital natives — young people born into a world of laptops and cell phones, text messaging and twittering — spend an average of 8 1/2 hours each day exposed to digital technology (id.). This exposure is rewiring their brain's neural circuitry, heightening skills like multi-tasking, complex reasoning and decision-making. But, Small concludes, there's a down side: all that tech time diminishes social oriented skills, including important emotional aptitudes like empathy. These are part of what in management studies is called emotional intelligence.

Emotional intelligence, indeed, plays a major role into recent leadership development research [18]: several research claims that emotional intelligence can correlate with less subjective workplace stress, better health and wellbeing or even significantly contribute to bottom lines business results. At the same time, claims surrounding the pliable nature of emotional intelligence since Daniel Goleman popular works [19], has led to the emergence of a veritable industry of human resource development professionals promoting the role of emotional intelligence assessment and enhancement in several sectors such as personal development, occupational and career assessment, occupational stress management, job performance and satisfaction and work-life balance. Some studies provided evidence that emotional intelligence contains strong links to leadership and executive competency [18].

Therefore digital natives need training about emotional intelligence. They indeed generally lack of social skills and they need to learn about such skills if they wish to become leaders.

On the contrary, digital immigrants seems not to be affected by a lacking of social skills; rather they can experience an enhancement of their capability: a recent UCLA study has assessed the effect of Internet searching on brain activity among volunteers between the ages of 55 and 76 — half of them well-practiced in searching the Internet, the other half not so. Semel Institute researchers used functional magnetic resonance imaging (fMRI) to scan the subjects' brains while they surfed the 'Net. The result: Researchers found that the brains of the Web-savvy group reflected about twice as much activity compared to the brains of those who were not Web-savvy [17]. According to Small "A simple, everyday task like searching the Web appears to enhance brain circuitry in older adults, demonstrating that our brains are sensitive and can continue to learn as we grow older"

These findings hold promise for older peoples' potential for enhancing their brainpower through the use of technology, said Small, an expert on the aging brain who has written several books to help people maintain vital brain function throughout their lives.

In conclusion, it seems that future holds a challenge for digital natives: if they wish to learn leadership abilities they must develop some emotional intelligence, otherwise leadership will be possessed by a handful of elder web savvy folks more able to internalize knowledge (because they are assisted by technology) and with better social skills (they learnt during along their life).

References

1. Lyotard, J.F. (1979) *La condition postmoderne*. Paris, Minuit.
2. Nonaka, I. and Takeuchi, H. (1995) *The Knowledge Creating Company*. Oxford U.P., Oxford.
3. Prensky, M. (2001a) Digital Natives, Digital Immigrants. *On the Horizon*, 9(5), 1-6
4. Prensky, M. (2001b) Digital Natives, Digital Immigrants, part II: Do they really think differently? *On the Horizon*, 9(6), 1-6.
5. Choo, C.W. (1998) *The Knowing Organization: How Organizations Use Information to Construct Meaning, Create Knowledge, and Make Decisions*. New York: Oxford University Press.
6. Choo, C.W. (2002) Strategic Management of Intellectual Capital and Organizational Knowledge. In *Sensemaking, Knowledge Creation, and Decision Making: Organizational Knowing as Emergent Strategy*. Oxford University Press.
7. Simon, H.A. (1947) *Administrative Behaviour*. New York, Macmillian.
8. Orlikowski, W.J. (2002) Knowing in Practice: Enacting a Collective Capability in Distributed Organizing. *Organization Science*, 13(3), 249-273.
9. Thompson, J.D. (1967) *Organizations in Action*. McGraw-Hill, New York.
10. Walsham, G. (2001) Knowledge Management: The Benefits and the Limitations of Computer systems. *European Management Journal*, 19(6), 599-608.
11. Laudon, K.C.,and Laudon, J.P. (2006). *Management Information Systems*. 10th Edition, Prentice Hall, Upper Saddle River N.J.
12. Polanyi, M. (1966) *The Tacit Dimension*. London
13. Nonaka, I. (1994) A Dynamic Theory of Organizational Knowledge Creation. *Organization Science*, 5(1), 14-37.
14. Nonaka, I., Konno, N. (1998) The Concept of "Ba": Building a Foundation for Knowledge Creation. *California Management Review*, 40(3), 40-54.
15. Hall, D.L. and James, R.T. (1998) Chinese philosophy. In E. Craig (Ed.), *Routledge Encyclopedia of Philosophy*. London: Routledge. Retrieved January 02, 2010, from http://www.rep.routledge.com/article/G001SECT1
16. EUROPEAN INNOVATION MONITORING SYSTEM (EIMS) (1994) Public Policies to Support Tacit Knowledge Transfer. *Proceedings of SPRINT/EIMS Policy Workshop*, May 1993.

17. Lin, J. (2008) *Research shows that Internet is rewiring our brains*. UCLA Today, Oct 15th 2008, Retrieved 6.01.2010 from http://www.today.ucla.edu/portal/ut/081015_gary-small-ibrain.aspx.
18. Lyons, D. (2008). Emotional Intelligence. In Marturano A., Gosling J. (Eds.) *Leadership the Key Concepts*. Routledge, London, 51-54.
19. Goleman, D. (1995) *Emotional Intelligence: Why It Can Matter More Than IQ*. Bantam Books, New York.
20. Kant, I. (1787). *Critique of Pure Reason*, Retrieved 3.01.2010 from http://humanum.arts.cuhk.edu.hk/Philosophy/Kant/cpr/
21. Lyons, D. (2008). Emotional Intelligence. In Marturano A., Gosling J. (eds.) *Leadership The Key Concepts*. Routledge, London, pp. 51-54.

Part V

ICT and Productivity

IS Success Evaluation: Theory and Practice

Angela Perego[1]

Abstract The assessment of Information Systems (IS) effectiveness and its contribution of business value to the firm has been widely debated among both business scholars and practitioners. However a robust and complete model with which to evaluate IS Business Value that practitioners can apply in their companies does not exist. As scholars' research has been unable to define quantitative and perceptual measures to assess the efficiency of IS, the issue of evaluating IS effectiveness remains unresolved. This lack of knowledge increases the difficulties companies face in the evaluation of IS Performance and in closing the perceptual gap that exists between IS management capability and the management capability of other company departments. Notwithstanding these challenges, the criticality of the issue leads companies to launch IS Performance Management Systems (PMS) implementations even though they cannot appropriately evaluate the results in economic terms. Firms are therefore very interested in improving their understanding of IS PMS design, implementation and evaluation processes. Furthermore, they seek guidance to help them during the critical challenges they will face and to exploit experiences and knowledge of other firms. This chapter contributes to the knowledge in the IS PMS field by bringing evidences and witnesses from the reality and providing companies with recommendations to facilitate the design and implementation processes and to improve their chances of success.

Introduction

Performance evaluation is critical for all business functional departments (accounting, marketing and operations etc.); each department is involved in performance measurement and must demonstrate its contributions to the firm [1-4]. In particular, the control and governance of internal services such as Information Systems (IS) has become quite critical in organizations due to the large degree of expenditure and investment. IS managers face mounting pressure to measure IS department performance, justify the appreciable investment they require to operate, and evaluate IS in terms of Tangible Business Value and Return on Investment (ROI).

In the light of the depicted scenario, IS Performance Management Systems (PMS) should help IS departments to evaluate the outcomes of activities, practices and processes at all levels of the IS organization. They should also help IS departments to face a serious credibility problem due to lack of management practices that can provide real benefits in business operations. Therefore IS PMS seem to be the right solution for the CIO and IS department's problems, but they are not so widespread in companies [5-6].

[1] SDA Bocconi School of Management, Milan, Italy, angela.perego@sdabocconi.it

Presently a robust and complete model with which to evaluate IS Business Value that practitioners can apply in their companies does not exist [8]. As scholars' research has been unable to define quantitative and perceptual measures to assess the efficiency of IS, the issue of evaluating IS effectiveness remains unresolved. This lack of knowledge increases the difficulties companies face in the evaluation of IS Performance and in closing the perceptual gap that exists between IS management capability and the management capability of other company departments. In addition, according to research in both PMS [2] and Management Control Systems [3], the difficulty in implementing this type of system has been determined by internal factors such as the culture and organizational tensions.

Notwithstanding these challenges, the criticality of the issue leads companies to launch IS PMS implementations even though they cannot appropriately evaluate the results in economic terms. A survey by Gartner [7] reveals that while Performance Management is a high priority for CIOs at least one half of the companies that implement PMS in the next two years will fail to realize the full benefits. Firms are therefore very interested in improving their understanding of IS PMS design, implementation and evaluation processes. They also seek guidance to help them during the critical challenges they will face and to exploit experiences and knowledge of other firms to improve their chances of success and their ability to evaluate IS performance.

Starting from the assumption that real-world experiences differ from theoretical explications, this research contributes to the knowledge in the IS PMS field by bringing evidences and witnesses from the reality through the case of the worldwide leader in the hearing aids retail and service market.

The structure of the chapter is as follows. The following paragraph will analyze relevant literature on the topic addressed in this chapter. Right after that, the research design will be described immediately followed by the case description and discussion. Some final remarks regarding the findings, the limitations, and future research plans, will conclude the chapter.

Theoretical Background

The assessment of IS effectiveness and its contribution of business value to the firm has been widely debated among both business scholars and practitioners. Interest in the debate has increased even though the conclusions of several studies in this area can be summed up using Robert Solow's famous remark: "*we see computers everywhere except in the productivity statistics*" [9].

Brynjolfsson called this phenomenon the "IT productivity paradox" [10] and suggested that traditional productivity measures may not be appropriate to estimate the contribution of IS to business outcomes.

Starting with Brynjolfsson's studies, several other researchers have tried to examine the relationship between IS investments and organizational performance. A plethora of different research methodologies has been adopted in this research stream that also shows contributions coming from several disciplines like economics, strategy, accounting, operational research and, of course, information systems [11-14]. Nevertheless the connection between IS and productivity is still elusive [15]. One reason could be the level of analysis at the organizational level, which makes it difficult to isolate the impact of any individual technology. In brief, it can be said that "*the more detailed the level of analysis, the better the chance to detect the impact, if any, of a given technology*" [16 p.275].

Other researchers have moved the debate "*from the question of whether IT creates value to how, when and why benefits occur or fail to do so*" [17 p.29] and focused their attention on the construction of the IS Business Value generation process. One of the first to move towards this new direction was Weill [18] who introduced the concept of "*conversion effectiveness*" that represents the aspects of the firm's climate which influence IS. In 1995 Markus and Soh gave an extremely relevant contribution to the debate proposing a theoretical model of IS value creation. Their model synthesized prior contributions in a chain of three different process models which would specify a sequence of necessary (but not sufficient) conditions that explains how the IS outcomes occur or not. "*[...] organizations spend on IT and, subject to the varying degrees of effectiveness during the IT management process, obtain IT assets. Quality IT assets, if combined with the process of appropriate IT use, then yield favorable IT impacts. Favorable IT impacts, if not adversely affected during the competitive process, lead to improved organizational performance*" [17 p. 39]. The main result of their study was to highlight the distance between IS investment and organizational performance. Since then, a lot of researchers have undertaken studies on the factors which lead to IS Business Value. A synthesis of the major highlights can be found in the "Integrative Model of IT Business Value" proposed by Melville, Kraemer and Gurbaxani [14]. They identified the organization as the locus of IS Business Value generation and pointed out IS Business Value is generated by the employment of IS resources and complementary organizational resources. They also emphasized the role of external factors (industry characteristics, trading partners and political, regulatory, educational, social and cultural context) in generating of IS Business Value.

A third research stream concerns IS Success measurement. The first study that sought to impose some form of order on IS researchers' choices of success measures was the paper of DeLone and McLean [19]. In their paper they proposed an IS Success Model based on six distinct constructs of Information System: System Quality; Information Quality; Use; User Satisfaction; Individual Impact; Organizational Impact. Pitt, Watson e Kavan [20] gave a relevant contribution to the development of the IS Success Model. They pointed out that IS department has expanded its role from product developer and operations manager to service provider. Therefore the quality of the IS department's services, as perceived by its users, is a key indicator of IS success which affects both use and user satisfaction. Grover [21] also, in his studies, gave some inputs to complement and extend DeLone and McLean's IS Success Model, building a theoretically-based construct space for IS effectiveness which encompasses three definitional dimensions: (1) evaluative referent; (2) unit of analysis and (3) evaluation type. Starting from the work of Grover et al. [21], Seddon et al. [22] proposed a new framework which summarized the seven questions proposed by Cameron and Whetten [23] in two dimensions: stakeholders corresponding to the point of view using in the evaluation, and system corresponding to the domain under evaluation. Recent studies have tried to empirically and theoretically assess these theoretical models of IS success in an IS use context [24] and address several areas of uncertainty with past IS Success research seeking to design robust, economical and simple models which practitioners can put into practice [8]. Finally, current research has deepened the relationships among constructs related to IS success and it has underlined the importance of user-related and contextual attributes in IS success [25].

A last research stream proposes the adoption of the Balanced Scorecard concept [26] to measure the value of IS and evaluate IS Performance. Martinsons et al. [27] developed a Balanced Scorecards for Information Systems that "*allows managers to see the positive and negative impacts of IT applications and IS activities on the factors that are important to the organization as a whole*" [27 p.85]. They pointed out that measurement is a prerequisite to management and, as a consequence, they proposed IS Balanced Scorecard as a strategic IS management tool that can be used to monitor and guide performance improvement efforts. In particular IS Balanced Scorecard becomes a IS PMS, which can be defined as the set of metrics able to quantify both the efficiency and effectiveness of actions [28], used to evaluate the outcomes of IS activities, practices and processes.

Reviews of the literature reveal several theoretical models aim at defining "appropriate" dimensions and measures to assess IS Success. In particular the final goal is to develop an "*algorithm for selecting the appropriate dimensions and measures*" [29] in order to provide the most relevant, reliable, and representative set of IS performance dimensions and measures referred to the specific internal and external environment of a firm. This scope implies that only one appropriate set of dimensions and measures exists for a company. Whereas individual, unit or department interests and the existence of organizational tension (inside the IS department or between the IS department and User Departments) also affect the design of the "appropriate" set leading people to take the defensive rather than promote a collaborative context [30].

In the following paragraphs we describe a case to show how many factors, especially "soft" factors, can affect the shape and the quality of the IS PMS in the real world.

MedicalSound Case

MedicalSound[2] is the worldwide leader in the hearing aids retail and service market. In 2008 it sold around 500,000 articles and had consolidated revenues of nearly 500 million euros. It is a multinational company and present in 10 countries with highly recognised brands. This is a peculiar characteristic of MedicalSound

[2] MedicalSound is a fictitious name.

because no other players can boast such a widespread diffusion throughout the world.

MedicalSound has the largest retail and service network with around 2,200 retail outlets, 3,000 service centres, 2,100 licensee network affiliates and 2,500 hearing aid fitting specialists.

Business Strategy is focused on the following points:

- Revenue growth supported by aggressive marketing strategies towards final customers and stronger relationships with the ENT community, and an aggressive acquisition campaign.
- Optimisation of the current market coverage through rationalisation and strengthening of the existing distribution network, and coverage improvement through local consolidation (e.g. France, Switzerland).
- Increasing Customer Satisfaction through the standardisation of fitting procedures, R&D on innovative application systems and fitting software, and technical and sales training of the frontline personnel.

IS has become essential in this context because the achievement of this business strategy implies increasing the business process efficiency in order to increase profitability, providing relevant data to businesses in order to improve their effectiveness (e.g. marketing actions), and integrating new companies in a short time so as not to spend too much time and resources on a transition period.

MedicalSound has its Headquarters in Italy, which delivers shared services (Supply Chain, Information Systems, Financial & Administration, Human Resources and Organization, and strategic marketing) to the ten country subsidiaries (included Italy). Each subsidiary has its own IS department which is sized according to the local market complexity, which hierarchically reports to the country manager and functionally to the IS Corporate department. The IS Corporate department is in charge of defining methodologies, standards and policies of providing software applications able to support the Sales and Marketing processes of subsidiaries, and of supporting the activities of shared services.

The IS Corporate department consists of 32 employees and is divided into 4 main units. Three of them refer to the main business processes (Finance, Control & Human Resources, Supply Chain and Services, Sales and Marketing) which are in charge of understanding user requirements and developing and enhancing specific business applications. The fourth is IT Infrastructure which is responsible for the IT architecture and providing technical support. Furthermore, there are two staff units: IT methodologies, Standards and Policies, and Country Integration Projects. The latter underlines the willingness of the IS Corporate department to support the acquisition strategy. Figure 1 shows the IS Corporate department organigram.

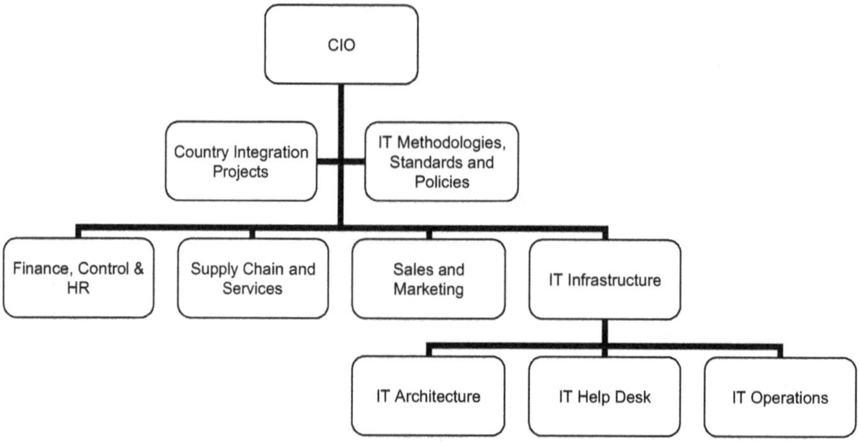

Figure 1: IS Corporate department organigram

Local IS departments support employees, retail outlets, services centres and licensee network affiliates. Whereas, the IS Corporate department supports employees of shared services functions and local IS organizations which should act as an intermediary for their local end users.

Objectives and Boundaries of IS PMS Implementation

The aggressive acquisition campaign has moved the equilibrium and routine of the IS Corporate department which was sized to serve a fairly stable number of users. The environment complexity has increased, and this new acquisition strategy has been required to perform new tasks for the IS department as well. Furthermore, some companies that were acquired performed very well, and as a result management was worried about effecting the revenues and profitability reduction, changing organizational structure, procedures or software applications due to corporate standards. The same issue was felt by country managers who had to maintain their business performance without relying upon their consolidated and tested organizational and technical structures.

Therefore, IS effectiveness has become a priority in order to guarantee that IS Corporate services were equal or better than previous local IS services, and thus the change of IS could not cause disorganization in the subsidiaries. At the same time top management required assurance of the IS department's ability to support the business strategy and of handling this extra work-load generated by the acquisition campaign.

In this stressful context, the CIO, in agreement with the CEO, decided to set an IS Service Level Agreement with country managers so as to avoid possible future organizational tensions.

Therefore, in October 2006, the CIO launched a project with the objective of defining relevant measures to assess IS service effectiveness, to compare the current IS performance with the defined measures, and finally, in agreement with the managing directors, to establish a value threshold for each measure which had to represent the "minimum" goal in terms of service quality that the IS department had to pursue and guarantee. These bases led to the adoption of several evaluation perspectives: the CIO's perspective was interested in assessing IS department efficiency and effectiveness and defining actions to improve them (e.g. acquiring new resources, optimizing the use of available resources, etc.); the CEO's perspective was interested in the overall IS performance picture and in the tangible IS contribution to the achievement of group business strategy. The domain under evaluation was the IS corporate department and IS corporate services. Local departments and their activities were outside the boundaries of this project.

The evaluation was conducted from both the organizational (group and subsidiaries) and individual perspective so as to build a complete picture of the effectiveness of IS services. The goal of arriving at an agreement makes the objective measures more relevant but the opportunity of using perceptual measures was not ruled out.

Finally, the intention was to conduct an evaluation every six months in order to verify the keeping of the agreement and monitor the IS performance improvements over time.

The Design Process

The project started with the analysis of documents which already existed at MedicalSound, in order to collect data about strategy, IS department organization, IS policies and processes and the like. The project team also interviewed the IS professionals responsible for the various IS areas so as to make an in-depth analysis of the practices and Management tools (e.g. Project Management, IS Cost Accounting, Help Desk Management and Application Management) adopted in the IS Corporate department. The data collection results for the IS Corporate department showed an extremely complex organization which had to manage different types of relationship. As a matter of fact, it had to interact, inside the company, with top management (CEO, country managers and shared services departments directors) and local IS departments, and outside the company with technological suppliers and partners.

The complexity of the relational environment has increased over the last few years with the acquisition campaign, and thus the IS Corporate department had started to tackle the new situation by changing its organisations, introducing new staff units (i.e. Country Integration Projects and IT Methodologies, standards and Policies) and also becoming a coordinator and controller of the various local IS departments. This process of change not only involved organizational change but also the improvement or development of management and monitoring tools which were not well-enough structured or complete. Top Management gave the IS Corporate department very clear goals, the achievement of which would have highly influenced its future credibility.

In this context the climate in the IS Corporate department was quite tense but the CIO sought to maintain a consensus on IS decisions and the actions to be performed. Tension was also caused by the different backgrounds of IS employees:

some of them were able and ready to change their roles and job contents, but others lacked the necessary managerial background to make this change.

After the context analysis, the team project was able to start the design process of the IS PMS adopting the Balanced Scorecard model. The project team initially focused on the "Business Contribution and Value" scorecard. According to the analysis, it identified the appropriate dimensions for this scorecard through contribution to achieving goals, the Business Value of IS projects and IS costs control. Thus, the following measures were defined:

- IS costs to support Success Key Factors (acquisition campaign, reinforcement franchising network, customer care and fitting device).
- Percentage of projects per business process.
- IS costs distributed across innovation, growth and run activities.
- IS costs for IS services.
- IS costs for compliance projects.
- Percentage of IS expenses above or within budget.
- Index of IS budget allocation among subsidiaries.

In order to measure the IS contribution to the achievement of business goals the project team used the percentage of IS costs per Success Key Factor, as there was no existing data on staff time saving, increased decision effectiveness, the improvement of the quality of business processes and the like. This solution assumed that IS impact depends on the degree of IS investments starting with the assumption that the IS Corporate department is efficient. This measure was considered acceptable because even if the company had had data on time or cost saving, cost reduction and the like, it would not have had the certainty that these results depended on IS investments. The data necessary to calculate the measures presented above should have come from IS Costs Accounting and Project Management Systems, and the project team was confident it would find them. The second analysed Scorecard was "Customer Orientation". In this scorecard the project team started to design the Customer Satisfaction dimension and thus find the corresponding relevant measures. In particular, the Customer Satisfaction dimension was translated into the following measures:

- User satisfaction index.
- Percentage of projects "on time" and "on budget" per type of project.
- Index of respect for the Service Level settled with users per IS service.
- Index of respect for business requirements defined by users.
- Collaboration with users index.

During the first meeting of approval by the CIO, he discarded the user satisfaction index as it was not a priority at that moment. As a matter of fact, the project's goal was to establish an IS Service Level Agreement with country managers in order to be in a position to pursue the defined IS Services quality and finally to have objective measures with which to evaluate the respect of settled quality levels. The CIO thus preferred to concentrate efforts on defining the quantitative and objective measures and postponed the customer satisfaction survey, which was an extremely time consuming activity as regards the size of the user population. The calculus of these measures required the definition of the IS Service Catalogue, then the design of appropriate measures representing the service quality for each IS service, and finally the establishment of a value threshold necessary to evaluate the achievement of the settled service quality. To feed the scorecard, the project team also required data on projects in relation to arranged time and costs, and defined business requirements arising from Project Management tools. The subsequent scorecard in the design process was the "IS Processes", which especially focused on System Quality, Speed of execution, Project Management Capability and IS staff workload. The project team identified the following measures as relevant:

- Unavailability of the server (percentage).
- Unavailability of the network (percentage).
- Response time.
- Number and severity of incidents and malfunctions.
- Number of application bugs.
- Average resolution time.
- Percentage of IS hours charged for innovation, growth, and run activities.
- Index of saturation of IS capacity.

In this scorecard, besides the data from Application Management and Project Management, data on IS staff time allocation and the availability of the server and network were necessary. The last scorecard was "Change and Innovation". The project team worked on three measurement dimensions: the organizational climate, the permanent education of IS staff, and the expertise and skill of IS staff. In particular, it decided to use the following measures:

- IS department turnover.
- Average age of IS staff.
- Number of educational days per person.
- Percentage of IS budget allocated to education.
- Number of years of IS experience per staff member.
- Percentage of necessary skills covered by IS staff.

The project Team did not expect a critical state to occur in order to be able to collect the necessary data to feed this scorecard.

At the end of this first part of the design process, the project team shared the set of measures with the CIO and the IS staff members. After that, IS staff members proposed changes, improvements, and the broadening of the proposed IS performance measures. Some changes aimed at using the data already available and thus rendering the IS performance management system more complete and rich without huge efforts. Whereas, other changes sought to rule some process measures out in order to guarantee buffer where to hide possible inefficiencies.

The Implementation Process

According to the results of the design process, the following actions were necessary to collect all the necessary data to feed the IS Performance Management System:

- data retrieval from Application Management, System & Network Management, Project Management, IS Cost Accounting, IS Human Resources Management and other tools identified in the previous stage;
- build two new tools: the IS Service Catalogue and IS staff timesheet.

The project team had some problems in performing these activities. As a matter of fact, some data was not available in management tools, for example the IS cost accounting system did not allocate IS costs per type of activity (innovation, growth and run) and per Success Key Factor. Other data was scattered over several spreadsheets or required manual elaborations to the project data. Therefore existing IS Management tools (e.g. IS Cost Accounting, Application Management, and System and Network Systems) were analyzed in-depth and the project team discussed the opportunity of improving them in order to collect more data and automatically feed the IS Performance Management System. According to the IS Corporate department's strategic role, the CIO and CEO considered the investment absolutely necessary in order to improve control capacity on IT infrastructure and application. A feasibility study was therefore started.

With reference to the construction of the two new tools, while the definition of the IS Services Catalogue and the determination of the value threshold for each IS service was defined as the first priority, the construction of the IS staff timesheet met some obstacles and thus an estimate was made in order to obtain the data necessary to calculate IS performance measures.

Table 1 shows the final set of IS Performance Measures implemented in MedicalSound.

Table 1: MedicalSound IS Performance Management System

"Business Contribution and Value"	**"Customer Orientation"**
Contribution to achieving business goals: *IS costs to support Success Key Factors.* *Percentage of projects per business process.* Business Value of IS projects: *Percentage of projects on Success Key Factors.* IS Cost control: *IS costs per staff member.* *IS costs distributed across innovation, growth and run activities.* *IS costs for IS services.* *IS costs for compliance projects.* *Percentage of IS expenses above or within budget.* *Index of IS budget allocation among subsidiaries.*	User Satisfaction: *Percentage of projects "on time" and "on budget" per type of project.* *Index of respect for Service Level settled with users per IS service.* *Average time to perform Ideation or Feasibility studies.* Partnership with user: *Index of collaboration with users.*
"Change and Innovation"	**"IS processes"**
Organizational Climate: *IS department turnover.* *Average age of IS staff.* Permanent Education of IS Staff: *Number of educational days per person.* *Percentage of IS budget allocated to education.* Expertise and skill of IS Staff: *Number of years of IS experience per staff member.* *Percentage of necessary skills covered by IS staff.*	System Quality: *Response time.* *Number and severity of incidents and malfunctions.* *Number of application bugs.* Project Management Capability: *Percentage of projects "on time".* *Percentage of projects "on budget".* Speed in execution: *Average resolution time.* IS Staff workload: *IS hours per business process.* *Percentage of IS hours charged for innovation, growth, and run activities.* *Index of saturation of IS capability.*

Discussion

The MedicalSound case describes the design process of a IS PMS and the factors that affect it. In particular, the analysis of the case shows how to start to define the IS measure set variables such as business strategy, organizational structure, size, and competitive environment are relevant, but the final set is affected by several variables related to IS department organization (role, size, maturity etc.) and organizational tensions (e.g. between IS department and User department).

The role of IS appears to be extremely relevant in the design of IS performance measures. In the case, IS played a strong strategic role, and as a result IS departments were able to translate Business strategy into IS strategy and link IS activities and projects to Success Key Factors. The perception of relevance and the motivation to design specific measures connected to Business Strategy were extremely high.

The Size and Structure of the IS department directly affects measures related to the Organizational Climate, Permanent Education of IS staff and Expertise and skill of IS staff. The Size has an indirect influence on the shape of the IS Performance Management System for two reasons. The first reason is that it affects the Maturity level of the IS department in terms of standards and policies definition, procedures formalization, and use of management tools. The second is related to internal relational complexity that increases with the size of the IS department.

The maturity of the IS department affects the shape of IS PMS in an extremely strong way because the availability of input data necessary to calculate the measures depends on it. Therefore, as MedicalSound case shows, the design of the IS performance measures can be an opportunity to verify and improve the supervision and the management of IS processes. As MedicalSound's CIO claimed, one of the main results of the design and development of the IS PMS is not only the definition of IS measures but the development of a solid system of IS governance and systems that produce input data.

The climate inside the IS department also affects the choice of IS Performance measures. A good climate avoids the likelihood of the IS staff considering the IS evaluation project as an exam, as occurred in MedicalSound case, and the IS Performance Management System as a control tool seeking to manipulate the design of the measures, especially referred to the efficiency of IS processes, so as to highlight only some aspects and not others.

The analysis of the case also shows that the climate between the IS department and user departments has an impact on the decision to share the results of the IS evaluation with users. However, an apparent good climate is not enough because power balances are also relevant in order to decide whether or not to involve users in the project. As matter of fact, when user departments are more powerful than IS department, IS department seeks to build trustworthy relationship with users through IS performance measures. This is evident in the case where IS department would have had objective data on which to discuss with user departments and define the quality value threshold beyond which users would have been satisfied. Furthermore, power can affect the choice of IS measures in order to maintain, as long as possible, the existing information asymmetry between the IS department and user departments. Therefore, IS department seeks to highlight not all possible process measures in order to have no controlled part of process which can guarantee buffer where to hide possible inefficiencies.

In addition, the MedicalSound case highlights Top Management support is crucial. On the one hand, IS department considered the Top Management support to be a guarantee that this project was the starting point of a change process and it was also confident that Top Management would have helped them to manage critical situations with user departments; on the other hand this factor forced it to speed up the design of the IS performance measures and extend the set of measures which would have been shared with user departments.

Finally the analysis of the case shows that the design of IS PMS triggers the opportunity to start activities of communication and internal marketing of IS to internal customers.

Conclusions, Limitations and Further Research

This research has attempted to contribute to the IS PMS field by bringing evidences from real-world experience. In particular it has analysed the MedicalSound case that describes the design process of a IS PMS and highlights the factors that affect this process.

The MedicalSound case has the limit to be conducted involving only IS staff in decision making process. We believe that the users' involvement would have changed the final IS Performance measure set because the user perspective would have been more relevant and the role of power balance would have been different. Therefore further research could involve both IS staff and users in order to investigate how the impact of variables analyzed in this research changes. In order to improve the understanding of IS Performance Management Systems, we also suggest that future research investigates the impacts of these systems on IS Management activities over time.

References

1. Bourne M, Franco M, Wilkes J (2003) Corporate Performance Management. *Measuring Business Excellence* 3(3):15-21
2. Ferreira A, Otley D (2009) The design and use of performance management systems: An extended framework for analysis. *Management Accounting Research* 20(4):263-282
3. Otley D (1999) Performance management: a framework for management control systems research. *Management Accounting Research* 10:363–382
4. Kaplan R (2009) Measuring Performance (Pocket Mentor). Harvard Business Press, Boston
5. Miranda S (2004) Beyond BI: Benefiting from Corporate Performance Management Solutions. *Financial Executive* 20(2): 58–61
6. Perego A (2006) IS Performance Management e misure dell'IT in azienda. *Proceedings of the Xth Italian Chapter of the Association for Information Systems* ItAIS, Milan, Italy, 26th-27th October
7. Gartner (2009) Gartner EXP Worldwide Survey of More than 1,500 CIOs Shows IT Spending to Be Flat in 2009. Press Release. Online at http://www.gartner.com/it/page.jsp?id=855612, Accessed 21 April 2010

8. Gable GG, Sedera D, Chan T (2008) Re-conceptualizing System Success: the IS-impact Measurement Model. *Journal of the Association for Information Systems* 9(7):377-408
9. Solow RS (1987) *We'd better watch out.* New York Times Book Review.
10. Brynjolfsson E (1993) The Productivity Paradox of IT. *Communications of the ACM* 36(12):66-77
11. Brynjolfsson E, Hitt L (1996) Paradox Lost? Firm-Level Evidence on the Returns to Information Systems Spending. *Management Science* 42(4):541-558
12. Lee B, Barua A (1999) An Integrated Assessment of Productivity and Efficiency Impacts of Information Technology Investments: Old Data, New Analysis and Evidence. *Journal of Productivity Analysis* 12:21-43
13. Brynjolfsson E, Hitt L (2003) Computing Productivity: Firm-Level Evidence. *Review of Economics and Statistics* 85(4):793-808
14. Melville N, Kraemer K, Gurbaxani V (2004) Information Technology and organizational Performance: an integrative model of IT Business Value. *MIS Quarterly Review* 28(2):283-322
15. Kohli R, Grover V (2008) Business Value of IT: an essay on expanding research directions to keep up with the times. *Journal of the Association for Information Systems* 9(1):23-39
16. Deveray S, Kohli R (2003) Performance Impact of Information Technology: is actual usage the missing link? *Management Science* 49(3):273-289
17. Soh C, Markus ML (1995) How IT Creates Business Value: A Process Theory Synthesis. *Proceedings of the Sixteenth International Conference on Information Systems.*
18. Weill P (1992) The relationship between investment in Information Technology and firm performance: a study of the value manufacturing sector. *Information Systems Research* 3(4):307-333
19. DeLone W H, McLean E R (1992) Information Systems Success: The Quest for the dependent variable. *Information Systems Research* 3(1):60-95
20. Pitt LF, Watson RT, Kavan CB (1995) Service quality: a measure of Information Systems effectiveness. *MIS Quarterly* 19(2):173-188
21. Grover G, Jeong SR, Segars AH (1996) Information Systems effectiveness: The construct space and patterns of application. *Information & Management* 31:177-191
22. Seddon PB, Staples S, Patnayakuni R, Bothwell M (1999) Dimension of Information System Success. *Communication of AIS* 20(2):2-39
23. Cameron KS, Whetten DA (1983) Some conclusions about organizational effectiveness. In: Cameron KS, Whetten DA (eds) *Organizational effectiveness: a comparison of multiple models.* Academic Press, New York
24. Rai A, Lang SS, Welker RB (2002) Assessing the validity of IS success models: an empirical test and theoretical analysis., *Information Systems Research* 13(1):50-69
25. Sabherwal R, Jeyaraj A, Chowa C (2006) Information System Success: individual and organizational determinants. *Management Science* 52(12):1849-1864.
26. Kaplan R, Norton D (1996) *The balanced scorecard: translating strategy into action.* Harvard Business School Press, Boston
27. Martinsons M, Davison R, Tse D (1999) The balanced scorecard: A foundation for the strategic management of information systems. *Decision Support Systems* 25:71-88.
28. Neely A (1995) Performance Measurement system design: theory and practice. *International Journal of Operations and Production Management* 15:80-116
29. Myers BL, Kappelman LA, Prybuto VR (1997) Comprehensive Model for assessing the quality and productivity of the Information System Function. Toward a Theory for Information Systems Assessment. In: Garrity E, Sanders L (eds) *Information Systems Success Measurement.* IDEA Group Publishing, Hershey
30. Perego A (2008) The Role of IS Performance Management Systems in today's enterprise. In: D'Atri A et al.(eds) Interdisciplinary Aspects of Information Systems Studies. Springer.

ICT, Productivity and Organizational Complementarit

Marcello Martinez[1]

Abstract Recent years have witnessed a surge in interest in Information Technology (IT) and its impact on productivity. The paper presents the analysis of the literature that has analyzed how firms' skills and organizational change affect the returns from investments in ICT.

According to the skill-biased technical change (SBTC) hypothesis technological change, and particularly the adoption of ICTs, increases the demand for skilled labour with respect to unskilled labour and leads to increasing wage inequality.

On the contrary the skill-biased organizational change hypothesis (SBOC) sustains that the adoption of new organizational systems based on decentralized decision-making and delayering calls for more skilled people. Because of the complementarity between new organizational systems and skilled labour firms that adopt the two complements are expected to outperform firms that use only one of them.

However SBTC and SBOC hypotheses are the two sides of the same coin. Drawing on the mixed empirical evidence reported in studies that have tried to test the SBTC, literature has introduced the concept of organizational complementarity between ICT and skilled labour. In this perspective, technological and organizational change together call for more skilled labour.

Economic Growth and Investment in ICT

The relationship between company investment in information and communication technologies and productivity is a key topic in studies of economics and business organization. However, up to the mid 1990s there was extensive discussion on the productivity paradox: as related by Nobel Prize winner Robert Solow, productivity increase was present everywhere except in statistics. Indeed, empirical research was unable to show a significant correlation or association between investments in ICT and productivity increase [1-4].

Several justifications have been advanced for this paradox [5]. Firstly, simple bivariate correlations between aggregate productivity and aggregate ICT capital stock do not take into account the impact of all controls which also affect aggregate productivity and are therefore likely to measure spurious effects [6]. Secondly, ICT investment has a positive effect on productive variety which may, in turn, negatively affect productivity. Third, productivity gains from ICT investment materialize only after time and depend significantly on network externalities and on changes in the complementary infrastructure [7]. Fourth, output measurement

[1] Dipartimento di Strategie aziendali Seconda università di Napoli, marcello.martinez@unina2.it

errors may affect estimates of the impact of ICT investment on output as quality improvements in products and in services are not fully reflected in sales. Lastly, since ICT accounts for a relatively small share of capital output, its increase has only small effects on aggregate output.

With a view to clarifying the debate, examination of the relationship between ICT and productivity should bear in mind that an increase in labor productivity can chiefly be generated by three causes [8]: first of all, by increasing the level of capital applied per unit of labor, a phenomenon called capital deepening; secondly, by increasing the quality of inputs, and labor in particular, as a result of education and training; lastly, by considering multifactor productivity (MFP) growth, which is the remainder of growth that cannot be accounted for by the first two factors. Reference to MFP is extremely significant insofar as it shows an improvement in models of production organization and/or product quality, the only phenomenon able to explain how, with the same input, higher output levels may be achieved.

To overcome the scientific difficulties arising from the productivity paradox, research approaches have been established that integrate macro-analysis with studies based on an analytical method and the micro-organizational level that collect data recorded directly by firms with official surveys or developed *ad hoc* on company samples or groups. Advances in computer technology have enabled large datasets on company productivity and IT to be amassed and also improved the ability of researchers to analyze such data. Micro-level data are now being used to study the relationship between ICT and company performance in a number of countries. These studies draw on both official and private data sources and use different methodologies. The underlying hypothesis is that productivity can be measured at the firm level, allowing businesses or policy makers to gauge firm performance, dispersion of performance, and productivity drivers at firm level.

Three main research strands may be identified in the literature on the impact of ICT on business organization models, which may be distinguished into three time horizons:

- studies investigating the relationship between ICT and productivity using the framework of hyperautomation (1985 – 1995);
- studies investigating the relationship between ICT and productivity using the framework of coordination cost reduction (1987 – 2001);
- studies investigating the relationship between ICT and productivity using the framework of organizational complementarity (1999 – 2009).

ICT and Hyperautomation

In this strand of studies, research on ICT and productivity has focused first and foremost on the potential effect of ICT upon the efficiency and effectiveness of organizational processes. The focus of such studies lies in transaction processing systems (TPS), information systems used to conduct operative and routine activity and to manage information exchanges for transactions undertaken within an organization, between organizations (*business to business*), and between end users and organizations (*business to consumer*). According to Zuboff [9] ICT allows hyper-automation of organizational processes (informate + automate) and enables labor to be replaced with capital (capital deepening). The use of TPS and their diffusion have led to the ***automation*** (*automate*, [10]) of many activities previously performed by a large number of employees, to simplification in execution, and to regulation of performance in keeping with set procedures to pursue objectives with regard to efficiency (cost reduction), quality, speed and flexibility. Underlying such workings of TPS are business programming systems, which define the rules according to which transactions and their relative operations must be carried out. In the case of production activities, for example, the systems indicate by means of optimization algorithms, for each unit of time, the quantities to be produced and the sectors involved, the plant used and delivery deadlines. With the application of TPS in organizations, structured decisions are made, emphasizing the use of procedures and routines such as organizational *decision-making* tools and institutionalized forms of knowledge (*knowing*). We are thus dealing with the effect of coordination that allows the impact of *procedural standardization to be amplified* within an organization.

However, the main contribution of TPS lies in their capacity to ***monitor the performance of automated activities***, collecting and processing (*On Line Transaction Processing* – OLTP) information on what activity and operation has been performed, who performed it, how it was performed etc., and to process the data gathered, by aggregating, comparing and storing (*informate*, [10]).

In conclusion, based on a method of case studies and longitudinal analysis, studies under the first approach show that the combination of two effects (automate and informate) allows hyperautomation and an increase in labor productivity at the level of the individual organization. However, their value in practice concerns effects derived from smart machines and hence from one type of information system, overlooking others of significant importance.

ICT and Coordination Cost Reduction (1987–2001)

Under the second approach, ICT systems allow a reduction in the information complexity of relations between organizational actors, increasing the elaboration capacity of parties to a transaction and thereby reducing the corresponding costs of coordinating and controlling their respective behavior. As a result, relationships that were once classified as having high information complexity and were thus better to manage using equity or non-equity mechanisms, may be more suitably governed with recourse to electronic relations. Underpinning this approach are chiefly the contributions by Malone, Yates and Benjamin [11], Gurbaxani and Whang [12], and Brynjolfsson and Hitt [13]. According to this approach, ICT is interpreted as having a two-fold role. First of all, ICT is a production technology that reduces technical specificity and allows the dependence between purchasers and suppliers to be reduced, also concerning relations that affect components designed and built *ad hoc*. Secondly, ICT is a coordination technology that reduces transaction and coordination costs within firms and between firms (knowledge level systems, management level systems, B2C, B2B, ERP, CRM), hence able to affect firm productivity directly.

Consistent with this function of ICT, Malone, Yates and Benjamin [11] developed their "move to the market hypothesis": ICT makes the use of market mechanisms to coordinate customer-supplier relations ever more attractive. Indeed, use of ICT systems favors:

- electronic communication, in other words the availability of more information in less time at lower cost
- electronic brokerage: ICT performs the role of intermediary between vendors and purchasers, facilitating trade;
- an increase in information processing capacity: information complexity is reduced, as are the costs coordination and behavior control.
- reduction in the dependence upon resource specificity: ICT increases product standardization and labor substitutability.

However, the literature is somewhat discordant on these points. Bakos and Brynjolfsson [14], Clemons, Reddi and Row [15] formulate the so-called *move to the middle hypothesis* that seeks to explain why, with the introduction of ICT, there has been no development in market mechanisms. Rather, the average number of suppliers to the same firm is lower and inter-organizational relations are long-term and stable. The chief explanations are as follows:

- ICT requires sunk costs and non-contractible investments arising from the performance of knowledge-intensive activities;
- - In products with a low degree of standardization, suppliers are assessed according to flexibility, reliability, and innovation, which emerge from long-term relationships.
- - The reduction in the number of suppliers increases the number of transactions for the supplier, reducing ICT investment costs per transaction.

To support this standpoint, it should be pointed out that, while in OECD-monitored countries 33% of firms with more than 10 employees use the Internet for purchasing and 17% for selling goods or services [16], as shown by Nurmilaakso [17] with a survey of 5,000 firms in 10 sectors and seven nations, productivity increases with the growth of Internet access, use of ERP and CRM systems and standard electronic commerce systems (EDI and B2B).

ICT and Organizational Complementarity

The third approach to studying the relationship between ICT and productivity focuses on the micro level and applies statistical analysis, reconciling two seemingly opposite approaches. Most of the literature on the organizational impact of

ICT [18] specifically concerns skill-biased technical change (SBTC) or skill-biased organizational change (SBOC). However, more recently attempts have been made to consider both the technical aspects of change and those more specifically organizational [19-21], with the pre-condition that research should be based on the hypothesis of complementarity [19] between the two types of changes.

Under the hypothesis of skill-biased technical change (SBTC), the adoption of ICT increases the demand in firms for more qualified staff [22-24] and reduces the demand for workers with operative duties. Indeed, the changes brought about are chiefly technological and modify operative procedures and processes within plants, industrial sites and factories. ICT are interpreted as a new technological paradigm that leads management and staff, over a substantial span of time, to try out new production systems and adapt to them. Studies consistent with the SBTC hypothesis have highlighted the indirect impacts and disequilibria caused by ICT upon the labor market. This was illustrated in Italy by the studies of Bratti and Matteucci [25], Manacorda [26], Erickson and Ichino [27], and Casavola et al [28] on the demand for white-collar workers and on wage rises granted to them according to the changes in competencies induced by the introduction of ICT.

By contrast, under the hypothesis of skill-biased organizational change (SBOC) greater importance is assigned to the relationship between organizational changes and the introduction of more skilled staff: firms that, after investment in ICT, adopt both new organizational models and more skilled staff manage to obtain greater productivity increases than those that have only made use of one of the two variables. One of the most extensively studied organizational changes [29] under this hypothesis is the decentralization of decision-making processes. For example, Caroli and Van Reenen [30] compare the costs and benefits of organizational decentralization brought about by ICT, observing that the presence of more skilled staff amplifies the benefits and reduces the costs of decentralization. Thus, according to this approach, the greatest productivity increases are obtained in firms that support organizational change by improving the skills of their own staff and are positioned among the more skill-intensive firms. By contrast, poorer results in terms of productivity are encountered among firms that are not skill-intensive. Clearly, to the extent that more skilled workers are better able to manage the greater quantity of information and manage horizontal and interpersonal relations, they tend to be more independent and motivated. Notable examples of studies carried out on the Italian system are those by Piva and Vivarelli [31] especially, and by Piva et al. [29].

Nonetheless, Bresnahan [19] showed the possible integration of the two previous hypotheses and introduced the concept of organizational complementarity between ICT and skilled labor. In this perspective, technological and organizational change together call for more skilled labor for several reasons.

First of all, ICT cannot completely replace human labor. If the effects of hyper-automation are encountered with transaction processing systems especially for simple, repetitive operational tasks, knowledge level systems and management level systems represent tools supporting decision-making processes performed by skilled, knowledge-intensive organizational positions, broadening their capacities and potential. Hence the organizational requirement for new professional positions, also at the lower levels of the organizational structure. Use of ICT increases the volumes of data and information transmitted within and between companies. This information flow, in turn, requires changes not only in coordination mechanisms (procedures, management systems) but also staff management competence, favoring more skilled tasks, but also decentralization of authority and more flexible forms of division of labor such as teamwork, multi-tasking, job rotation, just-in-time, and quality circles. Workers have to deal with greater autonomy, responsibility and uncertainty.

Secondly, there is the key distinction between industry and services: according to Bresnahan et al. [20] the demand for skilled workers is more likely to increase precisely in service companies or in industrial firms that change their organization toward greater decentralization, adopting integrated systems (ERP, MRP, CRM, supply chain management) that increase the value generated by services within their own business model.

Indeed, if we place organizational change at the centre of the analysis, the effects of ICT upon the demand for labor both directly and indirectly should be taken into consideration. The direct effects clearly stem from the fact that if new technologies are adopted, workers endowed with new skills are required. However, the indirect effects are caused by innovations in procedures, products and services that are developed at the level of the individual firm, according to a mechanism of recombination and co-invention, and that change the ability of workers to generate value for the firm. In actual fact, the complementarity hypothesis [20; 30] assumes that the relation between organizational skills and ICT adoption should be considered, with the analysis focusing on the effects produced by significant organizational changes. The solutions adopted by firms to re-combine their organizational structure with ICT are specific and vary across firms. The framework of organizational complementarity has been widely applied with success. Indeed, Bresnahan et al. [20] were able to show that doubling investment in ICT produces a 3.6% increase in productivity (sample of 300 US firms) but if the organization is flexible, the increase is 5.8%). Further, Brynjolfsson and Hitt [13] correlated ICT capital stock in individual firms with their labor productivity and their total factor productivity. Bloom, Van Reenen and Sadun (London School of Economics, [32]) showed the relationship between investment in hardware and productivity. Farooqui [33] (ONS, UK) associated an increase in firm productivity with an increase in investment in software and in its use by staff. Research carried out by the London Business School and McKinsey [34] shows that a 20% increase in productivity is achieved in firms if there are suitable managerial and professional skills in using ICT; it is reduced to 2% if firms are "poorly managed". Further, in younger firms the higher capacity of employees to use ICT systems has proved a more important factor of productivity increase than investment in ICT [33] Company productivity increases by 1.3% if the number of employees using computers increases by 10% [35], company productivity increases with the number of staff using the Internet [36], and value added per employee is greater in firms that have a higher percentage of staff able to use the Internet [33]. Nevertheless, studies carried out in several countries under the complementarity hypothesis [21] show mixed results. For example, in the USA and Australia significant relations have been found both between ICT and organizational change and between ICT and human capital [20;37]. Instead, in surveys of firms in Europe the chances of finding confirmation of the two hypotheses (SBTC and SBOC) at the same time are not so likely [38;39;30]. In this regard, the study by Bloom, Van Reenen and Sadun [32;40] of the London School of Economics is of particular significance. It is shown that what affects productivity much more is organization and management, with context being less important. Thus the hypothesis of natural advantages is not fully legitimate. The main conclusions of the above study are as follows:

- US firms have greater increases in productivity (labor and TFP) from investment in ICT than European firms;
- US firms operating in the UK have greater increases in productivity than other UK multinationals or those from other countries;
- US multinationals in the UK are more decentralized in organizational terms and have flatter structures, allowing greater diffusion of information;
- US multinationals in the UK are "better managed" and hence better able to manage organizational changes induced by the use of ICT (best practices are assessed on the basis of a model of organizational maturity drawn up and correlated with performance by Bloom and Van Reenen[32]);
- European firms have "inferior management performance" due to less competition and their family-run nature whereby the "first-born" succeeds the entrepreneur.

Research into organizational complementarity has focused on the large firms that clearly have greater need of information processing [41]. However, also in Italy, renowned for the major presence of small firms, studies and research have been carried out following the above approach.Trento and Warglein [42] observe the effects of organizational complementarity on productivity especially in large firms and on those processes which have already been formalized and standardized. Bugamelli and Pagano [43] point out a positive correlation between investment in ITC, human capital and re-organization also for Italian firms. In particular, there emerges a strong correlation between the choice of investing in TIC and re-organizing the production process. Moreover, investment intensity in ICT appears correlated with the level of human capital in the labor force. Matteucci and Sterlacchini [44] show that Italian manufacturing firms with greater ICT intensity (investment in ICT) have greater increases in productivity if ICT skills and organizational changes are adopted. Of interest are the findings of Giuri, Torrisi, Zinovyeva [18] from an analysis of 540 Italian manufacturing firms (source: Mediocredito Capitalia database). In SMEs, investment in ICT combined with organizational changes and investment in human capital does not produce significant effects on productivity. The limited size of the areas of organizational intervention reduces the effects of ICT. In medium-size firms the increase in productivity tied to ICT investment is amplified by the concurrent investment in human capital (skills). By contrast, organizational changes reduce rather than amplify increases in productivity tied to investment in ICT insofar as they make it too costly to implement new information technologies.

Conclusions

According to Zhen-Wei Qiang and Pitt [45] there are three channels through which ICT can influence economic growth:

1. TFP growth in ICT-producing sectors
2. Capital deepening
3. TFP growth through reorganization and ICT usage.

The growth of ICT-linked productivity has been recorded: it depends first of all on the growth of TFP in industries producing ICT, an explainable consequence of rapid technological progress. The most evident characteristic of this effect is the rapidly increasing computing power of new ICT products. The second channel where ICT can influence productivity is when higher levels of financial investment in ICT bring about new products and falling prices. This may lead to an increase in the real capital stock per worker—that is, ICT-related capital deepening across the economy (implying a lowering of the marginal cost of capital). The third possibility through which ICT acts on productivity concerns the potential that ICT has to significantly reorganize how goods and services are created and distributed. ICT applications can create new markets, new products and new ways of organizing how business operates.

One must look at how these technological advancements affect the entire economy rather than just focus on the benefits of improving technology in one ICT-producing sector. Such dramatic technological changes across the entire economy naturally affect TFP growth and demonstrate ICT's potential to stimulate productivity.

The third channel is more difficult to characterize, yet it may have the most profound long-term effects. The organizational complementary approach is able to present interesting results that are useful precisely in terms of this third relation, showing that mere implementation of ICT does not suffice to increase productivity. Indeed, it is necessary that these technologies are appropriately exploited by a competent management. Studies of organization and information systems are thus presented as an indispensable discipline, especially for a country like Italy in which significant public resources are often used to support investment in ICT in order to streamline, for example, public sector bureaucracy or support SMEs without suitable assessment of the management's capacity to make substantial gains in benefit.

References

1. Strassmann, P. A. (1990) *The Business Value of Computers: An Executive's Guide*. New Canaan, CT, Information Economics Press.
2. Loveman, G. W. (1988) An Assessment of the Productivity Impact of Information Technologies. *MIT Management in the 1990s*, Working Paper # 88 – 05, July 1988
3. Bender, D. H. [1986] Financial Impact of Information Processing. Vol. 3(2), 22-32
4. Roach, S. S. (1989) America's White-Collar Productivity Dilemma. *Manufacturing Engineering* , August , pp. 104.
5. Becchetti, L., Paganetto, L., and Bedoya, D.A.L. (2003) ICT Investment, Productivity and Efficiency: Evidence at Firm Level Using a Stochastic Frontier Approach. *Research paper CEIS*, n. 29.
6. Lehr, B., and Lichtenberg, F.(1999) Information Technology and Its Impact on Productivity: Firm-Level Evidence from Government and Private Data Sources, 1977-1993. *Canadian Journal of Economics*; 32(2), 335-62.
7. David, P. (1990) The Dynamo and the Computer: An Historical Perspective on the Modern Productivity Paradox. *American Economic Review*, 80(2), 355-61.
8. Dedrick, J., Gurbaxani, V., and Kraemer, K. L. (2002) *Information Technology and Economic Performance: Firm and Country Evidence*, Center for Research on Information Technology and Organizations, University of California, Irvine.
9. Zuboff, S. (1988) *In the Age of the Smart Machine: the Future of Work and Power*, Basic Books, New York, NY.
10. Zuboff, S. (1982) New Worlds of Computer Mediated Work, *Harvard Business Review*, September-October.
11. Malone, T. W., Yates, J., Benjamin, R. I. (1987) Electronic Market and Electronic Hierarchies. *Communication of the ACM*, June, 30(6)
12. Gurbaxani, V.,and Whang S. (1991) The impact of information systems on organizations and markets. *Communications of the ACM* 34(1): 59-73.
13. Brynjolfsson, E. and Hitt, L. (2001) Beyond Computation: Information Technology, Organizational Transformation, and Business Performance, *Journal of Economic Perspectives*, forthcoming.
14. Bakos, J. Y., and Brynjolfsson, E. (1993b) Information Technology, Incentives and the Optimal Number of Suppliers. *Journal of Management Information Systems*, 10(2) (Fall).
15. Clemons, E. K., Reddi, S. P., and Row, M. C. (1993) The Impact of Information Technology on the Organization of Economic Activity. The <<Move to the Middle>> Hypothesis. *Journal of Management Information Systems*, 10(2) Fall.
16. OECD (2009), OECD Science , Technology and 12 industry scoreboard 2009
17. Nurmilaakso, J.M. (2009) ICT solutions and labor productivity: evidence from firm-level data. *Electronic Commerce Research* 9, 173–181
18. Giuri, P., Torrisi, S. , Zinovyeva, N. (2005) *ICT, Skills and Organisational Change: Evidence from a Panel of Italian Manufacturing Firms*, LEM working paper #2005/11, Sant'Anna School of Advanced Studies, Pisa.
19. Bresnahan, T. (1999) Computerisation and Wage Dispersion: An Analytical Reinterpretation, *Economic Journal* 109, F390-F415.
20. Bresnahan, T., Brynjolfsson, E., and Hitt, L. (2002) Information Technology, Workplace Organization and the Demand for Skilled Labor: Firm-level Evidence. *Quarterly Journal of Economics*, Feb., pp. 339-376.
21. Arvanitis, S. (2005) Computerization, New Workplace Organization, Skilled Labor and Firm Productivity: Evidence for the Swiss Business Sector. *Economics of Innovation and New Technology*, 14, 225-249.
22. Machin, S.,and Van Reenen, J. (1998) Technology and Changes in Skills Structure: Evidence from Seven OECD Countries, *The Quarterly Journal of Economics*, November, pp. 1215-44.
23. Autor, D.H., Katz F.L., and Krueger A.B. (1998) Computing Inequality: Have Computers Changed the Labor Market? *Quarterly Journal of Economics*, 113, 1169-1213.

24. Acemoglu, D. (1998) Why do new technologies complement skills? Directed technical change and wage inequality. *Quarterly Journal of Economics* 113, 1055–1090.
25. Bratti, M.,and Matteucci, N. (2004) Is There Skill-Biased Technicological Change in Italian Manufacturing? Evidence from Firm-Level Data, *Quaderni di ricerca*, No. 202, Dipartimento di Economia, Università Politecnica delle Marche.
26. Manacorda, M. (1996) *Dualismo territoriale e differenziali di reddito. Un'analisi dell'andamento della dispersione dei redditi individuali nel Nord e Sud d'Italia*, mimeo.
27. Erickson, C.L., Ichino, A.C. (1994) Wage differentials in Italy: Market force, Institutions and Inflation in *Differences and Changes in the Wage Structure*, Freeman R. and Katz L. F.(eds), Chicago University Press and NBER, 105-127.
28. Casavola, P., Gavosto, A., and Sestito, P., (1996) Technical progress and wage dispersion in Italy: evidence from data. *Annales d'economie et statistique*, 41-42, 387-412
29. Piva, M., Santarelli E., and Vivarelli M. (2005) The skill bias effect of technological and organizational change: Evidence and policy implications. *Research Policy*, 34, 141-157.
30. Caroli, E. and Van Reenen, J. (2001) Skill-Biased Organizational Change? Evidence from a Panel of British and French Establishments. *Quarterly Journal of Economics*, Nov., pp. 1449-1492.
31. Piva,, M., and Vivarelli, M. (2004) The Determinants of the Skill Bias in Italy: R&D, Organization or Globalization? *Economics of Innovation and New Technology*, 13(4), 329-347.
32. Bloom, N., Van Reenen, J. and Sadun, R. (2005) It *Ain't What You Do, it's the Way that You do IT, Centre for Economic Performance*, London School of Economics: London
33. Farooqui, S. (2005) IT use by Firms and Employees, Productivity Evidence across Industries. *Economic Trends*, 625, 65–74
34. McKinsey (2004)
35. OECD (2004) Working Party on the Information Economy: New Perspectives on ICT Skills and Employment , DSTI/ICCP/IE(2004)10, Paris, December 2004.
36. Maliranta, M., and Rouvinen, P. (2004) *ICT and Business Productivity: Finnish Micro-level Evidence*. Office for Economic Co-operation and Development publication: The Economic Impact of ICT: Measurement, Evidence and Implications
37. Gretton, P., Gali, J. and D. Parham (2002), Uptake and Impacts of ICT in the Australian Economy: Evidence from Aggregate, Sectoral and Firm levels, Paper Presented in *The OECD Workshop on ICT and Business Performance*, Paris, December 9.
38. Bertschek, I. Kaiser, U. (2004) Productivity Effects of Organizational Change: Microeconometric Evidence. *Management Science*, 50(3), 394-404.
39. Hempel, T. (2002) *Does experience matter? Productivity effects of ICT in the German service sector*. Discussion paper 02–43. Centre for European Economic Research: Manheim
40. Bloom N., Sadun R., and Van Reenen J., (2007) *Americans do I.T. Better: U.S. Multinationals and the Productivity Miracle*, NBER Working Paper No. 13085.
41. Galbraith, J. R. (1977) *Organizational Design*, Addison Wesley, Reading, MA.
42. Trento, S.,and Warglein M. (2001), Nuove tecnologie e cambiamenti organizzativi: alcune implicazioni per le imprese italiane, *Banca d'Italia, Temi di discussion*, Number 428 – December.
43. Bugamelli, M., and Pagano P., (2001) Barriers to Investment in ICT. *Banca d'Italia, Temi di discussione,* Number 420 – October.
44. Matteucci, N., Sterlacchini, A. (2004) *ICT, R&D and Productivity Growth: Evidence from Italian Manufacturing Firms, EPKE Final Conference "Information Technology, Productivity and Growth*, London, 28-29 October.
45. Zhen-Wei Qiang, C., Pitt, A., and Ayers, S. (2004) *Contribution of Information and Communication Technologies to Growth W O R L D B A N K W O R K I N G P A P E R N O . 2 4*

Information Technology Benefits: A Framework

Piercarlo Maggiolini[1]

Abstract Why, since the first applications of ICT, was and still is so difficult – if not quite impossible – to evaluate the productivity of ICT? In our opinion, mainly because – before any quantification – we need a clear and systematic view of the different economic benefits of the different applications of ICT. We present here a realistic and powerful framework by considering the different benefits resulting from the applications of ICT. In this approach, a categorization of benefits is presented as a useful guide for anyone who has to decide on investments in ICT.

Introduction

Why, since the first applications of ICT, was and still is so difficult – if not quite impossible – to evaluate the productivity of ICT? (For a history and a state of art of the question of ICT productivity, more or less up to date, you can see can see [1-18]).

In our opinion, mainly because – before any quantification – we need a clear and systematic view of the different economic benefits of the different applications of ICT.

We first distinguish between the utilization of the Information and Communication Technology (ICT) in tasks where it is used as *production technology* and as a *work tool* and those where it is used as *organizational and mediating technology.* These are the two main manifestation of the ICT uses.

Benefits of ICT as Production Technology / Work Tool

This section is concerning the first use of ICT.

The earlier applications of ICT in business organizations were generally concerned with the administrative systems (accounting, wages, invoicing, etc.). In this context, ICT, that is to say, computer, can be considered office facilities – in the same way as typewriters, photocopiers, etc. Computers used for the production of documents *per se*, are real work tools, instruments, similar to other "production technology", as robots, CAD, CAM, etc. In this way they help to carry out activities previously performed with different technologies, manual or otherwise, and to replace both labour and traditional facilities.

[1] Politecnico di Milano, piercarlo.maggiolini@polimi.it

What are the benefits of ICT used substantially as production technology / work tool? They can be summed up as *reduction of costs of production* (see, for example, [19-22]), and, if we see administrative units as a particular type of service production units, as *savings of human work-time.* How do ICT achieves these economics of work time? In order to quantize this, it would be necessary to identify the factors that traditionally "consume" time. They include:

1) Many information processes are mainly *manual.*
2) They involves many transformations of information from one *medium* to another.
3) There are many *shadow activities.* These are the unforseen and unforseable time consuming activities that accompany any activity but do not contribute to the result: for example, errors in typewriting, or, when making a phone call, a misdialed number, a busy signal, a bad connection, interruptions, etc.

From this point of view, the ICT can improve efficiency by:

1) *Automation:* the benefits derived from the substitution or elimination of manual procedures; i.e., computer substitute manpower.
2) *Reduction on transformation of media:* a change of the medium that carries the message occurs in going from verbal to written, from handwritten to typewritten, etc. Reduction in these saves labour.
3) *Reduction of shadow functions:* we can reduce (and save labour time) errors in typewriting by using word processing systems, we can avoid potential unsuccessful – and time consuming – phone calls by using e-mail, and so on.
4) *Speed, timeliness:* immediate economics result from the reduction of idle or waiting time (labour saving) and thus the possibility of greater productivity. This is extremely important because it provides leverage by increasing all production factors that depend on "economics of speed". Such economics, though they bring a decrease in unitary costs, are fundamentally different from economics of scale. The increased total productivity of the factors in the case of the economics of speed is not achieved by adding more production factors but by speeding up the flow of goods through the processes of production and distribution and so permitting a steadier, more intensive use of the factors involved ([23]). When ICT systems are used as " work tools" (to produce and distribute, efficiently, data and documents) the approach used to evaluate economical implications and benefits of ICT is accurate but it is limited. In fact, it does not permit us to understand the real reasons that people use information, to understand more generally the role of information and communication in and between organizations. This makes difficult to understand (and consequently to achieve) the real benefits of ICT (such as stock reductions in since long time classical ICT application to production management). We must therefore examine the added value and hidden benefits of information and communication in and between organizations.

Benefits of ICT as Organizational and Mediating Technology

The Economic Functions of Information and Communication

In order to identify the *real* benefits of ICT we incorporate two different models of analysis of the benefits of information systems in organizations ([3;24]):

- The first is based on *decision making,* regarded as the main information-consuming and producing process in organizations ([25-26]).
- The second is based on the *transactional view* of the organizations and their information systems ([27-29]).

Information vs. Uncertainty

Galbraith [26] hypothesized that "*the greater the task uncertainty, the greater the amount of information that must be processed among decision makers during task execution in order to achieve a given level of performance*".

If there is good prior knowledge of the task with respect to its development, a large part of the activity can be predefined. If, on the other hand, the task is unknown, during execution more knowledge is acquired, consequently changes must be made to the allocation of resources, etc.

This implies a need to process information *during* the execution of the task. By these assumptions, the *uncertainty of the task* is what determines the information needs. Uncertainty implies a variety of events of states that the decision maker has to face while using a limited capacity for processing information.

But this is only of the possible causes of uncertainty (deriving from "nature": technology or environment), there are interpersonal relations which represent a distinct source of variety for the decision maker. This distinction between uncertainty of information regarding the *environment* and *other's behaviour* is useful and important [30]. The latter may be called "uncertainty of exchange" (transaction). It is useful to remember that the notion of *exchange* precedes that of the *organization* itself. Every transaction implies the importance of organizing and of social interaction between two or more individuals. Within the structure of the transaction, a decision maker reacts to others utilizing and communicating information, and if the relations exchange are sources of uncertainty, they also make it possible to acquire information. During the execution of the transaction, the information itself can be the object of exchange, deduced by observing the reciprocal behaviour, abstracted, distinguished, or communicated in some disguised fashion.

Organizing Economic Transactions

What are the major business decisions? According to Chander [41], Chandler and Daems [42], they are those of allocation of resources and monitoring and coordinating economic activities. Each economic system requires the resources to be *allocated* to the various units, the functioning and the performance of these units to be monitored, and the flow of goods, services, money and information between the units to be *coordinated.*

Because the transactions (the exchanges) between units are of vital importance, the most important function is that of *coordination.*

Any mechanism that improve the efficiency of transaction, speeds up the flow through the economic system, or allows a more intensive use of production factors is likely to improve the overall performance.

There are various ways of organizing these functions: the best known seems to be the *price system* (the *market).* Other ways are the "*hierarchies*" (the traditional firms), interagency arrangements *("federations")* and "*clans*" (see see [31-32;27;29]). The choice between these forms of organization does not depend only on *production costs* but above all on *transaction costs.*

The economic activity is carried out inside or outside the firm depending on relative importance of the costs of internal and external transactions; i.e., between the costs of internal coordination and monitoring and of the marketplace.

According to some economists (see, for example, Arrow [33], Coase [34]), *information* has a strategic role in the evaluation of the limit of economic activity in a market system. The possibility of using the price system to allocate, monitor and coordinate economic activity depends on the access of economic agents to information. When the access differs from one agent to another, the price system presents difficulties. Consequently the markets considered as information systems (and prices considered as transmitters of information) are costly and imperfect: transactions have an information cost.

Thus, when "hierarchical" organizational integration reduces costs, the "hierarchy" substitutes for the market; The hierarchical organization prevails when it is difficult to exchange on the market, because the costs of organizing (exchanges on) the market are too high.

Failures in the market mechanism are due to the difficulty for the potential sellers and buyers to find one another, to meet, to agree on the terms of the transaction, to define the contract of sale/purchase, and to monitor execution of the contract, etc. Then, an *administrative* mechanism is more efficient because it reduces the need to process the information by absorbing the uncertainty of the exchange.

But provision of that coordination, allocation. and monitoring of the resources within the "hierarchy" also has a cost: that of *coordination* (i.e., the cost of transactions within the organization).

For convenience, we distinguish the costs of coordination from those of transaction (external exchange with the environment), even if they are of the same nature.

From this point of view the *coordination and transaction costs* are those of collecting, processing, evaluating, and communicating information regarding the environment (and behaviour of the agents) inside and outside, respectively.

Coordination Costs

The subdivision of an activity into specialized subactivities poses the problem of coordinating these subactivities to assure execution of the overall activity. Thus the need is to create mechanisms that permit an action between a high number of interdependent parts. The various organization coordinating processes have, however, a limited validity and efficiency in the processing of the information needed to coordinate the interdependent roles.

According to Galbraith's analysis, organizations respond to uncertainty in two ways either by reducing the requirements of information processing (diminishing the quantity of information), or by increasing the capacity and consequently increasing the quantity of information processed and exchanged (see Table 1). We now briefly examine the principal ways in which the two types of behaviour can be put into practice.

Table 1: Strategies of reduction of uncertainty (from Galbraith [26])

I.	Reduce the need for information processing	1. Creation of slack resources 2. Creation of se!f-contained tasks 3. Investments in vertical information systems
II.	Increase the capacity to process information	4. Creation of lateral relations

Reducing the information requirements means reducing exceptions (the unforseen). In other words, there must be a wide margin of slack resources (financial and material, equipment and labour) or they must be organized with respect to their activity to guarantee a certain self-sufficiency (i.e., self-contained tasks).

In the first case, one is less demanding: later deadlines, high stock level, large production capacities to allow wide throughout variations, etc. Obviously the uncertainty is paid for by a higher resource cost.

In the second case, units are self-sufficient with respect to the output they produce. Typically one can transform a functional organization, oriented towards input resources. into a divisional organization, oriented towards outputs. Scale diseconomies and more specialized professional skills are the prices paid for greater self-sufficiency (and autonomy) with respect to the unforseen.

Increasing the capacity to process and communicate information means either investing in "vertical" information systems. or creating roles and organizational structures that facilitate "lateral" processing and exchange of information.

Classical management information systems supporting planning, coordination and control (from production management to warehouse control and so on) in a vertical fashion. In the second case, the organization must create and establish direct lateral contacts, provide liaison roles linking organization units, task forces, teams, and have integrating roles with matrix structures (see Table 2).

The price to be paid is the greater cost of information processing systems and greater organizational costs (*vis à vis* greater efficiency in the reduction of uncertainties).

Table 2: Lateral processes (from Galbraith [26])

1. Direct contacts (between managers who share a problem)
2. Liaison roles (linking organizational units)
3. Task forces (temporary groups created to solve problems affecting several organizational units)
4. Teams (permanent working groups for constantly recurring interdepartmental problems)
5. Integrating managerial roles (e.g. production manager, program manager, project manager. etc.)
6. Matrix organization structures

Benefits of ICT Supporting Coordination

The classical applications of ICT are the business and management information systems supporting operational or managerial activities (planning, coordinating, and control activities). What are the economical effects of the use of ICT in support of these systems?

Information and communication technology supporting coordination systems while reducing the scope of "bounded rationality" [25] of management, the costs of control, and the necessity to resort to slack resources and delegation of responsibility, favours strategies increasing the capacity to process and communicate information (type II in Table 1).

As illustrated in Table 3, the "vertical" information systems can render more efficient the functions of allocation (planning), coordination and monitoring within the firm. There is no doubt that, for example, the most specific and original office automation systems, those designed to support communications (e-mail, groupware and the various teleconference systems) allow the adoption of organizational strategies based on the easiest and most widespread *horizontal* communications, on modalities of self-coordination.

Thus strategy 4 (creating lateral relations) in the Galbraith's framework would be favoured (see tab.1). This strategy consists of using collective decision-making processes that selectively cut across lines of authority. This strategy lowers the level at which decisions are taken to coincide with the level at which information is first available.

In particular, among the lateral processes of Table 2, direct contacts, task forces, and teams are favoured and strengthened. In other words, the new communication systems (local area networks, Intranet) and telematics could reduce the necessity of intermediaries. either hierarchical or lateral.

Summing up, in these cases the economic benefits derive from a reduction of *coordination costs.*

Table 3: Effects of computer-based "vertical" information systems supporting planning, coordination and monitoring activities within organizations

- Possibility of faster planning cycles (faster reaction to changes to environmental conditions)
- Identifying and controlling the critical areas (reduction of reaction time with correcting actions)
- Simulating alternatives, studying interactions between firm subsystems, more accurate forecasting

Transaction Costs

Transaction costs are costs of collecting, processing, evaluating and communicating information about the environment external to the organization. In particular, such information refers to the condition of the market, the delivery terms of services and goods, the quality of products, and all the details necessary to define the obligation of parties in contracts.

More analytically it can be said that the cost of carrying out a transaction results in possible losses of resources due to a lack of information between the interested parties to the transaction itself.

There are three phases in the process of exchange (cf. Coase [35]):

a) *Research.* This involves the activities necessary to produce an interaction involving a minimum social unit (the contracting couple). It includes the exploration and identification of the alternatives of exchange. the identification of possible reciprocal advantages of the exchange. etc.
b) *Negotiation.* This involves activities related to the negotiation of the terms of the transaction and to the conclusion of the contract. Negotiating a contract means building a formal model of the exchange on which the parties can agree. In this model, the price and quantity are specified as well as aspects of behaviour of the parties. The process is described procedurally, including an estimate of future events that may involve the parties during the execution of the contract, as well as the actions that the parties should take in case certain circumstances arise.
c) *Contral and Monitoring.* These include the activities that make the model of the contract effective under conditions of uncertainty (for reaching agreement on adjustments and for put-ting them into practice). Furthermore, activities for monitoring deviations from the terms of the contract and any sanctions imposed to reestablish conditions must be specified.

The information system supporting transactions can thus be defined as a network of information and communication flows necessary to create, negotiate, monitor and control the exchanges [36].

Benefits of ICT Supporting Transactions

If one considers ICT as that which can render information flows and the communication necessary to create, install, control and monitor transaction faster, more regular and more efficient, then benefits derive from the reduction of the costs of transaction as they arise in the different phases of the exchange process.

More specifically, it can be said that the transaction costs depend principally on (see Williamson, [27]):

- the opportunistic behaviour of the participants in the transaction "*Opportunism is an effort to realize individual gains through a lack of candour of honesty in transactions*" (Williamson 1973, p.317)
- the numbers of potential participants;
- the non perfect and asymmetrical distribution of information between them: the "*information impactedeness* " of (Williamson [27]), There is information impactedeness when "*one of the agents to a contract has a deeper knowledge than does the other ... (and) it is also costly for the party with less information to achieve information parity*" ([21], p.316).

The use of ICT supporting *external economic transactions* of firms (web-based services as e-marketplace, e-procurement, etc.) tends to reduce the information costs of the transaction itself, thus reducing the importance of the factors (opportunism, small numbers, information impactedeness). (See [38-42])

Nolan's Curve Revisited

We do not intend to reexplain here Nolan's model (see [43-47]), known also as the "Stages of Growth" Model. Nolan's theory, perhaps the best-known and most widely cited model of IS evolution of in organizations, provides an insight into the way IS evolves in organizations. The Stages Theory is based on the notion that the complicated nature of computer technology would produce a body of knowledge on the effective management of IT within an organization. As a result, the assimilation of computer technologies, and more broadly, information technologies, required bold experimentation, out of which emerged different stages of organizational learning. Nolan's result correlates the evolution of the ICT budget and numerous other variables with time. In his investigations, the ICT budget evolved over time as a double S curve, which has six stages (a result of two successive and partly overlapping cycles of learning and assimilation by the firm). The first cycle is due to computer technology (stages 1-4) and the second to data resource technology (stage 3-6). Each cycle goes through four stages: initial, proliferation, control, and maturity.

The Stages Theory still has a strong influence and variations of the early models are widely used to describe technological and organizational trajectories for a range of technological implementations. For example: Knowledge Management [48], Intranet [49], e-Government [50,51], and Enterprise Resource Planning Systems [52]. This theory has been also widely used as a way of examining the adoption and progression of various aspects of Internet in organisations. Conceptual models depicting the stages involved in the development of Internet systems have appeared in the literature [53-55]. According with our theoretical framework and from our observation of ICT applications by enterprises, public administrations and especially by agencies which operate in telecommunication infrastructures and services, already 25 years ago ([56-57]) we could foresee a third cycle of innovation, a long time before the explosion of the Internet phenomenon. The subsequent advent and diffusion of telematics in broad sense and especially of a large varieties of web based information and communication systems opened this third cycle of innovation. Undoubtedly, telecommunications were and still are a large part of this kind of systems.

This third cycle of investments in information technology corresponds to the learning and assimilation of electronic communication technology, or telematics, and to the use of this to *support economic transactions,* particularly between economic agents on the market. We can therefore describe the evolution of the use of information technology in organizations in the following way (see Tab. 4):

- it passes from "*operational* " systems to *coordination* and *control* systems and then to systems supporting *transactions,* particularly on the market. It therefore passes from information technology as a *work tool,* as production technology, to informatics as *coordination and control information technology* and then to *technology of electronic communication* supporting transactions, exchanges;
- it goes from planning and managing *computer* resource to planning and managing *data* (data resources) and then to planning and managing *communications.* The emphasis is shifted from procedures and their mechanization to data and its support of electronic filing and automatic retrieval and then to communication and its support (telematics and local area networks);
- to the benefits that derive initially from the reduction of costs of *production* (also "production" of administrative services) as a result of economics of labour are later added those deriving from a reduction of *coordination* costs (to which are added those originating more specifically from a reduction in *transaction costs).*

Table 4: Cycles of investments in Information and Communication Technology

Ist cycle: *COMPUTER TECHNOLOGY* • "operational" systems (e.g. payroll) • computer as "work tool", ICT as "production" technology • added value: computerizing procedures • benefits: reduction of (information processing) "production" costs
2nd cycle: *DATA RESOURCE TECHNOLOGY* • "coordination and control" systems (e.g. production planning and control) • ICT as coordination and organizational control technology • added value: electronic memorizing data • benefits: reduction of "coordination" costs

Table 4: Cycles of investments in Information and Communication Technology

3rd cycle: *ELECTRONIC COMMUNICATION TECHNOLOGY* • "transactional" systems (e.g. e- mail, web based services) • ICT as mediating technology (particularly on the market) • added value: computerizing communication • benefits: reduction of "transaction" costs

References

1. Maggiolini, P. (1981) *Costi e benefici di un sistema, informativo*, Etas Libri, Milan
2. Francalanci, C. and Maggiolini, P. (1994) Measuring the impact of investments in information technologies on business performance. *Proceedings of the 27th Hawaii International Conference on Systems Sciences (HICSS)*, Wailea, Hawaii, January
3. Glucksmann, R., Maggiolini, P. and Pagani, D. (2004) *Gestione e strategie dei sistemi informativi*, Clup, Milan
4. Brynjolfsson, E. (1993) The productivity paradox of information technology. *Communications of the ACM*, 36 (12), 66–77.
5. Brynjolfsson, E. and Hitt, L. (1998) Beyond the Productivity Paradox: Computers are the Catalyst for Bigger Changes.*Communications of the ACM*, 41 (8), 49 – 55
6. Brynjolfsson, E. and Yang, S., (1999) The Intangible Costs and Benefits of Computer Investments: Evidence from the Financial Markets, *MIT Sloan School of Management*, December. http://digital.mit.edu/ERIK/ITQ00-11-25.pdf
7. Brynjolfsson, E. and Hitt, L. (2003) Computing Productivity: Firm Level Evidence. *MIT Sloan Working Paper No. 4210-01*. http://papers.ssrn.com/sol3/papers.cfm?abstract_id=290325
8. Dedrick, J., Gurbaxani, V. and Kraemer, K. (2003) Information technology and economic performance: A critical review of the empirical evidence. *ACM Computing Surveys*, 35 (1),1 – 28
9. Dos Santos, B. and Sussman, L. (2000) Improving the return on IT investment: the productivity paradox. *International Journal of Information Management*, 20 (6), 429-440
10. Melville, N., Kraemer, K. and Gurbaxani, V. (2004) Information Technology and Organizational Performance: An Integrative Model of IT Business Value. *MIS Quarterly*, 28 (2), 283-322
11. Oz, E. (2005) Information technology productivity: in search of a definite observation. *Information & Management*, 42 (6), 789-798
12. Pilat, D. (2004) The ICT Productivity Paradox: Insights from Micro Data, *OECD Economic Studies*, 38(1), Paris
13. Saunders, A. and Brynjolfsson, E. (2007) *Information Technology, Productivity and Innovation: Where Are We and Where Do We Go From Here?* Center for Digital Business MIT Sloan School WP 231, http://www.iii-p.org/research/IT%20Lit%20Review%20final%202007-03-30.pdf.
14. Thatcher ,M.E and Pingry, D.E. (2007) Modeling the IT value paradox. *Communications of the ACM*, 50 (8), 41 – 45
15. Triplett, J. E. (1999) The Solow productivity paradox: what do computers do to productivity. *Canadian Journal of Economics*, 32 (2),309–334. http://www.csls.ca/journals/sisspp/v32n2_04.pdf.
16. Yorukoglu, M. (1998) The Information Technology Productivity Paradox. Review of Economic Dynamics, 1(2), 551-592.
17. Willcocks, L.P. and Lester, S. (1997) In search of information technology productivity: Assessment issues. *Journal of the Operational Research Society*, 48 (11), 1082-1094

18. Willcocks, L.P. and Lester, S. (1999) *Beyond the IT Productivity Paradox*, Wiley, New York
19. Aral , S., Brynjolfsson, E. and Van Alstyne, M.W. (2007) *Information, Technology and Information Worker Productivity: Task level Evidence*. NBER Working Paper No. W13172
20. Bartel, A., Ichniowski, C., and Shaw,K. (2007) How Does Information Technology Affect Productivity? Plant-Level Comparisons of Product Innovation, Process Improvement, and Worker Skills. *The Quarterly Journal of Economics,* 122 (4), 1721-1758
21. Brynjolfsson, E. and Hitt, L. (1995) Information Technology as a Factor of Production: the Role of Differences Among Firms. *Economics of Innovation and New Technology*, 3 (3–4), 183 – 200.
22. Dewan, S. and Min, C. (1997) The Substitution of Information Technology for Other Factors of Production: A Firm Level Analysis. *Management Science*, 43 (12)
23. Valenduc ,G. (2010) Il ruolo delle tecnologie dell'informazione nell'intensificazione del lavoro, in Di Guardo, S., Maggiolini, P. and Patrignani, N. (ed.s) *Etica e responsabilità sociale delle tecnologie dell'informazione* (vol.2), Franco Angeli, Milan
24. Maggiolini, P. (2010). Informatica, organizzazione e lavoro, In Di Guardo S., Maggiolini P. and Patrignani , N. (ed.s) *Etica e responsabilità sociale delle tecnologie dell'informazione* (vol.2), Franco Angeli, Milan
25. Simon, H.A. (1976) *The new science of management decision,* Prentice-Hall, Englewood Cliffs
26. Galbraith, J.R. (1973) *Designing complex organizations,* Addison Wesley, Reading
27. Williamson, O.E. (1975) *Markets and hierarchies: analysis and antitrust implications,* Free Press, New York
28. Ouchi, W.G. (1979) A conceptual framework for the design of organizational control mechanisms. *Management Science,* 25 (9), 833 – 848
29. Ouchi, W.G. (1980) Markets, bureaucracies and clans. *Administrative Science Quarterly,* 25 (1), 129 – 141
30. Radner, R. (1968) Competitive equilibrium under uncertainty. *Econometrica,* 6 (1), 31-58
31. Chandler, A.D. (1977) *The Visible Hand. The Managerial Revolution in American Business,* Harvard University Press, Cambridge (MA)
32. Chandler, A.D. and Daems, H. (1979) Administrative coordination, allocation and monitoring: a comparative analysis of then emergence of accounting and organization in the USA and Europe, *Accounting, Organization and Society,* 4 (1-2), 2 – 20
33. Arrow, K.J. (1974) *The limits of organization.* W.W. Norton & Co., New York
34. Coase, R.H. (1937) The nature o the firm. *Economica N.S.,* 4 (16), 386-405
35. Coase, R.H. (1960) The problem of social cost. *Journal of law and economics,* 3, 1-44
36. Ciborra, C. (1981) Information systems and transactions architecture. *Journal of Policy Analysis and Information Systems,* 5 (4),305 – 324
37. Williamson, O.E. (1973) Markets and hierarchies – Some elementary considerations. *American Economic Review,* 63 (2),316 – 325
38. Ciborra, C. (1987) Reframing the role of computers in organizations — the transaction costs approach. *Office, Technology and People,* 3 (1), 17 – 38
39. Clemons E.K., Reddi S. P. and Row M.C. (1993). The impact of information technology on the organization of economic activity: the "Move to the middle" hypothesis, *Journal of Management Information Systems,* 10 (2): 9 – 35
40. Bakos Y. (1998). The Emerging Role of Electronic Marketplaces on the Internet, *Communications of the ACM*, 41 (8)
41. Francalanci,C. and Maggiolini, P.(1999) Measuring the Financial Benefits of IT Investments on Coordination. *Information Resource Management Journal,* January
42. Maggiolini, P. and Salvador Vallés, R. (2002) Évaluation des bénéfices de l'EDI: proposition d'un modèle fondé sur les coûts de transaction. *Proceedings of 7th AIM Conference "Affaire Electronique et Société de Savoir: opportunités et défis"*, Tunis, May
43. Gybson, C. and Nolan, R.L. (1974) Managing the four stages of Edp growth. *Harvard Business Review,* Jan.-Feb.

44. Nolan, R.L. (1979) Managing crises in data processing. *Harvard Business Review,* 57 (3), 115-126
45. Nolan, R. L. (1984) Managing the advanced stages of computer technology: Key research issues. In McFarlan, F.W. (ed.) *The Information Systems Research Challenge*, Harvard University Press, Boston, Mass., 195-215.
46. Nolan, R.L., Croson, D.C. and Seger, K.N. (1993). The Stages Theory: A Framework for IT Adoption and Organizational Learning. *Harvard Business School Note*, No. 9-93-141, Harvard Business School Publishing. Boston
47. Nolan, R.L. (2001) Information Technology Management from 1960-2000. *Harvard Business School Note*, No. 9, 301-147, Harvard Business School Publishing. Boston
48. Lee J-H, Kim Y-G., Yu S-H (2001) Stage Model for Knowledge Management. *Proceedings of the 34th Hawaii International Conference on System Sciences*
49. Damsgaard J. and Scheepers R. (2000) Managing the crises in intranet implementation: a stage model", *Information Systems Journal*,,10, 2, 131–150.
50. Layne K. And J. Lee J. (2001) Developing fully functional E-government: A four stage model. *Government Information Quarterly* 18, 122–136.
51. Solli-Sæther H. and Gottschalk P. (2010) The Modeling Process for Stage Models. *Journal of Organizational Computing and Electronic Commerce*, 20, 279–293,
52. Holland C.P., Light B. (2001) A Stage Maturity Model for Enterprise Resource Planning Systems Use. *The DATA BASE for Advances in Information Systems*, Spring (Vol. 32, No. 2)
53. Chan C. and Swatman P.M.C. (2004), B2B e-Commerce Stages of Growth: the Strategic Imperatives. *Proceedings of the 37th Hawaii International Conference on System Sciences*
54. Earl M.J. (2000) Evolving the E-Business. *Business Strategy Review*, 11, 2 , 33–38.
55. Raymond L. (2001), "Determinants of Web Site Implementation in Small Business", *Internet Research: Electronic Network Applications and Policy.* 11, 5, pp. 411–422.
56. Maggiolini ,P. (1984) La dimensione economica dell'automazione d'ufficio, in Bracchi G (ed.), *L'automazione del lavoro d'ufficio*, Etas Libri, Milan, 56-111
57. Maggiolini, P. (1986) Office Technology Benefits: a Framework. *Information & Management,* 10 (2),75-81

The Road Ahead: Turning Human Resource Functions into Strategic Business Partners With Innovative Information Systems Management Decisions[1]

Ferdinando Pennarola, Leonardo Caporarello[2]

Introduction

This chapter explores the interplay of two mainstream research areas: human resource management and information system deployment, both of which have relevant implications for organizations. As human resources management plays a critical role for an organization's success [1], challenges produced in the IS environment have significant impact for how human resources are managed. For many years, most of the human resources management initiatives have mainly focused on administrative aspects of HR (human resources) [2-3]. Although numerous studies have investigated the potential for human resource functions to be a strategic partner, human resources executives have not been perceived as strategic partners at all by their counterparts [4-5]. In this chapter, we argue that information technology offers the opportunity to free up HR from much of these administrative activities. Then, human resource functions could significantly focus on contributing to the organization's strategy [3]. The key is the adoption of modern human resources information system (HRIS) built to, 1) delploy a self-service HR infrastructure dedicated to administrative tasks, and 2) gather strategic data and information in order to contribute to the business strategy's formulation. The feasibility of such an interplay is acknowledged by the constant growth of the role that information technology (IT) is playing in business today, that has led to the development of new business models and new business processes [6]. In a modern business world, characterized by internationalization and cooperation between organizations from different industries, companies have to meet many different challenges, including:

- the integration of data sources, applications, platforms, and businesses;
- the technological and organizational flexibility needed to respond efficiently to changes in the marketplace;
- the creation of systems that are reliable, robust, and flexible, and that are able to keep pace with the changing needs of their users;

---

[1] This chapter draws its origin from previously published work done by the Authors (see references) and builds an updated perspective on the subject

[2] Department of Management, Bocconi University, Italy

- product and service quality;
- the possibility to rapidly roll out existing systems (not only IT, but mainly accounting/control and HR- related systems) into acquired organizations when an acquisition growth strategy is realized.

Many of the above mentioned challenges must be satisfied simultaneously, with very little compromises, and often this is an additional contest field for HR and IS managers as well. As such, companies are increasingly recognizing the importance of effective IS management [7]. The Lawler & Mohrman's study [3] shows how HR is most likely to be a full strategic partner when an integrated HRIS exists. The globalization of business, the development of more flexible organization structures, the further development of information technology are some of the drivers of the necessity for HR information systems [2].

In light of the above, the ultimate goal of managing information technology resources is to identify, select, and assess – and, when necessary, revise the initial decisions – a balanced, consistent set of IS products and services for both in-house users (employees and business owners) and external users (customers, suppliers, partners, and the community). Modern computing is also offering new platform development opportunities that can radically change the deployment of HR services throughout the organization: the cloud computing paradigm, for example, making available data and applications from any point of the network, is an additional proof of how HR functions can be freed of administrative tasks.

Background

At a first attempt, many organizations may be investing in IS to reduce transaction costs and downsize the HR function, instead of making it a strategic partner. However, as mentioned above, it is acknowledged that the HR function has a great potential contribution to the business strategy formulation.

In order to increase the strategic value-add of the HR function, the following considerations should be taken into account: 1) human resource is an information-centered activity; 2) IS can support the function to increase HR focus on critical aspects as capacity planning, organizational development and organizational designs; 3) IS can support the function to turn data into strategically valuable information; 4) IS can support the function to increase the business knowledge of HR professionals [2-3]. To make this happen, organizations should adopt IS governance systems that smooth the progress toward a full empowerment of company functions, among which we consider the case of the human resources.

Ultimately, managing IS resources implies a full understanding the needs of the business, investing in and coordinating the various IS components, and being able to alter the composition of IS resources, as well as to manage and control these resources and their relationship to the business as a whole. It follows, then, that IS governance does not limit itself to merely managing the current state of affairs, but also necessarily implies an ongoing analysis and revision of the needs, limitations, and opportunities provided by IS in relation to general business objectives [8].

Therefore, our first conclusion can be summarized as follows: appropriate models are required for effective IS resource management.

A number of authors [9-10] have shown how investments in IS resources can be beneficial to productivity, which does not necessarily mean an increase in productivity for the entire organization.

Below, we shall put forth a six-part model[1], based on the competitive forces model and applied to IS resources, which can be used as a general point of reference in managing IS resources in a manner that best supports a company's business activities (Figure 1).

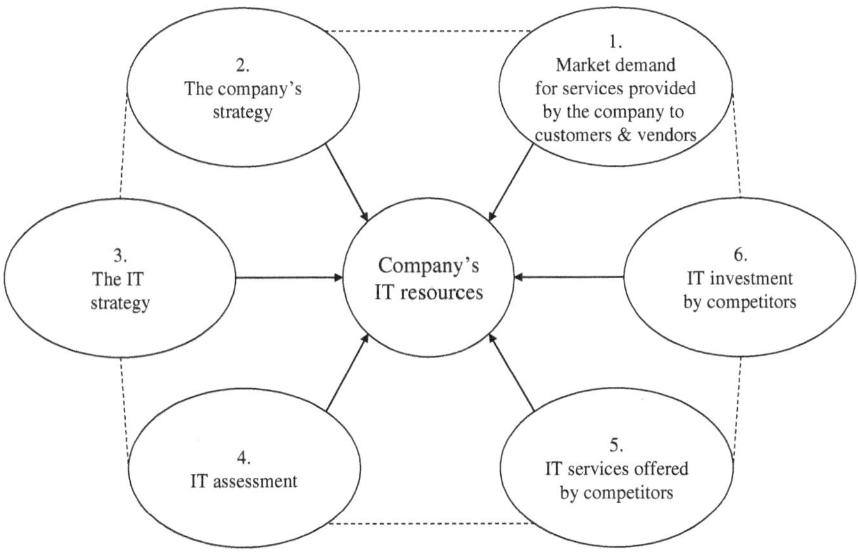

Figure 1: Competitive forces model for IS resources

The first part of the model requires that we identify the products and services currently provided to the organization's various stakeholders (both internal and external) in order to analyze any gaps between these and the users' actual needs.

The second and third parts concern with strategy:

- the strategy of the organization, the purpose of which includes determining which products and services are necessary in order to achieve general objectives;
- IS strategy, the purpose of which is to plan future needs in terms of IS initiatives and services that are in line with the organization's strategic goals.

The fourth part of the model highlights the importance of IS assessment in order to understand the level of the organization's technology and the results of the use of IS resources.

The two final parts then underscore the importance of the IS initiatives and services provided by the competition and of the related levels of spending and investment.

Finally, we want to deep our understanding of what it is commonly addressed as "IS resource management": IS management implies both an infrastructural dimension and an application dimension of the IS portfolio. IS managers have the responsibility to ensure that the appropriate IS infrastructures and applications are available for different projects committed by the other business functions.

IS Resource Management Strategies

IS resource management is a complex activity that goes beyond the mere technical aspects to include the even more important strategic, organizational, and financial aspects. For this reason, it is important to involve all of an organization's various levels of decision making, from analysis and definition of specifications to design and implementation. Everyone involved must also be clear on the elements needed to define IS resource management and on the effects of the various alternatives over the short, medium and long term.

At the strategy level, based on the observations of Coase [11] with regard to transaction governance[2], there are two possible forms of governance for an IS resource: turning to the market or using in-house resources.

Subsequently, the theory of transaction costs put forth by Williamson [12-13], which integrates Coase's observations, states that the choice between the market or in-house resources must be based on standards of organizational efficiency and on a comparative analysis of transaction costs and the following:

- costs of information and decision-making;
- costs of negotiation and distribution [14];
- costs of execution;
- costs of control;
- costs of change;
- economies of scale;
- economies of specialization;
- economies of communication, information, and control.

In essence, make-or-buy decisions (i.e.the choice between insourcing and outsourcing) are management decisions characterized by a certain complexity and uncertainty and are made under conditions of bounded rationality [15-16].

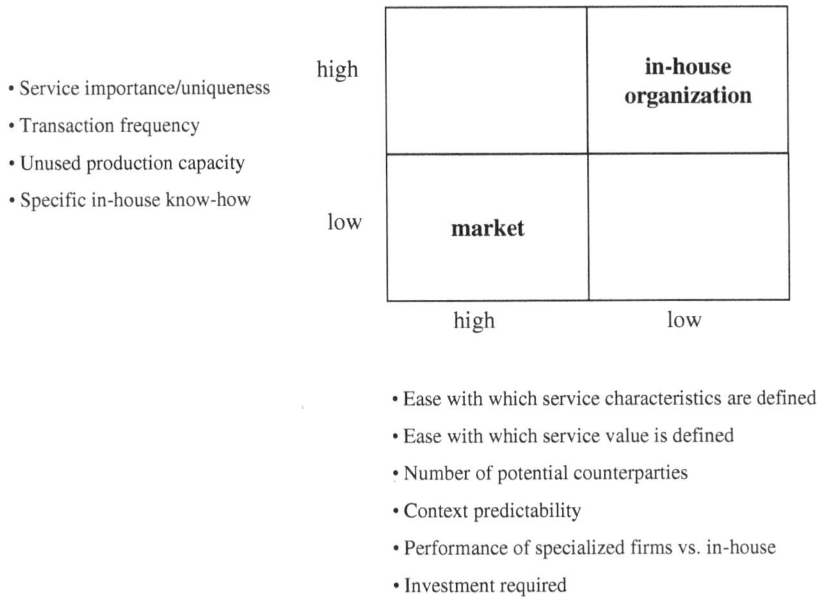

Figure 2: Variables in the make-or-buy decision

In information system management, such decisions have changed as technology evolved and as new models of organization and IS resource management were developed [17-18]. We can identify certain variables that impact on the make-or-buy decision, including: the importance of the service; the uniqueness of the service; the ease with which the service's characteristics and value can be defined; how often the transaction recurs; and the high performance of specialized firms as compared to in-house performance. Figure 2 presents these variables in a matrix in order to demonstrate how they affect the make-or-buy decision.

An organization may opt for a hybrid of the two options, which can be categorized based on two key aspects. The first is the level of competition in the marketplace, which can either be closed (in the case of a monopoly held by a single supplier) or open (i.e. multiple suppliers competing with each other for the services).

The second is the make-or-buy decision itself. By combining these two aspects, we get the various strategic orientations [17] for IS resource management as shown in Figure 3:

- in-house management, insourcing [19] and co-sourcing;
- full or selective outsourcing [20];
- joint ventures and consortia.
- These strategies are described below.

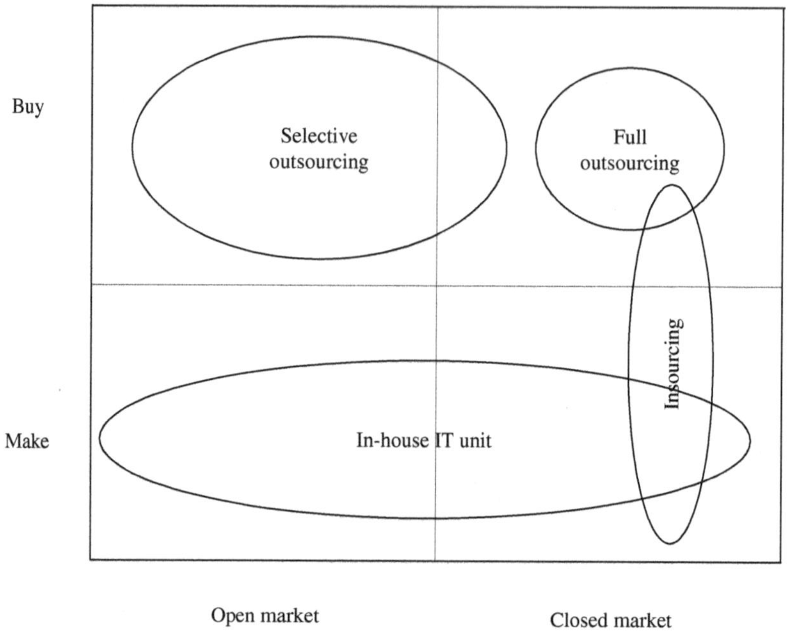

Figure 3: IS management strategies

In-house Management, Insourcing, and Co-sourcing

The strategy shown in Figure 1 as "In-house IS unit" represents the situation in which the realization and management of IS services are assigned to a department within a company, acquiring only the equipment and infrastructures from outside the company.

We then move up to "insourcing" (in its more specific sense for our purposes herein), whereby the IS function is delegated to a service company which is separate from but owned by the company to which the IS services are provided. "Co-sourcing", in turn, is selective application of insourcing and outsourcing (which will be discussed in greater detail below) for individual system components. Take, for example, a company which:

- defines user requirements and analyzes the project on an insourcing basis;
- outsources the development and implementation of the application software using highly specialized service providers.

Full and Selective Outsourcing

The term "outsourcing", which dates back to the 1970s, has established itself in the last decade and is used to indicate a situation in which a company delegates the management of one or more services (not just IS services, but any category of an organization's services) to an external vendor, i.e. shifting to outside sources that which was previously done in-house.

The various forms of this strategy can be categorized based on two key aspects: the type of activity outsourced and the number of activities outsourced.

For the former, we can distinguish between:

- the outsourcing of IS resources;
- business process outsourcing (BPO), wherein IS resources are typically a key component in the provision of the services themselves.
- For the latter, we can distinguish between:
- full outsourcing, whereby the company entrusts a single outsourcer with the entirety of an area or based on a specific service contract;
- selective outsourcing, where the company assigns certain IS or other services to one or more outsourcers, while keeping or more or less significant portion of the services in house.

The table 1 summarizes a number of the services that may be provided by an outsourcer.

Table 1: Typical outsourcing services

Type of service	Description
Application management	Including monitoring, maintenance, and upgrading
Infrastructure management	Including security, business continuity, and disaster recovery
Network management	Connectivity and management of related hardware
Workstation management	Including technical assistance, control, maintenance, and periodic updating of hardware and software
Contact management	User support
Systems integration management	The integration of (or creation of interfaces for) hardware and software components

Joint Ventures and Consortia

The joint venture strategy applies to situations in which IS is necessary to connect the company and the supplier. Such a strategy involves a long-term contractual relationship concerning specific projects that may be of critical importance to the company and for which the initial investment may be significant.

In this case, the IS function is delegated to a service company to receive the services together with an outsourcer (legally speaking, it is also possible to establish consortia or temporary groupings of firms).

The roles played by each of the parties varies: the company receiving the services, which may or may not hold a majority stake in the joint venture, is responsible for defining its own needs and guiding the implementation of new services by setting goals and priorities; the service provider, in turn, is responsible for managing operations related to design and delivery of the services themselves.

The IS service firm provides the company with its services based on formal contracts just as any other outsourcer would.

As opposed to insourcing, such a firm may also operate freely in the marketplace in order to promote the reuse of the solutions and infrastructures implemented and managed for the initial customer and to generate its own profits.

Specific Strategies of Application Management

Strategies for managing application software are strictly correlated with and dependent upon the general strategies for managing all IS resources.

In order to select the right strategy of application management, functional, technical, and financial analyses and comparison must be done right from the feasibility study phase and must take into account many factors, including: the total cost of ownership[4] of the individual solutions; the potential reuse by other companies; the technical skills available within the company; the portability and interoperability of the solutions; independence from a specific vendor or technology; specific need in terms of security and privacy; the availability of the source code of commercially available solutions and of those that are purpose-built.

The main strategies of application management are as follows:

- the development of custom-designed software, which is the most appropriate strategy for cases in which the procedures and activities to be computerized are specific to a given company and the software cannot, therefore, be reused by other companies, as well as when a great deal of personalization and integration with other functions and subsystems and extensive adaptation to the company's specific organizational model are required;
- the reuse of custom-designed software that was previously developed for one or more other companies and which is able to handle similar processes. This type of solution is advantageous in cases in which the existing software meets the company's primary needs, so it is deemed unnecessary to conduct analyses, define requirements, and develop software from scratch;
- acquiring a license to use proprietary software. This strategy may be justified in cases in which the processes and functions concerned are common to a broad number of companies, so vendors have created commercial software solutions (e.g. software for accounting, production, and sales). The better the commercial

product meets the needs of the processes to be computerized, the greater the benefits of such a solution;
- the purchase of open-source software. This strategy involves the use of software based on public domain source code that is open to all users, i.e. it can be viewed, altered, personalized, and redesigned to meet specific needs. It should be noted, however, that open-source software is not necessarily an "alternative" to commercial software;
- a strategy based on a combination of the any and all of the above strategies.

Application Service Providers

Another strategy for IS resource management is the use of Application Service Providers (ASPs), a form of IS management based on services provided over the Internet, rather than through possession of a full infrastructure or ownership of a software license.

As such, it is a sort of hybrid of other IS management strategies. What sets this strategy apart from the others is the new way in which the services are both provided to and used by the company concerned.

The main difference between ASPs and traditional outsourcing lies in their respective business models. In the case of ASPs, the applications (which are more or less standard) and services are provided to as many businesses as possible, whereas a traditional outsourcer seeks to provide services that are personalized and specific to each company, such as managing applications that are owned by the customer.

IS Resource Lock-in

The decisions made with regard to IS resources can result in limitations, or "lock-in", when it comes time for the company to adopt new IS solutions. The costs that a company will need to incur in order to switch from one solution to another are known as switching costs.

Types of lock-in include the following:

- database lock-in, where the cost of switching from one database architecture to another could be significant, in part due to the need to redesign and redefine data formats;
- loyalty lock-in, where the switch to another vendor could lead to the loss of benefits gained with the previous one;
- infrastructure lock-in, where the significant investment required for a certain infrastructure would make the cost of replacing IS significant, as well.

Impact on Human Resource Management

Nowadays, information technology is commonplace in nearly all areas of business (from orders management to production through customer relationship management, human resources management, and so on). For this reason, when speaking of IS resource management, we must also consider the aspects that characterize the given organization as a whole (industry, company size, products and services provided, corporate culture, organizational structure, etc.). As such, a contingency approach may be particularly useful.

For an example of how things are changing, we could look to the recent rethinking of IS service outsourcing decisions, as we are now seeing a number of organizations that are switching to insourcing the management of services that were previously outsourced. This may be happening because the outsourced service has become a core activity for the organization or because the quality and the control of the outsourced service have been found to be unsatisfactory.

This is just one example of how radically things continue to change in the world of information and communication technology. A more recent perspective is the one commonly titled "cloud computing": the availability of application services from any networked point, using any device, liberates the human resource function from routine tasks and it empowers users to access to HR services from anywhere and anytime, without necessarily the assistance of HR professionals. To a certain extent, the cloud computing solution represents an ASP approach, conceptually originated at the beginning of the spread of the Internet connections, revisited under the power of intra and inter organizational broadband available infrastructures. When both data and applications are available through the cloud, HR professional can focus their attention to process redesign, to deliver better services, and to improve productivity. This enables the alliance with business line managers and let the HR professionals to focus on the key business processes where their help is needed and most welcome.

Conclusions

The globalization of business, the development of more flexible organization structures, the further development of information technology are some of the drivers of the necessity for HR information systems. HRIS has the potential to be an enterprise-wide support system that helps achieve both strategic and operational objectives (Groe, et al., 1996).

The IS resources management is a complex process that goes beyond the mere technical aspects to include the even more important strategic, organizational, and financial aspects, as well.

For example, in terms of strategy, there are two forms of governance for IS resources: turning to the market (outsourcing) or using in-house resources (insourcing).

The decision between the two options is influenced by a number of variables, including: the importance of the service; the uniqueness of the service; the ease with which the service's characteristics and value can be defined; how often the transaction recurs; the number of potential counterparties involved; competitive uncertainty; and specific in-house know-how.

Taking all of these variables into account may lead to an orientation towards one of the two forms of governance, but not necessarily to an outright decision. Indeed, in many cases, a company may decide to adopt a sort of hybrid of a number of strategies, which include: internal management, insourcing, and co-sourcing; full and selective outsourcing; and joint ventures and consortia.

Two additional aspects that are important to IS resource management are: the lock-in effect, i.e. limitations or barriers that arise when it comes time for the company to adopt other IS solutions; and an analysis of the total cost of ownership (TCO) of IS resources.

References

1. Jackson, S., Hitt, M. and DeNisi, A. (eds.) (2003) *Managing Knowledge for Sustained Competitive Advantage: Designing Strategies for Effective Human Resource Management*. San Francisco: Jossey-Bass.
2. Groe, G. M., Pyle, W. and Jamrog, J. J.(1996) Information technology and HR. *Human Resource Planning, 19(1),* 56-60
3. Lawler, E. E. and Mohrman, S. A. (2003) HR as a Strategic Partner: What Does IS Take to Make IS Happen? *Human Resource Planning, 26(3),* 15-29.
4. Lawler, E. E. (1995) Strategic Human Resources Management: An Idea Whose Time Has Come. In B. Downie and M. L. Coates (eds.), *Managing Human Resources in the 1990s and Beyond: Is the Workplace Being Transformed?* Kingston, Canada: IRC Press, 46-70.
5. Lawler, E. E. and Mohrman, S. A. (2000) Beyond the Visions: What Makes HR Effective? *Human Resource Planning, 23(4),* 10-20.
6. Cline, M. K. and Guynes, G. S. (2001) A Study of the Impact of Information Technology Investment on Firm Performance, *Journal of Computer Information Systems*, 41(3), 15.
7. Broadbent, M. and Weill, P. (1997) Management by Maxim: How business and IS managers can create information infrastructures. *Sloan Management Review*, *38(2)*, 77-92.
8. Cegielsky, C., Reithel, B. and Rebman, C. (2005) Developing a timely IS strategy. *Communications of the Association for Computer Machinery*, *48(8)*, 113-117.
9. Hitt, L., and Brynjolffson, E. (1995) Productivity, business profitability and consumer surplus: Three different measures of information technology value. *MIS Quarterly*, *20(2)*, 121- 142.
10. Brynjolfsson E. and Yang, S. (1996) Information Technology and Productivity: a Review of the Literature. *Advances in Computers*, *43*, 179-214.
11. Coase, R. H. (1937) The Nature of Firm. *Economica*, *4*, 386-485.
12. Williamson, O. E. (1975) *Markets and Hierarchies: Analysis and Antitrust Implications*. New York: The Free Press.
13. Williamson O. E. (1980) The organization of work. *Journal of Economic Behavior and Organization*, *1*, 5-38.
14. Perrone, V. (1990) *Le strutture organizzative d'impresa*. Milano: Egea.
15. Loh, L., and Venkatraman, N. (1992) Determinants of information technology outsourcing: A cross-sectional analysis. *Journal of Management Information Systems*, *9(1)*, 7-24.
16. Simon, H. A. (1985) *Causalità, razionalità, organizzazione*. Bologna: Il Mulino.

17. Currie, W. L. and Willcocks, L. P. (1998) Analysing four types of IS sourcing decisions in the context of scale, client/supplier interdependency risk mitigation. *Information Systems Journal*, *8*, 119-143.
18. Shupe, C. and Behling, R. (2006) Developing and Implementing a Strategy for Technology Deployment. *The Information Management Journal*, *29(1)*, 52-57
19. Hirschheim, R. and Lacity, M. (2000) The Myths and Realities of Information Technology Insourcing. *Communication of the Association for Computer Machinery*, *43(2)*, 99-107.
20. Subramanyam, M. (2004). The impact of global IS outsourcing on IS providers. *Communications of the Association for Information Systems*, *14*, 543-557.
21. Laudon, K.and Laudon, J. (2005) *Management Information Systems*. Upper Saddle River, NJ: Prentice Hall.

Part VI

E-government

Barriers to e-Government Service Delivery in Developing Countries: The Case of Iran

Alinaghi Ziaee Bigdeli[1], **Sergio de Cesare**[2]

Abstract Similarly to many developed and developing countries today, Iran is transforming its provision of public services via a series of electronic government projects. Nearly 80% of such projects are related to e-service delivery. The realization and evolution of these projects represent a significant challenge due to a variety of barriers, both technical and non-technical, that hinder the successful introduction and expansion of e-government in Iran. The aim of this research is to investigate and analyze the barriers to e-service development projects in Iran. The research is based on primary data collected from eleven semi-structured interviews with high profile stakeholders in Iran's e-government projects and secondary data collected from governmental reports. The interviews focused on four types of barriers to e-service delivery projects as described by the literature. These include strategic, technological, policy and organizational barriers. Based on the results of the interviews conducted, a discussion follows which attempts to rank the barriers in each category and identify the relationships between them. This analysis can assist policy-makers in Iran in understanding the significance of each type of barrier in relation to current and future e-service delivery projects.

Keywords: e-Government, e-Service Delivery, ICT in Public Administration, Barriers, ICT in Developing Countries, Case Study, Iran

Introduction

Since the mid-1990s Information and Communication Technologies (ICTs) have been adopted by governments around the world in order to enhance their governing procedures [1]. The use of ICTs has helped governments to redesign the way in which they are organized and how they function so as to deliver more efficient public services to citizens. ICT adoption in government is potentially capable of achieving various goals such as increasing efficiency, enhancing accountability, and improving resource management [2]. Moreover, from a citizen's point of view, Signore et al. [3] emphasized that the main purpose of adopting ICTs by governments is to provide citizens with the opportunity to be more actively involved in decision-making processes. These reforms and changes have helped to generate new forms of administration, known as e-government.

E-government is a multidimensional and complex concept. As a consequence, the successful implementation of e-government systems requires a clear under-

---

[1] Brunel University, Uxbridge, UK, Alinaghi.Ziaee.Bigdeli@brunel.ac.uk
[2] Brunel University, Uxbridge, UK, Sergio.deCesare@brunel.ac.uk

standing of the characteristics that services of such systems must deliver [4]. The literature abounds with different perspectives on the concept of e-government. Some argue that e-government is about putting information and services online [5-6], while other researchers sustain that it is about optimizing governmental service delivery via the modernization of internal and external relationships through information technology [7-8]. One of the most important aspects of e-government is its interaction with citizens and businesses [7] in the form of electronic delivery of government information and services. According to a report by Iran's Supreme Council of ICT (SCICT), i.e. the highest decision making organization in the area of ICT policy-making in Iran, nearly 80% of e-government projects in the country are related to the delivery of information and services towards customers in an electronic manner. This high percentage underlines the importance of government to citizen (G2C) and government to business (G2B) connections in Iran.

Davison et al. [9] argue that the adoption of new technologies within governments is fairly time-consuming as it is faced with some significant barriers like privacy and security, insufficient technical knowledge of citizens and governmental employees, and the inadequate inclination of various stakeholders to change from government to e-government. The progression to e-government, as a means to increase efficiency and promote participation, does not happen just by computerizing processes and developing colorful websites. It is a progression that requires an appropriate plan and strategy, proper resource allocation and political support. Heeks [10] emphasizes that more than 80% of e-government projects in developing countries (DC) manifest some kind of failure. He identifies three gaps as the main causes of this high level of failure in DC. Firstly, many systems are designed by merely focusing on the technical aspects without any consideration of the softer aspects like people, culture, and politics (hard-soft gap). Secondly, governments try to set up systems originally developed for the private sector. This would be a cause of failure since the public and private sectors have fundamental differences (private-public gap). Lastly, an e-government system designed and prepared for a developed country cannot be simply deployed in a developing country. As such, local factors must be taken into consideration and in fact developed from that point of view (country context gaps).

Based on the discussion above, realizing e-government projects in Iran – as a developing country – becomes one of the major concerns for its government. It is difficult to analyze within a single study all aspects of e-government of a country as vast as Iran. As a result this research only focuses on e-Government service delivery towards Iranian citizens and businesses.

e-Government in Iran

History

The concept of electronic government is fairly new in the literature of Iranian administration, however the adoption of ICT to enhance government efficiency dates back to nearly 15 years ago [11]. During the last ten years the development of e-government systems in Iran has received attention by various authorities and government agencies.

The bureaucratic structure of Iran's public administration requires that most publicly funded plans and projects must be approved by the parliament. Table 1 presents different laws and policies that have been approved regarding e-government development in Iran.

Table 1: The List of Accreditations of e-Government in Iran [12]

Year	*Approved by*	*Accreditation Title*
2000	Iran's Parliament	Economic and Socio-cultural Development Policy
2002	The Administration Supreme Council	Public Sector Automation Policy
2002	The Boards of Ministries	General Guidelines of Using ICTs in Public Sectors
2003	The Board of Ministries	Specific Guidelines of Implementing and Developing ICTs in Government Agencies
2004	The Administration Supreme Council	The Plan of Sharing and Exchanging Citizens' and Businesses' Records within the Government Agencies
2005	The Board of Ministries	Privacy Laws and the Security of e-Transactions
2006	The Administration Supreme Council	The Guideline of Establishing and Developing e-Services Centers in Different States
2007	The Administration Supreme Council	National Guideline of Alteration from Iran's Government to Iran's e-Government

The government defined the following five objectives for e-government in Iran:

- To deliver information and services towards customers 24/7.
- To eliminate the physical interaction between the government and its customers.
- To deliver information and services in a quick and secure manner.
- To increase efficiency and effectiveness and reduce government costs.
- To increase transparency and accountability within the public sector.

Therefore, after publishing the policies, rules, objectives and goals the government started to develop an e-government plan during the last three years [12]. This initiative began by formulating guidelines and policies for the public agencies. These guidelines and policies primarily regarded the computerization of government departments, staff training and assistance in the design of public portals.

e-Government Service Delivery in Iran

The SCICT clarified that nearly 80% of e-government projects in Iran are related to G2C and G2B [13]. Two main objectives were defined in order to deliver government services towards citizens and businesses:

1. Design and implementation of a national portal to deliver services via the Web.
2. Equip 10,000 of Iran's villages and rural areas with an ICT Tele-Service Center.

National Web Portal (IranMardom.ir)

In relation to the first objective mentioned above the government is to design and implement a national Web portal containing a map of the Islamic Republic of Iran that will enable all citizens and businesses to request different electronic services in relation to a chosen city on the map [13]. The strategy adopted by the Iranian government to realize this project is to apply a simple and adaptive model as presented by Nobakht & Bakhtiari [12]. As it can be observed from Figure 1, the model consists of three layers. These layers are represented by: supporting activities, primary data and information and general procedures.

Figure 1: E-Government Service Delivery Model in Iran

Although the government published laws and policies regarding e-government service delivery, there is as yet no completed plan or strategy related to the supporting activities. This could be identified as a major problem while the government tries to apply the e-service model. On the other hand, four main projects regarding the integration of citizen and business records have begun. These projects mainly deal with developing Web-based databases for citizen and business identification, an online land registry and geographical information systems (GIS) for six of Iran's largest cities. Moreover, with reference to the general procedure, the government runs five projects with the aim: (1) to provide the infrastructure for digital signatures, (2) to design and implement an e-transaction system, (3) to develop the national data center, (4) to expand the national data network and (5) to develop the telecommunication infrastructure. The government categorized different services based on the needs of citizens and private businesses as summarized in Table 2.

The national portal called "MARDOMIRAN" (which means Iranian Citizens) was developed in 2008, however there is no written documentation related to the project and no reference to who was responsible for implementing it. This portal is in Farsi and consists of a map of Iran divided into 30 provinces. Iranian citizens and businesses have the opportunity to choose their own province and obtain different government services through the relevant ministry or government organizations. At present different services are delivered through this website, such as the renewal of driving licenses, international ID cards and passports.

Table 2: e-Service Types in Iran [14]

e-Service Categorization	
Citizens	*Businesses*
- Birth: birth certificate, citizen's ID	- Business registration
- Education: public education records/ certificate	- Property certificate
- Transportation: driving license, automobile ownership	- Tax: taxpaying/records
- Tax: paying tax, tax background records	- Funding registration
- Marriage certificate	- Trading: import/export registration
- Health: insurance records, medical ID	- New products registration
- Receiving pension	

Rural ICT Tele-Service Center

The second major objective regarding the delivery of e-government services is that of equipping 10,000 Iranian villages with an ICT Tele-Center initiated by the Ministry of Information and Communication Technology [14]. These centers will provide different governmental services such as Internet connection, postal services, bank services and tax services. Different government organizations, such as the Health Ministry and Agricultural Ministry, will be able to provide various services to the rural residences and decrease the amount of travelling to nearby cities. It is mainly the Ministry of ICT to be responsible for the project in terms of investment, financial support and development. The aim is to provide villagers with integrated information-based services and to increase the access of rural families to the telephone system and the Internet.

There are some important requirements to run such projects in Iran's rural areas. These include support from related government organizations (especially those responsible for rural areas) and the selection of experienced private companies to support the development of the projects [14]. Again, there is a lack of documentation on how the ICT ministry developed these projects; however, the first Tele-Center opened in Gharnabad village, near Gorgan city in the north east of Iran on 27th June 2004. The aims of this center are, among others, to provide a good environment for learning, finding jobs and delivering different government services. Gharnabad Tele-Center provides a variety of government organizations the opportunity to offer their services, thus gathering them in one place.

Research Design

A number of frameworks and models have been proposed by different academics regarding the barriers to the development of e-government projects. Most of the models, such as those proposed by Themistocleous & Irani [15] and Shang & Seddon [16], concentrate on just some specific obstacles of development projects. However, the framework presented by Lam [17] focuses on a wide range of barriers and considers four major areas: strategy, technology, policy and organizational barriers. Table 3 presents these four categories.

In this research, both primary and secondary data were used. The secondary data on e-government service delivery in Iran was collected mainly from governmental publications and reports as well as from censuses and surveys conducted by the Iranian government. The primary data was collected through eleven semi-structured interviews with high profile stakeholders in Iran's e-government projects, including five ICT professionals, and six IT managers. The questions of the interviews were formulated in relation to the framework's four categories of barriers as depicted in Table 3. This type of data collection was preferred due to the lack of written documents and governmental reports on challenges and barriers of e-service development in Iran.

Table 3: Barriers of Developing e-Government Projects [17]

Area	*Barriers*
Strategy	Lack of shared e-Government goals and objectives Over-ambitious e-Government milestones Lack of ownership and governance Absence of implementation guidance Funding issues
Technology	Lack of architecture interoperability Incompatible data standards Different security models Inflexibility of legacy systems Incompatible technical standards
Policy	Concerns over citizen privacy Data ownership E-Government policy evolution
Organization	Lack of agency readiness Slow pace of government reform Absence of an e-Government champion Legacy government processes Lack of relevant in-house management and technical expertise

Barriers of Developing e-Government Service Delivery

Strategy Barriers

As highlighted by Lam [17] and Ndou [4] one of the main strategy barriers is the lack of common objectives and having an unclear goal and vision. The respondents clarified that although their organizations had a published vision and objectives statement, they were still struggling on how those objectives would be achieved. As they stated, the SCICT issued a national vision with related objectives regarding the development of the national e-service portal. These objectives were related to different ministries and organizations that should support services on the Web site. Most of the objectives were too broad and more importantly they were not aligned with the ministries' organizational capabilities. The reason for this ambiguity is the lack of co-operation between the SCICT and the individual ministries or governmental organizations that provide and support the related services. Therefore, since the main stakeholders, such as ministry staff and their unions, are not getting involved in the definition of the e-service development vision, it would be difficult to promote a guideline on how those objectives would be achieved. One of the respondents, working as an IT manager in a ministry, stated that when the SCICT informed them of the e-service development vision, the ministry had several meetings with its IT department to try and align those objectives with their organization's capabilities. These attempts were reasonably time consuming.

Ebrahim & Irani [18] and Lam [17] clarified that as a result of this broad and unclear vision, ambiguity in roles and responsibility within an organization becomes a major barrier to the development of e-services; however the general feedback from the interviews illustrates that the ministries and organizations in Iran do not have problems regarding this issue. Some interviewees commented that the IT department within their organization had a clear responsibility of developing and supporting electronic services towards citizens and businesses. Others mentioned that their organization had an ICT section in order to expand the e-services based on their customers' needs. The ICT section is under the direction of the minister or the government organization's president. The reason that some of the government organizations are not faced with any challenges in terms of task responsibility is that within their IT department there is alignment between the national vision/objectives and their organizational capabilities. Therefore, different tasks can be assigned to experienced staff efficiently.

Almost all of the interviewees emphasized that financial barriers are one of the main obstacles of developing and expanding e-services within their organization. Traditionally, in Iran, the main financial resources come from central government. Two main issues regarding financial barriers can be observed from the interviewees' feedback. Firstly, the budget allocated by central government was less than the amount requested. Therefore, the organizations were not able to obtain any improvement on expanding their e-services. One of the interviewees argued that the cost of e-service development (which includes new hardware/software, maintenance, staff training, etc.) is fairly high and the allocated funds cannot cover these. Secondly, most of the organizations do not have a proper framework that allows them to control and manage their IT budget in order to meet their objectives efficiently. Many interviewees working in different IT departments stated that incompetent budget allocation represented a significant obstacle to development. They argued that since they had not prioritized tasks based on the vision, they were not able to dispense funds. Just one of the interviewees, an IT manager of one of the largest banks in Iran, stated that there was no financial issue in their organization regarding the allocation of funds. As he mentioned, major financial support comes from the central bank, hence there would be no problem in obtaining the level of budget requested. They prepare a development plan for the following year and based on this plan the required funding is usually provided.

Technology Barriers

Technology barriers can be considered as one of the most significant barriers of e-service development especially in developing countries. Previous literature emphasizes different aspects of this barrier. For example, Ndou [4] highlighted poor ICT infrastructure (lack of reliable networks and communication channels) as one of the main obstacles of development. In addition Lau [19] and Lam [17] highlighted that the lack of a common and integrated architecture and absence of a data standard can be recognized as a significant barrier to e-service development. Almost all interviewees noted that their organization is confronted with a series of technological barriers in relation to the expansion of electronic services. Some respondents argued that since there is a lack of technical and data standards among governmental organizations, they are not able to improve and expand their e-services. One of the basic requirements of the e-government service delivery project is having a technical standard in order to exchange data efficiently [17]. As an example, the Ministry of Economic Affairs and Finance decided to run a system that would enable citizens and businesses to pay taxes online (e-tax service). This system requires effective cooperation with the banking system in order to provide support for electronic payments. Since the programming frameworks that were adopted to design these two systems were not compatible with one another, the e-tax service had not been developed yet.

Poor ICT infrastructure can be identified as another technological barrier to e-service development in Iran. Some interviewees stated that a significant barrier to the expansion of e-services within their organization was the low speed, poor quality, and high cost of Internet connections in Iran. Based on the e-readiness analysis conducted by the United Nations in 2008, the telecommunication index of Iran is extremely low. This analysis showed that just a small portion of Iran's population has access to the Internet and to personal computers. Therefore, e-government services are not distributed equally among the citizens. The government has not been successful in deploying telecommunications equipment to small towns and villages; hence the digital divide is getting larger everyday in Iran. This is exactly what many researchers such as Ebrahim & Irani [18] and Ndou [4] have highlighted as a significant barrier to e-government development projects especially in developing countries.

Providing secure electronic service delivery in order to build trust and confidence between the government and citizens can be recognized as another major issue relating to technology barriers [17]. According to Ebrahim & Irani [18], since governmental organizations collect, process and utilize citizen/business information (such as personal information, financial information, health information, etc.), attention should be paid to considering security as a critical factor toward successful service delivery. Only one interviewee mentioned security as a technological barrier. The IT manager of a major bank in Iran stated that the organization developed a software called Customers Security System which protects and maintains information of citizens and businesses while they are using the online system. This software was developed with the help of an IT private company as a third party and it can enable a strong Secure Sockets Layer (SSL) available to all of the site's visitors during transactions.

Policy Barriers

According to Lam [17] and Lambrinoudakis et al. [20] the absence of customer privacy can be recognized as an important barrier to e-service development. Customer privacy is related to security issues which were analyzed above. Most of the interviewees argued that because there is no cyber law in Iran, it is hard to forge a trusting relationship between the government and citizens/businesses. This lack of trust among Iranian citizens and businesses is the major reason that few people request services electronically. Based on one of the author's experience, many Iranian citizens have realized that there are no policies in place to protect their sensitive information. Hence, they prefer not to use the government services electronically. Major banks in Iran are leading the way toward a change in attitude among citizens and business. These banks established some rules and policies with the help of Iran's judicial authorities in order to protect the customer privacy.

Developing a national portal offering different services of a variety of government organizations requires effective cooperation and coordination among them [21]. One of the main indicators of this kind of cooperation is sharing and exchanging data between the ministries and organizations. Many governmental organizations consider themselves as the owner of the data and therefore they do not consent to share such data with other agencies; this attitude definitely hinders the delivery of e-services and has its roots in a lack of policy [17]. However, feedback from the interviews conducted, show that in general there is no obstacle regarding the sharing and exchanging of data among governmental organizations in Iran. A number of interviewees argued that there is in fact effective cooperation among different government organizations to support and develop back-office tasks in order to improve service delivery. For example, for different services (e.g., paying tax, renewing driving license and passport, etc.) the related governmental organizations can obtain the citizen/business data from the National Organization for Civil Registration who is the largest owner of citizen and business records.

Organizational Barriers

Other significant barriers to developing e-government projects, as expressed by different researchers, are organizational barriers. Different academics focus on different aspects of this type of barrier. Heeks [22] and Bonham et al. [23], for instance, highlighted the lack of IT training programs as a major organizational obstacle to e-government service development. Lam [17] and Li & Steveson [24] also place emphasis on the cultural issues that affect e-service development processes. Based on Lam's framework, interviewees responded to this issue from four points of view: lack of organizational readiness, absence of a champion and top management support, slow pace of reform, and change challenges in their organization.

In relation to organizational readiness to develop and expand electronic services, almost all of the respondents identified the lack of IT skills and knowledge among the staff and top management as the major obstacle. They stated that staff had been trained based on a seven-staged certificate called ICDL (International Computer Driving License), which helps to acquire a very basic knowledge of computer skills. This level of knowledge would not be sufficient for a development process since IT technologies change day by day. As the interviewees believe, the learning process is very low in Iranian organizations. McClure [25] believes e-service development requires specific IT skills (such as systems analysis and design, network construction, applications integration, etc.) that are mostly absent in government organizations.

Respondents also expressed some external issues that affected the readiness of their organization to expand their e-services. First, the speed of the Internet in Iran is quite low and the government has a fear of high speed Internet these days. Based on an interviewee's view, this low speed affects back-office tasks and cooperation between different governmental departments and organizations. Second, the readiness of governmental organizations is hindered by the sanctions imposed by the U.S. government. As one of the interviewees clarified, e-service development requires accessibility to new hardware and software technologies that are mostly produced in the United States. Organizations cannot purchase this equipment directly from the vendors and they are required to make contracts with second and third hand distributors at higher prices. Therefore, e-service development projects would be costly and in some cases small government organizations cannot afford the required resources.

Change challenges can be declared as another important organizational barrier to e-service development. Based on the interviewees' responses, two main types of change challenges to e-service development can be identified: resistance to change and lack of top management support. First of all, most of the organizations are faced with resistance from their employees to expand and develop e-service processes. As the interviewees clarified, there are three main reasons for this resistance. First, employees resist any IT change as their knowledge about it is quite low. As a result of this lack of awareness, they have a fear of losing their job thinking that they will be replaced by computers or other new technologies. Lastly, sometimes new systems and applications are developed by unskilled IT people, therefore staff resistance would be caused by the systems' greater complexity of use and lower user-friendliness.

Another change challenge that emerged from the interviews is the lack of top management support. Since IT knowledge among key decision makers and heads of organizations is considerably low, these managers frequently resist any IT change. One interviewee argued that whenever the organization needs to focus on and develop an electronic service that is based on customer needs, the top managers refuse to accept it. It requires several meetings between them and the IT and marketing departments in order to discuss the benefits of the new service that ultimately may or may not be approved. This reluctance from the heads of organizations may possibly affect the behavior of staff as well since this induces the belief that top managers are not concerned about IT change. Ebrahim & Irani [18] believe that this resistance to IT change by high-level management is due to two reasons: lack of IT knowledge and the perception of losing power and viability.

Discussion and Conclusion

The government in Iran has started to implement and develop electronic government projects. According to the Supreme Council of ICT nearly 80% of those projects are related to e-service delivery towards citizens and businesses highlighting the importance of e-service development among Iranian ministries and organizations [13]. This paper makes important contributions in understanding the challenges of e-government service development in a developing country such as Iran by identifying and analyzing the barriers of e-service delivery projects. This analysis was conducted by through applying Lam's conceptual model on e-service delivery initiatives in Iran. The data was gathered via governmental documents and reports as well as eleven semi-structured interviews with a various ICT managers involved in e-government projects in Iran.

Based on the in-depth discussions carried out during the interviews and the opinion of the interviewees, we attempt to firstly, rank the barriers in each of the four main categories as summarized in Figure 2. Secondly, we aim to identify the relationship between these obstacles in each category. These relationships would assist governmental decision-makers in understanding and possibly prioritizing the challenges (or barriers) among the many perceived obstacles that e-service delivery projects can potentially encounter. Therefore, this study highlights areas in which efforts should be directed to address the underlying problems.

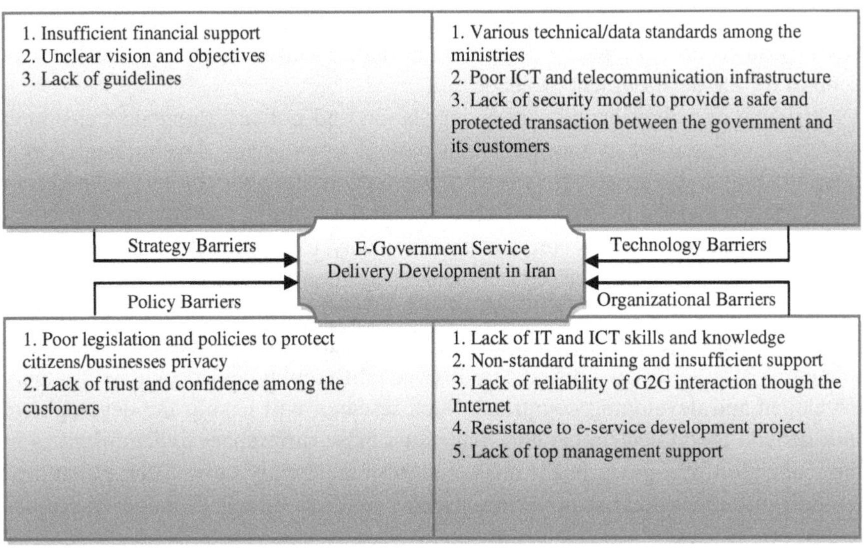

Figure 2: Barriers to e-Government Service Delivery in Iran

In relation to strategy, almost all of the interviewees agreed that insufficient financial support had the most significant impact on service delivery and development.

Since there is uncertainty in the defined long and short-term visions, policy makers are not able to allocate sufficient funds for the development projects. Comprehensive planning and strategy is missing on how to approach the whole issue. Although the government has set up an ICT plan and a national committee to deal with e-government issues, a systematic and coordinated approach towards ICT is absent. Moreover, since ICT and the use of e-services is an unknown phenomenon among the majority of the population, it is often not high on the political agenda and therefore fewer funds are allocated for this purpose.

As far as the technology barrier is concerned, lack of technical and data standards among government's entities is identified as the main bottleneck for e-service delivery and development. This may be primarily due to the poor ICT and telecommunications infrastructure in developing countries and secondly to the lack of sufficient IT knowledge and skills among civil servants.

This lack of knowledge was emphasized as the key organizational barrier to e-service delivery development. It does not just mean lack of basic knowledge and education on ICT, but it also entails a lack of perception and awareness amongst the champions, stakeholders and those who are actually involved in e-service delivery and development. It is interesting to note that most of the discussions about other perceived barriers eventually returned to this lack of awareness and correct knowledge about ICT and its use. Furthermore, it can be learnt that updated IT/IS systems which are used in developed countries have been employed and implemented in government organizations. However, since there is a lack of knowledge, standard training and lack of top management support those systems are no longer in use. Resistance to change has been realized as another barrier to e-service delivery development. The discussions show the politicians and decision makers are not yet mentally ready to change the current procedure and situation. Therefore, it would lead to unwillingness to accept new ideas with reduced top management support for the development projects.

In terms of policy barriers, poor legislation and policies to support customer privacy is recognized as the main impediment to e-service development. Legal infrastructure and administrative reform is a precondition for any ICT related processes. Since there is no such infrastructure in the country, the government is not able to serve services in a secure and protected way. Consequently, this may lead to reduced trust and confidence of customers in the adoption of e-services.

The findings described in this paper are related to an individual country case study (i.e. e-service delivery in Iran). Further research is being conducted in order to identify similarities and differences between different types of countries (namely developed and developing countries). Such research will lead to the development of a general theoretical framework that can expose differences and similarities in the realization of e-government projects across apparently very different national realties; differences that span various aspects such as culture, IT maturity, politics and so on.

References

1. Siau, K. and Long, Y. (2004) A stage model for e-government implementation. Paper presented at the *15th Information Resource Management Association International Conference (IRMA'04)* New Orleans, LA., 886-887.
2. Heeks, R.B. (2002) *Reinventing Govrnment in the Information Age,* Routledge, London, UK.
3. Signore, O., Chesi, F. and Pallotti, M. (2005) E-Government: challenges and opportunities. *Proceedings of the CMG Italy XIX annual conference.*
4. Ndou, V. (2004) E–Government for developing countries: opportunities and challenges. *EJISDC,* 18(1), 1-24.
5. Fountain, J. and Osorio, C. (2001) Public sector: Early stage of a deep transformation. *The Economic Payoff from the Internet Revolution: what lies ahead?/Robert E.Litan and Alice M.Rivlin*
   Manufacturing: lowering boundaries, improving productivity/Andrew McAfee Automotive industry: innovation and economic performance/Charles H.Fine(TRUNCATED), pp. 235.
6. West, D.M. (2004) E-government and the transformation of service delivery and citizen attitudes. *Public administration review,* 64(1), 15-27.
7. Fang, Z. (2002) E-government in digital era: concept, practice, and development. *International Journal of The Computer, The Internet and Management,* 10(2), 1-22.
8. Chircu, A.M. and Lee, D.H.D. (2005) E-government: key success factors for value discovery and realisation. *Electronic Government, an International Journal,* 2(1), 11-25.
9. Davison, R.M., Wagner, C. And Ma, L.C.K. (2005) From government to e-government: a transition model. *Information Technology & People,* 18(3), 280-299.
10. Heeks, R.B. (2003) *Most eGovernment-for-development projects fail: how can risks be reduced?* Institute for Development Policy and Management.
11. Sharifi, H. and Zarei, B. (2004) An adaptive approach for implementing e-government in IR Iran. *Journal of Government Information,* 30(5-6), 600-619.
12. Nobakht, M. And Bakhtiari, H. (2008) *E-government and a Fusibility Study of Developing of it in Iran,* Azad University: Vice Chancellor of Research, Tehran, IRAN.
13. SCICT (2008) *Report on Current Situation of Electronic Government in Iran,* Supreme Council of ICT, Tehran, IRAN.
14. SCICT (2009) *Rural ICT Strategic Plan.* Available: http://scict.ir/Portal/File/ShowFile.aspx?ID=1e3c7ef9-7b0b-49bd-8d4d-ed67f39eec7c Accessed: 2010, 02/02.
15. Themistocleous, M. and Irani, Z. (2001) Benchmarking the benefits and barriers of application integration. *Benchmarking: An International Journal,* 8(4), 317-331
16. Shang, S. and Seddon, P.B. (2000) A comprehensive framework for classifying the benefits of ERP systems. *Americas Conference on Information Systems*, pp. 1005
17. Lam, W. (2005) Barriers to e-government integration. *Journal of Enterprise Information Management,* 18(5), 511-530.
18. Ebrahim, Z. and Irani, Z. (2005) E-government adoption: architecture and barriers. *Business Process Management Journal,* 11(5), 589-611.
19. Lau, E. (2003) Challenges for e-Government Development, paper presented at the *5th Global Forum on Reinventing e-Government.*
20. Lambrinoudakis, C., Gritzalis, S., Dridi, F. and Pernul, G. (2003) Security requirements for e-government services: a methodological approach for developing a common PKI-based security policy. *Computer Communications,* 26(16), 1873-1883.
21. Burn, J. and Robins, G. (2003) Moving towards e-government: a case study of organisational change processes. *Logistics Information Management,* 16(1), 25-35.
22. Heeks, R. (1999) *Reinventing government in the information age: International practice in IT-enabled public sector reform,* Routledge.
23. Bonham, G.M., Seifert, J.W. and Thorson, S. (2001) The transformational potential of e-government: the role of political leadership. *Proceedings of the 4th Pan European International Relations Conference.*

24. Li, F. and Steveson, R. (2002) Implementing E-Government strategy in Scotland: current situation and emerging issues, *2nd European Conference on E-Government, St Catherine's College, Oxford, United Kingdom, 1-2 October 2002*Academic Conferences Limited, pp. 251.
25. McClure, D.L. (2000) Electronic government: Federal initiatives are evolving rapidly but they face significant challenges, *Statement of David L.McClure, US General Accounting Office, before the Subcommittee on Government Management, Information and Technology, Committee on Government Reform, House of Representatives.*

Framing the Role of IT Artefacts in Homecare Processes

Maddalena Sorrentino[1]

Abstract Based on the preliminary results of a case study, this qualitative research explores the meaning of the technological decisions implemented by a voluntary care association, which we will call Gamma. A provider of home assistance to terminally ill patients living in Lombardy (Italy), Gamma recently introduced an IT artefact to support its socio-care teams, equipping all the members with a Personal Digital Assistant (PDA) to remotely access the patients' electronic medical files, which are then updated in real time after each home visit. The article uses organisation studies to respond to two questions: how is the relationship between the technological and the organisational choices shaped by the new device? In what terms does the IT artefact help *make the difference*, or influence the decision processes at the diverse levels? It is argued that the artefact enters the caring processes as an additional source of regulation. The PDA makes the difference in terms of broadening and extending the control exercisable by Gamma's management, but also enables the care providers to affirm their autonomy.

Introduction

The overall epidemiological and technological scenario in developed countries demands a health service whose offering can be structured into a coordinated "network" of the organisations and institutions responsible for ensuring that citizens receive continuity of assistance at the different levels and intensity of healthcare [1, p. 190]. The populations of the more industrialised regions are ageing rapidly and progressively. In addition, the effect of extending the lifespan of people suffering from chronic or degenerative diseases has created new patient categories to which the public health service must deliver integrated response strategies aimed at continuing and constant care.

The demand for integrated health and social services is significant in the palliative care sector. Palliative care is offered to patients diagnosed with life-threatening diseases – mainly tumours and, to a lesser extent, AIDS and neurological diseases – whose life expectancy is reduced to a matter of weeks. Such conditions require the provision of specific local services, from assistance in the home to hospices, integrated with the hospital in a continuum of care [2], which can offer adequate responses to both the patients and their families. This is a field where care prevails over treatment.

[1] Università degli Studi di Milano, Milan, Italy, maddalena.sorrentino@unimi.it

Lombardy, home to almost 10 million people, was the first Italian region to implement (in late 1998) concrete initiatives in the palliative care sector. The region has between 40,000-54,000 patients in the terminal stage of their illness, i.e. those with a life expectancy of less than three months, who require care and assistance every year.

Home palliative care is distinguished by its multidisciplinary features with the work organised and assigned to a team made up of several types of professionals, underscoring the special conditions in which the palliative care organisations are called to operate. The work practices implemented by those who interact with the patients and their families, along with the uniqueness and complexity of the issues dealt with, provide a fertile and interesting terrain for organisational reflection. The selection, the combination, and the sequence of the services implemented, which vary in kind and in time [3], are determined by patient feedback. That means the team's activities are guided by the patient's physical and mental conditions, translating into intense relations in a highly uncertain and ambiguous scenario. But what happens when an IT-based artefact enters the caring process?

The purpose of this paper is to highlight and understand – based on the preliminary results of a case study still in progress – the meaning of the technological decisions implemented by a private care association, given the pseudonym of Gamma, which provides home assistance to terminally ill patients living in the Italian region of Lombardy. Gamma recently introduced an IT artefact to support its socio-care teams, equipping each member with a Personal Digital Assistant ("PDA", also called a palm organiser) to remotely access the patients' electronic medical files, which are then updated in real time at the end of every home visit.

From the technological standpoint, Gamma's decision was not especially original. PDAs were first used in the medical field around ten years ago, when they were initially adopted for diary management, and later for processing clinical data, both within the healthcare structures and between geographically remote units [4]. On the other hand, from the organisational perspective, the issue is significant because it touches Gamma's 'technical core' [5, p. 43]. Following Cook et al. [6, p. 197], changes in the in the service/production activities of the healthcare sector are particularly expensive and complex to implement, not only due to the specialisation of productive inputs, "but they are also the types of changes that the professionals in the organisation (e.g. physicians and nurses) care the most about". The Gamma case thus opens valuable horizons for researchers interested in analysing the organisational response to IT implementation.

This article seeks to add to our understanding of the organisational implications of the PDA. Specifically, it asks how this artefact is relevant to Gamma's structuration choices, by which we mean the coordination and control actions performed in this organisational setting. Therefore, the field of interest is the relationship between technological change and organisational change, a theme of fundamental importance yet highly difficult to address because it is a generator of contradictions, misunderstandings, and even "illusions" [7, p. 164], also in the current debate. Two interrelated questions will guide the discussion: how is the relationship between the technological and the organisational choices shaped by the new device? In what terms does the IT artefact help "make the difference", or influence the decision processes of the different organisational levels?

We have used multiple data sources (interviews, various documents, official reports) to develop the qualitative case study proposed here. We point out that analysing the impact of the IT artefact on the clinical outcomes is beyond the scope of this contribution.

The article is structured as follows. After the introduction, the first section outlines the theoretical background. The next section focuses on the research method and data, while the section after provides a short description of the research setting. The choices made by Gamma are then commented. The preliminary findings of the study are summarised and discussed in the last section, which also sets out their implications.

Theoretical Background

The relationship between technological change and organisational change has always been a major cause for reflection, as attested to in an article published in 1958 in the *Harvard Business Review* [8] only four years after the launch of the first commercial computer application (i.e., a payroll management program implemented by General Electric). Since then, numerous proposals have been formulated with the aim of interpreting the phenomena that accompany the introduction of technologies to organisations.

Many studies have significantly contributed to the generation of a considerable amount of research over the years. However, the overall picture we have today is highly heterogeneous, given that the research settings adopted make it hard to assess the theoretical proposals: each time the dependent variable is the organisation: "the organisations must adapt to technological change" [9, p. 333]. Proponents of this school tend to attribute a predominantly explicative role to the intrinsic traits of the technology or artefacts, such as the absence of personal or social cues and the presence of new features [10, p. 125]. On the other hand, alternative perspectives claim that the dependent variable is the technology: "[technology] is the means to achieve the goals of those who use it" [11, p. 102]. This view argues that the social outcomes do not depend on the capabilities of the technology as such, but on the result of the behaviours and personal beliefs of the users.

The limitations of the predominant literature have been the object of a number of contributions with a critical accent (see, for example: [12-16]). Among many such voices, the reflection proposed by Masino [7, p. 71] stands out because it spotlights the conceptual question. The first observation made by this author is that the studies that pose the problem of the relation between technology and organisation in terms of "technological imperative" and those that support the so-called "organisational imperative" – despite being based on opposing assumptions – both share a common denominator in that they perceive the technology "object" and the organisation "object" as distinct and separate entities. That separation (actually a *reification*) leads to the attribution of a presumed, as it has never been demonstrated, capacity to solve organisational problems. In addition, the predominant rhetoric on organisational change helps to fuel the illusion that the technologies are always and anyway an opportunity to emancipate working conditions and practices. Ultimately, Masino (ibidem, p. 166) confutes the mainstream's presumption that technology is neutral when it affirms the superiority of technical rationality over organisational rationality, and over the rationality and interests of the parties.

Therefore, is it possible to capture the overall sense of the organisational change by using an interpretive key that avoids misleading simplifications? The answer, once again, can only be found on the conceptual side. Mainstream literature relies on opposite ways of perceiving organisational change. A framework that does not conceptually separate the two environments is the Theory of Organisational Action (TOA) [3; 17]. According to this proposal, technology is understood as technical knowledge, not as an element *outside* the organisational process but, to all effects and purposes, an *intrinsic* choice of the organisation, a bounded rational decision made by actors in a framework of constraints and opportunities.

Artefacts embed multiple technologies and help perform numerous tasks [18, p. 318]. Specifically, IT artefacts translate past knowledge accumulated into a visible form and guide the representation of the knowledge in the definition of a problem. They help achieve particular tasks and actions and are considered as good solutions for recurrent problems [18].

Simon [19, p. 6] observes that an "artefact can be thought of as a meeting point – an "interface" … – between an "inner" environment, the substance and organisation of the artefact itself, and an "outer" environment, the surroundings in which it operates. If the inner environment is appropriate to the outer environment, or vice versa, the artefact will serve its intended purpose". The appropriateness of which Simon says is not absolute and unchangeable, and excludes deterministic relations between organisations and actors and between structure, technology and environments reduced to "things" [3, p. 71]. From that perspective, to understand the way in which the artefacts influence organisational regulation, we need to distinguish between the decisional processes of the design, adoption and use of artefacts.

Research Method and Data

To explore the role of the IT artefact in Gamma's structuration choices a case study [20] was conducted. This research-in-progress is based on the data collected in seven semi-structured interviews with two doctors, two nurses, and the family of a patient assisted by Gamma at home. Of the care givers, the doctors and nurses were chosen as they are the key reference points for both the patient and their family. To elicit an understanding of current practices, the interviews were guided by the following objectives: collect, through the words of the care givers concerned (doctors and nurses), opinions on the use of the PDA and understand how it influences the care processes.

Each 90-minute interview was transcribed and used (in two cases) for a follow-up interview (about one hour long), to validate and comment the impressions received. Additional information was obtained from official documents, Gamma's website and that of the IT supplier who developed – for the association – the application software to support the care teams.

The Case Study

Gamma is an "Onlus" (an Italian acronym for a "not-for-profit socially useful organisation") that for more than 20 years has been providing integrated and regular (weekends and public holidays included) home care free of charge to patients in the terminal stage of irreversible diseases. Gamma operates in Milan and about 50 other municipalities in Milan province, providing local services through its own pain-relief and palliative-care specialist teams (composed of about 70 professionals in total, paid but not employees of Gamma), made up of doctors, nurses, social workers, psychologists, personal hygienists and physiotherapists. The teams visit the patient at home at least twice per week and are supported by more than 100 volunteers. Gamma operates in conjunction with Italy's public health service structures which entrust it with the care of those patients to whom they can no longer give a hospital bed. As soon as a patient enters Gamma's care, the association ensures the ongoing involvement of a general practitioner ("GP") and the definition of a personal program – consisting of diverse levels of "care intensity" – by the medical team, which can be redefined at any time to meet the changing needs of the patient and their family. Gamma has capacity to care for up to 160 patients per day, guaranteeing coverage 365 days per year backed by a 24/7 on-call telephone service. It also supplies various healthcare materials to ensure the patient the appropriate overall level of home assistance.

Gamma introduced a computerised solution based on a PDA, a handheld device with wireless connectivity. Each PDA is installed with special software enabled with a multidisciplinary clinical records function. The PDA enables the data collection and specifies the services provided to the patient and family. That information, duly transmitted and received in wireless mode, immediately updates the personal files of the patient's care giver and the central database where all the medical records of Gamma's patients are stored.

In short, the new artefact enables the care givers to:

- record the services provided by each professional, making the relative information immediately accessible to all the care givers;
- communicate in real time and from wherever they are directly with the Gamma central database;
- print out at the patient's home the description of the care-giving processes and practical information of use to the family members involved in the care plan;
- keep the family's GP informed of the clinical decisions made concerning his/her patient.

The IT solution was created by a specialist software house that, guided by Gamma, performed the functional analysis and developed the application programs. The system was piloted, the users trained and, after a last fine-tuning, the application was rolled out. Although the electronic file was designed to resemble the traditional paper medical record or "chart" (PDA use was made compulsory in 2004), the computerised version expanded the scope of the chart, sparking additional opportunities. For example, the PDA systemises and supports the collection of the clinical data both at the time the patient enters Gamma's care and after the home visits made later. The software is programmed to alert the user to any input errors and runs checks on the coherence of the information entered. The central archive (hosted by the remote server) enables several people to share information at the same time without risking its integrity. In addition, the use of a standard archive format and structure facilitates the reuse of the information for management, administrative and scientific research purposes.

The PDA has replaced the previous paper files, the originals of which were kept at the patient's home. In the past, the completeness of these documents varied considerably from one case to the next, therefore, the effective usefulness of their information content depended on the care giver's personal attitude and focus on their manual compilation. The IT system produces detailed reports on the usually complex and demanding therapies and medications given to patients with life-threatening diseases. This functionality is highly appreciated by the patient's family. For instance, printing the file update directly from the PDA removes any transcription errors and eliminates the risk of misinterpreting the GP's handwriting. No less important, the report gives key practical information on the telephone numbers and shifts worked by the respective care givers.

The central database enables the doctor and the duty nurse (on call weekends and public holidays) to consult the patient's records and use the information to determine and implement the best response to a specific circumstance even if they have no direct knowledge of that patient. One particular benefit of the procedure is that it prevents unnecessary hospitalisation and visits to A&E. In addition, the contents of the patient's medical records can be used by the professionals who stand in for absent colleagues, while the patient's GP can use the system documents as support information.

Each team attends a weekly meeting at the Association's HQ to discuss the more important aspects of their respective cases, drawing on the data contained in the electronic archives. The meetings enable the professionals to update patient diagnostic and therapeutic programs, protocols and guidelines, share information on the services given or completed, evaluate their congruency, and report key aspects. Monthly meetings – attended by all the local care teams – are held at head office and led by a Gamma manager (the socio-healthcare director) in a format that ensures the assessor's direct interaction with the person assessed, in line with the 'peer review method' [21].

Commentary

Using a non-deterministic way of approaching organisational phenomena enables us to interpret the Gamma case by concentrating on the decisional processes (*design*, *adoption* and *use*) in which the technological artefact is "organisationally relevant" [22] as it is the bearer of rules originated by diverse sources at different levels. These decisions triggered opportunities and constraints that were absorbed into the [17] care process, contributing to its structuration.

The ***design*** process involved several bounded rational decisions to materialise the designers' technical knowledge, whose bounded and intentional rationality led to the definition of the architecture, the equipment features, the technical standards, the type and format of the data, the user interface, etc. By choosing a handheld device like the PDA, Gamma's top management has assigned a crucial role to aspects such as: portability and, therefore, information access anywhere and at any-time [23], and inter-professional communication among spatially distributed co-workers. The small size of the device means it has been given a menu interface and requires the use of a special pen directly on the screen. The team workers also have a portable printer linked to the PDA for generating paper copies of the patient's updated file, usually at the end of each visit.

The central database containing both the historical archives and the current patient records is kept in the server of an external supplier in ASP (Application Service Provisioning) mode, which means the external supplier hosts the techno-logical facilities (processors, infrastructure, databases, programs and computer files) and makes them accessible to authorised users via secure connections. Given the nature of the information managed (the clinical file is a public act with sensitive data), Gamma is legally responsible for the treatment of the data collected.

Gamma's top management wanted to retain strategic control over the applica-tion design processes of the software solution despite commissioning an external supplier with its development. Likewise we can interpret Gamma's decision to out-source the technical management of the programs and equipment, choosing a con-tractual formula that curbs running and maintenance costs.

The ***adoption*** processes, also guided by bounded and intentional rationality, defined the recipients of the artefacts and the timing and methods of use of each user category. Gamma's management held the multidisciplinary team care pro-cesses the determining level for harnessing the potential fostered by the new sys-tem. The system calls for each professional to record the services and processes they carry out each time. Adoption of the PDA, preceded by training courses and practice sessions, subjects the medical team's field of action to a new, heterony-mous constraint: the obligatory use of the tool every time they are called to assist or when a decision is made regarding the patient. In parallel, this user constraint has generated a new rule for Gamma's managers: the obligation to check that the sys-tem is used according to the conditions established by the internal norms. The arte-fact introduces a kind of HQ-operated "remote control" on the care team personnel. In turn, the remote control is the result of the architectural decisions applied to the design process: standardising the contents of the clinical file has created a kind of "common language" that didn't exist before, thanks to which documentation that meets minimal qualitative standards is produced along with all the advantages of conserving, reproducing and transmitting the information. Prior to 2004, such information was difficult to obtain but, today, management can use the data as a basis for assessments, to monitor particular situations or individual cases or to support decisions on the general organisation of Gamma's activities. More rules (in the form of authentication procedures) were also introduced to ensure secure access to the system and archives.

Finally, the ***use*** process, the real crux, marks the moment in which the artefact become an integral part of the team's work process. In this sense, the 'artefact-in-use' fully expresses its organisational relevance [7]. The users, based on their own bounded rationality and personal beliefs, have "appropriated" the system and gradually grasped its possibilities and constraints. This explains why, without fail, it generates forms of self-regulation that contrast sharply with the official provisions.

The new system imposes an order on the data selection and processing: inputting data into the system has to be done in the precise sequence established by the software program and cannot be modified by the user. The design and adoption choices mean that entering data to the system is slower than using a PC keyboard.

The medical condition of a patient is reported through the collection (guided by the system) of several closed answers to preset questions. The user can enter text notes (via the PDA's small keyboard) to enrich the standard Q&A information, although, in practice, this option is little used due to the user's poor keyboard skills. Sometimes, the note-taking window is too small to adequately communicate a specific situation: "I can't key in detailed notes, it would take me too long", observed one doctor. As a result, the information entered in parts of the patient record can appear, too generic or impersonal, which reduces an individual's perception of the usefulness of the PDA. In other words, to fit the limited computational and physical capabilities of the device, the software 'shapes and squeezes' [19] the reality. The artefact returns a hyper-simplified patient "picture" compared with the actual situation of each patient treated, it records "only what can be articulated" [24, p. 25]. "It's like asking us to play Beethoven's Fifth Symphony with a whistle", remarked one nurse.

The use of the PDA tool in the complex social practice of medicine and nursing – we underscore that this latter field is where patient interaction takes on a holistic connotation [25] – requires a material time (for logging on to the system and to enter the data) that cannot be compressed in which the professional is exclusively focused on the technical-procedural aspects. The GP perceives that the PDA distances him/her from the main reason for their visit to the patient, creating an element of unease: "I feel like the gas inspector", said one doctor. The room for interaction is filled instead by the professional's total focus on the "machine". On the other hand, before the advent of the IT system, the care giver kept up their dialogue with the patient also during the manual compilation of the paper charts. "In the eyes of the patient or their family, the time dedicated to the PDA eats into the time of the visit", observed one nurse. It is an added burden that often causes embarrassment: "When I get out the PDA at a patient's home, I explain that I have no choice", one doctor told us.

The electronic medical record is used in tandem with the other communication means, such as the telephone and the e-mail, or direct personal contact. The PDA enables the doctor, for example, to follow changes in patient conditions reported by another professional and to control the treatment or indicate the most suitable procedures remotely. The care giver can also enter confidential notes in "freehand", using that part of the file not accessible to the patient. Each member of the team is kept abreast of the actions of the other members.

Generally, we can say that the IT system orients the medical team's actions in the "desired directions" [22]. Management has established some heteronymous user rules for the artefact. In parallel, its introduction has given the users room for self-regulation. If, on the one side, the updating of the patient file is performed systematically by all the professionals after each home visit, on the other, the electronic file is less frequently updated after the doctor/nurse has been in phone contact with the patient or a family member. "Minor changes are rarely recorded", affirmed one GP. Generally, the decision not to use the PDA is more frequent in all those cases in which the care giver perceives the artefact as incapable of bringing concrete improvements in the form of lowering the margin for error, less cognitive effort, better service to the families and patients.

It remains to be seen in which way the concerted action of the socio-care teams – using the IT artefact – comes about through coordination. Above all, we underscore that the selection, combination, and sequence of the actions implemented, variable in type and timing, are determined by patient feedback, which means that the team's work is guided by the patient's physical and mental conditions. Creating intensive relations [5] in a highly uncertain and ambiguous scenario. Under these conditions, the adoption by all the members of the team of "mutually consistent decisions" [26, p. 190] can only proceed through reciprocal adaptation, which are also "privileged moments of the production and transmission of new information"[3, p. 68].

Also after the introduction of the IT artefact, the goal of the Gamma's 'technical core', i.e. the integrated care processes, remained the same: to ensure the active, continuing and total care of patients at home, meant as a place for the humanisation of treatment, pain-relief and other symptoms. In terms of the coordination between the various care givers, the need to directly exchange information remains: "Dialogue with colleagues is irreplaceable", reported one doctor. The healthcare and the socio-care dimensions interweave continuously, both during the provision of the service (i.e. at the patient's home) and at Gamma's head office, nevertheless the 'relational density' [7] between the care givers diminishes when the artefact tends to absorb a good part of the social relations that were essential before its arrival. For example, if the patient needs a wheelchair or a special mattress, the program enables the automatic transmission (at a few clicks by the doctor or nurse) of the detailed request to the operations centre, whose staff take care of such needs – from its initial purchase or reuse and deposit in the association's warehouse through to delivery to the patient's home. The same standard procedure can be used to send a request to a social worker, for example, to support the patient's family in dealing with administrative practices, or to a psychologist or spiritual counsellor.

Head office meetings are organised with unchanging regularity. Investments in operational upgrades, training and internal communication continue as before. The decisions are made, as usual, by each professional, although the external visibility of the actions and outcomes of the care processes has been heightened (see the paragraph above on the architectural decisions). The care givers are aware they are being observed remotely and thus adapt their working patterns (e.g. input of data at the point of care) to those dictated by Gamma's management. The artefact has introduced a heteronymous constraint into the organisational workflow, which is delegated to the subjects of the constraint itself. Managerial control of the care-giving processes extends and reinforces itself in an indirect way.

Conclusions

This paper has explored the importance of the technological artefacts on organisational processes by tracing the key steps in Gamma's experience. Fundamentally, this study indicates that assumptions about a straightforward causal relationship between the IT solution deployed in the integrated home care processes and organisation processes are oversimplified and misleading. The interpretive key adopted to understand this case differs from both the objectivist and the subjectivist proposals. Specifically, it distinguishes three decisional processes analytically: the decisions of the design, adoption and use of IT artefacts. The meeting of these processes – interacting and in continuous evolution – derives a notion of technology undistinguishable from the other organisational decisions.

In seeking to answer the first research question on the shaping of the relationship between the technological and the organisational choices, the Gamma case indicates that the innate nature of (information) technology leads to change that cannot be grasped and understood through dichotomist approaches (centralisation vs. decentralisation; autonomy vs. heteronomy; control vs. independence, etc.). Indeed, our analysis has highlighted the diverse, also opposing, effects in line with the decisional levels (and actors) in question.

As to our second research question on how the technological solution helps "make the difference", or influences Gamma's care practices, we have seen that the IT artefact enters the work process as a bearer of constraints and opportunities. Constraints because it limits the decisional alternatives, opportunities because it unfolds new possibilities of action and decision for the actors in conditions of bounded and intentional rationality. The PDA did not significantly change the logic of the multidisciplinary teams. However, the artefact has changed the way in which the clinical information is treated. Information that – we shouldn't forget – translates into crucial decisions from the administrative and managerial perspectives. In turn, these latter also become premises for other interrelated processes of action and decision.

How does this research enhance our understanding of the social impacts observed in the Gamma case? From a theoretical standpoint the TOA opens up horizons that cannot be adequately grasped and understood through dichotomist approaches. For example, the TOA can help us to analyse the spaces of action and decision generated by the process of organisational regulation to clarify the meaning of the outcomes of technological change. On a practical level, the study suggests how the rules laid down by management do not always "work" as expected. Planners make their move, i.e. design solutions and implement artefacts in everyday practice, while those who are affected by them alter their own behaviour. The use of the PDA *makes the difference* because it broadens Gamma management's power of control, but at the same time there is always room for the care providers to become 'themselves designers who are seeking to use the system to further their own goals … in the changed environment' [19, p. 153-4].

The analysis has its limitations, above all, the small sample size. Flick [27] proposed that a researcher could stop collecting interview data at the point of 'theoretical saturation', namely, when no further data are being found that add to the theory that is being developed. This study has a lot of ground to cover before achieving Flick's cut-off point. The gap will be the object of future study, which will take two directions: conduct at least 30 to 50 interviews and include other categories of stakeholders, comprising Gamma's top management and the external provider who developed the software application.

We believe other interesting insights could be provided by the field studies that investigate the relations with the other organisational process levels that shape the action of Gamma. Recently, the Association opened a residential centre (hospice) in Milan to assist about 20 patients whose medical condition is not compatible with staying at home. The services offered by the new structure focus less on the medical profile and more on the care and relational side. And, like home care, this new service also demands the work of a team of different PDA-enabled specialists. The kind of strategy implemented by Gamma could be read as an enlargement of the organisational domain (the organisation operating intensively on the client seeks to place their boundaries around that client [5, p. 43]). An interesting way to extend the research would be to analyse the crucial constraints and contingencies that ensue from this extension of the organisation's technical core.

Therefore, this study is merely the point of departure in a research pathway that has yet to bear its ripest fruit.

References

1. Cicchetti, A., et al. (2005) L'analisi dei Network Organizzativi nei Sistemi Sanitari: il caso della Rete di Emergenza della Regione Lazio. *AIES, Associazione Italiana di Economia sanitaria*. Genova
2. Venturiero, V., et al. (2000) Cure palliative nel paziente anziano terminale. *Giornale di Gerontologia*, 48, 222-246
3. Maggi, B. (1990) *Razionalità e benessere: studio interdisciplinare dell'organizzazione*. Etas, Milano

4. Shah, S. 2001) Grassroots Computing: Palmtops in Health Care. *Journal of the American Medical Association*, 285(13), 1764-1769
5. Thompson, J.D. (1967) *Organizations in Action*. McGraw-Hill, New York
6. Cook, K., et al. (1983) A Theory of Organizational Response to Regulation: The Case of Hospitals. *Academy of Management Review*, 8(2), 193-205
7. Masino, G.(2005) *Le imprese oltre il fordismo*. Carocci, Roma
8. Leavitt, H. and Whisler, T. (1958) Management in the 1980's. *Harvard Business Review*, (Nov-Dec), 41-48.
9. Cyert, R.M. and Kumar, P. (1994) Technology Management and the Future. *IEEE Transactions on Engineering Management*, 41(4), 333-334
10. Markus, M.L. (1994) Finding a happy medium: explaining the negative effects of electronic communication on social life at work. *ACM Transactions of Information Systems*, 12(2), 119-149
11. Kraemer, K. and Dutton, W. (1979) The interests served by technological re-form. *Administration & Society*, 11(1), 80-106
12. Hickson, D.J., Pugh, D.S. and Pheysey, D.C. (1969) Operations Technology and Organisation Structure: An Empirical Reappraisal. *Administrative Science Quarterly*, 14(3), 378-397
13. Attewell, P. and Rule, J. (1984) Computing and Organizations: What we Know and What we Don't Know. *Communications of the ACM*, 27(12),1184-1192
14. Markus, M.L. and Robey, D. (1988) Information Technology and Organizational Change: Causal Structure in Theory and Research. *Management Science*, 34(5), 583-598
15. Orlikowski, W. and Baroudi, J. (1991) Studying Information Technology in Organizations: Research Approaches and Assumptions. *Information Systems Research*, 2(1), 1-28
16. Sorge, A. and Van Witteloostuijn, A. (2004) The (non)sense of Organisational Change: An Essai about Universal Management Hypes, Sick Consultancy Metaphors, and Healthy Organisation Theories. *Organization Studies*, 25(7), 1205-1231
17. Maggi, B. (2003) *De l'agir organisationnel: un point de vue sur le travail, le bien-être, l'apprentissage*. Octarès, Toulouse
18. Ponte, D., Rossi, A. and Zamarian, M. (2009) Cooperative design efforts for the development of complex IT-artefacts. *Information Technology & People*, 22(4), 317-334
19. Simon, H.A. (1996) *The Sciences of the Artificial*, 3rd ed. MIT Press.Cambridge, Massachusetts
20. Myers, M.D. (2009) *Qualitative Research in Business & Management*. SAGE
21. Rebora, G. (1999) *La valutazione dei risultati nelle amministrazioni pubbliche: proposte operative e di metodo*. Guerini e Associati, Milano
22. Masino, G. and Zamarian, M. (2003) Information technology artefacts as structuring devices in organizations: design, appropriation and use issues. *Interacting with Computers*, 15(5), 693-707
23. Prgomet, M., Georgiou, A. and Westbrook, J.I. (2009) The Impact of Mobile Handheld Technology on Hospital Physicians' Work Practices and Patient Care: A Systematic Review. *Journal of the American Medical Informatics Association*, 16(6), 792-801.
24. Tsoukas, H. (2005) *Complex Knowledge. Studies in Organizational Epistemology*. Oxford University Press, Oxford
25. Nicolini, D., Bruni, A. and Fasol, R. (2003) *Telemedicina: una rassegna bibliografica introduttiva*, in Quaderno n. 29. 2003, Dipartimento di Sociologia e ricerca sociale, Università degli Studi di Trento, Trento
26. Simon, H.A. (1997) *Administrative Behavior*. 4th ed. The Free Press, New York
27. Flick, U. (2002) *An introduction to qualitative research*. 2nd ed. SAGE, London

Tracing Diversity in the History of Citizen Identifiers in Europe: a Legacy for Electronic Identity Management?

Nancy Pouloudi[1], **Eirini Kalliamvakou**[2]

Abstract Secure and interoperable e-government identity management practices and transactions are essential in supporting the free movement of people, products and ideas across the European Union. As a result there is significant interest and investment in this area, with open architecture solutions being proposed to support electronic cross-border identity management services. In our engagement with GUIDE ('Creating a European Identity Management Architecture for eGovernment'), an EU-funded project that provided specifications for such a solution, we explored the influence of 'softer' issues, related to organizational, legal and societal aspects of identity management. This chapter reports on our findings on the role of the social context of the European Union in the understanding and acceptance of electronic identity management services by citizens. Our approach entailed looking at six, geographically spread and culturally diverse EU countries to investigate the interplay of social context and history on the perceptions of identity management in society. This chapter reports on current citizen attitudes towards identity management in these countries, as influenced by historical circumstance. We argue that efforts to coordinate identity management at the European level need to respect and accommodate historical and cultural conditions that have shaped the diversity in current national practices.

Introduction

The facilitation of cross-border movements and transactions has been a key priority for the European Union (EU). The extended country membership of the EU today, the technological capabilities available as well as the increasing importance of e-government services, and e-commerce more broadly, have brought cross-border electronic identity management to the forefront. Indeed, the EU has made a multi-million euro investment in this area of research through a number of initiatives and research projects (e.g., FIDIS[3], PRIME[4], GUIDE[5]).

A recent paper on identification and interoperability of e-government systems [1] presented current systems of identification in 18 EU member states. It recognized that: "heterogeneity results obviously from the different national, legal,

---

[1] Athens University of Economics and Business, Athens, Greece, pouloudi@aueb.gr
[2] Athens University of Economics and Business, Athens, Greece, ikaliam@aueb.gr
[3] http://www.fidis.net/
[4] https://www.prime-project.eu/
[5] http://www.guide-project.org/

political, and historical frameworks, on one hand, and the actual chosen solutions for identity management, on the other hand" (p. 49). However, further evidence and analysis of the historical circumstances leading to the diversity is rather limited to date.

This chapter reports some of the findings from our involvement in the GUIDE (Creating a European Identity Management Architecture for eGovernment) project. Aiming to deliver specifications for an open architecture that supports secure and interoperable e-government identity services and transactions, the project also investigated the broader societal context for identity management in the EU. The GUIDE project also recorded significant diversity in current practices of identity management and explored its implications for interoperability in cross-border applications. Drawing from the sociological study of identity management conducted within the project [2], this chapter sheds light on the research findings that concern the link between historical conditions and current identity management practices. To this end, we explore how current perceptions on identity management and the use of identifiers have evolved in six culturally diverse countries of the EU.

The next section presents our research approach, focusing in particular on the selection and preparation of the six cases. Subsequently, we present the main findings for each country, leading to an overview of the distinct practices and an analysis of the relationship between current practice and historical circumstance. The chapter concludes by identifying key areas on which policy makers should focus, to develop and adopt viable solutions for identity management.

Research Approach

Our intention has been to investigate the diversity in the use of identifiers in the European Union and its relation to historical circumstance. As an exhaustive study of all Member States was not possible, we selected six countries that arguably form a representative picture of the diversity across the EU, taking advantage of access to expert opinion. In particular, we ensured that information on the actual use of identifiers as well as the historical perception on identity in the country was provided by experts in identity management research or practice who also had experience of residency in the country in question and access to original sources (e.g., legislation, stakeholder reports, national press).

The six countries selected are geographically dispersed so that different cultural and historical backgrounds of Northern, Southern, Eastern, Western and Central Europe are incorporated in the study. Also, all countries exhibit characteristics of interest in terms of their approach to identity management. **Denmark**, as a Scandinavian country, is considered to be at the forefront of both technological as well as social issues of identity management. **Germany** is a federated state and therefore offers an interesting profile in terms of the complexity of inter-state information exchange. **Hungary** has a different perspective of identity since it does not allow for single identifiers to be used. The **UK** has developed e-government systems in place but has a history of resistance to the use of identity cards. **Greece** has a distinct profile concerning identity issues due to a history of military regime, foreign occupations and the large impact of religion in the formation of national identity. Finally, **Estonia** is a new nation that appears keen on implementing modern schemes regarding identity management.

Our research approach includes data collection based on expert opinion from the six countries on the actual, present use of identifiers, as well as reports on societal reactions that have resulted from the implementation of identity management practices. Also, through a short historical background account regarding identity management in each country, we extracted the historical perceptions of identity and identifiers. This allowed us to draw conclusions on whether and how a country's historical background has indeed affected its current decisions for identity management. Such decisions may involve both policy making and current implementation of identity management systems and processes.

In order to obtain symmetrical accounts for all countries, we designed a template for data collection by the experts. This is organized in five sections, reflecting our research scope:

(a) **Historical account of data collection on identity:** This is an introductory section, providing a historical account of how current identity schemes and beliefs surrounding identity have come into place.
(b) **About identity:** This section aims to provides the 'official' perspective of what constitutes identity and identification, the description of the authority in charge. It also presents major changes to identity management and the reasons for these changes.
(c) **Identity management in e-government:** Presents the identifiers used in e-government and the issues that arise in the process.
(d) **Societal attitudes regarding identity management:** This section depicts citizen attitudes towards various identity management schemes and initiatives
(e) **Conclusions-Concerns:** A set of initial conclusions and an account of major concerns that derive from the above sections

The authors of this chapter coordinated the research and write up of the Greek case and set it as benchmark for the authors of the other cases. Where possible, we triangulated the expert reports with a variety of relevant sources, including official publications and activist groups' reports. Nonetheless, we deliberately invited the experts to provide their interpretation on why certain points in time were considered important for identity management and to draw their own conclusions (fifth section of the template). Although we are aware that this may have introduced further bias to the accounts gathered, we considered the expert insights valuable for our analysis. Indeed, we were not aiming at providing a 'dry', objective account of historical data but rather at flagging a variety of issues, historical circumstances, cultural influences and reactions that may be witnessed when identity management schemes are planned or implemented. This data collection strategy also led to the identification of factors that play a major role in identity management. From these accounts we drew conclusions on practices and issues pertaining to identity management in each country and comparatively derived common elements and differences from our cross-country analysis, thus contributing to a better appreciation of the contextual nature of identity management.

Research Findings: the Use of Identifiers in Context

This section presents an overview of the use of identifiers in the identity management schemes of the countries selected, as well as the issues of concern in each country. A brief historical account is provided for each country at the end of the section in Table 1a and 1b, focusing on how the current identity management came to be, revealing the social and cultural context that, we argue, has influenced the use of identifiers. The countries are presented in alphabetical order.

Denmark

Denmark utilizes a single unique identifier, the Central Persons Register (CPR) number, since 1968. It is issued by the Ministry of the Interior to all citizens immediately after birth or at registration on immigration. It is used for identification towards all authorities, social security, health, tax and address registers. Danes feel confident about the government handling their personal data and being able to obtain services through all levels of public administration using the CRP. There is a general feeling that the benefits to the individual citizen are far greater than the risk of too much control in the hands of the State. Citizens may be reluctant to give their CPR-number over the phone or in shops but not to public authorities. It seems that the Danish culture of high level social security has made it acceptable to have authorities look into all aspects of a citizen's life. Although the trust towards the government's identity management practices is high there are requirements regarding security of data. There should be provision for the level of transparency of use and recording of personal data so that security is not affected. In addition, since the unique identifier is easy to remember, therefore easy to guess, there should be provision for the level of security, for example additional authentication numbers. In 1979 the Act on public registers was implemented (regulations to control the storage and communication of data that can be used to refer to individuals). In 2000, the law was revised in order to comply with EU regulations.

Estonia

The young Estonian state adopted practices similar to those in the Scandinavian countries by introducing the personal identification code in 1992. This is a unique identifier issued at birth or on immigration, valid for life, which is written also on every ID document used in everyday transactions, and all citizen personal data kept by other authorities is connected to that code. The identifier facilitates identification towards all authorities and is also used electronically along with other authentication passwords. Citizens occasionally have to prove that a certain personal identification number belongs to them and for that ID card, driving license and passport offer complimentary authentication. Along with the codes, the population counting database was also established in 1992. Data comes from local municipalities, vital statistics departments, courts, citizenship and migration boards and other state institutions. The chief processor of the register is the Ministry of Internal Affairs although, since 1994, the Ministry outsourced keeping and processing the database to Andmevara Ltd. The data on the register is used by public and local authorities and private companies. Since 1997, the data can be accessed and used online. Data regarding the personal identification number is kept in a central database with strict access rights; however, the code itself is public. The Population Register (the main national register) manages the formation and issuing of the codes. The register is regulated by the personal Data Protection Act, Databases Act and Population Register Act. There is also the Data Protection Inspectorate for national supervision of processing and keeping databases of personal data and access. Whenever sensitive personal data is processed there is an account of that in the data protection supervisory office. Public discussion regarding ID cards took place in 1998 with pilots in 1999. In 2002, the first ID cards were issued. These can be used electronically, are the major form of identification and contain the personal identification code. The ID cards comply with EU regulations. In 2005 the ID cards were used to carry out the first elections using e-voting in Estonia. Estonians have accepted this kind of identification as it has proven to be very comfortable to use. However, constant public attention and a lot of media coverage have resulted in increasing awareness regarding processing and protection of personal data. People are getting more interested and concerned about how their personal data is treated and the potential from misuse, the number of cases (also increasing in complexity) that the a Protection Inspectorate is solving increases.

Germany

Throughout its changing history, Germany has had a stable, consistent identity management scheme [3]. Compulsory registration of individuals was introduced under the Reich Registration Law of 1938. Since then the German ID card has not undergone any changes except in 1987 when the ID card was produced in a machine-readable format [4]. Germany's historical and social background has formed an identification scheme that is application-specific (different identifiers for different occasions which are not stored in the same database) and does not utilize a unique, permanent individual's number. Each identifier is used on specific occasions, such as the identity card number, the social security number, the tax registration number. The protection of personal data is ensured through the restricted access to personal details and the time frame of each number's validity. It is forbidden by German constitutional law for the identity card number to be used as a database field key on central government databases. German citizens generally demand concrete justification of any activities concerning identity management and security issues and also voice their need for the basic human right of "information self-determination" to be taken into account. There is a shared mentality against any kind of centralization, with security, trustworthiness and credibility being central issues in such a debate. However, transparency and open discussions have led to German citizens developing considerable trust towards the State regarding identification initiatives. The protection of personal data, avoiding invasion of privacy and the potential abuse of information and protecting the legitimate interests of the state or third parties (national security), is approached by the German federal state through adequate technical and legal frameworks [5-6].

The identification landscape may be different in the future, though, as there are plans for central registration of German citizens via a lifelong tax identification number [7]. This will be assigned at birth and stored centrally and updated through local registration authorities. During the reform of the federal organization of the German State in 2006, the legislative competence for citizen registration was moved to the federal authorities. There are plans to centralize the system of citizen registration by adding a central registration index containing data about German citizens to today's local registration databases[6].

Greece

Multiple identifiers are used in Greece, with identity card number and tax registration number used most often for transactions with the public sector. Some transactions (e.g., bank transactions or registration with phone and electricity companies) request both identifiers. Identity cards were introduced and made obligatory in 1945. New identity cards were issued in 2000. These have the name of the bearer also in Latin characters to comply with EU and international regulations. They no longer include the fingerprint, full name of spouse, maiden name, profession, home address and religion, information included in the old identity cards. The latter are nonetheless still widely used. The tax registration number is the only identifier stored electronically. However, the lack of uniformity in its issuance limits its applicability as a unique single identifier. In Greece, there is a pressing need for uniformity and interoperability (since most public authorities do not share systems and information) but at the same time special provision is needed regarding the retention of data records, privacy and the protection of civil rights and liberties. At the same time there is limited trust towards the government, a national trait attributed to the troubled modern history of the country [8].

Hungary

Three main identifiers are used in Hungary (identity card number, personal identification number, social security identification number), as it is unconstitutional to keep a unique number for each citizen. The personal identification number was abolished in 1992 but it still exists in Hungary, although it is rarely used. Only the social security identification number is issued at birth. Different identifiers are used for clearly defined different purposes and there is no interoperability. The Office of

[6] http://www.fidis.net/resources/deliverables/privacy-and-legal-social-content/d133-study-on-id-number-policies/doc/15/

Data Protection and Freedom of Information of Hungary did an analysis around 1998 to monitor the public's opinion regarding identity management schemes which concluded that there was a general distrust towards the state while the fear of centralization was also highlighted [9]. Cultural and historical characteristics show that there is great sensitivity in the Hungarian society towards data protection and the right to information self-determination. Also, any attempt of the state towards centralization is viewed as a potential danger and restriction of civil liberties. This is probably the main driver behind the 1992 Act foregoing the unique identifier and ruling it unconstitutional in favour of multiple identifiers. However, the Hungarian people seem to embrace initiatives such as e-taxation systems or electronic signatures.

United Kingdom

The UK has a number of identification documents (National Insurance Number, National Health Service Number, passport number, driver's license, birth certificate) used for various purposes, presenting a fragmented identity management process between the citizen and multiple services. There is no single identifier; however, on March 30 2006 the ID Cards Act became law [10-12]. The proposed identity card will contain large sets of data that will also be recorded in a new national centralized database [13].Opinion polls and studies show that the population is largely concerned with monetary costs [14] as well as the perceived invasion of privacy, especially through the inclusion of biometric data in the scheme [15-17]. A study conducted by the London School of Economics in March 2005 [18] concluded that citizen opinion actually supported the goals of the ID card but was concerned and in cases opposed to the method of introduction. There was also a distinct lack of trust in core elements of the proposed scheme and the public "has little or no confidence in the Government's ability to introduce a national ID card system smoothly". A substantial concern voiced in various opinion polls throughout the years has been the perceived invasion of privacy posed by the introduction of ID cards [19-21], especially through the inclusion of biometric data in the scheme. There is a feeling of uncertainty and mistrust in the public and private sector about the collection and management of information. Further opposition to ID cards comes from civil rights groups that fear that ID cards will increase discrimination and racism, as well as increase friction amongst ethnic minority communities.

Table 1a: The use of identifiers in context

	Current use of identifiers and ID documents	*Relevant historical circumstance (on identity & the use of identity documents)*	*Recent developments and citizen reactions*
Denmark	Single identifier: Central Persons Register, in use since 1968	Citizen registration dates back to the 16th century (church registers). ID cards were first introduced in World War II.	High level of trust to government agencies.
Estonia	Single identifier: Personal Identification Code In use since 1992; on all ID documents Extensively used in e-government	Long history of foreign rule throughout the centuries – Russian and German influence in the use of names until 1917; followed by 'Estonianisation' in the 1920s and 1930s; followed by Soviet norms (obligatory use of father's name) imposed since 1940s when Estonia was annexed by the Soviet Union. A new identification scheme followed the foundation of the Estonia state(1991)	Strong sense of independence, and self-regulation; autonomy is celebrated. Wide acceptance of the Personal Identification Code – seen to reflect the country's progress to efficient governance. Some concerns on data protection emerged since incidents of misuse have been reported.
Greece	Multiple identifiers; ID card no. and tax registration no. most commonly used, often in combination ID cards are compulsory	Long history of foreign occupation under the Ottoman empire (ending in 1821) result in a close link between the ethnic and religious identity of Greeks, nourished by the Church. ID cards have been obligatory since 1945 (originally introduced by German occupants in World War II to identify Greeks with a Jewish religious affiliation). Civil war (1945-49) brings polarization in society and lack of trust towards the state. Surveillance and exile for political reasons continue until the end of the military regime (1967-1974). New ID cards were introduced in 2000, with certain data types (including religious affiliation) removed.	Church-led mass reaction to the removal of the religion field in the new ID cards ('the Greek Orthodox identity is integral part of the Greek identity'); unsuccessful petition to maintain an option for registering religion as a field on ID cards. Reactions to the Schengen Convention by the Church and left wing parties. Concerns include centralized control, surveillance and electronic filing (bringing memories of civil liberties' loss under the military regime), but also superstition. Widespread mistrust towards the Greek state, reflected in all modernization efforts; partly related to the surveillance practices of the past, partly to widespread clientelism, partly to perceived inefficiency of government services.

Table 1b: The use of identifiers in context

	Current use of identifiers and ID documents	*Relevant historical circumstance (on identity & the use of identity documents)*	*Recent developments and citizen reactions*
Germany	Domain specific identifiers; ID card no. cannot be used as a database key field on central government databases (the ID card is machine-readable since 1987)	ID cards date back to Bismarck's time. Compulsory registration of individuals was introduced under the Reich Registration Law of 1938.	A new machine-readable ID card was introduced in West Germany in 1987, following a lengthy and controversial legislative process and public opposition. There is a conscious adoption of identification schemes that minimize risks of centralization and surveillance, practices linked to 'a darker past' (namely the Nazi era)
Hungary	3 main identifiers: ID card no., personal identification no., social security identification no. Unconstitutional to keep a unique no. for each citizen	Following a long history of foreign rule, and bringing together contesting ethnic and religious groups the Hungarian state was established in 1920. Following World War II the country was occupied by Soviet troops and remained under communist regime until 1989 ('Goulash Communism', a metaphor for a more liberal regime since the 1960s). Despite the more liberal regime, a general distrust towards the state and centralized practices developed and is still present.	
UK	Multiple identifiers. Identity Cards Act (30 March 2006) [22] makes ID cards compulsory for anyone getting a new or renewed passport from 2008 (not implemented yet)	Earlier ID card schemes (adopted during the two world wars) abandoned due to public resentment	Strong public debate on the new Act, with vocal activist groups arguing against the ID card scheme. Their concerns include cost, privacy, potential misuse and discrimination of minority groups and show a lack of trust in the government's ability to manage data efficiently in the National Identity Register

Discussion

While it is difficult to present the long and complex history of European countries in a short space, the review in the previous section demonstrates eloquently the diversity in identity management practices and shows that this is often tied to the country's history. In particular, three distinct approaches to the use of identifiers can be observed:

A single unique identifier, valid for life used for all identification purposes
This is the case in Denmark and Estonia and is characteristic of all Nordic countries. The choice to use a single unique identifier is driven primarily by efficiency and effectiveness concerns and is the product of a conscious decision made by policy makers. The use of this single identifier in Denmark shows robustness and citizens feel safe as long as they use it cautiously. Estonians, conversely, have been enthusiastic adopters of the single identifier, as it was closely related to the effort to reinvent the Estonian identity since the independence of their state. However, instances of misuse and abuse have been reported, making citizens more conscientious, over time, of identity management security issues.

Several identifiers, partially related, are used by government agencies
This is characteristic of countries where there are multiple, and often incompatible, approaches to identity management in the public sector. Greece and the UK, where this practice has been observed, both seem to use identity management systems that have – to date – emerged through practice rather than planning. Thus, different agencies may follow different rules. This situation is complemented by a general feeling of distrust in the way the public sector handles citizen data. Greek citizens find public services extremely slow, bureaucratic and inefficient; the collection of the same information by several agencies is deemed frustrating. At the same time, having experienced a totalitarian regime in the relatively recent past, Greeks are worried about data collection by the state and possible surveillance if data is integrated. Ironically, the compulsory use of multiple identifiers in transactions reflects a symmetric lack of trust of the state towards the citizen. The attitudes of British citizens can also be considered as paradoxical. For example, the use of CCTV is widespread and accepted, despite the controversies [23]. Yet, the use of an identity card has been strongly resisted. Citizens in both countries share a concern about identity management schemes, but the nature and leadership of the respective debates have been markedly different. Most characteristic is that while political activists and academics have played a leading role in the UK, in Greece, the Church has been a protagonist.

Explicit legislation against a single identifier, limited number of identifiers
The final distinct approach to identity management in Europe is the practice followed by Germany and Hungary. Both countries' history includes periods of totalitarian regimes, when single identifiers were in use. These were subsequently abandoned in favour of decentralized identity management schemes that would not

bring to mind practices of past eras. Thus, on the one hand, the German constitution prohibits the electronic central storage of a single unique identification number because such a practice is associated to practices employed in the Nazi era. Hungary, on the other hand, abolished in 1992 the single unique identifier that was in use by the communist regime (personal identification number) and replaced it with a system that uses three unrelated identifiers for different kinds of transactions (certification of personal identity, certification of residence, certification of payment of health-related taxes).

It follows from the previous analysis that differences in culture, social organization and historical background play a significant role in the choice of countries on what identity management schemes to propose and implement. The evidence from the six countries quite clearly indicate a close connection between national historical circumstance and the use of identifiers. For example, there are instances where the use of identifiers is associated with a 'darker past', such as the experience of a totalitarian or foreign regime. In such cases, the countries are eager to disassociate their current practices from this past experience. What is fascinating though, is that the way this intention is reflected on the use of identifiers may be radically different (e.g., Hungary vs. Estonia). Additional factors that seem to play a role in current identity management practices, and the use of identifiers in particular, include the general efficiency of the state, citizen trust towards the state and the power and identity of activist groups in the counties. Such country specific particularities could lead to contradicting demands and requirements about identity management.

Along the same lines, even the concerns voiced by citizens and non-governmental organizations (NGOs) regarding identity and identity management reflect the differences in culture and historical evolution of every nation, as well as their probability of adapting and accepting a homogeneous and unified identity management system. Hence, we can note variations in the issues that concern citizens and governments, although there are some common underlying concerns. Security requirements regarding data collection and processing appear to be common for all countries. However, a distinct and very important difference is that in some countries respect of data privacy and security are considered given, revealing trust towards the government on behalf of citizens (Denmark and Germany are good examples, even though the use different approaches) while in other countries there are stronger concerns voiced.

This diversity implies that a common, pan-European approach to identity management is difficult to accommodate. Identity is strongly related to social, political, historical and cultural backgrounds and so its formation, representation and management are to be approached with more than strictly technical criteria. It becomes evident from our study that even inside the national bounders of a country, new identity management initiatives are viewed with scepticism by the public when they do not fully correspond to the country's collective identity and profile. In a pan-European scale this scepticism is even greater because in order for common ground to be found, several profiles have to work together and this created problems.

Conclusion and Implications for Policy Makers

Our analysis shows that the public may be sceptical to new identity management initiatives, particularly where they don't correspond to the country's collective identity and history. Not surprisingly, this scepticism is greater with EU initiatives, as the centre of decision making is more remote and therefore less understood. The implication for identity management is that the accomplishment of a common approach is challenging. The way policy makers respond to this complex environment will be critical for the development and adoption of appropriate, acceptable solutions. Our analysis of current practice and citizen response to such practice indicate a number of key areas on which policy makers should focus to achieve appropriate identity management solutions.

First, at project level, it may be the case that over-ambitious implementation plans should be replaced by application-specific identity management solutions. The different identity management practices currently in place attest that there is no "universal" best practice and that suitable solutions are contingent on the broader cultural and social climate. As a result, it makes sense to form multidisciplinary teams when discussing and deciding on e-government and identity management issues. These should ensure that socio-economic criteria be taken into account in selecting and implementing identity management systems, alongside technological and security requirements.

Second, at the political level, decisions pertaining to this standardization regarding identity management need to be made at the highest political level. In other words, the governments of Member States need to commit to such decisions to provide the legal frameworks and signal political commitment to ensure future compliance. However, Member States have their own practices and internal organization, influenced by their historical and political context. Their day-to-day "way of doing things" may interfere with and jeopardize efforts of standardization across Europe. Directives for harmonization, standardization and cross-border interoperability need therefore to acknowledge diverse practices and accommodate them, respecting the subsidiarity of each national government.

Finally, at a societal level, policy makers need to orchestrate efforts to raise citizen awareness concerning identity management initiatives both at the national and the EU level. It is often the case that the societal upheaval following a government's decision is caused by uncertainty or misconceptions. Citizens are sometimes prone to criticizing an initiative without having the necessary information or knowledge themselves but based on hearsay and rumours or the interests of a particular vocal stakeholder group involved in the debate. This signals the need (alongside the ethical responsibility) for governments to inform the public about identity management practices, regulations, benefits and costs. Raising awareness gives the citizen a stronger sense of assurance and therefore, trust towards new practices increases as well as the probability of a smooth adoption, or, conversely, triggers healthy and justified resistance.

In tandem with awareness creation, a key political action for policy makers is to actively include stakeholders and NGOs. Several activist groups voice concerns regarding civil rights when a new initiative concerning identity management is about to be introduced. Also, several organizations that form the stakeholders for identity management practices demand inclusion in decision making. Since, as we discussed earlier, different cultural and historical backgrounds mean different perceptions regarding participations and trust, this might be an opportunity to promote a "trust development process" where all relevant parties can be aware and allowed to participate.

Acknowledgements

This chapter has been developed in the framework of the IST project GUIDE (IST-2003-507498), which has been funded in part by the European Commission. The authors would like to acknowledge the contributions of their colleagues from University of Surrey, Budapest University of Economic Sciences and Public Administration, Estee-Taani Kommunikatsioon, and DeCon ApS. We would also like to extend special thanks to Elpida Prasopoulou and Chrysanthi Papoutsi, who worked as researchers for GUIDE at the Athens University of Economics and Business, for their help and constructive comments. We would also like to thank the participants at the Identity Workshop in Arona, Italy in May 2008 for their comments; Jim Backhouse, Kieron O'Hara, Lothar Fritsch and Wainer Lusoli in particular. The authors are solely responsible for this document; it does not represent the opinion of the Commission, and that the Commission is not responsible for any interpretation of data generated in GUIDE.

References

1. Otjacques, B., Hitzelberger, P., and Feltz, F. (2007) Interoperability of e-government information systems: issues of identification and data sharing. *Journal of Management Information Systems*, 23(4), 29-51.
2. GUIDE Consortium. (2007) *Sociological study of Identity Management issues in Europe* (Deliverable No. D2.1.2): Athens University of Economics and Business (Deliverable leader).
3. Schmidt, M. G. (1998) *Sozialpolitik in Deutschland. Historische Entwicklung und internationaler Vergleich.* 2nd rev. ed., Opladen: Leske + Budrich.
4. Leisering, L. (2000) *Germany – Reform from Within.* In Alcock P. and Craig G. (eds.) (2001). International Social Policy: Welfare Regimes in the Developed World. London: Palgrave.
5. Achelpöhler, W. and Niehaus, H. (2004). Data Screening as a Means of Preventing Islamist Terrorist Attacks on Germany, Part 1 of 2. *German Law Journal*, 5(5), 2. Available at: http://www.germanlawjournal.com
6. Drews, H. L. (2003) *Data Privacy Protection in Germany: The effects of the German Federal Data Protection Act (Bundesdatenschutzgesetz) from the perspective of Siemens AG*. Munich. February 2003. Available at http://www.industry.siemens.com
7. Perera, R. (2001) Proposed German law foresees biometric IDs. 8 November 2001. Available at: http://cnn.com

8. Mouzelis, N. (1978) *Modern Greece: Facets of Underdevelopment.* New York: Holmes & Meier.
9. Karvalics, L. Z.(1998) Information society development in Hungary. Research for Information Society. *Proceedings*, Warsaw.
10. Arnott, S.(2005) ‘Experts say ID cards timetable needs rethink.’ Originally published in *IT Week*, 15/06/2005. Accessed at http://www.itweek.co.uk/2138041 on 30/06/2008.
11. House of Commons. (2008)‘Identity Cards Bill’. United Kingdom Parliament. Accessed at http://www.publications.parliament.uk/pa/cm200405/cmbills/008/2005008.htm on 30/06/2008.
12. Wadham, J., Gallagher, C. and Chrolavicius, N. (2006) *Blackstone's Guide to the Identity Cards Act 2006.* Oxford University Press.
13. Blunkett, D. (2003) ‘*Identity Cards. The next Steps.*’ The Stationery Office, London.
14. BBC News Online (2006a). '*ID card costs 'are already £32m*'. http://news.bbc.co.uk/1/hi/uk_politics/4742556.stm. Accessed 30/06/2008
15. BBC News Online (2008) '*Q&A: Identity card plans*'. http://news.bbc.co.uk/1/hi/uk_politics/3127696.stm. Accessed 30/06/2008
16. Gentleman, A. (2003, November 15). ID cards may cut queues but learn lessons of history, warn Europeans. *The Guardian.* Retrieved from http://www.guardian.co.uk/world/2003/nov/15/eu.humanrights
17. Grossman, M. W. (2005) *Identifying Risks: National Identity Cards.* Lecture delivered at the University of Edinburgh on January 19, 2005. Available at: http://www.law.ed.ac.uk
18. ‘*The Identity Project. An assessment of the UK Identity Cards Bill & its implications.*’(2005) London School of Economics, London.
19. BBC News Online (2004) '*ID cards 'could worsen racism'*. http://news.bbc.co.uk/1/hi/uk_politics/3455685.stm. Accessed 30/06/2008.
20. BBC News Online (2006b) '*What data will ID cards store?*'. http://news.bbc.co.uk/1/hi/uk_politics/4630045.stm. Accessed 30/06/2008.
21. The Economist (2003). *Prepare to be scanned.* 4 December 2003. Available at: http://www.economist.co.uk Accessed 30/06/2008
22. House of Commons (2008) ‘*Identity Cards Bill*’. United Kingdom Parliament. Accessed at http://www.publications.parliament.uk/pa/cm200405/cmbills/008/2005008.htm on 30/06/2008
23. O’Hara, K., and Shadbolt, N. (2008) *The Spy in the Coffee Machine: The End of Privacy as We Know It.* Oneworld Publications.

The Self-Organizing Map in Selecting Companies for Tax Audit

Minna Kallio[1], **Barbro Back**[1]

Abstract Today, Tax Authorities receive the tax reports from companies to a large extent in digital form from the companies in Finland. Most of the tax reports are processed routinely i.e., a computer program checks that the taxes paid in advance are the correct ones and if not, the company either receives a tax return or is asked to pay the difference and there is no need for a tax audit. However, there is a small percentage of companies that need it. Most of these companies – for some reason – have not reported all their income items or have reported cost items that do not belong to their report. This could be unintended or it could be fraud. The problem is to find this percentage from the mass of tax reports. So far, the tax auditors or tax inspectors have used their past experience and posed queries to the data base, where the reports are stored, to find the ones that need a tax audit. This is not necessarily the most effective way of finding the tax reports that need a tax audit. Different data mining tools might aid in this process and make the selections of companies that need tax audit more effective. The aim of this paper is to investigate how well an unsupervised neural network method – the self-organizing map (SOM) – can perform in the task of finding the companies that need to be tax audited. SOM is a data driven approach without a need to have predefined rules or sets of values. A real data set is used and the results are compared to the results that the tax inspectors have received with their methods.

Acknowledgments

The authors gratefully acknowledge the financial support from The Finnish Funding Agency for Technology and Innovation (grant no. 33/31/08) for the empirical studies in this research.

Introduction

Today, Tax Authorities receive the tax reports from companies to a large extent in digital form from the companies in Finland. Most of the tax reports are processed routinely i.e. a computer program checks that the taxes paid in advance are the correct ones and if not, the company either receives a tax return or is asked to pay the difference and there is no need for a tax audit. However, there is a small percentage of companies that need it. Most of these companies – for some reason – have not reported all their income items or have reported cost items that do not belong to

[1] Department of Information Technologies, Åbo Akademi University, FIN-20520 Turku, Finland

their report – it could be unintended or it could be fraud. The problem is to find this percentage from the mass of tax reports. So far, the tax auditors or tax inspectors have used their past experience and posed queries to the data base, where the reports are stored, to find the ones that need tax auditing. Tax officials select companies for a tax audit according to their internal guidelines, which at the moment often is past knowledge and queries to data base that contains the information about companies. The selection process may not be complete due to constraints on time, effort and money. Also, the selection process might not pick the best possible candidates for a tax audit, due to the multitude of indicators for possible fraud.

A fraud, or fraudulent financial reporting, is a widely discussed topic in literature and can be defined for example as "intentional or reckless conduct, acts or omissions that result in materially misleading financial statements" [13]. Another way is to say that a fraud has happened when the financial statement does not anymore "present the true picture" [16]. From the point of view in taxation, both intentional and un-intentional errors and frauds should be detected and that is a complicated context, where some data mining methods might be an aid.

In this study, we employ the technique of self-organizing maps (SOM) [10] to cluster the companies in groups. SOM belongs to the family of neural networks. There are two main types of neural networks – supervised and unsupervised methods. SOM is an unsupervised method. Unlike supervised methods, which require that the data contains examples; certain kind of inputs are followed with certain outputs, the SOM learns to cluster the data based on the similarities and differences of the input variables. The main idea of the SOM is to project multi-dimensional data to a two-dimensional map. In the map similar cases are situated close to each other and thus creating clusters. This algorithm has been implemented in several software packages. We have used a software package called Viscovery SOMine [2].

The aim of this paper is to investigate how well SOM – can perform in the task of finding the companies that need to be tax audited. If the model is good it can be used to find the companies that need to be audited and to better allocate resources i.e., to give the tax inspectors more time to concentrate on tax audits with larger returns by selecting the right companies to be inspected in depth. The rest of the paper is organized as follows. In Section 2, we briefly describe related works both in data mining in taxation and in detecting frauds. In section 3, we introduce the methodology of this research. In section 4, we describe how the model in this study is created. Section 5 presents the results. Section 6 concludes the paper.

Related Works and Relevance of this Study

Data Mining in Public Administration and Taxation

Our research is similar to the research done by Danziger et al. [6] as it deals with the impacts that information technology has on public administration.

---

[2] www.eudaptics.com

Danziger et al. [6] define four categories on which information technology has impact i.e., *capabilities, interactions, orientations* and *value distribution*. They further divide the capabilities into three areas: *information quality, efficiency* and *effectiveness*. All these areas are potential outcomes of a data mining application development generally and as well in this research. The target of the research is to improve the information quality, to find out more about the data in use; more than conventional methods can show. The efficiency is expected to improve, as new tools are available for the tax auditing process and data mining applications in this context impact on the effectiveness, as the process is directed based on better decision making and planning.

Data mining might also influence the orientation in taxation. We can see the taxation data also as a model in which the relationships and patterns are found and shown. This fact offers us a groundbreaking view to see the taxation data as an entity, the characteristics of which, for example the scene over whole business line, can be taken into consideration as one single case is approached during the taxation process. This option emphasizes that the result of the whole yearly taxation process is more important than one single minor detail in one case, although we have to remember that the before mentioned result is literally a sum of its details.

Taxation gathers a mass of information and the taxation process consists of several sub processes and follows a complex set of rules. Thus it offers an excellent field for data mining research. Researchers [9] have studied decision trees to fuse a set of rules to define whether emigrants and immigrants have the residential status to be taxed. Another application has used decision trees in order to find a model that classifies companies, with positive recovery, separate from the ones with negative recovery. Recovery was defined as "the amount of evaded tax ascertained by the audit "[3]. DeBarr and Eyler-Walker [2] have studied the problem of using abusive tax shelters by first visualizing all relationships taxpayers and their families have with different partnerships, trustees and corporations and then modeled the tax shelter risk of individuals. Bakin et al. [1] have had an approach similar to our research. They have found it infeasible to go through all tax returns and developed a model to classify cases after the probability of fraud in them.

Data Mining in Fraud Detection

The research of Spathis et al. [17], and Spathis [16] searched for factors that affect the likelihood of falsified financial statement, FFS. They used ratios as variables in their model. The statement was defined to be falsified when assets, sales or profit is overstated or liabilities, expenses or losses are understated [16]. Referring to the literature of published research they rank some accounts to be manipulated or falsified more likely than the others. Those variables are for example sales, accounts receivables, and inventory. They started with seventeen ratios and examined them using correlation analysis and performed t-tests to find out the statistical significance of them and ended up with ten ratios.

Kotsiantis et al. [12] also had a goal to identify factors, which auditors could use in their work for detecting financial frauds and errors. They used different kind of machine learning algorithms to test the factors. In their study they collected

23 variables representing profitability, leverage, liquidity, efficiency, cash flow and financial distress.

SOM, the data mining method, which we have employed in this research, has also been studied in auditing research. Koskivaara [11] found SOM useful in finding otherwise hidden patterns or as well to be used as a data mining technique in a continuous monitoring and controlling tool. Koskivaara also brought out the possibility to employ unsupervised SOM clustering as a supportive phase before a supervised data mining model is used.

SOM has been employed as a clustering and visualizing tool to group similar companies as to certain features and to analyze the clusters created by the data driven method. Eklund [8] has used SOM in financial benchmarking. The research was based on data from the biggest companies in pulp and paper industry. The model showed how the companies performed compared to each others during 1998-2002.

Tan et al. [18] have employed the SOM to conduct a quantitative analysis of financial statements in credit rating classification. They have combined the quantitative model with qualitative analysis, which is based on facts like company strategy or economic market outlook. In the model, they used 18 different financial ratios as attributes and trained a map in which they were able to find clusters defining the profiles of companies like "healthy, large and stable, average, small, underperformers, unstable".

Denny et al. [5] have studied the context of compliance and fraud in taxation. They have visualized taxation data with self-organizing maps. Their main interest was to identify and analyze the changes regarding the clustering. They compared the data from year 2006 to year 2007 and found a change in clusters that was dependant on changes in the politics of the Australian Government.

Methodology

Self-Organizing Map, SOM

SOM is a neural network algorithm which maps multidimensional data to a two-dimensional map. SOM is used as a data analysis method in different data mining tasks like clustering, visualization, data organization, characterization and exploration. It is based on unsupervised learning, which means that the learning process is data driven and no predefined values are provided. The goal of unsupervised learning is to find a novel structure in the data and not to learn to follow rules, which are known to be connected to certain output values.

SOM is a neural network consisting of two layers; an input layer and an output layer, without any hidden layers. The neurons are arranged in hexagonal or rectangular arrays, which most commonly are two dimensional. The software package which we use in our research uses the hexagonal array, which is commonly used. For each neuron there is an associated weight vector, the dimensionality of which is equal with the dimensionality of input data, which is also processed as vectors.

As the algorithm operates the input data is compared to the weight vectors and the best matching weight vector, the winner neuron, is found based on Euclidian distance between the data vector and the weight vector. The second step is to update the network; the neurons in the neighbourhood of the winner neurons are tuned to the input data vector. These steps are repeated for the each input data vector until the stopping criterion is reached.

The Self-Organizing Map was developed and introduced in 1981 by Teuvo Kohonen [10] The latest published information on the web site of Helsinki University of Technology had discovered almost 8000 published research papers, where SOM is included. In an earlier published bibliography Oja et al. [http://www.cis.hut.fi/research/som-bibl/] have divided SOM papers into several categories after the context of them and found only 73 of 3339 (~2%) belonging to category of business applications. The main use of the algorithm had until then been on technical area. Despite of that Smith [15] in studying neural networks in business argues that SOM is the most common unsupervised method. It has been found to be a robust method with a valuable contribution in applications also in business field. As Vesanto [19, p.111] also has noticed, "SOM has proven to be a valuable tool in data mining and KDD with applications and financial data analysis". The approach of this preliminary research is emphasized on the application in the context of taxation and introduces SOM as an unchallenged method of data mining in taxation.

The key feature of the tool is the data driven method in exploring the data. Although the taxation process is directed, following laws like pre-defined rules, the whole process itself as well as the taxation data is quite complicated, containing a large variety of cases; both so-called routine cases and cases, which can be defined fraudulent. The fraud may be intentional or unintentional, but those cases should be selected and inspected by Tax Authorities.

Selecting the Companies

The data of the research is real data from corporate taxation. The research is limited to one business line and includes one form of enterprises; partnerships. The data is from year 2004 and contains only Finnish companies. At that time foreign companies were not operating to a larger extent in Finland – as they do now – and therefore they were not included. The small, one-man companies were also excluded, although they are quite many. A computer-aided tool to compare those could be very useful, but the large group of different cases each having just a minor share for the amount of collected taxes gave a reason to omit them at this stage of the research.

The data in the study consisted of 4355 companies and it was labeled; we knew whether a company had been tax audited that year or not and we also knew the result of each tax audit, whether the taxation had been increased or decreased. 107 companies had been inspected and their tax amount had been corrected. The data did not include several companies that had been audited and found "clean" and therefore we chose to use as comparison group 207 uninspected companies although we did not know their status according to the need to be inspected for sure.

Creating the Model

The goal is to develop a model, which uses the Self-Organizing Map and supports in selecting the companies to be inspected. The first phase is to select the variables, i.e. the attributes for the map. The next step is to pre process the data and then to train the map. For training of the map we need a sample that contains both companies with an inspection result that differs from zero and ones with a result zero i.e. there is nothing to change in the taxation, here considered also as a clean result. Through the training of the map we want to find a cluster – a key cluster- where all companies that have an inspection result unequal to zero should be found in the best case. Then the rest of the companies could be fed to the final map and we can see which uninspected companies are similar to the ones in the key cluster.

The attributes were first chosen based on discussion with the Tax Authorities, who have the domain knowledge. Based on the discussion, we selected eight variables. They were facts on which the Tax Authorities have concentrated their inspection choice lately, like salaries, debts and so on[3]. In the model each chosen attribute was divided by the turnover, which is one of the most usual ways to decrease the influence of company size.

We started the modeling of the map with five attributes, and trained the map with a randomly chosen set of instances, companies. Then we enlarged the set of attributes. We added the remaining three ones and used the original training set to be able to see the change created by the new features. We also tested the maps by using the rest of the data, outside the training sample, as a test set.

Next we used again the first set of attributes and tested how much the results of the map change as the control data set changed. We divided randomly all uninspected partnership companies of the whole data set to 20 groups and combined each group with the inspected ones. Thus, we received 20 training sets to compare. As the test results of the first two maps seemed to introduce the "over learning" problem we picked still one map with a different result to show that the problem of over learning can also be avoided in a model.

Results

Map 1

In Figure 1, the feature planes, the final map and the identified clusters A-F are displayed.

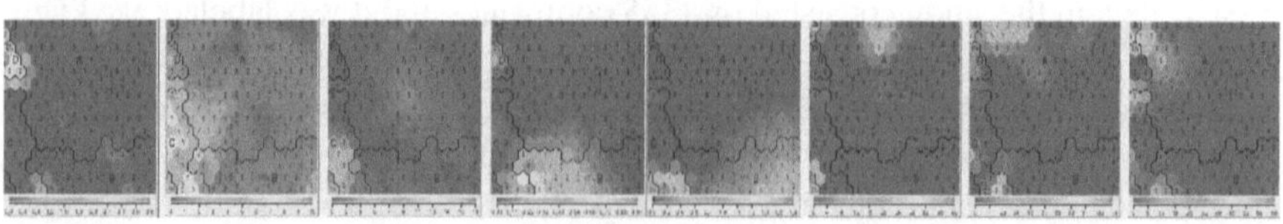

Attribute 1 Attribute 2 Attribute 3 Attribute 4 Attribute 5 Attribute 6 Attribute 7 Attribute 8

---

[3] We are not allowed to reveal the attributes

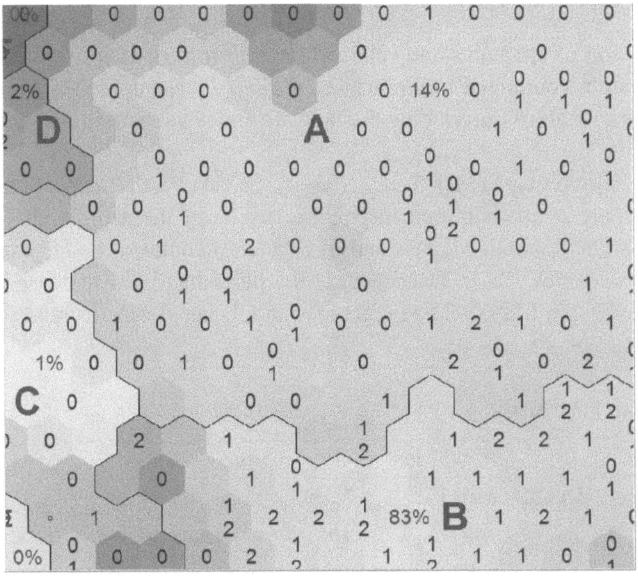

Figure 1: Feature planes connected to Map 1 and Map 1. Companies which are placed to the map are symbolized as follows: 0= not inspected, 1=inspection result low, 2=inspection result high. The percentage marked in each cluster is the share of inspection results of the sample in each cluster.

The characteristics of the different clusters are identified using the eight feature planes in Figure 1 -one feature plane for each attribute. The feature planes show the values of the different attributes as they are distributed across the map. Warm colours (red – yellow) on the feature planes illustrate high values, whereas cool colours illustrate low values (blue -black) on the chosen attributes. Attribute 1 has a high value in the first feature plane in Clusters F and C. Attribute 2 has high value in Cluster C and so on.

Figure 1 shows that cluster B contains most of the inspected companies 83% i.e. a fairly good result. Attributes 4 and 5 have high values in Cluster B. Cluster D is clearly an outlier because it has only one inspected company that forms the whole result; the 2% shown on the map. The feature that led to the cluster was later left away from the attribute list, but at first we were interested to see, whether this feature would correlate with the inspection result or other exceptional values. Cluster A has high values on attributes 6 and 7. It is a large cluster and it contains 14% of the inspected companies, but most of the companies are uninspected in this cluster i.e. not captured by the methods Tax Authorities have used. Given that the Tax Authorities methods are correct there was a need to try to improve the performance of Map 1.

Map 2

We enlarged the collection of attributes and selected three new attributes from the before mentioned research, conducted by Spathis et al.[17]. The sample size was still 314 companies. As a result of introducing the new attributes the map improved considerable.

Table 1 compares the two maps (Map 1 and Map 2). In Table 1 the inspection result is a perceptual share of the summed inspection results of the sample. The key-cluster is still cluster B for both Maps 1 and 2. Cluster B contains the largest percent of inspected companies. Table 1 shows that the percentage has increased from 83% in Map 1 to 93% in Map 2. The percentage in Cluster A has decreased from 14 to 6%.

Table 1: The results of Map 1 and Map 2

	Results in %		Results in #		Action
	Map 1	Map 2	Map 1	Map 2	
Cluster A	14 %	6 %	166	166	not inspected
			43	32	inspection result low
			5	2	inspection result high
Cluster B	83 %	93 %	11	13	not inspected
			39	50	inspection result low
			15	18	inspection result high
Cluster C	2 %	2 %	9	16	not inspected
				3	inspection result low
			1	1	inspection result high
Cluster D	1 %	0 %	16	3	not inspected
			3		inspection result low
Cluster E	0 %	0 %	3	6	not inspected
Cluster F	0 %	0 %	3	4	not inspected
Sum	100%	100%	314	314	total

The next step was to investigate how well the maps generalize to the whole line of business of partnership companies. We fed the rest of the data consisting of 4041 uninspected companies to the maps. In doing so we received the results: In Map 1 1334 companies are placed to the key-cluster B and in Map 2, the result of which is a somewhat better according to the sample, as many as 2270 companies are placed into the key-cluster B. However this is clearly not a good result. This indicates that a possible over training has taken place.

Examining the Results – Samples 1-20

We evaluated Map 1 by examining the same eight attributes in 20 different samples. Each sample had the same inspected companies, but the comparing, randomly chosen ones were divided to 20 samples which varied in each map. Very small companies, those with a turnover under 10 000 € were excluded. That was partly because the values in proportion to turnover may be quite exceptional when the turnover is so low. Those companies are outliers in the sample. To exclude the outliers is one phase in a knowledge discovery process although of course sometimes also valuable information may be excluded [14]. The companies were sorted by the turnover to avoid samples with only small or big companies, and every twentieth company was chosen. The turnover was here used as an argument also as all attributes are ratios in proportion to turnover. Each sample was then used together with the inspected companies and the data was used as input for training the map.

We examined the maps assuming that companies with a need to be inspected should be organized in the same cluster i.e., the key-cluster. Table 2 lists the results of the key-cluster in each map. The columns in Table 2 are: results; the share of correct results, true positives; the number of inspected companies clustered in the key-cluster and false positives; the number of uninspected companies, true negatives; the number of companies clustered to another cluster and false negatives; the number of inspected companies clustered outside the key cluster. All inspected companies have an inspection result unequal to zero that means that the taxation has always been changed at least somehow, if the company has been inspected. We cannot regard every uninspected company, which has been clustered to the key cluster as a clean company, i.e. the methods that the Tax Authorities use might not be perfect. Thus, the results may be even better than what is shown in the Table 2. The samples in *Table* 2 are sorted by the results.

The results of the maps are not perfect, but on the other hand if the model clusters about 23 percent of inspected companies, which bring almost 70 percent of the result, we can assume that there might be a useful pattern to be discovered and developing a model will be productive.

Finally, we chose Sample 8, to test the model with the rest of the data. The results of the chosen map were quite in the middle or slightly below the lower half of results as shown in *Table2*. The rest of the data; that is the pre defined attributes of all partnership companies, with a turnover over 10 000 Euros, was fed to the map.

Only 264 of 3815 companies were placed in the key-cluster. As the rest of the data contains only un-inspected cases, the inspection result could not change; it is still the original 64% of the inspection result of the sample. We were here mainly interested in how many companies seem to follow same features as the inspected ones in the key cluster. The next question that arises is, whether they also have a need to be audited and how much this auditing could increase the inspection result. The map based on Sample 8 generalizes much better than Maps 1 and 2. The before mentioned *over training* has not taken place in training the maps.

Table 2: The uninspected partnership companies have been divided to 20 samples. Each sample is combined with the inspected ones and used as an input data in the self-organizing map

Map	Results	True positives	False positives	True negatives	False negatives
Sample3	69 %	25	24	177	76
Sample10	68 %	22	23	178	79
Sample18	68 %	20	12	189	81
Sample2	68 %	19	17	184	82
Sample19	68 %	20	23	178	81
Sample14	68 %	20	14	187	81
Sample1	68 %	19	22	179	82
Sample17	68 %	22	17	184	79
Sample12	68 %	12	30	171	89
Sample11	67 %	21	37	164	80
Sample9	66 %	21	24	177	80
Sample7	65 %	18	22	179	83
Sample6	65 %	14	11	190	87
Sample8	64 %	17	13	188	84
Sample5	63 %	19	20	181	82
Sample15	50 %	20	14	187	81
Sample4	50 %	17	13	188	84
Sample20	48 %	17	23	178	84
Sample13	47 %	20	19	182	81
Sample16	40 %	16	30	171	85

Discussion and Future Research

The results with the samples are good but the model does not generalize well in particular concerning Maps 1 and 2. There could be several reasons for this:

a) We have over trained the map.
b) We have chosen the wrong attributes,
c) We have used a wrong share of inspected in relation to uninspected companies for training the map,
d) There are too many companies in the population that should have been inspected by the Tax Authorities, but were not and are therefore labeled wrongly in our material as clean companies.

Over training According to Kohonen [10] 'over learning' or 'over training' is possible when the learning of the neural-network continues after the optimum is reached the code book vectors of the map become too tuned for the training data – here the sample- that the ability of the algorithm to generalize for the rest of the data suffers. Our result that about one third or over the half of companies should be inspected by Tax Authorities differs strongly from information, which is known in practice. However 264 extra that have to be inspected is a much more promising result.

Choice of attributes Our choice of attributes does not seem to fit the smallest companies. There is a need to investigate more regarding them.

The share of inspected companies and uninspected companies needs to be investigated more. There is a great amount on this in the literature concerning bankruptcies that could be researched.

Inspected versus uninspected companies. The problem with whether uninspected companies really are clean needs to be solved. This is not an easy task how this could be done and we are working on it how this could be done in an cost effective way.

We have also started to investigate limited companies and we have promising results from that group. When the models have the right attributes and are specified to certain groups of companies, we can call them prototypes. The next phase is then to test the prototypes using different data sets, in cooperation with the users. With satisfactory results, a cost-benefit analysis of the use of the model can be made. A final phase would then be turning the model into a software product and that way reach the goal that Danziger et al. [6] outlined in his research i.e. improve the efficiency through better planning and decision making.

References

1. Bakin, S., Hegland, M., Williams, G. (1999) *Mining Taxation Data with Parallel BMARS* in http://citeseer.ist.psu.edu/cache/papers/cs/28534/http:zSzzSzresearch.cmis.csiro.auz SzgjwzSzpaperszSzatobmars.pdf/bakin99mining.pdf, 06.06.2006.
2. DeBarr, D., and Euler-Walker Z., (2006) Closing the gap: Automated screening tax returns to identify egregious tax shelters. *SIGKDD Explorations*, 8(1), 11-16.
3. Bonchi, F., Giannotti, F., Mainetto, G.,and Pedreschi, D., (1999) *Using data mining techniques in fiscal fraud detection*, in Mukesh Mohania and A Min Tjoa eds., DaWaK'99, LNCS 1676, 369-376,Heidelberg, www.springerlink.com 11.09.2006.
4. Bonner, S. E., Palmrose, Z-V., and Young S. M., (1998) Fraud type and auditor litigation: An analysis of accounting and auditing enforcement releases. *The Accounting Review, 73*(4), October, 503-532.
5. Denny, Williams. G. J.,and Christen P., (2008) Exploratory hot spot profile analysis using interactive visual drill-down self-organizing maps. Advances in Knowledge Discovery and Data Mining:12th Pasific-Asia Conference, PAKDD 2008, Osaka, Japan, May 2008.
6. Danziger, J. N., Andersen K., (2002), The impacts of information technology on public administration: an analysis of empirical research from the "golden age" of transformation. *International Journal of Public Administration,* 25(5), 591-627.
7. Eilifsen, A., Knivsflå, K. H., and Sættem F., (1999) Earnings manipulation: cost of capital versus tax. *European Accounting Review,* 8(3), 481-491.
8. Eklund, T., (2004) *The Self-organizing Map in Financial Benchmarking.* TUCS Dissertations No 56.

9. Fisher, R., (1997) Determination of residence status for taxation law: Development of a rule-based expert system, Melbourne, Australia. *ACM Press*, 161-169.
10. Kohonen, T., (2001) *Self-Organizing Maps*, 3rd ed.Springer Verlag, Berlin.
11. Koskivaara, E., (2004) *Artificial* ***Neural Networks for Analytical Review in Auditing.*** Turku School of Economics and Business Administration. Series A-7:2004.
12. Kotsiantis, S., Koumanakos, E., Tzelepis, D., and Tampakas, V., (2006) Forecasting fraudulent financial statements using data mining. *International Journal of Computational Intelligence,* 3(2), 104-110.
13. Lange, G. A., (2001) *Fraudulent financial reporting* in Encyclopaedia of business and finance ed. by Kaliski Burton S., USA.
14. Pyle, D., (1999) *Data preparation for data mining*, USA.
15. Smith, K., (2002) *Neural Networks in Business: Techniques and Applications*, USA
16. Spathis, C. T., (2002) Detecting false financial statements using published data: some evidence from Greece., *Managerial Auditing Journal,* 17(4), 179-191.
17. Spathis, Ch., Dumps', M., and Zopoudinis, C., (2002) Detecting falsified financial statements: a comparative study using multicriteria analysis and multivariate statistical techniques. *The European Accounting Review,* 11(3), 509-535.
18. Tan, R. P. G. H., van der Berg, J., and van der Berg, M., (2002) Credit Rating Classification Using Self Organizing Maps, in *Neural Networks in Business: Techniques and Applications Smith Kate*, ed., USA, 2002, 140-153.
19. Vesanto, J., (1999) SOM-based data visualization methods. *Intelligent Data Analysis,* 3, 111-126.

Digitization as an IT Response to the Preservation of Europe's Cultural Heritage

Claudia Loebbecke[1], Manfred Thaller[2]

Abstract This paper examines the potential for preserving Europe's cultural heritage in a digital world. After an extensive literature review on the economics of museums and the digitization of cultural heritage, it highlights national and international political initiatives to create cooperative cultural heritage systems. As a mean of achieving global integration while simultaneously keeping institutional independence, this work proposes 'Digital Autonomous Cultural Objects (DACOs)' as reference architecture. This paper illustrates the contribution of DACOs with two real-life projects serving as proof-of-concept. Finally, the paper offers some 'Lessons Learned' and an outlook to wider preservation of Europe's cultural heritage in the digital world.[3]

Introduction

Under the term 'cultural heritage object' we subsume all objects that are represented in libraries, archives and museums and that are of cultural or historical value. This definition covers tangible goods like writs, pictures or statues as well as music or films. A Cultural Heritage System consists of several digitized cultural heritage objects about a special topic which are represented with their contexts to a public audience. Digital Cultural Heritage Systems aim at preserving cultural heritage objects for the future and providing access to them via networks. Overall, the creation of Cultural Heritage Systems and digitized cultural heritage raises the question whether they will be an add-on to traditional museums or even replace them.

Until recently, the visual reproduction of objects was more expensive than publishing a description of these objects. Therefore, important objects were 'edited' in the digital world; the most important ones were 'scanned' with the remainder being left untreated. Due to new digitization technologies and cheaper storage, this 'rest' of objects has become increasingly smaller. Hence, further successful digitization could lead to some hundred of millions of easily and freely combinable digital objects of cultural heritage, which may or may not replace traditional museums, archives and libraries [e.g, 1-2].

---

[1] University of Cologne, Pohligstr. 1, 50969 Koeln, Germany, claudia.loebbecke@uni-koeln.de, Tel. +49-221-470 5364, Fax -5300, www.mtm.uni-koeln.de

[2] University of Cologne, Albertus-Magnus-Platz, 50923 Koeln, Germany, manfred.thaller@uni-koeln.de, Tel. +49-221-470 3022, Fax -7737, www.hki.uni-koeln.de

[3] A previous version of this article has appearerd in the proceedings of the European Conference of Information Systems 2005 in Regensbourg

In this context, we aim at developing concepts for the preservation of Cultural Heritage in the digital world which will have to fulfill three main objectives:

(1) Provide accessible source material at least one order of magnitude larger than traditional forms of publication,
(2) Allow for cataloguing by access information,
(3) Offer digital representations going beyond print possibilities.

As contribution of this paper to introduce conceptual components addressing the above objectives, we propose the concept of Digital Autonomous Cultural Objects (DACOs).

The remainder of the paper is structured as follows: In the next section we offer a literature review on three relevant bodies of literature. We then introduce national and international political initiatives in Europe, all aiming at the preservation of Europe's cultural heritage. After a short section to prototyping as research method in the field of system development, we then introduce the concept of Digital Autonomous Cultural Objects (DACOs) as technical proposition. We introduce two real-life DACO applications and conclude with 'Lessons Learned' and a brief outlook.

Literature Review

Out of three bodies of literature, (1) Cultural economics or museum economics, (2) Organizational approaches for Europe-wide access to digitized cultural heritage, and (3) Information Systems and Computer Science, we introduce major themes relevant for this work.

Cultural Economics or Museum Economics

One relevant body of literature on the digitization of cultural heritage stems from the field Cultural Economics, which can be traced back to the work of Baumol and Bowen [3]. More recently, Hutter and Rizzo [4] present an introduction to the field; Throsby [5] and Blaug [6] offer literature surveys on the field of cultural economics.

Shortly after Baumol and Bowen [3] had introduced Cultural Economics, Peacock [7], Montias [8], and Peacock and Godfrey [9] dealt with Museums Economics. More generally oriented monographs on Museum Economics [e.g., 10-13] were complemented with more specific works. For instance, Robbins [14] and Johnson and Thomas [15] concentrate on political issues in the context of museum economics and develop suggestions for economic research. Other authors [e.g., 16-20] mainly discuss entrance fees for public museums in particular. Schuster [21] focuses on hybrid forms between public and private museums, while Meier and Frey [22] recently have examined the case of private art museums.

Museum Economics are to be distinguished from sociological approaches [e.g., 23], anthropological approaches [e.g., 24] or art historic approaches [e.g., 25] of studying cultural heritage. Illustrations of the struggles between the three disciplines can be found in Feldstein [26] and Grampp [27-28].

Organizational Approaches for Europe-Wide Access to Digitized Cultural Heritage

A second body of literature turns to organizational options for developing and managing an infrastructure that offers Europe-wide access and data maintenance and allows initiating precautions concerning long-term material access. Relevant organizational issues covered in the literature specifically refer to (1) who selects which cultural heritage objects to be digitized, (2) who digitizes, and (3) who controls the access.

Due to market failures and some public-good characteristic in cultural heritage objects [e.g., 29-30; 3], the provision of cultural heritage objects could be below the social optimum. Hence, for the selection of cultural heritage objects, the value of individual cultural heritage objects has to be determined. In this context, literature [e.g., 31] distinguishes between cultural and the economic value.

While the cultural value – extensively discussed for instance by Connor [32] – is difficult to operationalize [33], the economic value is expressed numerically, usually in financial terms. Several scholars deal with different economic techniques and approaches accessing the individuals' satisfaction deriving from cultural property in its non digitized version [e.g., 34-35; 30). These methods include the (1) concepts of willingness-to-pay, (2) impact studies, and (3) Contingent Valuation.

To assess the willingness-to-pay for cultural heritage objects, most studies use either the travel cost approach [e.g., 36-39] or the hedonic market approach [e.g., 40]. The travel cost approach measures the effort people are willing to spend to visit a cultural heritage object. It assumes that the cultural heritage object is the only reason for the journey. However, this approach has several limitations [e.g., 12], for instance, it does not cover all non market values of the cultural heritage object [41]. The hedonic market approach measures the value of a cultural heritage object by looking at private markets which indirectly reflect the utility persons enjoy. It does not reflect upon all social values of the cultural heritage object either. Furthermore, its reliability highly depends on the ceteris paribus assumption.

Impact studies [e.g., 42] measure the revenue derived from a cultural heritage object. The revenues stem from, for example, transportation fees, entrance fees, meals in the restaurant, gifts, and any kind of other income that can be ascribed to the cultural heritage object. Unfortunately, revenue per cultural heritage object does not reflect the social value of the object and thus is inadequate.

The most common evaluation method is Contingent Valuation [e.g., 43]. It uses sample surveys to elicit the willingness-to-pay for cultural heritage objects. The questionnaire involves a hypothetical situation; the term 'contingent' refers to the constructed or simulated market presented in the survey. For example, Martin [37] and Santagata and Signorello [44] use Contingent Valuation to measure the willingness-to-pay for a museum. For specific applications of Contingent Valuation to culture see e.g., Navrud and Ready [35] or Noonan [45]. Its limits are highlighted by Throsby [33].

After having decided on who selects cultural heritage goods for digitization and having chosen the cultural heritage goods to be digitized, the next question is who digitizes them. This question has been for instance addressed by Waetzold [46] who states that such work cannot be delegated to graduate assistants or trainees as it includes important decision for example concerning color reproduction and by Hanappi-Egger [47] who illustrates the importance of the stakeholder approach in this context.

Concerning the questions who shall control the access to the digital cultural heritage based on which approach, two bodies of literature are available. The first one, mainly stemming from the political and social sciences [47-48] leads us back to the systems theory work as put forward by Luhmann [49]. The computer science literature on access control [e.g., 50-54] suggests Role-Based Access Control (RBAC) as introduced in 1992 by Ferraiolo and Kuhn [51]. RBAC (also called role based security) has become the predominant model for advanced access control because it reduces the complexity and cost of security administration in large networked applications and thus alleviates the administration of users and resources. With RBAC, each user role has a set of privileges for operating on some resources. Access permissions are only associated with roles rather than with individual users; hence, the administrative complexity is greatly reduced [e.g., 55]. More specifically, the literature [e.g., 56-57] suggests Policy-Driven RBAC (PDRBAC) for controlling the access in our context where the Internet in general and the proposed infrastructure in particular support large numbers of both users and resources and the mapping of users to resources can change dynamically.

Information Systems and Computer Science

Thirdly, in the field of technically oriented information systems and computer science research, the creation of digital collections has become fashionable during the last years. As the digital collections are supposed to fulfill the functions of traditional ones – such as collection, conservation, study, interpretation, and exhibition [58] or using Weil's [59] terminology, preservation, research, and communication. Such functions of traditional collections serve as anchor point for developing basic requirements for digital collections or 'virtual heritage' [60].

Frequent information systems and computer science conferences investigate technical solutions for translating the fulfillment of these traditional functions into the digital world. Regular conferences in the field, all with numerous scientific contributions, are the Conferences of the International Committee for Documentation of the International Council of Museums (ICOM-CIDOC) (www.cidoc.icom.org/conf1.htm), the International Conference on Hypermedia and Interactivity in Museums (www.archimuse.com/conferences/ichim.html), Electronic Imaging & the Visual Arts, Museum Computer Network Conferences (www.mcn.edu/conferences/), and Museums and the Web (www. archimuse.com/conferences/mw.html).

Political Initiatives Concerning the Digitization of Cultural Heritage

In recent years, the creation of Cultural Heritage Systems and the digitization of cultural heritage were supported by politics on a national and international (EU) level.

National Initiatives

Many European countries started initiatives to make significant parts of their national treasures accessible on the Internet in digitized form. In doing so, the particular digitization projects reflect the different national styles to approach the nations' culture.

In the United Kingdom, a national digitization policy was proclaimed and termed mandatory for every institution. Nevertheless, there is still no single national portal. France, with the 'Gallica' of the 'Bibliothèque Nationale' (gallica.bnf.fr/) has opted for a massive centralized national effort at creating a digital library.

German digitization projects reflect the country's federal system. Many digitization projects have been conducted independently on state level. Recently, efforts have been started to bundle them into a small number of national portals (see Table 1 in the appendix for an overview of the single library digitization projects funded by the German National Research Council).

Considering the different national digitization initiatives, European policy should aim at establishing an infrastructure that guarantees the interoperability of the national cultural policies. Europe's diversity does not allow for favoring one of these policies over another. For example, it would be neither possible nor desirable to describe Spanish's past by German conceptual categories. Rather, a European policy should try to preserve national traditions and spirits by handling the respective traditions subsidiary.

For example, in all European countries manuscripts are identified uniquely by traditional, national referencing systems. They follow their own principles and models for digitization. However, a unified European Digital Manuscript Library will only be feasible if all libraries make their digitized manuscripts accessible as objects that can be accessed via an approved protocol.

European Commission Initiatives

Part III, Title III, Chapter V, Section 3, Article III-181 of the EU draft constitution (e.g., www.budobs.org/eu-const-culture.htm) explicitly states that the "conservation and safeguarding of cultural heritage" is of "European significance".

In the EU, European research activities are structured around consecutive four-year 'Framework Programs (FPs)'. Already in the 'Fifth Framework Program of the European Community for Research, Technological Development and Demonstration Activities' (1998-2002) (europa.eu.int/comm/research/fp5/fp5-intro_en.html) the 'Information Society Technologies Program (IST)' was established as one of seven priorities. The IST is divided into four actions which comprise interaction of information and knowledge. The third key activity, which deals with the interaction of knowledge and information, also assesses cultural heritage or 'Cultural Heritage Systems (CHS)' as a key activity. The IST project has been continued in 'The 6th EU Framework Program for Research and Technological Development (FP6)' (europa.eu.int/comm/research/fp6/) which intends to improve the integration and co-ordination of the largely fragmented European research within the European Research Area (ERA).

Concerning the digitization of cultural heritage, European Commission activities include, for example, the project 'Digital Heritage and Cultural Content (DigiCULT)' (www.cordis.lu/ist/directorate_e/digicult/index.htm) which aims at developing advanced digital library services through standards, infrastructures, and networks. DigiCULT encompasses several sub-projects, some of which have been continued beyond the funding through DigiCULT. Such projects include 'ECHO – European Cultural Heritage Online' (hecho.mpiwg-berlin.mpg.de/home) and 'E-Culture Net' (www.eculturenet.org/). 'E-Culture Net' particularly aimed at developing the European Research Area (ERA) for digital cultural heritage. It included the 'Distributed European Electronic Resource (DEER)' that later developed into 'Distributed European Electronic Dynamic (DEED)'.

Major examples of ongoing development initiatives are the EU projects, EPOCH and BRICKS, both funded in the FP6. The overall objective of the EPOCH network (www.epoch-net.org) is "to (…) increase(e) the effectiveness of work at the interface between technology and the cultural heritage of human experience represented in monuments, sites and museums". BRICKS (www.brickscommunity.org) "aims at integrating the existing digital resources into a common and shared Digital Library", while respecting the European cultural **diversity**. Its 'bottom-up' approach is "based on the **interoperability** of a dynamic community of local systems" as to "maximise (…) the use of existing resources and know-how, and, therefore, national investments".

Overall, European cultural heritage programs have so far concentrated on investigating technical standards or on testing modes of co-operations between institutions.

Digital Autonomous Cultural Objects (DACOs) as Reference Architecture

The provision of digital cultural heritage objects for access by research or the interested public is frequently seen as a sub-field of the research on digital libraries (e.g., http://www.delos.info/). As far as not specimen of the monolithic concept of a digital library [61], cultural heritage servers can usually be subsumed under one or the other of the distributed concepts. Within production systems relatively conservative ones, like harvesting mechanisms, still predominate (e.g., the projects initiated by the Open Archives Initiative (OAI) (www.openarchives.org/). Systematically, the approach described hereafter could be summarized under 'preparation of web services for the provision of cultural heritage material'. We avoid this term however, as in the cultural heritage domain the most prominent technical advisory body, The Office for Library and Information Networking (UKOLN) (www.ukoln.ac.uk/interop-focus/gpg/) quite consistently uses the precise technical term (as for instance implied by the World Wide Web Consortium (W3C) Web Services Description Language Standard www.w3.org/TR/wsdl) 'web services' in a loose and almost colloquial meaning.

Research Approach: Developing a Reference Architecture

As we "build and evaluate" [62, p. 254], our research aims at establishing a reference architecture derived from an analysis of existing academic prototypes and few existing commercial products. The viability of the reference architecture is validated using a proof-of-concept approach with two prototypical implementations which are shown below. Following March & Smith [62, p. 254], we strive to "create models, methods, and implementations that are innovative and valuable".

Further, we also expect this design effort to foster theory building [e.g., 63] in the field of system design. To serve this ambition, with additional implementations coming up, we continue to apply and test the reference architecture.

The DACO Concept[4]

DACOs represent cultural heritage objects digitally such that they can be easily integrated into other web services.

To allow for such integration, two main requirements have to be fulfilled: (1) Functional completeness allowing extended navigation, and (2) 'unobtrusiveness' meaning that DACOs integrate into overarching constructions like frames, but do not take over the website linking to them.

The presentation of each cultural object commonly account for about 90% for the representation of the cultural heritage object. Approximately 10% are needed for several navigation elements and an idiosyncratic emblem of the providing (and sometimes even the sponsoring) institution. DACOs can also be applied for three-dimensional objects: In a co-operation between the British Museum in London, UK, and the Acropolis at Athens, Greece, the British Museum could provide access to the digital versions of its repository of European artefacts from many national traditions. These artefacts (e.g., the Elgin Marbles) could then be used to reconstruct the Acropolis as a 3D model in virtual space.

DACOs are characterized by a common behavioral code that provides for informing about cultural objects on request. The code involves the object wrapping itself in mark-up language. It also provides a persistent addressing scheme allowing for control of the individual institution holding the good as well as a mapping scheme. Thus, even if the technology (e.g., HTML, XML, SGML, VRML objects, Flash movies, SVG constructions) can be chosen by the individual institution, the

[4] The DACO concept goes back to Thaller [2].

structure of basic elements integrated into a DACO is predetermined. A single DACO may be saved on the server of the holding institutions.

Cultural heritage brokers, connected to all servers, integrate many DACOs of different institutions (DACO providers) into specialized interfaces, thus serving the interests of laymen and researchers. The communication between the servers takes place via the DACO protocol consisting of several XML-codes transmitted via Hyper Text transfer Protocol (HTTP). When addressed by a broker, the DACO server describes itself through providing a list of supported 'access venues' (e.g., titles, authors, years, etc).[5] The access venues can be used by the broker to develop a search mask.

Users access this data via a broker. They see an index of all available DACOs and after, appropriate specification, a HTML-Site containing all relevant DACOs to the special task is displayed. Users select a single DACO represented in the page of the broker as the broker receives the URL of exactly that object as well as information about which kind of DACO will be received (e.g., XML, HTML or Flash).

DACOs in Practice Two Case Studies

Cologne Diocesan- and Cathedral-Library

An example DACO application implies digitizing the complete holdings of medieval manuscripts of the Cologne Diocesan- and Cathedral-Library (www.ceec.uni-koeln.de). The project idea was to test whether complete holdings – instead of individual objects – could be digitized and then replace the 'default medium of scholarship'. The purpose of this project was not to reproduce what could be done in print, but to open material for study not accessible by traditional technology. Therefore, the aim was to provide the complete library content of incunabula online in a sufficient quality for all types of research.

A Digital Cultural Heritage System was built consisting of about half a million freely addressable DACOs. During the years 2001 to 2004 about 420 codices comprising 130,000 pages were digitized in different resolutions. The common resolution of the scanned codices' pages is up to roughly 4,000 by 3,000 pixels, allowing for extensive paleographic research (e.g., exploring the writing direction of the writing element). An average manuscript page consists of 35MB to 48 MB of data, large format codices even of 120 MB. All codices together require storage of approximately 3.5 TB to 4.5 TB, equaling approximately 6,000-8,000 CD-ROMs.

---

[5] An example of this kind of description terms is the CIDOC Conceptual Reference Model (CRM) to be found under cidoc.ics.forth.gr. The primary author of the CRM, Martin Doerr [64]strongly emphasises the character of the CRM as an intellectual way of describing cultural heritage data. If one looks at truly native XML data bases capabilities, however, it becomes possible to use the CRM not only as abstract, but indeed as concrete data model for an information system. Regarding the understanding of the relationship between XML data bases and other abstract constructs expressible in XML, which is required by that, see Thaller [65].

With steadily decreasing prices for storage capacity and good project management, the costs for digitizing a single page in the aforementioned quality is down to about one Euro per page.

Further, additional tools are provided allowing for browsing through the manuscripts like in traditional libraries. A native ‘dynamic’ XML database administers all codicological manuscript descriptions since the 18th century. For some codices those descriptions amount to the equivalent of fifty printed pages.

‘Dynamic’ means that links are automatically generated for the references of the descriptions to individual manuscript pages. Thus, even if a multi-page description looks like a direct transcript of the traditional writing, it is a result of a database query that represents a specific intellectual view of a specific research tradition. For example, if one codicological study claims that only the time of a manuscript’s origin but not the place of origin is known, but another study gives time and place of the origin, the place of origin will be presented to the user on the screen in all cases. The user can specify a preference order (or use a pre-specified system wide preference order assigned to the individual study) no matter whether the time of origin is presented from the first or the second study or even from all previous researchers. Several search tools are then designed on such descriptions.

Furthermore, the users can download several tools which measure the performance of typical types of codiological / palaeographic work (e.g., measurement of single characters). As far as available without copyright restrictions, the main scientific literature to work with the codices is also made available in digital form.

Using the concept of DACOs, one URL of the library dissolves into about 600,000 URLs of individual references to a specific cultural heritage object that can be referenced directly from any other cultural heritage resource. This is due to the various views of the metadata and different resolutions.

Most of the traditional references to the codex under discussion are linked to its actual pages. In order to allow authors from any external server setting such links, a worldwide standard has to be created for addressing a specific manuscript. In this context, the system ‘Permanent Universal Resource Identifiers’ used for identifying single items of cultural heritage would have to be transformed into a ‘Permanent Universal Resource Locator’.

In the case of the Cologne Diocesan- and Cathedral-Library, a quotation is linked to the address of ‘kn28-0124_25v%22’. The tag can be explained as follows: ‘kn-’ is the siglum of the library in the German library system, ‘0124_’ the number of the codex and ‘25v’ the folio reference. Therefore, the traditional quotation would be ‘Folio 25v of Codex 124 of the Cologne Diocesan- and Cathedral-Library. Together with the additional wrap up (could be easily supplied by a lookup mechanism), the complete address is ‘www.ceec.uni-koeln.de/ceec-cgi/kleioc/0010KlCEEC/exec/pagemed/%22|kn28-0124_25v%22’. When accessing this address from another DACO, the complete virtual CEEC library could be explored as proper navigation tools have been installed on the same site.

Concerning the ‘user acceptance’ of this DACO approach, we expect positive feedback especially from the academic community even if user satisfaction for this DACO application digitized Cologne Diocesan- and Cathedral-Library is hard to measure properly: The majority of pages contain the discussion of canonistic laws in Latin or medieval handwriting, being useful mainly for academic researchers. However, there are also many visits from curious laypersons, which make it difficult to properly assess the intensity of manuscripts uses.

Distributed Digital Incunabula Library

The 'Distributed Digital Incunabula Library' (inkunabeln.ub.uni-koeln.de/vdib/) is developed as a prototype for the digitization of all German incunabula. Incunabula, Latin for cradle, are books printed between 1454 and 1500. Worldwide, approximately 550,000 incunabula (approximately 27,000 writings) have been preserved. The Distributed Digital Incunabula Library project, organized as a joined project between two libraries, the 'Koelner Universitaets- und Stadtbibliothek' and the 'Herzog August Bibliothek Wolfenbüttel', has demonstrated that the necessary DACO servers can be build fast and at reasonable price. Within the Distributed Digital Incunabula Library, as described in the previous section, a broker directs users to the library holding the digital copy of the cultural heritage objects.

The two libraries involved hold together approximately 5,800 copies incunabula (including duplicates). Out of these, 350,000 pages (ca. 2,000 – 3,000 titles) have been selected for the current pilot project, of which ca. 40 % have been digitized in the first ten months of a two year project. When completed, the 350,000 pages could represent as much as six percent of the titles of incunabula preserved world wide.

Obviously, beyond tackling the technical challenges, cost plays a major role in pushing such a digitization effort forward. The most important cost factors have been (1) content and subject classification, (2) workflow/data importation, (3) raw digitization, (4) storage capacity, and (5) development and maintenance of the WWW server. The content and subject classification is based on the already existing Incunabula Short Title Catalogue (ISTC) which has been in development at the British Library since 1980.[6] The raw digitization of the single pages was conducted using a Nikon DXM 1200. A book cradle allows for photos in an angle of 45 degrees (see Figure 1) to treat the incunabula carefully while simultaneously saving time and money. The pages are scanned in a 24 bit color scheme using a resolution of 3800x3072 pixel (i.e. about 300 dpi for DIN A3) leading to a (uncompressed) data file size of 34 MB. With such a digitization procedure more than 80% of existing incunabula can be digitized leading to about 12 TB raw data volume (or 24 TB with a complete backup at an additional storage place). Considering all cost components, the costs for one page amount roughly 0.75 € (plus metadata and work environment).

[6] See inkunabeln.ub.uni-koeln.de/vdib/dokumentation/introistc1.html for an introduction to the ISTC. The project specific Illustrated ISTC dynamically creates links between the newly digitized DACOs and the catalogue entries at the moment a new DACO is uploaded onto the server. The search tools based on the Illustrated ISTC can be integrated in all common German On-line Public Access Catalogue (OPAC). After digitization, a Table of Contents (ToC) Editor checks the new DACOs for quality and assigns the ISTC numbers to the single objects.

Figure 1: Book cradle for 45 degrees photos (Source: www.image-engineering.de).

Lessons Learned and Outlook

In earlier times, the description of cultural heritage objects has been cheaper than their visual reproduction. However, with the advent of modern digital technology, reproducing visual appearance of text has become cheaper than its description. What has been published by highly developed technologies of the last decades is already available as digital objects. Therefore, following the experiences of the prototypes discussed above, scientists should turn new technologies to those types and amounts of material that could not have been publicly available until ten years ago. Consequently, in the near future, many institutions will present their cultural heritage objects as online content; DACOs could contribute to achieve and maintain independent, individual and unrestricted cultural heritage institutions as well as a global comprehensive Cultural Heritage System.

Overall, the digitization of cultural heritage objects can be seen from two points of view: On the one hand, one may interpret digital cultural heritage objects as equivalent to their non digitized counterparts, as digital facsimiles, just being 'more beautiful' and after intensive development (e.g., word-based linking) able to imitate the possibilities of printed objects on the screen. On the other hand, one may consider digital cultural heritage objects as something substantially new, which make the largest possible amount of sources available through digital corpora with flat access tools. Such digital corpora hold significant new technical potential beyond print offerings. From both viewpoints, the digitization of cultural heritage should be a quest of every researcher and layperson and be emphasized and fostered by politics on a national and international level.

In any case, following up on the European draft constitution, political support needs to go beyond the development of technical solutions: Several activities seem necessary to make progress towards a European infrastructure and a Europe-wide strategy for digitizing European Cultural Heritage: At least, all European institutions holding digital cultural heritage should be able to integrate their objects into a large scale Cultural Heritage System regardless of their individual political and technical solutions. Therefore, it will have to be defined – beyond current prototypes described in this work and first pilot projects, how a Cultural Heritage Server has to react when asked for access by foreign institution. While the actual definition is a technically oriented design issue, its acceptance and implementation will need political and public support throughout the European Union. Such support should start with some initial encouragement for additional pilot systems showing the possibility of integrating resources drawn from different servers in various cities and countries.

References

1. Loebbecke, C. (2004). *Digitizing European Cultural Heritage: Opportunities and Challenges, E-Culture, U-Tourism, and Virtual Heritage Workshop*, Washington D.C., USA, December.
2. Loebbecke, C., Thaller, M. (2005) *Preserving Europe's Cultural Heritage in the Digital World*, European Conference on Information Systems (ECIS), Regensburg, Germany, May.
3. Baumol, W. and Bowen, W. (1966). *Performing Arts: The Economic Dilemma.* The Twentieth Century, New York.
4. Hutter, M. and Rizzo, I. (1997). *Economic Perspectives on Cultural Heritage.* Macmillan Press Ltd., Basingstoke.
5. Throsby, D. (1994). The Production and Consumption of the Arts: A View of Cultural Economics. *Journal of Economic Literature*, 33, 1-29.
6. Blaug, M. (2001). Where are we now on cultural economics?. *Journal of Economic Surveys*, 15 (2), 123-143.
7. Peacock, A. (1969). Welfare Economics and Public Subsidies to the Arts. *Manchester School of Economics and Social Studies*, 37 (December). 323-35.
8. Montias, J. (1973). Are museums betraying the public's trust? *Museum News*, 25-31.
9. Peacock, A. and Godfrey, C. (1974). The Economics of Museums and Galleries. *Lloyds Bank Review*, 111 (January), 17-28.
10. Frey, B. and Pommerehne, W. (1989). *Muses and Markets: Explorations in the Economics of the Arts.* Blackwell, Oxford.
11. Heilbrun, J. and Gray, C. (2001). *The Economics of Art and Culture.* Cambridge University Press, Cambridge.
12. Throsby, D. (2001). *Economics and Culture.* Cambridge University Press, Cambridge.
13. Weil, S. (2002). *Making Museums Matter.* Smithsonian Books, Washington.
14. Robbins, L. (1994). Unsettled Questions in the Political Economy of the Arts. *Journal of Cultural Economics*, 18 (1), 67-77.
15. Johnson, P. and Thomas, B. (1998). The Economics of Museums: A research perspective. *Journal of Cultural Economics*, 22, 75-85.
16. Robbins, L. (1971). Unsettled Questions in the Political Economy of the Arts. *Three Banks Review*, 91, 3-19.
17. Frey, B. (1994). Cultural Economics and Museum Behaviour. *Scottish Journal of Political Economy*, 41(8), 325-52.
18. O'Hagan, J.W. (1995). National Museums: To Charge or Not to Charge?. *Journal of Cultural Economics*, 19, 33-47.

19. Steiner, F. (1997). Optimal Pricing of Museum Admission. *Journal of Cultural Economics*, 21, 307-33.
20. Bailey, J. and Falconer, P. (1998). Charging For Admission to Museums and Galleries. *Journal of Cultural Economics*, 22, 167-177.
21. Schuster, J. M. (1998). Neither Public Nor Private: The Hybridization of Museums. *Journal of Cultural Economics*, 22, 127-150.
22. Meier, S. and Frey, B. (2003). Private Faces in Public Places: The Case of a Private Art Museum in Europe. *Cultural Economics*, 3 (3), 1-16.
23. William, R. (1982). *The Sociology of Culture*.Fontana Paperbacks, London
24. Keesing, F. (1958). *Cultural Anthropology: The Science of Customs*. Stanford.
25. Fowler, P.J. (Ed.) (2003). *World Heritage Cultural Landscapes*. UNESCO World Heritage Center, Paris.
26. Feldstein, M. (1991). *The Economics of Art Museums*. University of Chicago Press, Chicago.
27. Grampp, W. (1989). *Pricing the Priceless. Art, Artists and Economics*. Basil Books, New York.
28. Grampp, W. (1996). A Colloquy about Art Museums: Economics Engages Museology. In: Ginsburgh, V. and Menger, P. (Eds.). *Economics of the Arts: Selected Essays*. Elsevier, Amsterdam et al., 221-254.
29. Baumol, W. and Bowen, W. (1965). On the Performing Arts: The Anatomy of their Economic Problems. *The American Economic Review*, 55 (2), 495-502.
30. Poor, P. and Smith, J. (2004). Travel Cost Analysis of a Cultural Heritage Site: The Case of Historic St. Mary's City of Maryland. *Journal of Cultural Economics*, 28, 217-229.
31. De La Torre, M. (2002). *Assessing the Values of Cultural Heritage*. Getty Conservation Institute, Los Angeles.
32. Connor, S. (1992). *Theory and Cultural Value*. Blackwell, Oxford.
33. Throsby, D. (2003). Determining the Value of Cultural Goods: How Much (or How Little) Does Contingent Valuation Tell Us?. *Journal of Cultural Economics*, 27, 275-285.
34. Frey, B. (1997). Evaluating Cultural Property: The Economic Approach. *International Journal of Cultural Property*, 6 (2), 231-246.
35. Navrud, S. and Ready, R. (2002). *Valuing Cultural Heritage: Applying Environmental Valuation Techniques to Historic Buildings, Monuments and Artifacts*. Edward Elgar, Northampton.
36. Huszar, P. and Seckler, D. (1974). Effects of Pricing a 'Free' Good: A Study of the Use of Admission Fees at the California Academy of Sciences. *Land Economics*, 69 (1), 1-26.
37. Martin, F. (1994). Determining the Size of Museum Subsidies. *Journal of Cultural Economics*, 18, 225-270.
38. Forrest, D., Grime, K., and Woods, R. (2000). Is it Worth Subsidising Repertory Theatre?. *Oxford Economic Papers*, 52 (2), 381-397.
39. Ward, F. and Beal, D. (2000). *Valuing Nature with Travel Cost Models: A Manual*. Edward Elgar, Northampton.
40. Rosen, S. (1974). Hedonic Prices and Implicit Markets: Product Differentiation in Pure Competition. *Journal of Political Economy*, 82 (1), 34-55.
41. Smith, V. (1993). Nonmarket Valuation of Environmental Resources: An Interpretive Appraisal. *Land Economics*, 69 (1), 1-26.
42. Rogers, J. (1995). The Economic Impact of the Barnes Exhibit. *Final Report prepared for the Ontario Ministry of Tourism and Recreation.*
43. Throsby, D. and Withers, G. (1985). What Price Culture?. *Journal of Cultural Economics*, 9, 1-34.
44. Santagata, W. and Signorello, G. (2000). Contingent Valuation of a Cultural Public Good and Policy Design: The Case of 'Napoli Musei Aperti'. *Journal of Cultural Economics*, 24, 181-204.
45. Noonan, D. (2003). Contingent Valuation of Cultural Resources: A Meta-Analytic *Review of the Literature. Journal of Cultural Economics*, 27, 159-176.

46. Waetzold, S. (1971). Museum und Datenverarbeitung. Zum Bericht der Arbeitsgruppe Museumsdokumentation. *Museumskunde*, 40.
47. Hanappi-Egger, E. (2001). Cultural Heritage: The Conflict between Commercialisation and Public Ownership. *Working Paper*, Vienna Technical University, Vienna. www.oeaw.ac.at/ita/access/hanappi_egger_txt.pdf, download on September 22, 2004.
48. Dempsey, L. (2000). Scientific, Industrial and Cultural Heritage: A shared Approach: A research framework for digital libraries, museums, and archives, Ariadne Issue 22, www.ariadne.ac.uk/issue22/dempsey/intro.html
49. Luhmann, N. (1987). Soziale Systeme. Suhrkamp Publishing, Frankfurt.
50. Barkley, J. (1995). Implementing Role Based Access Control Using Object Technology. *First ACM/NIST Workshop on Role-Based Access Control*, hissa.ncsl.nist.gov/rbac/rbacot/titlewkshp.html.
51. Ferraiolo, D. and Kuhn, R. (1992). Role-Based Access Control. *Proceedings of the 15th NIST-NSA Nat. (U.S.) Computer Security Conf.*, 554-563.
52. Giuri, L. and Iglio, P. (1996). A formal model for role based access control with constraints. *Proceedings of the Computer Security Foundations Workshop, IEEE Computer Society*, Washington D.C., 136-145.
53. Sandhu, R., Coyne, E., Feinstein, H., and Youman, C. (1996). Role-Based Access Control Models. *Computer*, 29 (2), 38-47.
54. Neumann, G. and Nusser, S. (1997). A Framework and Prototyping Environment for a W3 Security Architecture. *Proceedings of Communications and Multimedia Security, Joint Working Conference* IFIP TC-6 and TC-11, Athens, Greece
55. Ferraiolo, D., Kuhn, D., and Chandramouli, R. (2003). *Role Based Access Control.* Artech House, Norwood, MA.
56. Lin, A. (1999). *Integrating Policy-Driven Role Based Access Control with the Common Data Security Architecture.*HP Laboratories Bristol HPL-1999-59.
57. Moffett, J. and Sloman, M. (1994). Policy Conflict Analysis in Distributed System Management. *Journal of Organizational Computing*, 4 (1), 1-22.
58. Noble, J. (1970). Museum Manifesto. *Museum News*, April, 27-32.
59. Weil, S. (1990). *Rethinking the Museum: And Other Mediations*. Smithsonian Institution Press, Washington.
60. Addison, A. (2001). Virtual heritage: technology in the service of culture. *Proceedings of the 2001 Conference on Virtual Reality, Archeology, and Culture Heritage*, 343-354.
61. Goncalves, M.; Fox, E. and Watson, L. (2004). Streams, Structures, Spaces, Scenarios, Societies (5S): A formal model for Digital Libraries, portal.acm.org/citation.cfm, download on November 11, 2004.
62. March, S. and Smith, G. (1995). Design and Natural Science Research on Information Technology. *Decision Support Systems*, 15(4), 251-266.
63. Walls, J., Widmeyer, G. and El Sawy, O. (1992). Building an Information System Design Theory for Vigilant EIS. *Information Systems Research*, 3 (1), 36 – 59.
64. Doerr, M. (2003) The CIDOC conceptual reference module: an ontological approach to semantic interoperability of metadata. *AI Magazine*, 24 (3), 75-92.
65. Thaller, M. (2004b). A Note on the Architecture of Computer Systems for the Humanities. Dino Buzzetti, D. Pancaldi,, G. and Short, H. (eds.): *Digital Tools for the History of Ideas, Office for Humanities Communication series*, Vol. 17, 49-76, London

Kolibri 360 GmbH
Ferdinand-Jühlke-Straße 7
99095 Erfurt, Deutschland
produktsicherheit@kolibri360.de